SAVING THE PEO1

NADIA MARZOUKI
DUNCAN McDONNELL
OLIVIER ROY
(*Editors*)

Saving the People

How Populists Hijack Religion

HURST & COMPANY, LONDON

First published in the United Kingdom in 2016 by
C. Hurst & Co. (Publishers) Ltd.,
41 Great Russell Street, London, WC1B 3PL
© Nadia Marzouki, Duncan McDonnell, Olivier Roy and the
Contributors, 2016
All rights reserved.
Printed in India

The right of Nadia Marzouki, Duncan McDonnell, Olivier Roy
and the Contributors to be identified as the authors of this
publication is asserted by them in accordance with the
Copyright, Designs and Patents Act, 1988.

A Cataloguing-in-Publication data record for this book
is available from the British Library.

9781849045209 *hardback*
9781849045162 *paperback*

This book is printed using paper from registered sustainable
and managed sources.

www.hurstpublishers.com

CONTENTS

v

CONTENTS

ACKNOWLEDGEMENTS

This book began its genesis when all three co-editors were colleagues at the European University Institute (EUI) in Florence. It has been produced within the framework of the ReligioWest Research Project led by Professor Olivier Roy, based at the EUI and funded by the European Research Council, under the European Union's 7th Framework Contract Ideas.

In addition to the contributing authors, there are many people we would like to thank for their help in bringing the volume to fruition: first, the anonymous reviewers whom we asked to comment on the initial drafts of the country case-study chapters; second, the secretaries at the EUI who provided important logistical assistance on numerous occasions; finally, Ciarán Burke for his invaluable assistance with the editing of this volume.

Nadia Marzouki, Paris   December 2015
Duncan McDonnell, Brisbane
Olivier Roy, Florence

LIST OF TABLES AND FIGURES

Tables

Figures

ix

CONTRIBUTORS

Zoltán Ádám is Assistant Professor at the Department of Comparative and Institutional Economics at Corvinus University in Budapest, Hungary. He holds a PhD in economics from Debrecen University, where he wrote his dissertation on the political economy of the Hungarian post-communist transition. His research interests include the social and economic factors behind the authoritarian turn in Hungary and other semi-peripheral countries, the rise of majoritarian populism and the new forms of institutionalised state capture.

András Bozóki is Professor of Political Science at Central European University in Budapest. He has authored or co-authored seventeen books and edited or co-edited twenty-three volumes. These include *The Roundtable Talks of 1989: The Genesis of Hungarian Democracy* (2002), *The Communist Successor Parties of Central and Eastern Europe* (2002), *The Future of Democracy in Europe* (2004), *Anarchism in Hungary: Theory, History, Legacies* (2006) and *25 Years after the Fall of the Iron Curtain* (2014). He has been a recurrent visiting professor at Columbia University. He was founding editor of the Hungarian *Political Science Review* and Chairman of the Hungarian Political Science Association.

Dani Filc is Associate Professor at the Department of Politics and Government, Ben-Gurion University. Among his publications are the books *The Power of Property: Israel in the Globalization Age*, edited with Uri Ram (Van Leer Jerusalem Institute, Hebrew), *Hegemony and Populism in Israel* (Resling, Hebrew), *Circles of Exclusion: The Politics of Health-Care in Israel* (Cornell University Press) and *The Political Right in Israel* (Routledge). He is currently the head of the Center for Health, Society and the Humanities at Ben-Gurion University and co-chair of Physicians for Human Rights-Israel.

Leila Hadj-Abdou is a Research Fellow at the Department of Politics, University of Sheffield (UK). She specialises in international migration politics and the governance of ethno-cultural diversity. Prior to coming to Sheffield, Leila held positions at the School of Advanced International Studies (SAIS) in Washington DC and the University of Vienna. She has been a visiting researcher at University College Dublin, the Centre National de la Recherche Supérieure (CNRS) in Paris and the Institute for Higher Studies in Vienna. She holds a PhD from the European University Institute.

Nadia Marzouki is a Research Fellow (Chargée de Recherche) at the CNRS and a consultant for ReligioWest, at the European University Institute. Her work examines public controversies about Islam in Europe and the United States. She is also interested in religious conversions to Evangelical Christianity and debates about religious freedom in North Africa. She is the author of *L'Islam, une religion américaine?* (Le Seuil, 2013). She co-edited, with Olivier Roy, *Religious Conversions in the Mediterranean World* (Palgrave Macmillan, 2013).

Oscar Mazzoleni is Professor of Political Science and Director of the Research Observatory for Regional Politics at the University of Lausanne, Switzerland. He has previously taught at the University of Sorbonne I, Science Po-Paris, Geneva and Turin. He has published numerous books, articles and chapters on European political parties. His most recent books are the edited volumes *Understanding Populist Party Organisation: The Radical Right in Western Europe* (Palgrave Macmillan, 2016, with Reinhard Heinisch) and *Regionalist Parties in Western Europe: Explaining Failure and Success* (Ashgate, 2016, with Sean Mueller).

Duncan McDonnell is Senior Lecturer in the School of Government and International Relations at Griffith University in Brisbane. He was previously a Marie Curie Fellow at the European University Institute. With Daniele Albertazzi he has co-authored *Populists in Power* (Routledge, 2015) and co-edited *Twenty-First Century Populism* (Palgrave, 2008). He has published widely in journals such as the *European Journal of Political Research*, *Political Studies*, *West European Politics* and *Party Politics*. He is currently working on a book with Annika Werner about the European-level alliances formed by radical right populist parties.

Timothy Peace is Lecturer in Comparative Politics at the University of Stirling (UK). He completed his PhD at the European University Institute

(EUI) and has held positions at the University of Edinburgh and the University of Padova in Italy. His research investigates the relationship between religion and politics in Europe and his publications include *European Social Movements and Muslim Activism* (Palgrave, 2015) and *Muslims and Political Participation in Britain* (Routledge, 2015).

Olivier Roy is Professor at the European University Institute (Florence) where he heads the Mediterranean programme at the Robert Schuman Centre for Advanced Studies and the ReligioWest research project (funded by the European Research Council). He has been a Senior Researcher at the CNRS since 1985, Professor at the Ecole des Hautes Etudes en Sciences Sociales since 2003 and visiting professor at Berkeley University (2008/2009). He is the author of *The Failure of Political Islam* (Harvard University Press, 1994), *Globalized Islam* (Columbia University Press, 2004), and *Holy Ignorance* (Hurst/Oxford University Press, 2010).

Ben Stanley is Lecturer at SWPS University of Social Sciences and Humanities, Warsaw. His primary research interests are the theory and practice of populism and the party politics of Central and Eastern Europe (particularly Poland). He has published on these topics in the *Journal of Political Ideologies, Party Politics, Democratization, Communist and Post-Communist Studies* and *Europe-Asia Studies.*

Stijn van Kessel is Lecturer in Politics at Loughborough University, UK. His main research interests are populism and the discourse and electoral performance of radical parties. He published his monograph *Populist Parties in Europe: Agents of Discontent?* with Palgrave Macmillan in 2015. In addition, he has published in edited books and in journals such as *Government and Opposition, Acta Politica* and *Journal of Political Ideologies.*

1

POPULISM AND RELIGION

Nadia Marzouki and *Duncan McDonnell*

The sustained rise of populists across Western societies represents a relatively recent historical phenomenon. Until the end of the 1960s, populists were rare occurrences in established democracies, with only sporadic cases such as Pierre Poujade in France and George Wallace in the United States. The ensuing decades, however, have witnessed their increasingly widespread emergence and, in many cases, consolidation. First came the anti-tax populist parties in early 1970s Scandinavia, followed by the creation of extreme-right movements which would also come to be considered populist such as the Front National (FN—National Front) in France. These trends continued in the 1980s, both with the founding of new parties like the ethno-regionalist populist Lega Lombarda (LL—Lombard League)[1] in Italy, and the transformation of more traditional right-wing parties like the Schweizerische Volkspartei (SVP— Swiss People's Party) and the Freiheitliche Partei Österreichs (FPÖ—Austrian Freedom Party) into radical populist parties. Finally, since the 1990s, we have seen many other successful newcomers like the UK Independence Party (UKIP), Law and Justice (PiS—Prawo i Sprawiedliwość) in Poland, Geert Wilders' Partij voor de Vrijheid (PVV—Party for Freedom) in the Netherlands and the Tea Party (TP) movement in the United States. Given this ongoing

1

trend, Western democracies without strong populists have now become the exception rather than the rule.

As the above list indicates, the most important new populists of the past four decades in established democracies have been almost exclusively right-wing. These have based their appeal on the claim that a homogeneous 'good' people is suffering due to the actions, from above, by elites and, from below, by a variety of 'others'.[2] Populists express strong moral judgements in decrying this state of affairs, portraying society in Manichean terms as divided into a good 'us' and a bad (even 'evil') 'them'. In defining both of these categories, religious identities often play an important role. Populists can deploy a mixture of national, ethnic, class, regional and religious identities in order to define who belongs within the category of 'us' and—by extension—who is consigned to 'them'. This use of religious identity in turn raises the issue of how populists interact with Church authorities—who could, of course, be considered part of the elites within societies—and how Church leaders react to populists and the use they make of religion. Nonetheless, despite the large volume of scholarly work on right-wing populism in Western democracies over the past three decades, the relationship between religion and right-wing populists, as Cas Mudde notes, 'has received only scant attention in the literature so far'.[3]

This book focuses on precisely that relationship. Over the course of the ensuing chapters, our contributors look firstly at how populists conceive of 'the people' and 'others' in terms of their religion and, secondly, at the relationship between Churches and populists. As we will see, the populist use of religion is much more about 'belonging' than 'belief' and revolves around two main notions: 'restoration' and 'battle'. What has to be restored is usually described as the importance afforded within society to a particular native religious identity or set of traditions and symbols rather than a theological doctrine with rules and precepts. This restoration, however, requires battling two groups of 'enemies of the people': the elites who disregard the importance of the people's religious heritage, and the 'others' who seek to impose their religious values and laws upon the native population. In the remainder of this introduction, therefore, we will devote some time to considering 'the people' and 'the others' (or 'us' and 'them'), before briefly outlining the cases covered in the book and the main points of the subsequent chapters.

'Us' and 'Them'

Like many political science concepts such as 'liberalism' and 'socialism', 'populism' has suffered at the hands of media commentators and politicians who continue to use it excessively and with little clarity.[4] Although academics have also often employed the term in inconsistent and undefined ways in order to denote any kind of appeal to 'ordinary people', an increasing consensus has emerged among scholars of populism in recent years concerning its key elements.[5] As Margaret Canovan observes, 'all forms of populism without exception involve some kind of exaltation of and appeal to "the people" and all are in one sense or another anti-elitist'.[6] This is the basis for one of the most-cited definitions of populism, that of Cas Mudde, who views it as 'an ideology that considers society to be ultimately separated into two homogeneous and antagonistic groups, "the pure people" versus "the corrupt elite", and which argues that politics should be an expression of the *volonté générale* (general will) of the people'.[7] While we broadly agree with Mudde, we feel that in the case of right-wing populists (as almost all the parties discussed in this book are), there is an additional essential component beyond this antagonistic relationship between a 'good people' and a 'bad elite': the presence of 'others' who threaten the well-being of the people. We therefore follow the definition proposed by Daniele Albertazzi and Duncan McDonnell, for whom right-wing populism is 'a thin-centred ideology which pits a virtuous and homogeneous people against a set of elites and dangerous "others" who are together depicted as depriving (or attempting to deprive) the sovereign people of their rights, values, prosperity, identity and voice'.[8]

Albertazzi and McDonnell's conceptualisation of populism is in line with that of scholars like Mudde and Ben Stanley who understand populism as a 'thin-centred ideology' that is found only in combination with 'thick' ideologies of the left and right or with other thin ones (like nationalism).[9] As Hans-Georg Betz and Carol Johnson have argued, like all ideologies, populism proposes an analysis designed to respond to three essential questions: 'what went wrong; who is to blame; and what is to be done to reverse the situation?'[10] For populists, the answers can broadly be summed up as: (1) the government and democracy, which should reflect the will of the people, have been occupied, distorted and exploited for their own interests by elites; (2) the elites and 'others' (those not of 'the people') are to blame for the current situation (inevitably portrayed as a crisis which is going to get much worse); and (3) the people must be given back their role as rightful sovereign before it is too late.[11] While populists preach impending doom, however, they also offer salvation and exculpation. Populism and its leaders promise the people, as Francisco Panizza says, 'emancipation after a journey of sacrifice'.[12] In the meantime, they provide immediate exculpation by telling people that the ills

3

of the country are not their fault. Rather, these righteous, clean-living citizens are said to be the prime victims of the elites and 'others'.

The existence of a virtuous and homogeneous 'people' is central to populism. For populists, the people constitutes an inherently good community—with 'community' being a place where, as Zygmunt Bauman explains, there is mutual trust and where 'it is crystal-clear who is one of us and who is not'.[13] This view of the people as an exclusive, morally upright community recalls what Paul Taggart refers to as the populist 'heartland' in which 'a virtuous and unified population resides'.[14] The evocation of the 'heartland' is closely tied to the anxiety expressed by right-wing populists about the replacement of the supposedly plain, unambiguous and united society of the past with the increasingly polluted and blurred society of the present. Indeed, according to right-wing populists, the people risk losing their very identity due to elite-promoted phenomena like globalisation, immigration and multiculturalism. The nostalgic celebration of an idyllic past of course also serves to increase the persuasiveness of calls for cultural re-awakening and re-conquest.

Such calls are often linked by right-wing populists to the defence of native religious identities and symbols, which are said to be under threat from elites and 'others'. Many populists have stressed the need to re-assert these identities and symbols in order to fight back against the undermining of native identity that comes with secularism, immigration and multiculturalism. This 'restorationist' discourse of populists is based on a particular conception of culture as a set of codes.[15] For populists, culture does not designate complex and historically embedded modes of producing meaning, memories and social arrangements. Rather, it is the opposite of complexity, and can be reduced to a simplistic and easily recognisable series of codes of behaviour and symbols (for example, the crucifix). These codified symbols and attitudes are also key instruments in distinguishing between those who can be included among 'the people' and those who have been deemed impossible (and undesirable) to integrate. Restoration, as we have noted, is accompanied by the idea of an essential 'battle' which must be waged. Hence, right-wing populists have actively participated in campaigns to defend local spaces from 'alien' religions and to keep 'native' religious symbols in public places (with the consequent reinforcement through such campaigns of who is 'us' and who is 'them'). For example, the Lega Nord (LN—Northern League) in Italy, the Tea Party in the US, the French Front National, the Swiss People's Party, the Austrian FPÖ and the Dutch PVV have all fought against the construction of mosques and/or minarets, arguing that they are a threat to the purity and integrity of the native community's territory and identity (in addition to mosques being supposed hotbeds of terrorist activity). This understanding of culture and religion, in turn, is inseparable from a conception of 'us' that emphasises a homogeneous *ethnos*, rather than a pluralist *demos*.

As for the enemies of the people in right-wing populist discourse, these consist of elites and 'others'. The former are charged with being, at best, distant from the people and incompetent (and, at worst, downright corrupt), while the 'others' are made up of those whose identity, behaviour or beliefs preclude them from being considered part of the natural community formed by the people. For contemporary right-wing populists in Western democracies, the main 'others' are almost always immigrants and, in particular since 9/11, Muslims. Muslims allegedly want to impose their religious values and traditions on the people as part of a surreptitious 'Islamisation' plan. Moreover, they are said to receive the support of liberal elites (who are accused of always favouring minority rights over those of 'the people'). Ideas of invasion, infiltration, contagion, conspiracy, replacement and impending irreversible crisis represent key components of the populist imaginary, and all of these are present in the notion that a deliberate process of Islamisation is occurring under our noses in many Western democracies.

With the spectre of Islamisation, populists have thus succeeded in marrying the old Orientalist condemnation of the innate hypocrisy of the 'Moor' with contemporary concerns about immigration, international terrorism and the circulation of jihadists from Europe to the Levant (and vice versa). An important effect of the success of the notion of Islamisation is the normalisation of the idea according to which Muslims are incapable of distinguishing between their political views and their theological beliefs. Conflating religious radicalism and political radicalism, the proponents of the Islamisation paradigm contend that Muslims who practice a conservative form of piety will inevitably endorse radical views about domestic and foreign politics. As Olivier Roy notes, this argument stands in contrast to the sociology of radicalised individuals who resort to violent action. As Roy explains:

> the relatively high percentage of converts among terrorists indicates that radicalisation is not the consequence of a pervasive, long-term religious indoctrination in the midst of a local Muslim community, but is the result of an individual and sudden decision to go for action. Conversely, many so-called religious fundamentalists are perfectly quietist in political terms.[16]

Although populists claim that any place or category of population could be an instrument of Islamisation, they particularly focus on schools and mosques, and on issues such as gender relations. Schools are an important battleground, since, firstly, the religious traditions of native children are allegedly being respected less and less (e.g. the recurrent claims by populists about nativity plays being banned) and, secondly, children risk being brainwashed by Islamists who want schools to promote their beliefs and practices (e.g. by providing Halal food in canteens).[17] The incessant polemics about headscarves and burqas in French schools reflect the same concerns about protecting children. As mentioned earlier, protests against mosques and/or minarets also represent an attempt to re-appropriate public spaces, while populist warnings about the danger of Western women being converted, abducted, forcibly married, brainwashed or physically hurt by Arab Muslim males echo colonial and Orientalist fantasies about the enslavement of white women. While extreme, it is important to note that these right-wing populist arguments about Islam and Islamisation are not entirely exceptional. In fact, some of them have become quite mainstream in public debates, with a vicious circle now established in many countries between populist and mainstream discourses, whereby one enables the other. Last but not least, the media has of course also played a central role in amplifying the theme of the Islamic threat.

Linked to the Islamisation thesis is another argument that has gained strength in right-wing populist discourses over the past decade: that Islam is not a religion. Rather, populists claim that it is a legal and military code and/or a political ideology that underpins the plan to conquer Western liberal democracies. This definition of Islam as a non-religion also serves as a rhetorical strategy that allows populists to deny the legitimacy of claims to religious freedom, and more generally, the rights of Muslims living in Western countries. After all, so the logic goes, how can Muslims claim a legal right to practise their religion when what they are practising is not a religion in the first place? More broadly, the distinction between what counts as religion and non-religion also contributes to further 'othering' and alienating Muslims: in this way, they appear not only as citizens who cannot be integrated, but as people who do not even have a genuine religion. As shown by several of our contributors, the attention devoted by populists to the legalistic and ritualistic aspects of Islam—fed by countless books and supposedly expert reports on 'what Sharia is' and 'what the Quran really says'—consolidates this image of Muslims as individuals whose religious practice is based only on violent superstitions and plans for domination. Moreover, if we accept this view of Islam, then every single Muslim becomes a potential threat, since they all adhere to what is in reality a political/military ideology and programme. In other words, there can be no such thing as 'moderate Muslims'. They thus provide a perfect 'dangerous other' for the definition of right-wing populism discussed above.

Cases and Chapter Outlines

All of the countries examined in this volume officially adhere to a secular relationship between religion and politics, although the particular form and history of this relationship varies significantly from case to case. For example, while the constitutions of France and the United States define a strict separation between the state and religious institutions, in Britain there are established Churches and in Italy the Concordat affords the Catholic Church a series of special rights and privileges. As for Israel, it defines itself in its Basic Laws (Constitution) as a 'Jewish and democratic state'—a phrase that has led to heated controversies about the position of religious minorities there.[18] These differences notwithstanding, all Western societies have become secularised to greater and lesser degrees.[19] While the secularisation of France, Britain and the Netherlands is a well-advanced phenomenon, similar changes are affecting countries that have traditionally been marked by a stronger level of religiosity, or lived religious practice. For example, the number of people claiming no religious affiliation has significantly increased in the US, while in Poland sociologists have noted that—notwithstanding the high level of declared religious belonging—younger generations are undergoing a process of secularisation.[20]

As the chapters in this book show, the relationship of populist movements to religion is far from uniform and has varied considerably over time. In most of the cases examined, the turn to religion—where there has been one—occurred around the end of the 1990s and the beginning of the current century. Before that, some right-wing populist parties included a significant number of representatives and members who opposed traditional faiths and Church leaders. For example, neo-pagans celebrating the strength of pre-Christian Europe were prominent alongside conservative Catholics among the founding groups of the French Front National; in Austria, the FPÖ initially had a strong anti-clerical component; in the 1990s, the LN in Italy even went through a phase of promoting neo-pagan type rituals; in the Netherlands, neither the Lijst Pim Fortuyn (LPF—Pim Fortuyn List) nor the PVV has given precedence to Christian values over libertarian views on ethical, economic and social issues. Indeed, given that Church leaders can be considered part of society's elites and that they usually advocate charity and acceptance of immigrants, there are many obvious reasons why right-wing populists could come into conflict with Christian Churches (while at the same time defending their symbols).

We also find that right-wing populists do not always agree on what exactly comprises the religious identity that the people need to reclaim. This may be defined by populists as Christian, Judeo-Christian or Judeo-Christian-Humanist. In the FPÖ's 1997 manifesto, for example, Christianity was defined as the 'spiritual foundation of Europe' and was equated with Western values. By contrast, Geert Wilders has referred on many occasions to the 'Christian/Jewish/Humanistic' culture of the Netherlands. The case of the French Front National is different again, since it mostly speaks of national identity rather than Christian identity, and has cast itself as the only remaining guardian of *laïcité* (state secularity). Indeed, its attempt in recent years to combine the call to reclaim *laïcité* with a celebration of the Christian roots of France has resulted in a complex and ambivalent discourse. Meanwhile, in Israel, the call of the Shas Party to restore 'the Crown to its Ancient Glory' is essentially a reaction to conflicts about the place and status of Mizrahi Jews in Israeli culture. Shas' use of religion, as Dani Filc's chapter shows, is designed first and foremost to assert the need of its 'people' for inclusion and for their acceptance by Ashkenazi elites as full partners within a common Jewish political and religious identity.

While noting the tendency of right-wing populist parties to denounce Islam as the evil 'other', the volume also seeks to explore variation among populist discourses and strategies concerning religion. This is why the study of populists in eight European democracies (Italy, Austria, Switzerland, the Netherlands, France, Britain, Hungary and Poland) is supplemented by the analysis of two non-European, but still Western, cases: the Tea Party in the US and the Shas Party in Israel. These allow us to explore the extent to which populist arguments regarding religion are circulating beyond Europe. On this point, we find that, despite the important differences among the political contexts and histories from which right-wing populists have emerged, there has been a significant standardisation of their approach to religion over the past fifteen years or so.

Authors of the country case studies were asked to consider a number of common topics in their chapters. These included providing answers to the key questions below. In this way, we hope to provide comparable analyses of how right-wing populists make use of religion in a range of Western democracies.

• Do populists conceive of 'the people' in terms of religious identities and values? If so, how is this expressed?

- Do populists propose themselves as the political defenders of a religiously-defined 'people' against religiously-defined 'others'?
- How do populists characterise the religious 'other'?
- How are relations between Church authorities and populists and have they changed over time?

As regards the individual country chapters, the first, by Duncan McDonnell, discusses the LN, which has very clearly used religion for political gain. In particular since 2000, the party has defined its 'people' as virtuous northern Italians who are attached to their Catholic heritage and its main 'dangerous other' as Muslim immigrants who seek to impose their own traditions and laws through 'Islamisation'. McDonnell then discusses the relationship between the LN and the Church, which has gone from one of outright confrontation in the 1990s to one involving mutual recognition of each other's roles and tentative agreement on a range of issues at times during the 2000s, before moving back to a more confrontational relationship since Matteo Salvini took over as leader at the end of 2013.

In Chapter 3, Leila Hadj-Abdou focuses on the case of one of the most successful radical right populist parties in Europe over the past three decades, the FPÖ. She traces and explains the move of a party, which traditionally included a fierce anti-clericalist component, towards a pro-Christian stance. Hadj-Abdou shows that the reference to Christianity is essentially used in an instrumental way by the FPÖ to give more weight to its anti-Islamic agenda. As she argues, this agenda is based on the notion that Islam is a threat to national security and to the survival of Austrian cultural identity.

Oscar Mazzoleni discusses in Chapter 4 how the denunciation of the supposed Islamic invasion has become an important theme for the Swiss SVP. Advocating a policy of assimilation for Muslims, the SVP view of Islam is closely linked to its critiques of multiculturalism and the naiveté of the left. The party's defence of Christianity, on the other hand, focuses on religion as an identity marker, as shown by the emphasis placed on national symbols such as the cross on the Swiss flag. Moving on to the SVP's role in the anti-minaret campaign, the chapter explores the arguments made by party leaders in support of the referendum, and explains why Catholic and Protestant Churches opposed it.

In Chapter 5, Stijn van Kessel examines the two populist parties that have enjoyed the greatest degree of electoral success to date in the Netherlands: the LPF and the PVV. He shows how, instead of using religion as a means to conceive of the 'ordinary' people, both parties have deployed religion mainly to identify those who do not belong to the 'people' ('the others'). Van Kessel also analyses the ambiguity of Wilders' positions on moral issues, which combine elements of liberalism and conservatism. By contrast, the PVV's denunciation of Islamisation is very clear. The chapter also provides a detailed analysis of the complex relationship that the PVV cultivates with Judaism and Israel.

Olivier Roy shows in Chapter 6 how the Front National's conception of religion is situated at the crossroads between three major traditions: neo-paganism, neo-Maurrasianism[21] and *laïcité*. The chapter argues that while the Front National has relaxed its stance on family issues such as gay marriage and abortion, it has maintained the same anti-immigration position since the late 1970s. Over the past fifteen years, however, the enemy has been increasingly defined as 'Muslim' rather than simply as 'migrant'. The categories of religion and culture have thus replaced that of race. Defending Christianity as an identity marker rather than as a faith or a set of values, the FN has had a vexed relationship with the Catholic Church, having criticised it both for being the embodiment of the establishment and for leaning toward leftist values on immigration.

In Chapter 7, Timothy Peace analyses the relationship to religion of three very different British populist parties. The case of Respect, which actively cultivated support from British Muslims, shows that left-wing populists can also be tempted to make strategic use of religion. However, UKIP—although it has constructed a close link between its anti-immigration discourse and its anti-Muslim agenda—does not give religion a central place in its programme. Finally, in the case of the extreme-right British National Party (BNP), Peace finds that while the party has done much to exploit the issue of religion, especially in terms of how it defines 'the other', it retains a rather secular basis and does not easily define the people as Christian.

Ben Stanley in Chapter 8 examines how in post-communist Poland populist parties have appealed to an inward-looking and nation-centric brand of Catholicism. The chapter looks at two parties, the Catholic Liga Polskich Rodzin (LPR—League of Polish Families) and the Prawo i Sprawiedliwość (PiS—Law and Justice party), both of which have invoked religious values and identities to consolidate narratives based on the dichotomy between the good people and the evil elite. Stanley shows how these parties brought the divide between 'open' and 'closed' Catholicism into the mainstream of party politics. However, as he notes, the extent to which the Polish party system has consolidated around this new line of competition remains a matter of debate.

In Chapter 9, Zoltán Ádám and András Bozóki argue against the notion of a strong relationship between populism and religion in Hungary, where right-wing populists have kept their distance from Catholic and Protestant Churches. However, even in the context of a highly secularised society, both the governing right-wing populist Fidesz party and the far-right Jobbik have introduced some Christian references and symbols into their rhetoric. Both parties interpret and appropriate Christianity within the framework of an ethno-nationalist understanding of 'the Hungarian people' and their rejection of migrants and Roma. Ultimately, Ádám and Bozóki contend that Hungarian populism itself can be understood as a nationalistic surrogate religion.

In Chapter 10, Nadia Marzouki examines the close links between Christian nationalism and the critique of liberal elites in the discourse of the Tea Party in the United States. A heterogeneous movement based on the combined action of grassroots activists, wealthy foundations and conservative media, the Tea Party has an equivocal relationship to religion. While some of its followers hold libertarian views on issues such as marriage, abortion and religious freedom that are consistent with their socio-economic outlook, a significant number of the TP's leaders and followers have stressed the need to defend American Christianity and fight against Islamisation.

In Chapter 11, Dani Filc examines the case of the ultra-orthodox Shas Party in Israel, which campaigns for greater inclusion and recognition of the Mizrahi Jews. The chapter explores the complexity of Shas' platform, which is based on a combination of inclusionary and exclusionary features. Economically, Shas' vision is quite inclusive, given that it supports welfare, solidarity and redistribution. However, the party also vehemently criticises the presence of refugees, asylum seekers and migrant workers in Israel because, as non-Jews, they are said to represent a threat to the survival of the Jewish people.

Finally, in the concluding chapter, Olivier Roy emphasises once again how religion is essentially a matter of identity for populist parties: they place Christendom above Christianity. Indeed, this nationalist, culturalist and localist use of Christian symbols can also be found in mainstream party rhetoric and court judgments. By contrast, the Churches insist on revitalising belief (rather than simply 'belonging') and on giving a spiritual content to norms, values and symbols. Hence, although populist parties and Churches may seem to share a similar objective of 'defending' Christianity, many Church leaders are concerned that depriving religious symbols (like the crucifix) of their spiritual content and turning them into cultural symbols (as both courts and politicians have done) serves to detach them from faith and religious practices.

2

THE LEGA NORD

THE NEW SAVIOUR OF NORTHERN ITALY

Duncan McDonnell

The Lega Nord (LN—Northern League) presents us with a very clear example of a right-wing populist party which has used religion to define both 'the people' and 'the others'. This has been particularly the case since the turn of the twenty-first century, with the LN consistently casting itself as the saviour of a culturally Catholic northern Italian 'people' which is said to be under threat, from below, by Muslim immigrants seeking to dominate the native population and, from above, by secular elites at national and supranational levels who do not respect the traditions or identities of the people and instead privilege the rights of 'others'. Compounding matters, with the exception of some individual clergymen, the Church—according to the Lega—has too often sided with elites and 'the others' against the people, leaving the party as the sole constant defender (and saviour) of ordinary northern Italians.

Although the specific configuration of 'people', 'elites' and 'others' outlined above especially characterises the Lega since 2000, the party's attempt to position itself as the saviour of northern Italians is nothing new. Founded in 1991 by Umberto Bossi, who served as party leader until 2012, the Lega united a series of regionalist leagues that had emerged across northern Italy in the mid-1980s. As discussed in the first section of this chapter (A New Faith), the party offered a form of exculpation for northern Italians by depicting them as the victims of a morally bankrupt national political system, an inefficient state and a backward, criminal south. The problems of Italy were not the fault of northerners, according to the Lega. Rather, northerners were said to be suffering, while elites and 'others' benefited at their expense. This exculpation was combined firstly with the attempt to create an intense personal bond with the party and its mission among supporters and, secondly, with the use in the second half of the 1990s of pseudo-pagan rituals and rhetoric about the attachment of 'the people' to the purported northern Italian 'nation' of Padania.[1] These latter features remained until the party's re-establishment of an alliance with Silvio Berlusconi's centre-right coalition in 2000 (after six years of standing alone). Thereafter, the territorial reference point of Padania, the pseudo-pagan elements and the criticisms of southern Italians were all either heavily toned down or dropped.

Although southern Italians had been the principal 'other' for the LN prior to 2000, they were not the only ones. The Lega had also warned of the dangers posed to northern communities by undesirable foreign immigrants—especially those from northern and sub-Saharan Africa and from Eastern European countries like Albania. While the party continued to oppose immigration in general following the new alliance with the centre-right in 2000, the predominant 'other' in LN discourse very clearly became Islam and immigrants of that faith. As discussed in the second section of this chapter (A New Crusade), the Lega has positioned itself over the past fifteen years as the main defender of the Catholic traditions and identity of northern Italians in the face of alleged threats from Muslim immigrants and secular elites. This defence has primarily centred on struggles concerning local spaces (such as opposition to the construction of new mosques), symbols (the crucifix in schools) and official recognition (the European Convention's failure to acknowledge Europe's 'Christian roots'). These campaigns have also gone hand-in-hand with the attempt—akin to those of right-wing populists in other established democracies—to portray Islam as a threat to liberal democracy and as incompatible with Western cultures.[2]

The party's more belligerent stance towards Islam since 2000 has thus been framed in terms of a defence of the people's Catholic identities, traditions and democratic rights not only from the threats posed by Muslim immigrants, but also from elites in Rome and Brussels who side with 'the others' against 'the people'. This defence can also be seen in the LN's opposition over the last decade to reforms in Italy on ethical questions such as euthanasia and civil unions (whether between same-sex couples or not). In part due to the closeness between the Lega's stances and those of the Catholic Church on some of these issues, the relationship between the party and the Church also changed. As discussed in the third section of this chapter (The Lega Nord and the Church), while in the 1990s the LN condemned the Vatican and senior clergy *en masse* as another elite which stood against the people, this position became more nuanced in the 2000s, with the party praising some high-ranking members of the Church (usually those who agreed with the LN on questions concerning immigration and Islam, or at least did not strongly oppose the party) and continuing to denounce others (usually those who opposed the LN's stances on immigration and Islam).

To understand this changing relationship, it is important to bear in mind that the Italian Church was faced for the majority of the first decade of the twenty-first century with a situation unlike that of its ecclesiastical counterparts in most other European countries: not only was the Lega Nord a party which regularly secured between 4 and 10 per cent of the vote in general elections (see Figure 2.1)—and well over 20 per cent at times in major northern regions like Lombardy and Veneto—but it was also a member of national-level coalition governments from 2001 to 2006 and from 2008 to 2011. In addition, given that LN representatives held ministries like Justice (2001–2006) and the Interior (2008–2011), the party was able to wage considerable influence over key areas of government policy.[3] For most of the past fifteen years, the Lega has therefore been a political actor that was extremely difficult for the Church to ignore. That said, the changes in leadership, both in the Vatican and within the Lega Nord since 2012—combined with the LN's return to more hard-line policy positions and parliamentary opposition—have meant that the relationship between the party and the Church runs much less smoothly in 2015 than was the case a few years previously.

A New Faith

As Ilvo Diamanti has argued, Umberto Bossi 'redefined the concept of territory' within Italian politics in the late 1980s and early 1990s.[4] Although small regional movements had existed in peripheral and/or linguistically distinct areas of Italy like Sardinia, Trentino-Alto Adige and the Aosta Valley, the

Fig. 2.1: General Election Results of the Lega Nord, 1992–2013

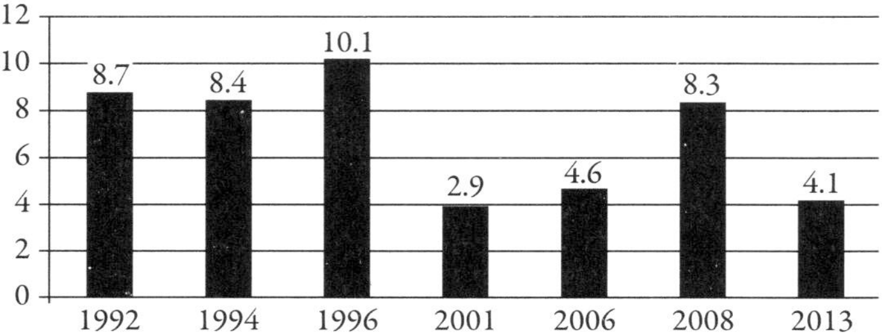

Note: General election results refer to the proportional parts of the elections for Italy's lower house, the Camera dei deputati (Chamber of Deputies).

Source: Electoral archive of the Italian Interior Ministry, *www.elezionistorico.interno.it.*

economic and cultural differences between north and south had never been politicised by the existing parties. The Lega focused on precisely these differences. It was thus what Paul Lucardie, in his classifications of new political parties, terms a 'prophetic party' in that it developed a new ideology around a new issue.[5] This new ideology is best conceptualised by Alberto Spektorowski's definition, which catalogues the party as 'ethnoregionalist populist'.[6] The Lega appealed to a distinct northern 'people', conceived of as 'a single entity, ethnos and demos together, an idealised community'.[7] As summed up in one its most famous slogans, 'padroni a casa nostra' ('masters in our own homes'), the party said it was fighting to return the democratic rights to this community allegedly taken away by bad elites and further undermined by the presence of undesired 'others'.

The Lega thus offered a new identity and 'a new source of self-respect' to those in northern regions which had traditionally been strongly Catholic and who had voted for decades in large numbers for the Democrazia Cristiana (DC—Christian Democracy), the confessional party that dominated Italy for over four decades until its collapse under an avalanche of corruption scandals in the early 1990s.[8] As Piero Ignazi observes, the Lega's 'offer of an ethnic identity, while highly problematic given the looseness of real distinctive elements, met the need for symbolic references in an area formerly moulded by the Church's presence and, at the time, affected by the rise of secularisation'.[9] Moreover, it was an area which, by the end of the 1980s, had become increasingly disillusioned with its existing political representatives (and those of the DC in particular), who were seen as far away in Rome, corrupt, inefficient, too pliant before the demands of the wasteful south and unconcerned with the problems of the productive north.

The Lega did not just propose a new territorial and ethnic identity. It also proposed a party identity which was extremely strong and contained religious overtones. We can see this, for example, if we look at the annual LN rallies in the small Lombardy town of Pontida—termed 'sacred ground' by the party as it is said to have been the site of a pledge between Lombard towns in 1167 to combat the Holy Roman Empire of Federico Barbarossa (with the Lega therefore casting itself as the modern successor to those northern rebels against Roman rule). The Pontida rallies have regularly featured mass oaths of loyalty to the party, the leader and the cause of northern autonomy.[10] They are also where key changes in party strategy have been announced, with the sacredness of the location supposedly conferring legitimacy upon them.[11] Yannis Stavrakakis notes the intensity 'of the investment leaders and followers exhibit in their identifications' towards populist movements and we can see this very clearly at Pontida.[12] Take, for example, Bossi's appearance at the 2005 meeting after he had been absent from public life for a year following a stroke.[13] Introducing him, Daniele Belotti (a Lega regional councillor) told the crowd: 'he is our guide, our hope of freedom, our hero, our leader'. In the official party newspaper *La Padania* the next day, Igor Iezzi wrote that the crowd could feel the atmosphere of 'a page in history being written. The hundred thousand have tears in their eyes.' In the same edition, we read that the meeting in Pontida is a day of coming together for those who 'have bound themselves irrevocably by oath to their movement and their great leader'.[14]

Populism often uses language, imagery and rituals that are typical of religious movements and the above examples from Pontida reflect this. Indeed, at times during the 1990s the party went further by using rituals and language resembling those of New Age and neo-pagan groups. These were particularly associated with the 'Padania' secessionist stance adopted by the LN in the latter half of the decade: for example, beginning in 1996, at the end of each summer Bossi collected water in a ceremony at the source of the Po river in Piedmont and brought it to Venice where he would pour it into the sea in a solemn ritual during the party's annual September rally in the city. The religious symbolism of this act, explicitly stated by Bossi, was that the water made the people of the north 're-born'.[15] After all, it was no ordinary water, but that of a river frequently described by the Lega as 'Dio Po' (the God Po) or the 'sacred Po'. This type of pseudo-pagan language was consistent with how Bossi and other senior figures in the Lega presented their own religious beliefs and

17

practices in these years. For example, Bossi said: 'I believe in God. It is a God that is everywhere, in water and fire, in the air that we breathe. [...] I think my beliefs are a kind of Pantheism.'[16] Similarly, leading party representative Roberto Calderoli was married in 1998 according to what was termed a 'Celtic rite', featuring the taking of an oath in front of a 'purifying fire' and the exchange of bracelets rather than rings.[17] The Lega during these years thus proposed (albeit not very coherently) a form of belonging—to both the party and the supposedly 'Celtic' Padania—which was in opposition not just to the existing political allegiances, but also to the existing main religious faith in the north of Italy, Catholicism.

Neither the Lega's secessionist nor its pseudo-pagan turns held the same appeal for the wider northern public as federalism, however. Although the ritual of collecting water from the Po continued until Bossi stepped down as leader in 2012, the other neo-pagan elements and the call for Padanian independence largely disappeared before then, especially after the party resumed its alliance with the Berlusconi-led centre-right coalition in 2000. In exchange for the promise of 'devolution' (which had quite a different meaning in the Italian context to that in the UK), the Lega abandoned its independence claim. In sum, the party's efforts in the 1990s to establish a new territorial cleavage within Italian politics and a strong attachment to the party among supporters had been successful, but the attempt to establish a new 'faith' in a Padanian nation (with its accompanying pseudo-religious baggage) was not. As we shall see in the next section, in the 2000s the Lega would revise its offer, placing itself not in opposition to the traditional Catholic identity of the north, but as its sole true defender.

A New Crusade

Although the Lega had always looked unfavourably on Muslim immigration, this became a far more important question for the party in the 2000s. There are three main explanations for this development. First, the increased focus on the issue was due to the opportunity provided by the 9/11 attacks to strongly associate Islam with anti-Western sentiments, extremist ideologies and terrorism. Second, having noticeably reduced its emphasis on southern Italians as a dangerous 'other' due to the re-establishment of the coalition with the centre-right (which contained parties such as Berlusconi's Forza Italia that relied also on the south for votes), a gap opened up for a new principal 'other' in the Lega Nord's discourse. Muslims provided a perfect fit. Third, the Lega's shift responded to the move of another member of the centre-right alliance, Alleanza Nazionale (AN—National Alliance), from its former far-right positions towards more moderate conservative ones in the early 2000s. This created the possibility for the LN to gain ownership over the interconnected immigration and security issues, both of which were rising in salience among the public.[18] As Emanuele Massetti shows, using data from the Italian National Election Studies: 'in 2001, 59.8 per cent of voters thought (strongly or fairly strongly) that immigrants represent a threat to public order and security'. Moreover, in all three general elections held in Italy during the 2000s, over 10 per cent of voters considered immigration one of the two main problems facing the country.[19]

For most of the decade, the Lega was thus able to present itself as leading a new and crucial battle within Italy against the dangers to identity and security posed by Islam and Muslim immigration. As the LN Minister for Justice in the 2001–2006 government, Roberto Castelli claimed: 'it is clear that we are at the forefront in this country in the fight against clandestine immigration, fundamentalism and Islamic terrorism'.[20] Moreover, even when Muslims were not accused of being terrorists, they were still charged with wishing to colonise and oppress native cultures as part of the process of 'Islamisation' supposedly occurring in Europe (see the discussion of this in the preceding chapter). For example, the LN local leader in Emilia-Romagna, Angelo Alessandri, talked of the need for the party to defend northern identity against 'Muslims and all those who want to suffocate us'.[21] As we will see, the idea of an essential 'new crusade' against Islam and Islamisation—with no quarter given—underpinned LN rhetoric and policy on a series of questions after 2000.

Overall, the Lega's position on immigration tallies with what Hans-Georg Betz and Carol Johnson describe as 'selective exclusion', according to which 'certain groups cannot be integrated into society and therefore represent a fundamental threat to the values, way of life and cultural integrity of the "indigenous" people'.[22] The LN's conceptualisation of 'selective exclusion' was clearly religiously based, with Muslims—as the religious group supposedly least capable of integrating with native Italian communities—very firmly at the top of the party's list of undesirables. Likewise, its conceptualisation of which immigrants could best be included was also religiously based. For example, the party's junior minister in the 2001–2006 government, Stefano Stefani, proposed that if immigration really was necessary for the economy, then it would be better to encourage the return of those of Italian (and hence Catholic) heritage in South America with whom there are 'common cultural, historical and religious roots', since 'not all immigration is the same, not all those who want to enter the country are equal'.[23]

As regards those Muslims already living in Italy, the Lega adopted a position of utter intransigence on issues such as the construction of mosques and other perceived concessions to Muslims by the Italian state. As Chantal Saint-Blancat and Ottavia Schmidt di Friedberg note, 'mosque construction always transmits the message that the new community is "here to stay"' and can therefore trigger new fears about societal change among the native population.[24] The Lega played on such fears, particularly after 2000, with a series of high-profile campaigns against plans to build new mosques in northern Italy. For example, the party organised a series of very strong protest actions from October 2000 onwards against proposals for a new mosque in the outskirts of Lodi (a small town in Lombardy). These took the form, firstly, of a march, followed by the 'pollution' of the intended site with pig urine and then the 're-consecration' of the land by a Catholic priest who said mass there.[25] Such extreme attempts to reclaim public spaces for the native Catholic community from the supposed Muslim invaders were also, of course, designed to attract copious media attention (which they duly did).

A similar case that received considerable publicity occurred in Milan, where the Lega was at the forefront of efforts to close the mosque in via Jenner. This eventually happened in 2008 on public order grounds, with the LN taking the credit not only because it had spearheaded the campaign, but also because it was its minister for the interior, Roberto Maroni, who oversaw the order to close the mosque.[26] Recalling the party's slogan of being 'masters in our own homes', Bossi commented at the time: 'this is our home. We are not going to make a present of our country to anyone.'[27] To underline its total refusal to concede public space for Muslims to practise their religion, the Lega then opposed the construction of any new place of worship for Muslims in the city. As the party's MEP from Milan (and leader since December 2013), Matteo Salvini, asserted in 2010: 'The mosque is not a priority and we cannot give space to those who use their religions to impose a backward way of life.'[28] The presence of mosques was thus framed not only in terms of a security issue (in line with the idea that they are 'breeding grounds for terrorism'), but also in terms of invasion and a hostile attempt to force a non-Western (and hence inferior) culture on the native people—in a word: Islamisation. The evocation of this threat was also accompanied in LN protests with frequent references to the Battle of Lepanto in 1571 between Christian and Ottoman forces, thus reinforcing the idea of a militant Islam intent on conquering Europe once again.

The increased importance attached by the party to Islam, Muslim immigration and the defence of native religious culture was very clear in the Lega Nord's 2006 general election campaign, when it published five key points on which it said its participation in another centre-right coalition government would depend. First among these was 'the defence of the Christian roots of Europe and opposition to fundamentalism'. Launching the Lega's campaign that year, the LN Minister for Reforms, Roberto Calderoli, stated: 'we will go amongst the people to defend our Christian roots and our identity'.[29] He also took to wearing a T-shirt in public—and especially on television—with the slogan *orgoglioso di essere cristiano* ('proud to be Christian') printed on it. Calderoli thus completed a remarkable conversion from being a groom in a pagan-style wedding in 1998 to a vigorous defender of Christianity just eight years later. While this may be an amusing personal history, Calderoli's behaviour in the first half of 2006 had very serious consequences: following an appearance on television in which he revealed that he was wearing a T-shirt displaying an image of the prophet Muhammad, protests were held outside the Italian consulate in Benghazi (Libya) on 17 February at which eleven people were killed and many more injured.[30]

Despite its rhetoric about being proud to be Christian, what the Lega appears to be defending when protesting against new mosques in Italy are 'Christian' spaces rather than actual Christian values. Theirs is a battle about symbols and 'who belongs' (plus, of course, who does not) rather than beliefs. We can see this also in the attention the party has devoted since 2000 to defending the presence of crucifixes in public places, particularly school classrooms. As Luca Ozzano and Alberta Giorgi observe, the LN has used the crucifix as 'a symbol to support in order to defend Italy and "western civilisation" from an alleged Muslim "invasion"'.[31] In 2002, the party presented a proposal to make the presence of the crucifix obligatory in all schools and public offices, since it was said to be 'an essential part of the historical and cultural heritage of our country'.[32] This enabled the Lega to kill two birds with one stone, given that its defence of the crucifix could be cast as protecting the people's Christian traditions from the twin threats posed by Islam on the one hand, and secular elites on the other. As regards the latter, the judgment of the European Court of Human Rights (ECHR) in November 2009 that the Italian state could not make the exhibition of religious symbols in public schools obligatory provided another excellent opportunity for the Lega to pose as the defender of the people's religious symbols and traditions. As Ozzano and Giorgi document, the ECHR ruled—in response to a case brought by a naturalised Italian citizen who had been born in Finland—that the presence of the crucifix in public schools could be considered discriminatory.[33] For the Lega, this was yet another example of unwanted—and undemocratic—supranational interference in Italian affairs.

Throughout the first decade of the twenty-first century, the LN criticised European elites for not respecting the people's religious identity. In particular, the failure to explicitly recognise 'the Christian roots of Europe as a fundamental characteristic of our history' in the European Convention was condemned by the party.[34] As the Lega explained in a 2003 policy document, it considered Europe to be 'a coming together of different peoples who are united by their common attachment to Christianity'.[35] It is interesting also to note here that in its criticisms of the Convention the party only mentions 'Christian roots' and not 'Judeo-Christian roots'—the latter had in fact been the wording favoured by most others calling for a reference to religious identity in the European Convention. Given that what unites Europe for the Lega is its Christian heritage, it is no surprise to find that the party has also regularly linked religion to its opposition to Turkish EU accession. For instance, a policy manual used in preparatory courses for LN members aspiring to stand for public office explained that:

> Turkish accession would cause the collapse of the very concept of a Europe founded on certain cultural and spiritual roots. Roots which, we repeat once again, are Christian. For this reason, we believe it should be carefully taken into account that the vast majority of Turkish society are Muslim.[36]

The document adds that the party will continue to oppose Turkey joining the EU because it stands 'against the Islamisation of Europe and of our country'.[37] This idea of a creeping and aggressive 'Islamisation' of northern Italy recurs frequently in LN official documents and campaigns. Take, for example, the following passage from the above-mentioned manual, which has also appeared in several other policy papers produced by the party:

> Today the Islamic communities present on Padanian territory are increasingly trying to impose measures in our schools which are unacceptable for our students such as the removal of the crucifix from classrooms, the disappearance of the traditional Christmas crib, the placing of boys and girls in separate classes, the banning of the use of food such as ham in canteens, and the introduction of the chador (and even the Burqa). They are thus mapping out a dangerous path towards the progressive abolition of the most basic civil rights.[38]

This type of claim—common to many right-wing populist movements in Europe—is accompanied by allegations such as that 'there are thousands of cases in which Koranic law is prevailing over that of the host country'.[39] These provide the justification for the Lega's warning that we are facing 'a loss of Christian and Western identity due to the aggressiveness of the Islamic community'.[40] The co-existence of Muslims and Christians in both Italy and Europe is thus portrayed in terms of a 'clash of incompatible civilisations', with Muslims (helped by the complicity of secular elites) supposedly intent on subjugating the native Christians. Under its new leader Salvini, the Lega's stance on Islam has hardened further, especially in the wake of terrorist attacks. For example, after the *Charlie Hebdo* shootings in Paris in January 2015 Salvini stated: 'Islam is dangerous: there are millions of people around the world, including some living next door to us, who are ready to slit throats and kill in the name of Islam.'[41] Interestingly, as we will see in the next section, although senior figures within the Italian Church hierarchy have opposed the Lega's characterisation of Muslim immigrants and Islam, there have also been some who have been more pragmatic and even supportive.

The Lega Nord and the Church

The relationship between the Lega and the Catholic Church has ranged from one of open conflict at times to an uneasy truce and even agreement at other moments. In the 1990s in particular, the Lega fiercely attacked both the Vatican and the Italian Church hierarchy as being among those elites acting against the interests of the northern people. First, the Church was criticised for its close ties to the DC and other corrupt elites which had dominated the country since the end of World War II. Second, the Lega denounced what it saw as the Church's welcoming attitude to the arrival of immigrants in Italy, irrespective of the social consequences for northern communities. To take one very early example of such criticisms: at a rally in December 1989, Bossi—leader at the time of the Lega Lombarda (Lombard League)—claimed that one of the key sponsors of immigration, in addition to the left and big capital, was 'the Church, shut in its wealthy palaces, which has lost all credibility and needs to fill its empty seminaries with priests whom these days it can only find in the Third World'.[42] No Italian politician had ever dared to speak about the Church in these terms. Nor did Bossi shirk from singling out popular individuals within the Church for extremely strong criticism, including even Pope John Paul II. For example, in 1997, he claimed that 'the Polish pope has invested in temporal power, in the IOR and in the likes of Marcinkus. He has invested in politics and forgotten his spiritual and evangelising roles'.[43] In sum, the Church was accused by the Lega not only of having abandoned the 'people', but of having become a corrupt political elite itself which sided with 'others' (immigrants and southerners) against the northern people in order to pursue its own aims. Given that the Church no long stood with the people, the Lega thus claimed to be the only force battling to save the north from the threats posed to its traditions and wellbeing.

If the above were not enough to keep the LN and the Church on a frequent collision course, the Lega in the 1990s was also calling into question the unity of Italy, something the Catholic Church held as a value and in which it had a vested interest. As Enzo Pace explains, the Church saw itself as one of the key creators and shapers of post-war Italy, a country united (in the Church's view) by Catholicism.[44] Since the Lega was gaining support in those areas of northern Italy where the DC had traditionally done extremely well and the local populations were considered to be strongly attached to the Church, the party's rhetoric and electoral success positioned it as an important challenger to the Church's influence in society. Furthermore, as we have seen, high-ranking members of the Lega in the 1990s even endorsed types of neo-pagan religious practices rather than paying lip service to Catholicism—as right-wing (and many left-wing) Italian politicians have tended to do. Indeed, before the party's neo-pagan turn, Bossi and other key LN figures had frequently suggested that northerners held values closer to Protestantism (in particular, self-reliance, hard work, entrepreneurship, responsibility) than Catholicism (in which supposedly lazy, inefficient, corrupt southerners exploited Catholic values of 'solidarity' and 'charity' to force northerners to support them). On this point, it is also worth noting that individual LN representatives (including Bossi) expressed support on numerous occasions for those priests who followed Marcel Lefebvre and his rejection of the changes introduced by the Second Vatican Council.

The Lega's 'theological challenge' (such as it was) to the Church largely disappeared after 2000 when it re-joined the centre-right alliance and then entered government in 2001. The party's relationship with the Church began to change in these years. Although the first signs of this could be seen when the Lega was part of the 2001–2006 government, the rapprochement quickened noticeably in the second half of the decade. There are several reasons for this mutual shift. First, the Lega's opposition to the exclusion of references to Europe's 'Christian roots' in the European Convention was perfectly in line with the Vatican's position on the issue. Second, as a party which spent most of the decade in government and, after 2008, saw its vote rise considerably and one of its main figures (Roberto Maroni) become Minister of the Interior, the Lega was now a far more powerful political actor than in the second half of the 1990s. Third, as Massetti explains, after 2005, 'the new course in the Catholic Church inaugurated by Pope Benedict XVI and the new Secretary of State, Cardinal Tarcisio Bertone' saw ethical questions like abortion, euthanasia, artificial insemination and civil unions (including between homosexuals) take centre stage.[45] On all of these, the Church found a willing ally in the Lega Nord. Likewise, the second half of the 2000s also saw what Massetti terms 'a marked decrease in official Catholic criticism of the government's anti-immigrant policies'—something that obviously pleased the Lega, since it was the main sponsor and author of these policies.[46]

The Church thus increasingly recognised the Lega's support in defence of Christian identity and ethical issues, along with its role as a key institutional interlocutor and representative of millions of northern citizens. We can see this more conciliatory position (and the logic underpinning it) in the comment after the Lega's success in the 2010 regional elections by Archbishop Rino Fisichella, President of the Pontifical Academy for Life and a very visible figure within the Church in Italy. When asked whether the stance of the Lega on immigration posed problems for the Church, he replied:

> First of all, I believe that we need to acknowledge the Lega's success, its presence for over two decades in parliament, and its strong roots at local level which allow it to hear directly about problems present in the social fabric. As regards ethical questions, it seems to me that there is full agreement between the Lega and the Church's thinking on these. As regards immigration, we need to be able to combine the needs of citizens with those of employers: this means acknowledging the dignity of the human being which must be respected, but also that the Church can never oppose a request for legality.[47]

As we can see, not only did Fisichella publicly state that the Lega and the Church were in harmony on ethical issues, but he also appeared (at least partly) to validate the LN's stance on immigration, given the emphasis the party places on the 'legality' of immigration. While Fisichella's comments can be viewed as a pragmatic attempt to put the Church's relationship with a key government party on a solid non-confrontational footing, other senior members of the Church in Italy have gone further, expressing opinions on Muslim immigration which closely resemble those of the LN. Take, for example, a pastoral letter in September 2000 by the former Cardinal of Bologna, Giacomo Biffi, which attracted extensive media coverage. In it he says that Muslim immigration merits special attention since:

they have a different diet (which is not in itself such a problem), a different day of worship, a family law which is incompatible with ours, a conception of the woman which is very far from ours (they even accept and practise polygamy). Most importantly, they have a vision of public life which is rigorously fundamentalist. Indeed, the perfect synergy of religion and politics is an indisputable and indispensable element of their faith, even if they usually wait until they have come into power to proclaim and apply this.[48]

Biffi warns in the same letter that the existing 'culture of nothing' (in other words, secularism) in Europe 'will not be able to withstand the coming ideological assault of Islam' and that only by rediscovering its Christian roots will Europe be able to ensure 'a different outcome to this inevitable clash'.[49] As we can clearly see, this type of view dovetails perfectly with those of the Lega discussed in the previous section. Indeed, rather than right-wing populism hijacking religion, we might see Biffi's letter as a curious case of religion hijacking right-wing populism.

Of course, we cannot speak of the Church as a unitary actor in its responses to Muslim immigration or to the Lega's stances on this issue. While many within the Italian clergy have either tried to ignore the party or have walked the Fisichella line of non-confrontation and partial agreement, there have also been high-ranking figures within the Church who have adopted positions clearly in contrast with those of the LN. For example, two former Cardinals of Milan, Carlo Maria Martini (1980–2002) and Dionigi Tettamanzi (2002–2011), were both outspoken in their defence of rights for members of the Roma community and Muslims. In each case, these led to fierce responses from the LN. In December 2009, the Lega's newspaper *La Padania* ran an article about Tettamanzi asking whether he was 'a bishop or an imam?' and accusing him of being open to 'the presence of mosques in every quarter'. It added that the cardinal did not seem preoccupied by 'what in theory ought most to interest the Church', in particular the ECHR judgment concerning crucifixes and the rise of Islam.[50]

Of course, this is a relationship in flux, which depends also on who is leading both the Church and the Lega in a given period. Under the papacy of Pope Francis, the new LN leader Matteo Salvini initially sought to avoid conflict. When the pope chose for his first official trip outside Rome to visit immigrants held in detention centres on the island of Lampedusa, Salvini was quick to say that he liked the new pope, and that people should not use his visit to Lampedusa for political ends.[51] However, their very different stances on the 2015 refugee crisis in Europe have brought the Lega and the Church into open conflict once more. In June 2015, Salvini commented: 'the pope says we should ask for forgiveness for those who close the doors to refugees. I ask myself how many refugees there are in Vatican City and how many millions of bogus refugees the pope thinks Italy and Europe can welcome.'[52]

Just as Bossi had done before him, Salvini too has sought to differentiate between the 'bad' elites of the Church hierarchy and 'good' local northern priests. Hence, in April 2015 he said in a radio interview: 'I talk to parish priests, not important bishops living in 300 square metre homes, perhaps with housekeepers.'[53] For its part, the Church has also been more inclined in recent times to issue harsh criticisms of the Lega. The General Secretary of the Italian Episcopal Conference, Nunzio Galantino, was clearly alluding to the LN when he referred in August 2015 to 'worthless populists who, just to win votes, say incredibly stupid things' about migrants.[54]

Conclusion

As we have seen in this chapter, religion has been used for many years by the Lega Nord to define 'us' and 'them'. In particular since 2000, the party has defined 'the people' as virtuous northern Italians who are attached to their Catholic heritage and Muslims immigrants as 'dangerous others' who seek to impose their own traditions and laws through 'Islamisation'. These have become core elements of the Lega Nord's ideology and campaigning strategies. However, as we have also seen, the party's defence of 'the Christian people' focuses more on symbols and the question of 'who belongs' (and does not belong) than on Christian beliefs. Hence, its 'new crusade' has been centred on issues such as opposition to the construction of mosques, support for the maintenance of the crucifix in public buildings and criticism of the failure of elites to acknowledge Europe's Christian roots. Indeed, these roots, according to the Lega, are the key common link between the different nations of the continent. The 'people'—whether northern Italian, Italian or European—are thus defined in terms of residual Christian identities rather than current, actively practised Christian values (especially since these would presumably involve attributes like compassion and charity to foreigners). At the same time, the principal 'other'—the Muslim—is defined in terms of a hostile identity and a series of purported negative values (sexism, extremism and anti-democratic sentiments). These combine to make the Muslim immigrant impossible to integrate within Western societies.

Massetti observes that the presence of a 'virtually mono-religious and mono-confessional (Catholic) tradition has not helped in accepting the ongoing transformation of Italy into a multi-ethnic/multi-religious society,[55] and the Lega has certainly used both this tradition and the transformation brought by immigration to its political advantage. Although the party initially did not position itself as the defender of Catholic traditions against secular elites and immigrants, but rather focused on 'the southerner' as its key 'other', and dismissed the Church as another block of elites acting against the interests of the people, it changed strategy after 2000. In the ensuing decade the party not only used religion far more to frame issues and set the political agenda, but—especially during its years in government—the LN and the Church moved from a position of confrontation to, at times, mutual recognition of each other's roles and tentative agreement on a range of issues. While this relationship has since returned to a more confrontational footing and appears susceptible to change depending on events and specific leaders, what seems unlikely to change is the Lega's religiously-based conceptualisation of 'people' and 'others' that has served it so well over the past fifteen years.

3

THE 'RELIGIOUS CONVERSION' OF THE AUSTRIAN FREEDOM PARTY

Leila Hadj-Abdou

The Freiheitliche Partei Österreichs (FPÖ—Austrian Freedom Party) has been one of the most successful populist right-wing parties in Europe over the past three decades. From the late 1980s onwards, it witnessed a remarkable rise, which led to its participation in national government after the 1999 general election.[1] Even after having to cope with dramatic losses at the ballot boxes in 2002, which ultimately caused the party to split in 2005 into the Alliance for the Future of Austria (BZÖ), led by Jörg Haider,[2] and the FPÖ, now led by Heinz-Christian Strache, the far right recovered. In the 2013 general election, the FPÖ gained 20.5 per cent of the vote, while the BZÖ received only 3.5 per cent (BMI 2013). The rise of the FPÖ was accompanied by some remarkable programmatic developments, among which was the adoption of a pro-Christian stance. In the party manifesto, adopted in 1997 under Haider's leadership, a commitment to Christianity was included. This commitment has been further strengthened since. For instance, when the decision of the European Court of Human Rights (to remove the Christian crucifix from public schools in order to guarantee children's right to a secular education) in the *Lautsi v. Italy* case sparked a Europe-wide debate, the Freedom Party took a clear pro-religious stance.

This evolution is highly puzzling for two reasons: first, the party had traditionally been characterised by a fierce anti-clericalism. In terms of political ideology, the FPÖ represents the 'third camp' which developed in the nineteenth century as a political movement advocating the idea of Pan-Germanism. Anti-clericalism is a central pillar of the ideology of the pan-German movement. In line with its ideological roots, until 1997 the party had never openly departed from its anti-clerical stance. Second, this 'conversion' happened at a time when the Catholic Church had lost a significant degree of support among the Austrian population. The decline was triggered by several cases of child abuse committed by representatives of the Church, which were made public from the mid-1990s onwards. In 1995, it was revealed that the Primate of the Austrian Church, Hans Hermann Gröer, had committed sexual abuse. Within a month, the Gröer affair had caused 5,500 Austrians to leave the Church.[3] Such incidents were often played down by the Church. Not least as a consequence of these and other scandals, the number of people leaving the Catholic Church increased steadily, reaching a peak in 2010, when 85,960 people left.[4] Furthermore, not only are the numbers of those faithful to the Catholic Church in decline, but so too are the numbers of those professing any religious belief at all. The European Values Survey shows that since the 1990s the number of people who perceive themselves as religious has constantly decreased. While in 1999, 82.9 per cent of Austrians declared themselves to believe in God, this number had decreased to 73.3 per cent by 2008.[5]

Given the ideological roots of the party, as well as the societal context, the 'religious conversion' of the Freedom Party is therefore surprising at first glance. This chapter aims to explore the role that religion plays within the Austrian populist right and tries to understand how this 'religious turn' can be interpreted. It is guided by the assumption that religion does not represent a core element of the party's ideology in the sense that religious dogmas do not determine its fundamental ideas about how society should work. Instead, it is argued that (a) the adaptation of the party position on religion is an expression of the transformation of the FPÖ from a traditional far right niche party into a right-wing populist political force, and that (b) religion is used in an instrumental way within the framework of the party's anti-Islamic agenda.

The chapter is divided into the following sections: in the first section, the evolution of the party in terms of its position on religion is traced. I argue that the religious repositioning is closely related to the party's endorsement of Austrian patriotism, founded on the legacy of the old imperial Austria and its mission to be a 'bulwark of Christianity'. In the second section, I discuss the evolution of the party's anti-Islamic agenda. In this section, religion is shown to be primarily used as a tool to stir up anti-immigrant sentiment and to legitimize claims for the restriction of immigration. In the third section, relations between the Church and the party are discussed and conflicting issues are pointed out. This section reflects on the fact that although there is some exchange and ideological overlap with conservative parts of the Church, dissent and conflict override any consensus between the Austrian clergy and the party. Finally, it is worth noting that although the Austrian radical right has been split into two parties since 2005, the focus of this chapter is restricted to the Freedom Party (FPÖ). This reflects the fact that the FPÖ is the more relevant party in terms of electoral strength (see Figure 3.1). Moreover, in the 2013 general elections, the BZÖ failed to gain any seats in the national parliament. Both parties are characterised by very similar rhetoric and similar ideas.[6]

The Evolution of the Freedom Party: from an Anti-Clerical Right-Wing Niche Party to a Successful Pro-Christian Populist Party

Historical Anti-Clerical Roots and Liberal Rapprochement

According to Ludger Helms,[7] two kinds of right-wing populist parties can be distinguished: the first type comprises parties which are newly founded, and

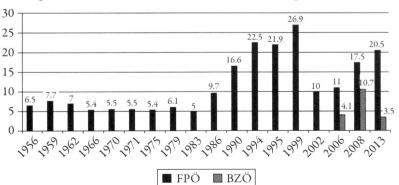

Fig, 3.1: General Election Results of the Austrian Far Right, 1956–2013

Source: Elaboration of data from the Austrian Federal Ministry of the Interior (BMI).

the second are parties which emerge as a result of the transformation of an established party into a populist radical right party. The Austrian Freedom Party belongs to the second category. While it was founded in 1956, its ideological roots date much further back as an offshoot of the German nationalist movement. This movement is also called 'the third camp', as it has traditionally been the third force in Austrian politics, beside the Catholic Conservatives and the Social Democrats. One central, unifying element of the movement, apart from its pan-German orientation, was its anti-clericalism. This strong anti-clerical position, which characterized the Freedom Party for many decades, resulted from the formation of the third camp in opposition to the Habsburg Empire. For centuries the *raison d'être* of the empire had been its role as a defender of Christian Europe against the East,[8] thus championing the Christian West (*Abendland*). 'This was the only principle that gave the Habsburg Empire, this patchwork in the middle of the European map, some form of [character logically legitimating its existence],' Weiss argues.[9] With the French Revolution of 1789, the idea of Europe replaced the idea of a Christian *Abendland*. The Habsburg concept of the Christian West 'became an imaginative construction that no longer fitted the historical reality'.[10] The German nationalists of the nineteenth century despised the supposed backwardness of Catholic Austria, while they associated the German Empire with progress and economic success.[11] In contrast to the other political camps in Austria, overall the Freedom Party remained loyal to its German national roots and, in line with this, maintained its anti-clerical position. This dogmatism isolated the party considerably, and as a result weakened its political influence.[12]

While the first discussions about opening up the FPÖ ideologically and giving it a more liberal make-up emerged in the mid-1960s, it was not until the late 1970s that a liberal ideology gained any momentum within the party. During this period, an initial rapprochement with Christian Churches also took place. Two Christian working groups, one Catholic and one Protestant, were set up within the party in the early 1980s.[13] According to Friedhelm Frischenschlager, a leading FPÖ politician at the time, the creation of the working group 'Freedomite Catholics' aimed to reduce the prejudice and misunderstandings which had hampered dialogue with the leadership of the Catholic Church ever since the foundation of the Freedom Party.[14] The opposition to totalitarian, anti-liberal and collectivist ideas and state-forms was identified by Frischenschlager as a common denominator of Catholicism and the party.[15] The rapprochement with the Church was limited, however. For example, the party continued to disagree with the Church on the question of abortion.[16] Moreover, the ideological broadening of the party was confined to its leadership. At grassroots level, a strong orientation towards traditional, German nationalist, anti-clerical ideas prevailed.

New Orientation under the Leadership of Haider

The ideological gap between the management and the grassroots levels of the FPÖ resulted in an abrupt change of leadership. At a party congress in 1986, a liberal-minded group led by Norbert Steger was pushed out of the party and Jörg Haider was declared the new party leader. Paradoxically, although it was the party's traditional (anti-clerical, pan-German) elements that enabled him to first take power, it was Haider who eventually achieved a break with these traditions. He realised that in order to boost the party's electoral strength it had to be radically refashioned since the national cleavage had become increasingly irrelevant. In the late 1980s, only 6 per cent of the Austrian population perceived themselves as German.[17]

In order to broaden its appeal, the FPÖ distanced itself from its German nationalist roots over the course of the 1990s, with the former pan-German ideology widely substituted with Austrian patriotism. This programmatic shift was additionally triggered by the fact that Austria in the early 1990s faced decisive demographic and political changes which provided fertile ground for political mobilisation based on claims of identity: firstly, after the fall of the Iron Curtain in 1989, Austria witnessed a significant increase in immigration. Between 1987 and 1994, the number of foreigners residing in Austria doubled.[18] This development was accompanied by a considerable anti-immigrant backlash.[19] Secondly, in 1995 Austria became a member of the European Union. The accession process also promoted concerns about a potential loss of Austrian identity, which the major parties—the Austrian People's Party (ÖVP) and the Social Democrats (SPÖ)—could not sufficiently address. During the early 1990s especially, the ÖVP had developed a strong self-image as a pro-European party, which was beginning to override its previous commitment to Austrian patriotism.[20] The SPÖ also placed strong emphasis on Europe, and largely refrained from focusing on national identity.[21] The FPÖ clearly tried to fill this political vacuum.

In times of such far-reaching change, the party promised its potential voters 'a return to the national roots in the sense of an idealised status quo ante,' as Reinhard Heinisch puts it.[22] While the FPÖ has historically developed itself in opposition to the old, Catholic and conservative Austria, the party's success in the 1990s was widely based on the invocation of precisely this 'good old' Austria. 'What we need is a clear return to these values and virtues [...] that have been lost in the past [...],' Haider emphasised.[23] In a nutshell, the Freedomites cast themselves as true representatives of the Austrian people and their traditional values and needs, and as a voice against those who were depicted as endangering the preservation of these values and the fulfilment of these needs: most notably, political elites and immigrants. In line with this new image, Haider described himself in interviews[24] as the 'chosen' one, the 'icon of civil resistance'.

Being a declared advocate of the 'people', the new FPÖ on the one hand had a strong 'egalitarian' agenda,[25] which manifested itself in its articulated hostility against the political elite and those societal groups that benefited from the status quo. This 'egalitarianism', on the other hand, was combined with an anti-egalitarian stance against immigrants, a stance based upon the classical right-wing populist understanding of the 'demos' as 'ethnos'.[26]

Endorsement of Christianity, a Dimension of Austrian Patriotism

The transformation of the party under Haider culminated in the adoption of a new party programme in 1997, which, for the first time at that level of the party, displayed a strong commitment to Austrian patriotism as well as to Christianity. In the manifesto, the party explicitly distanced itself from anti-clericalism, which it defined as 'outdated' in light of 'the changed role of ecclesiastical and religious institutions'.[27] Instead, Christianity was identified as the 'spiritual foundation of Europe'[28] and was equated with Western values.[29] These values were depicted as being endangered by 'the increasing fundamentalism of radical Islam which is penetrating Europe, as well as hedonistic consumption, aggressive capitalism, increasing occultism, pseudo-religious sects and an omnipresent nihilism [...]'.[30] Christian Churches were defined as the 'ideal partners' for the Freedom Party in preserving these sets of values, 'even if they sometimes take other positions on political issues'.[31] This endorsement of Christianity was not meant to convey an ideological congruence with Church dogmas. Instead, the significance of Christianity in the party manifesto was confined to an understanding of religion as culture, an idea which in turn aimed at mobilising demands based on identity. The reference to Christianity as the 'spiritual foundation of Europe' reasserted the Habsburg conception of Europe as the Christian West. It complemented the Freedom Party's claim to be the new, true defender of Austrian identity in times of increasing European integration and ethno-cultural diversification. In line with this new vision, one of Haider's stock phrases in the 1990s in his fight against immigration was: 'We did not fight the Turkish wars in order to let Turkish immigrants now come into Austria, but in order to keep them out.'[32]

These programmatic changes, however, became a matter of fierce contestation within the party, reflecting the allegiance of the majority of party members to the German national roots of the FPÖ. The Viennese branch of the party, in particular, was among the strongest opponents of the endorsement of Christianity in 1997. The Freedom Party was about 'Honour, Freedom and Fatherland' and not about 'Poverty, Chastity, Obedience,' argued Rüdiger Stix, a Viennese Freedomite politician.[33] After the draft of the new party programme was made public, a call was circulated within the party to protest against these new developments. Among those supporting this call was Heinz-Christian Strache, the future leader of the FPÖ.[34] The adoption of the manifesto eventually provoked some party members who were deeply committed to the anti-clerical tradition of the FPÖ to renounce their party membership.[35]

While the new profile did not necessarily resonate with the party's ideological roots or the convictions of its members, it was sufficient to mobilise the Austrian electorate to vote for the FPÖ. In fact, the subsequent 1999 general election produced the best result in the history of the party to date (see Figure 3.1). It is important, however, to stress that it was not the religious segments of the Austrian electorate to whom the party was appealing. Although the FPÖ was able to slightly increase its vote share among religious people, it continued to be a party mostly voted for by the secular population. Among the majority of voters with religious affiliations, the Austrian People's Party (ÖVP) has been, and remains, the most attractive party (see Figure 3.2). The FPÖ's real winning formula was thus not its appeal to Christian voters, but its ability to mobilise those who felt inclined towards the 'idealised status quo ante', of which Christianity represented a symbol. Apart from a successful attempt to attract new voters, this 'religious conversion' also reflected the office-seeking character of the Freedom Party in the 1990s. According to Richard Luther, the reference to Christianity served also to facilitate cooperation with the ÖVP, which was regarded by the FPÖ as a potential coalition partner.[36]

The Construction of a New Outsider Group: from 'Bogus Asylum Seekers' to the Threat of 'Muslim Immigration'

Alongside its new commitment to Christianity, the FPÖ in the 1990s also made Islam a key concern. While immigrants from Muslim backgrounds,

Fig. 3.2: Voting Behaviour of Voters with Strong Denominational Affiliation by Political Party, in Percentages, 1990–2006

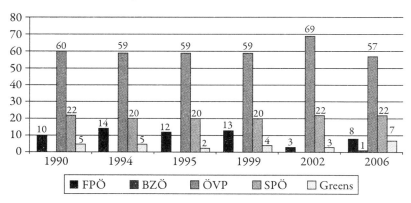

Source: Plasser and Ullram 2008, p. 64.

particularly those from Turkey, had been the subject of FPÖ anti-immigrant rhetoric in the past, the 1990s clearly marked a shift in party discourse as (Turkish) immigrants began to be seen as the Muslim 'other'. 'The social order of Islam is diametrically opposed to our Christian values,' Haider stated in his first book, *The Freedom I Mean*.[37] It is important to note, however, that despite this new attention to Islam and Christianity other themes such as 'bogus asylum seekers' and 'criminal aliens' dominated the political rhetoric of the party. The reticence towards 'playing the Islamic card' more heavily during Haider's leadership, Hödl suggests, might be a side-effect of Haider's political connections during these years with the Libyan president Muammar al-Gadaffi and the Iraqi president Saddam Hussein.[38]

During the populist radical right's participation in national government (2000–2007), Islam was not a major issue either, although targeting Islam was, in an ambivalent manner, part of the party's rhetorical repertoire. After the attacks on 11 September 2001, the Freedom Party positioned itself against a 'global condemnation of all members of the Islamic religious community', and stated firmly that religious freedom and respect for members of all religious communities were cornerstones of the party's ideology.[39] In 2004, too, the FPÖ did not utter a single word of protest when the ÖVP Minister of Education, reacting to a school conflict over Muslim veiling, issued a decree endorsing the Islamic headscarf as an expression of religious freedom.[40] On other occasions during the same period, however, the FPÖ regularly targeted Islamic practices, including the wearing of the Muslim headscarf. The party in sum followed a double strategy, which reflected its difficult position as a member of government. On the one hand, it wanted to prevent the alienation of its voters, who were attracted by the radical nature of its claims. On the other, it had to compromise its political standpoints and to de-radicalise its rhetoric in order to maintain a good basis for cooperation with its coalition partner, the ÖVP. The FPÖ also had to cope with the situation of being the subject of international attention.[41] In response to international protests about the FPÖ's participation in the ruling coalition, the government had signed a declaration promising to avoid racism and xenophobia, and to act in full accordance with European values.[42]

From the mid-2000s onwards, however, following the party's split—into the Alliance for the Future of Austria (BZÖ) and the Freedom Party (FPÖ)—Islam became one of the most prominent issues in the political mobilisation of the latter. The split resulted from the pressure of incumbency and the dramatic decrease in votes in the early 2000s. At the 2002 general election, the FPÖ took only 10 per cent of the vote. Inner conflicts emerged, which eventually led to the bifurcation of the radical right in 2005. The BZÖ, under the control of Jörg Haider, stayed in government until 2007, and in that role still came under pressure to tone down the radicalism of its political agenda. The Freedom Party, now led by Heinz-Christian Strache, went into opposition. Strache used the issues of Islam and Muslim immigration as means of sharpening the political profile of the FPÖ against its political competitors. Since the Islamic religious community is officially recognized in Austria, the anti-Muslim agenda did not merely suit the traditional anti-immigrant orientation of the party: it also had the potential to strengthen anew the party's image as being against the status quo and the rules set by the political establishment. The FPÖ's strengthened anti-Islamic agenda also matched the increasing level of anti-Muslim sentiment within the Austrian population. In the 1999 European Value Survey, 15 per cent of Austrian respondents said that they did not want to live next door to a Muslim. In the 2000s, this number more than doubled. In 2008, 31 per cent of respondents stated that they did not want to have a Muslim neighbour.[43]

In essence, the anti-Islamic agenda of the FPÖ under Strache relies on two main arguments. The first argument is that fundamental Islam poses a threat to national security. The second argument is that Islam is a fundamentally alien culture, which threatens the cultural identity of the Austrian nation state. The concept of cultural identity as used in the party's discourse remains rather vague. While it relies strongly on the abstract notion of 'Christian western values', it is, however, also partly based on liberal values, such as gender equality.[44] Cultural identity is also equated with national customs, such as the consumption of pork. Claims used in political campaigning like 'Free Women Not Forced Veiling' (*Freie Frauen statt Kopftuchzwang*), which was used in the general elections in 2006, co-exist with statements from party representatives, such as 'Pork Chop Not Minaret' (*Schweinskotelet statt Minarett*).[45] The party thus combines forms of cultural 'othering' with illiberal liberalism, the idea that some immigrant cultures—particularly Muslim ones—contradict liberal universal values, and thus do not belong in the liberal societies in which they now live.[46] In the rhetoric of the FPÖ, Islam is constructed as a monolithic entity, endorsing a culture which is irreconcilable with that of Western societies.[47] The party's solution, to address both cultural and security threats, is to restrict immigration. In other words, Islam is used in the party's rhetoric as a simple synonym for unwanted immigration and immigrants. Several of the party's anti-immigrant campaigns have relied on explicit slogans, such as *Pummerin statt Muezzin* ('Church Bells, not Muezzin', 2005 Viennese local elections), *Daham statt Islam* ('Home, not Islam', 2006 general election) and *Abendland in Christenhand* ('The West in the Hands of Christians', 2009 European parliament elections). These slogans were, moreover, accompanied by pictures of Christian and Islamic motifs. While the former were meant to symbolise the deficiencies caused by the political opponent, the latter were meant to refer to the patriotic position of the FPÖ.

Christianity and Islam have thus been used within the framework of the anti-immigrant agenda to signify the 'good us' in opposition to the 'evil them'. The anti-Islamic agenda has also been used by the party to underline its opposition to Turkey's entry into the European Union. A referendum launched by the party in 2006 on the question of Turkey's EU membership used the image of a woman wearing the European flag as a full veil. In relation to the question of whether Turkey (and its migrant community) belongs in Europe, the Freedom Party again made strong reference to Austria's historic past as a Christian bulwark against the Ottoman Empire. The perceived threat of a looming third Turkish siege, invoking the collective memory of the occupation of Vienna in 1529 and 1683 by the Ottoman Empire, became a central theme of the party's rhetoric.[48]

Although the party on the one hand relies strongly on references to Austria's past, on the other it shares a common discursive repertoire with the populist right in Europe. In particular, the theme of Islamic oppression of women, and the perceived threat of the imminent Islamisation of Europe, are common discursive concepts of the European populist right.[49] Sharing a mutual conception of the 'enemy', the anti-Islamic agenda has allowed many parties on Europe's populist right to strengthen transnational ties and foster an exchange of ideas. The political transnational platforms 'Cities against Islamisation' (founded in 2008) and 'Women against Islamisation' (founded in 2012), which were launched under the initiative of the Belgian Vlaams Belang, in close cooperation with the Austrian Freedom Party,[50] represent paradigmatic examples of this evolution. More recently, the FPÖ has used occasions such as the 2015 *Charlie Hebdo* attacks to make the argument (alongside its political allies in Europe), that Islamic radicalism constitutes a Europe-wide problem which demands Europe-wide solutions. It has therefore called for a revocation of the Schengen agreement.[51]

The anti-Islamic agenda is thus not restricted to domestic politics, and the FPÖ also pushes this agenda within the European Parliament (EP). A study of religion in the European Parliament[52] showed that 70 per cent of all parliamentary questions relating to religion from Austrian members of parliament were asked by Freedomite deputies.[53] Almost all of the religiously related questions posed by the FPÖ in the EP concerned the issue of Islam.[54] The strengthened anti-Islamic agenda of the FPÖ under Strache was also accompanied by a shift in the party's position regarding certain 'European' immigrant groups. Ex-Yugoslavs, who had previously been viewed as a threat by the party, were suddenly no longer seen as a problem. In the 1990s, the FPÖ under Haider was still stigmatising immigrants from the former Yugoslavia as thieves.[55] However, immigrants from Serbia in particular began to be depicted in the official party rhetoric as integrated into Austrian society, on the grounds that they shared a common Christian, Western heritage.[56] In 2010, the FPÖ announced the establishment of the 'Christian Freedomite Platform for a Free Europe of Sovereign Peoples' (CFP), which was to be presided over by a Serbian immigrant. The organisation is meant to act as a support for Christians who are forced to leave their homelands.[57] In line with this self-presentation as advocate of persecuted Christians, in the wake of the Syrian refugee crisis, the party has also repeatedly advocated that Austria should primarily grant Christian rather than Muslim refugees protection status.[58] During the European refugee crisis in 2015, the FPÖ repeatedly warned that the incoming Syrian refugees would further increase the threat of Islamic terror. It consequently renewed its calls for the reintroduction of border controls at Austria's borders in order to protect the country from the Islamic State.[59] The strong anti-refugee position adopted by the FPÖ proved highly successful, given that the party gained 30.8 per cent of the votes in the 2015 local elections in Vienna.

In sum, from the mid-2000s onwards, the term 'Muslim' has, to some extent, replaced the term 'immigrant' in the party's rhetoric. It serves as a means to divide those who are supposedly Europeans, and hence can be part of the Austrian nation, and those who are not. 'Islam' functions as an empty signifier, ascribing a combination of naturalised cultural attributes to Muslims that have little to do with religious beliefs, or even being a believer.[60] The Austrian populist right is certainly not the only actor in Europe to have contributed to the 'othering' of Muslims, but it has done so in a more provocative and outspoken manner than many others. For example, in a seminar held in 2009 at the educational institute of the FPÖ, participants were taught that 'if cardinals are raping children, they do it despite their religion; Muslims rape children because of their religion'.[61]

The anti-Islamic agenda allowed the party to successfully address the various segments of the Austrian electorate characterised by one common denominator, namely a strong cultural identification with Christianity. Consistent with the Freedomite concept of religion, the majority of voters who can be successfully mobilised by the 'Christian', anti-Islamic agenda of the FPÖ see religion predominantly as equivalent to culture: according to Zulehner's findings, 40 per cent of Austrians belong to the category of 'militant cultural Christians' (*kämpferische Kulturchristen*).[62] People belonging to this category vote mainly (but not exclusively) for the populist right.[63] These developments, in particular the strengthened transnational engagement and the incorporation of certain 'European immigrants' into the group conceived of as 'us' by the party, also highlight the fact that the party's focus on religion represents an expression of a post-national, Europeanised era. The preservation of national identity postulated by the populist right becomes entangled with the ongoing formation of a European identity. The FPÖ is not merely the self-appointed champion of Austrian patriotism: the religious framing allows the party to portray itself, in the same vein, as the defender of Europe.

Relations between the Church and the FPÖ

How has this new religious conception of identity promoted by the FPÖ affected relations between the party and the Christian Churches? As mentioned previously, when the FPÖ adopted its pro-religious programme in 1997, Churches were defined as the ideal partner to safeguard the Christian West. The Church's reaction to this new position was not entirely clear-cut. To be more precise, a division existed between those who reciprocated the party's approach and those who were more sceptical about the FPÖ's religious 'conversion'. This, of course, merely mirrors the internal heterogeneity of the Church, which represents a wide spectrum, from liberal to ultra-conservative. As Burchianti and Itcaina have pointed out, the Catholic Church is characterised by a certain tension between 'compassion for the excluded and a fear of the religious rival'.[64]

The FPÖ has found some allies among ultra-conservative clerics. In particular, the Bishop of the Diocese of St Pölten, Kurt Krenn, backed the FPÖ on several occasions. In 1993, for instance, he arranged for Haider to have a private audience with the pope.[65] This certainly helped Haider to promote himself as a serious politician. After the 1999 general election, the bishop also openly supported the participation of the FPÖ in government. As he said: 'I hold Haider in high esteem. [...] If he can move things forward they should let him.'[66] Other representatives of the Church, however, have held a more negative attitude towards the party, interpreting the new rapprochement of the FPÖ as an abuse of religion. For example, in a rather explicit press statement responding to the endorsement of Christianity in the 1997 party manifesto, the Austrian Conference of Bishops declared that they did not want to be used in an instrumental way by the FPÖ.

The issue of migration has represented a continuing point of contention between Church representatives and the party. On the occasion of the 'Austria first' referendum, which was launched by the FPÖ in 1993 to demand that immigration be halted, the party was widely criticised by many high-ranking Austrian clerics.[67] The FPÖ's 1999 electoral campaign, which extensively used the notion of 'overforeignisation' (*Überfremdung*), raised new protests from Church representatives.[68] In response, Haider tried to depict the Church as a part of the establishment which had given up its mission to fight against social ills, while portraying the FPÖ as the only remaining true defender of the socially weak groups within Austrian society.[69] The FPÖ's rebuttal of criticism by the clergy thus mirrored that of the Northern League in Italy (see Chapter 2). Another of Haider's strategies was to use theological terminology in order to defend the party's anti-immigrant position. In a paper in which Haider explained the relationship of the FPÖ to the Christian Church, for example, he explicitly referred to a passage on the order of charity from the text *Summa Theologica* by Thomas Aquinas.[70] In this paper, Haider also argued that Aquinas emphasised that we must love those nearest to us, including fellow citizens, more than strangers.

In the 2000s, the friction between the Church and the FPÖ increased still further. In particular, Strache's brandishing of a Christian cross in public in 2008 in order to protest against the construction of mosques met with disapproval from various Church representatives as an abuse of Christianity. Another disputed issue was the FPÖ's anti-Islamic slogan, 'The West in Christian hands', which was used during the 2009 European Parliament election campaign. The slogan was condemned by several clerics, and also led to the issuing of a common press statement by the Ecumenical Church Council, an association of fourteen Christian Churches, which declared that it was opposed to any exploitation of the Christian faith during electoral campaigns.[71] The conflict was sparked again during the 2013 general election campaign. The Freedom Party had chosen the slogan 'Love your neighbour', to which it added the following phrase: 'For me these are our Austrians'. Church representatives criticised the limitation of this Christian commandment to Austrians.[72] The conflict between the Church and the party also manifested itself in December 2012 when protesting refugees found shelter in a church in Vienna. In reaction to the Church's support for the refugees, the FPÖ placed an advertisement in a widely distributed free newspaper, accusing the Catholic Church of being 'delinquent' and supporting 'bogus asylum seekers'. It also claimed that new Church leadership was needed.[73] These divergent positions and conflicts between the Church and the FPÖ mostly related to immigration politics. Yet the party also made its disapproval of the Church known on other occasions. For instance, in 2009, in the wake of the European Court of Human Rights' decision in the *Lautsi v. Italy* case in favour of the removal of the Christian crucifix, the Freedomite deputy Werner Neubauer, a leading FPÖ politician, blamed the Church for supposedly not raising its voice on the matter, and called the Church, 'alongside neo-liberal elements of the EU', the 'coffin-nail' of 'Western, Christian ideas'.[74]

Notwithstanding the above incidents and criticisms, it should be noted that the FPÖ has not challenged the hegemonic position of Christian Churches in Europe. Nor has it questioned the institutional arrangements from which the Church benefits.[75] Rather, the FPÖ has presented itself as the real guardian of Christianity. Or, put more bluntly, the FPÖ has claimed to be more Christian than the Church itself. Strache, like Haider before him, has consistently made use of religious terminology. For instance, he defended his widely criticised use of the crucifix in 2009 with the argument that he had never misused it, but had instead employed it as a symbol of 'redemption and deliverance' in a cultural sense.[76] Although 'redemption' for the FPÖ has primarily meant 'redemption' from the cultural 'other' rather than redemption through the Holy Spirit, its position has indeed moved substantially closer to Christian dogmas on some critical ethical issues. In 2006, Strache initiated a debate on Austria's abortion law, proposing to restrict the time period during which abortions were legally permissible,[77] an initiative which was widely rejected by all other political parties, including the Christian Democratic People's Party. In the current 'Handbook of Freedomite Politics', the official guidebook for party officials, it is stated that, because of abortion, 'the female uterus [is] the place with the highest probability of death'.[78] In these guidelines the party proposes several measures to combat abortion, such as the introduction of official nationwide statistical documentation for abortion rates, and the establishment of a foundation for the protection of human life.[79] The party moreover explicitly condemns homosexual partnerships and the adoption of children by same-sex couples.[80]

The ideological convergence with the Church on these issues is, however, at odds with the resurgence of an anti-clerical, German nationalist spectrum within the party leadership. When transforming the party into a modern populist force, Haider reduced the share of members of German national fraternities to 11 per cent.[81] After the 2008 general election, however, more than a third of the thirty-four FPÖ deputies in national parliament belonged to these same duelling German national fraternities. Indeed, the most influential political and administrative posts within the party were occupied by fraternity members.[82] The ideological dominance of anti-clerical German nationalists within the party is also reflected in the new party manifesto, which was adopted by the Strache-led FPÖ in 2011. In contrast to the 1997 manifesto, it contains no major references to Christianity. The only paragraph that mentions Christianity is to be found in the chapter on identity.[83] This chapter emphasises that the Freedom Party is committed to a 'European world-view' (*europäisches Weltbild*). This world view is defined as a 'cultural Christianity' (*Kultur-Christentum*) 'which is based upon the division of state and church'.[84] The manifesto, moreover, stresses the importance of negative religious freedom.[85] The weight of Christianity in the political programme was thus considerably weakened when compared to the previous manifesto adopted under Haider. Its significance is explicitly restricted to its function as a marker of cultural identity. Given these developments, it remains highly questionable whether the party indeed ever went through a profound 'religious conversion' which would justify the argument that the FPÖ had truly incorporated religious beliefs and values.

Conclusion

This chapter has looked at why the Austrian Freedom Party, a party which had traditionally been deeply committed to an anti-clerical agenda, endorsed Christianity at a time of drastic decline in the popularity of the Catholic Church. In order to make sense of this initially surprising development, several factors must be taken into account. Firstly, the 'religious conversion' happened during the transformation of the party from a German nationalist niche party into a populist force. One core feature of populist parties—and the FPÖ is a paradigmatic example of this—is to radically adapt their programmes in order to maximise voter appeal. The FPÖ in the early 1990s had come to realise that in a nation that had ceased to define itself as German, and had built up a strong national identity of its own, German nationalism was not the way to win over voters. The consequent detachment from German nationalism, and the simultaneous adoption of Austrian patriotism paved the way to change the party's position on religion. This invocation of Christianity served the FPÖ in strengthening its new self-image as a party of Austrian patriots. The new emphasis was not intended to signify belief—rather, it was intended to signify belonging to the Austrian nation.

Secondly, in times of increasing European integration, the endorsement of 'Christianity' as part of the party's new identity concept enabled its agenda to be linked to the emerging European identity. From the mid-2000s onwards, Christianity in the rhetoric of the FPÖ served as a demarcation line between those who supposedly 'belonged' in Europe and those who did not. The abstract notion of the 'Christian West' functioned as a bridge connecting Austrian identity to Europe. Thirdly, the new commitment to Christianity suited the FPÖ's anti-immigrant agenda extremely well. The construction of Islam, and consequently of Muslim immigrants, as potential threats to the country's Christian identity legitimised the Freedom Party's claims for restrictions to be placed on immigration. The new focus on Muslim immigrants, however, not only enabled the party to foster its anti-immigrant profile, but also facilitated the targeting of new groups of naturalised (ex-Yugoslav) immigrant voters, since they had come to be seen as 'one of us' by virtue of sharing the same religion.

The fact that Christianity was used predominantly in a culturally laden, exclusionary way also explains why the religious positioning of the party did not bring it any closer to the Catholic Church, but rather increased the friction between them. Apart from the ultra-conservative spectrum of the Church, the party was not able to convince the majority of Austrian clerics of its religious 'conversion'. The issue of migration, in particular, was a continuous source of disagreement between the two actors. In order to deflect criticism from the clergy, the party tried to denigrate the Church as a part of the establishment responsible for the demise of the 'West'. In that way, the party further accentuated its populist self-image as a party of 'true democrats', voicing popular opinion and grievances.

Having examined the 'religious conversion' of the Freedom Party, it can be concluded that the success of the Austrian populist right is certainly not due to a revival of religious belief in Austrian society, but rather to the existence and ongoing reaffirmation of boundaries within society. Closely intertwined with an anti-Muslim agenda, religion has served the FPÖ as a tool to exclude the 'other', and to distinguish itself from its political opponents. In sum, this chapter has shown that the inclusion of religion in the programme of the Freedom Party is to be understood as a populist mobilisation strategy rather than an indicator of adherence to a faith. Since the link with religion is not a core element of the Freedom Party's ideology, but more a vote-maximisation strategy, its relevance may change, and the party agenda may shift away from religion again at some point. However, taking into account the fact that 'Muslims have become desirably undesirable'[86]—a sentiment which was successfully stirred up by the populist right and which has contributed to its electoral strength—it might be too presumptive to conclude that any such shift in agenda will happen in the near future.

4

POPULISM AND ISLAM IN SWITZERLAND

THE ROLE OF THE SWISS PEOPLE'S PARTY

Oscar Mazzoleni

In Switzerland, as elsewhere, the fall of the Berlin Wall in 1989, the accelera-
tion of globalisation and the attacks of 11 September 2001 have all combined
to bring about a major change in the relationship between religion and politics. Like other Western European countries in the first decade of the twenty-
first century, Switzerland witnessed the emergence of a new configuration
conducive to the exploitation of Islam in the strategies of right-wing populist
parties. The specific features of this mobilisation depend upon political, cultural and institutional factors which contribute to determining the content of
political discourse and the style of populism in each individual country. How
and why has the main Swiss right-wing populist party, the Swiss People's Party,
placed religious issues within its political agenda? Does this represent a rediscovery of religious faith? Or is it just another example of the manner in which
such parties present themselves as defenders of the 'true' people, of the 'true'
nation, of the 'true' values which various 'enemies' (namely the establishment
and foreigners) are said to have betrayed or cheated?

This chapter focuses on the Schweizerische Volkspartei/Union démocratique du centre/Unione democratica di centro (SVP—Swiss People's Party), which has been the strongest party from an electoral perspective in Switzerland over the past decade. Via the first popular vote in Europe designed to prevent the construction of minarets, the SVP placed the fight against 'Islamisation' high on its agenda. The first part of this chapter discusses the party's main characteristics, analysing them in relation to its conception of the Swiss people and, in particular, the 'Christian' people. The second part analyses the role of Islam in the SVP's election campaigns. The third part looks at the party's role in the anti-minaret campaign. The fourth part poses a range of questions concerning the political opportunities offered in Switzerland by mobilisation against Islam, with particular reference to Islam's public image and the popular initiative that enables changes to be made to the Swiss Constitution.[1]

Electoral Success, Radicalisation and Populism

The SVP enjoys a unique position in Western European politics. It is the only radical right populist party in the last two decades in Western Europe to have established itself as the strongest national party. This is due primarily to the resources at its disposal. Thanks to a mobilisation capacity unequalled among its competitors[2] and strong leadership under billionaire Christoph Blocher, the SVP has been Switzerland's biggest party, at least in terms of votes and seats won in the National Council, since 2003. To put this into perspective: in 1991, the party won just 11.9 per cent of the vote, before beginning its remarkable electoral rise, which reached its zenith in 2015, when it received 29.4 per cent (see Table 1).

This advance has been accompanied by a profound transformation in the SVP's support base and ideological profile. Its roots are those of a traditional agrarian party founded in the second decade of the last century. Until recently, the SVP was only represented in about half of the country's cantons, which were predominantly Protestant in composition. In the first decade of this century the party made inroads into the other cantons, including those whose populations were mostly Catholic.[3] Another feature distinguishing the SVP from other Western European populist parties is its unbroken participation in the federal government: apart from an eleven-month period in 2008, it has been a minority party in broad coalitions comprising the Liberal, Christian Democrat and Socialist parties since the 1950s.[4] Its participation in the federal government has not been affected by its ideological radicalisation. Without ever presenting itself as a religious party, in the 1990s what may now be called the 'new' SVP underwent a marked radicalisation. Traditionally a moderate centre-right party, in the last two decades it has moved appreciably to the right, in particular advocating restrictions on immigration and asylum.[5]

Table 4.1: Percentage Strength of the Main Swiss Parties in Federal Parliamentary Elections (Lower Chamber), 1991–2015

Year	Swiss People's Party	Liberal Party	Christian Democratic Party	Socialist Party
1991	11.9	21.0	18.0	18.5
1995	14.9	20.2	16.8	21.8
1999	22.5	19.9	15.9	22.5
2003	26.7	17.3	14.4	23.3
2007	28.9	15.8	14.5	19.5
2011	26.6	15.1	12.3	18.7
2015	29.4	16.4	11.6	18.8

Source: Federal Office of Statistics, Berne.

A crucial feature of the 'new' SVP's discourse is the sacralisation of the 'Swiss people' as a national entity, the character and cohesion of which are threatened from outside by the danger of invasion on the part of groups which do not observe—or which reject—the Swiss rules of co-existence. In its interpretation of the Swiss socio-economic, cultural and political crises of the 1990s and 2000s, the SVP gave centre stage in its agenda to the country's struggle for independence from the European Union and resistance to rising immigration. It did this in the name of defence of Swiss 'exceptionalism': the combination of a specific institutional structure (federalism, direct democracy, foreign policy neutrality) and an affluent society. These go toward constructing the principal elements of the 'new' SVP's 'winning formula'.

Foreign Cultures versus Swiss and Christian Culture

The perceived threat to national identity, criticism of the establishment and the desire to impose changes appealing to popular sovereignty shape the way in which the general theme of immigration is approached. The SVP demands greater restrictions on the presence of foreigners and 'false' refugees, and on 'foreign criminals' and naturalisation. Over the years, it has launched a number of popular initiatives and referendums on these questions, taking up at least some of the demands that have been made since the 1960s by minor parties and other political movements, the platforms of which emphasised imposing restrictions upon the number of foreigners coming to Switzerland.[6] Although the SVP has rarely won such initiatives and referendums, its repeated campaigns have kept these issues at the centre of national political debate and ensured that the party has been identified with them in the eyes of the public.

While the questions of Europe and immigration have been the pillars of the 'new' SVP's agenda for the last two decades, other issues, such as the defence of traditional education against the anti-authoritarian legacy of 1968 and the question of Islam, did not appear on its agenda until the end of the 2000s. This was reflected, first, in its support for the campaign against minarets, resulting in a ban passed in 2009, and then in the party's programme, which, having concentrated on 'excessive immigration', 'foreign criminals' and 'bogus asylum seekers', introduced a new element. For the first time, the party took up religious questions, focusing on a specific community rather than a collection of groups and heterogeneous communities. Hence, in the run-up to the 2011 federal elections, the SVP was the only major party whose manifesto contained a chapter devoted to religion, and Islam in particular. More recently, during the 2015 federal election, this theme has again been underlined.[7]

At the centre of the SVP's portrayal of Islam is the threat posed by it endangering Swiss 'values' and the Christianity that Switzerland embodies. Rather than religious faith, the values said to be in danger are those of democracy, tolerance and freedom. In its 2011 programme (and again, four years later) the party stated: 'The SVP is committed to upholding Switzerland's Western, Christian culture. It forms the basis for our identity and our coexistence. It is no accident that our country's national emblem contains a cross.'[8] The appeal to the cross on the Swiss flag—a religious symbol and a mark of identity, as stated in the party's manifesto—seems to be an attempt to impose a definition of Swiss identity upon the Swiss people through religion, which is understood less as the experience of faith than as a moral and legal norm.[9] It should be noted, however, that there is some oscillation between the defence of Swiss values and those of Western Christianity, which is inconsistent with the party's discourse, focused principally until a few years ago on the defence of Swiss national integrity. Thus, the party states:

> Our freedom of worship and of conscience accords everyone in our country liberty of thought, writing, speech and religion. Under our Constitution, churches and religious communities therefore enjoy freedom to promulgate their beliefs and carry on their religious activities. But the boundaries of this tolerance lie at the point where religious communities hold it in contempt or even openly oppose it.[10]

For the SVP, Protestantism and Catholicism are strictly related to Switzerland's democratic legacy, as well as its prosperity:

> The development of democracy from ancient ideas can only be understood with the transition to individual responsibility. Furthermore, the Protestant work ethic is the foundation for an entrepreneurial and also performance-driven society. We derive reasonable thought, creativity and innovation from Western Christian principles. After all, entrepreneurship and progress are rooted in the hope of a prosperous future. In the same way, the Catholic principle of subsidiarity and the stressing of the value of the individual within Creation had and continue to have a substantial influence on Switzerland and Swiss federalism. Individuals should assume responsibility for their problems and, if possible, resolve them themselves.[11]

By contrast, the anti-Islam claim fits with the SVP's agenda, above all because it ties in with the struggle against foreign invaders and the inability of immigrants to accept and be integrated into 'Swiss culture'. Muslims are generally presented as immigrants whose values are incompatible with those of the host country. For example, the SVP says:

> It is estimated that over 400,000 Muslim believers live in Switzerland today. Clearly, only a small minority sympathises with extreme Islamist ideas. But Muslim immigrants often come from countries in which there is no democratic rule of law. They bring with them ideas of law and order that are incompatible with our legal system and our democratic rules. Radicalisation and isolation trends are problems that should not be underestimated. In our country, too, there are individuals and groups who sympathise with a radical Islam. At the same time, Islamic communities are raising their voices and calling for recognition as legal entities under public law or training for their spiritual leaders at our universities. These challenges and the demand for special legal treatment should not be naively accepted without criticism.[12]

According to the Swiss Statistical Office, Muslims accounted for only about 5 per cent of the resident population in Switzerland in 2010, and just 12 per cent of these had Swiss nationality.[13] Nonetheless, the SVP manifesto concentrates on Muslim immigration and naturalisation, arguing that: 'Anyone who fails to support our free and democratic principles without reservation must not be granted Swiss citizenship.' The SVP therefore calls for a policy of assimilation of Muslims and rejects any kind of multiculturalism. It argues:

> Just as we adapt to the rules of Islamic states when we are guests there, we must systematically insist on reciprocity here. Parallel societies with their own legal systems cannot be tolerated. Our legal order based on freedom must on no account give way to Sharia law; our courts must not accept an Islamic 'cultural background' as a reason for imposing a milder sentence. Toleration and even encouragement of practices such as forced marriages, 'honour killings', blood

feuds, female circumcision, marriages involving minors or polygamy are totally unacceptable in our country.[14]

Again, with regard to Islam, the SVP criticises elites such as 'the left', journalists and 'public offices responsible for the defence of gender equality' for their excessive tolerance. Hence, in the 2011 manifesto, the party stated: 'The craven and cowardly attitude of certain politicians, journalists and representatives of the Church is a matter of concern. The left, feminists and even equality offices generally choose to remain silent.'[15] Representatives of Catholic and Protestant Churches are also criticised by the SVP due to their alleged inability to confine themselves to their proper tasks and their unjustified interference in public life. In fact, in recent years Swiss Catholic and Protestant Churches have expressed positions on immigration and asylum policies that strongly differ from those expressed by the SVP. Hence, just as we saw with regard to the Lega Nord in Italy (see Chapter 2), the SVP has made pronouncements about what the role of the Churches should (and should not) be:

> The task of the Churches is to offer people support and genuine assistance in their lives, by spreading the word and providing pastoral care. Politicians should not preach from the pulpit, and neither should preachers use it to engage in politics. The SVP is opposed to biased pronouncements by Church functionaries based on left-wing ideology, because they divide our national Churches. It is also opposed to egalitarian, socialist interpretations of the Christian message, which accords great importance to the free development of the individual.[16]

It is particularly interesting to observe that the struggle against Islamisation has entailed an attempt to engage with questions previously of little concern to the party: not only religious freedom, but also gender equality and the defence of Swiss liberal democracy. In this regard, the question of Islam has afforded the SVP the opportunity to speak to potential supporters outside its usual constituency, setting itself up as a guarantor of liberal democracy and gender equality, both of which are traditionally considered to be values more at home on the left.

The Campaign against Minarets

The tools of direct democracy have been the SVP's weapon of choice in the fight against Islam. Thus far, it has been via the anti-minaret campaign that the 'new' SVP has most effectively tested its arguments against Islamisation. In its support for the campaign, in which the party cast itself as acting virtually alone against the establishment and in defence of endangered values, the SVP again appealed to the idea of a Christian Swiss people in danger. It was also this campaign which forged the position, expressed in the party's 2011 election manifesto, that 'the construction of minarets is an expression of a desire for religious and political power and must therefore be rejected'.[17]

From Uncertainty to Support

Nonetheless, the SVP's support for the anti-minaret initiative, launched in 2007, was initially limited and marked by hesitancy on the part of the party's head office. Given its participation in government, the novelty of religion as an issue to be addressed by the party, and the danger of being accused of damaging Switzerland's image (thus risking an Arab commercial and financial boycott), the SVP's national leadership never gave the anti-minaret campaign its unconditional support. Indeed, at the time of its launch, the party's assembly of delegates preferred to put its weight behind a 'competing' campaign for the expulsion of 'foreign criminals' from the country. It was not until two years later that the party's federal parliamentary group and assembly of cantonal delegates clearly came out in support of the campaign to ban the construction of new minarets throughout the entire country, though its headquarters made no direct or financial commitment to this initiative.[18]

However, in addition to its aversion towards immigration and multiculturalism, a series of new factors contributed to convincing a clear majority of the SVP to support the anti-minaret campaign. In the first place, the party observed that the initiative enjoyed considerable public support, as evidenced by the 113,500 signatures collected in its popular initiative in June 2008. Having by no means been assured of achieving such levels of support, the initiative had been promoted by a committee composed of fourteen SVP members and two from the Federal Democratic Union (a small evangelical party).[19] SVP support was also a consequence of local mobilisation campaigns—some organised by SVP members, others mounted independently by Christian organisations—against the construction of new minarets in a number of areas of Switzerland; without the participation of these Christian groups the campaign would probably not have got off the ground. The political controversy over minarets dated back to 2005, to the granting of planning permission for a minaret in Wangen (Canton Schwyz), and continued in 2006 concerning projects in Langenthal (Canton Berne) and Wil (Canton St Gallen). In 2007, a few months before the launch of the national campaign, there was a proposal to open an Islamic centre, with a minaret, in the capital,

Berne.[20] During the same period, the ideological mobilisation was given intellectual impetus in journals and other publications distributed, above all, in those German-speaking areas which had for some years shown concern over the dangers of Islam. This took the form of right-wing and extreme right-wing propaganda reflecting a desire following the fall of communism to develop opposition to the hegemony of the great powers (the European Union and the United States) and Islam and to assert patriotic and nationalist values.[21] These circles were swift to interpret Samuel Huntington's 'clash of civilisations'[22] as a confrontation between religions.

Not only did the question of Islam appeal to more traditional concerns (fear of immigration and foreign cultures), but it also held the potential to reach new segments of young and female voters (by focusing on accusations of a lack of respect for women's dignity in Muslim cultures). It should also be borne in mind that the strategy of the 'new' SVP had always been to avoid finding itself wrongfooted by those movements further to the right, and there was a danger that the small but determined Federal Democratic Union—a religious party which sponsored initiatives to assert an unbending evangelical Christianity[23]—might make electoral capital out of a successful anti-minaret campaign.

Political Players and Churches in the Public Sphere

Having followed the usual procedures, and after being shunned by the government and all its participating parties except the SVP, the popular initiative was launched in November 2009. The campaign organised by the committee included a nationwide display of posters depicting a Muslim woman, whose face and body were completely covered in black, near minarets—also black— rising above the Swiss flag in such a way as to resemble threatening missiles. Their purpose was to represent the minaret as the symbol of Islam's ambition for dominion. The initiative committee's argument ran as follows:

> The minaret represents [...] a claim that fundamentally knows no tolerance, that divides the world into the faithful [Muslims] and infidels [everybody else]. The minaret is therefore the symbol of a quest for political-religious power that contemplates no freedom of worship.[24]

On a more general level, the minaret was presented as the manifestation of a conflict of values between Islam and the rules of co-existence underpinning Swiss democracy. With arguments similar to those espoused by Huntington, the promoters of the initiative accentuated the profound conflict between Islam and the West. In an interview given during the collection of signatures, one of the campaign's main proponents, Christian Waber of the Federal Democratic Union, even claimed that 'Islam aspires to world domination [...] Islam is a declaration of war on other faiths.'[25]

Besides the federal government, the popular initiative's opponents comprised centre-right parties, parties on the left, a range of humanitarian nongovernmental organisations and the Catholic and Protestant Churches, which intensified their public pronouncements in the months and weeks leading up to the vote. In an official press release, the Swiss Catholic Bishops' Conference explained its opposition to the campaign as follows:

> It is a political question that regards a religion and the corporative rights of religions. Like bell towers, minarets are a sign of the public presence of a religion. [...] A general prohibition on the construction of minarets would undermine the efforts of those who wish to establish an attitude of reciprocal openness to dialogue and mutual respect. In this regard too, fear is counter-productive. [...] Though acknowledging the real difficulties in the co-existence of religions, for the sake of consistency with the Christian values and democratic principles of our country, we call for a rejection of the initiative.

The Swiss Federation of Evangelical Churches echoed these sentiments, pointing out that the minaret constituted the expression of a religious belief and, as such, was worthy of respect. The success of the initiative would jeopardise religious peace and would not help Christians who were being persecuted in some Muslim countries.[26] Opposition was also expressed by Switzerland's various Jewish organisations in the name, among other things, of the equality of all religions. It was necessary in their view to

> take seriously the disquiet of the Swiss people, worried by the spread of extremist ideas. Far from being a solution to the problem, the prohibition of minarets would arouse feelings of exclusion and discrimination on the part of Muslims in Switzerland.[27]

During the campaign, criticism was also voiced by some leading members of the SVP, in particular the party's federal government representative, Ueli Maurer, and one of its foremost economists, the entrepreneur Peter Spuhler. Indeed, the latter said that in the event of a successful constitutional change boycotts would have to be expected and that there would be a serious risk of economic sanctions against Switzerland.[28]

An Inconclusive Success?

On 26 November 2009, the popular initiative against the construction of minarets was approved by a clear majority of voters (57.5 per cent) and an overwhelming majority of cantons (it was rejected in only four out of twenty-six cantons and semi-cantons). The result was a surprise for supporters and opponents of the initiative alike, since opinion polls had written it off as a probable failure. At 53 per cent, the turnout was higher than average for this type of vote. Surveys showed that the cultural, social and political composition of those in favour and against the ban was in some respects similar to that on popular initiatives and referendums on immigration and asylum seekers.[29]

The SVP, and above all its leaders active in the anti-minaret campaign committee, claimed the victory as their own, trying to capitalise on its political success. Since 2009, there have been local propositions such as parliamentary calls in the Cantons of Aargau and Ticino for a ban on the burqa. In the latter canton, in September 2013, a popular initiative supported by 53 per cent of the population introduced a ban on people covering or hiding their faces in public, with the campaign focused on a burqa ban. Two years later, after the official recognition of this ban by the Swiss Constitution, the national committee that won the minarets initiative launched a new popular initiative in September 2015 to introduce burqa and veil bans at national level.

Conditions Rendering Mobilisation Possible

The development and success of any political actor are determined by a complex combination of factors. In an attempt to understand how and with what degree of success a political actor can mobilise opinion on a particular issue, two related dimensions must be considered: firstly, the characteristics of the actor itself, its resources and its pronouncements—the extent to which it is able to identify and respond to forms of latent social unease; secondly, the external conditions, or the political, institutional, cultural and religious opportunities onto which the actor's strategies can be grafted, including its ability to position itself, through alliances and competition, with respect to other political actors.

With the above in mind, we can now consider what conditions—aside from its own resources and capacity for mobilisation—enabled the SVP to mobilise opinion around the struggle against Islamisation in politically successful terms. At least three factors may be proposed: (1) the appearance of the conflict between Islam and the West as a subject of public debate in the first years of the twenty-first century; (2) the weakening of the public role of religion in the years preceding the emergence of the question of Islam; and (3) institutional opportunities, in particular the ready availability of the instruments of direct democracy.

The Public Portrayal of Islam

As observed above, one of the themes prominent in the SVP manifesto and the anti-minaret campaign was Islam's supposed desire to suppress Swiss democracy. There can be no doubt that mobilisation over the minaret question and the heated debate about Islam in Switzerland were, in part, the fruit of the 11 September 2001 attacks and more recently the *Charlie Hebdo* killings as well as the international fallout from these events. The spread of unease about profound socio-economic, demographic and cultural changes, the arrival of millions of people from Africa and the Middle East, the 'war on terror' and the increasing number of Muslims all over Europe coincided with a heightened public interest in Islam, identified as a threat to the West in general and Switzerland in particular.[30] From the 1960s to the 1990s, the construction of mosques and minarets in Switzerland had aroused no political controversy.[31] Although occurring later than in other European countries,[32] the negative portrayal of Islam in the Swiss public sphere was a consequence of international developments in the first decade of the twenty-first century, as shown by studies on media coverage,[33] and the question of Islam was highlighted more by parties of the populist right than those of the centre-right or left.[34]

The Weakening of the Public Role of Religion

As observed above, the anti-minaret campaigners and the SVP manifesto attempted to impose an image of religion as a strictly private matter, as part of a strategy designed to oppose any form of religious interference in public norms (which, according to the SVP, should be reserved for political actors). In other words, the sphere of religion should not affect the rules of co-existence; otherwise, there would be a danger of civil and religious conflict. The injunction to stay out of politics thus applied as much to the Christian religions as it did to Islamic movements. The SVP's stance on the public sphere and religion should be seen in the light of the ambivalence which remained— and in some respects has remained to this day—in the Swiss constitutional and legislative system, where increasing tolerance and recognition of religious freedom stand alongside unchanging legal constraints. Until a few decades ago, as a consequence of religious conflicts going back to the nineteenth century, the federal Constitution laid down a series of constraints on a number of religious communities, in particular Catholics and Jews. They have since been removed from the Constitution, but the regulation of relations between Church and state is still left to the cantons, some of which have retained constraints on religious communities because certain practices are deemed to be disrespectful of public morals. In some Protestant cantons, for instance, there remain limits on the exercise of the priesthood—in Geneva Canton, it is still illegal for priests to wear a cassock in public.[35] Such juridical ambivalence reflects the tension between an active state role in regulating religious matters and the consideration of religion as a private sphere within which a liberal democratic state should not legislate. According to some surveys, this ambivalence is also present in public opinion, not only because—like elsewhere in Europe—the de-institutionalisation of religion has been accompanied by the appearance of new religious movements,[36] but also because the idea of a public role for Churches in general seems to arouse negative feelings.[37]

In the 1980s and 1990s, religious questions faded from prominence in Swiss public life.[38] In all the main political parties this was accompanied by a tendency to present religion as a private matter and by the parallel assumption that the role of Churches should be confined to the non-political sphere. Bearing witness to this trend is the development of the main Christian-based political party, the moderate centrist Christian Democratic Party—represented in the federal government since the late nineteenth century—which has gradually abandoned religious questions in its election manifestos since its re-foundation in 1971. Though retaining its Christian basis, the party asserted an increasing degree of independence from ecclesiastical organisations.[39] When events at the beginning of the twenty-first century drew attention to Islamist terrorism, the Federal Democratic Union, and later the SVP, were able to legitimise their anti-Islamic stance in the name of the necessary separation of religion from the public sphere. This disqualified the representatives of the Christian Churches from standing in opposition to the anti-minaret campaign, but it also neutralised *a priori* an argument that might have been used against the Christian Democratic Party, which opposed the ban on minarets in the name of religious freedom and human rights, though without seeking the support of the Catholic or Protestant Churches.[40] It is no coincidence that in their analysis of the result of the popular initiative the Protestant Churches judged the role of the 'established political parties' against the initiative to have been 'superficial' and incapable of mounting an effective opposition, because the latter were no longer used to dealing with religious issues.[41]

The Instruments of Democracy as a Political Opportunity

The other major condition conducive to the SVP's mobilisation on the question of Islam derived from Switzerland's employment of direct democracy. While in the past the use of these mechanisms as a protest strategy was mostly character-istic of parties and movements of the left, the 'new' SVP with its populist dis-course has marked an increase in their deployment by the radical right. Oskar Freysinger, an SVP member of the federal parliament, was a leading promoter and an active campaigner in the anti-minaret initiative. In his comment on the result of the vote, he emphasised that the use of initiatives and referendums had highlighted the true interests of the people, seen as a homogeneous entity, against the elites:

> Two camps emerged: the elite who said that direct democracy was anti-democratic and against human rights, which is a total paradox, and the defenders of popular rights, who, while recognising that it is not ideal, nonetheless think that the system is the best possible, because it allows people to feel involved and to have an outlet of expression. [...] In fact, Switzerland, at the heart of Europe, has just given an incredible lesson in civic spirit, against the politically correct, against the elites, against the media and against the monumental pressure of uniform thought.[42]

Switzerland was the first European country to organise public debate and decision-making on the question of immigration. This process began in the 1960s.[43] Likewise, the question of Islam entered the political arena not only through the mass media, but also by means of the mechanisms providing for direct democracy. One example was the vote held on questions concerning the relationship between Church and state and on immigration, in particular on naturalisation. In 2003, on the occasion of a popular initiative regarding the recognition under public law of non-Christian religious communities in the Canton of Zurich, 'Islam' became the campaign's overriding issue; the oppo-nents of recognition succeeded in focusing attention on the 'danger' that madrasas might benefit from state subsidies. In a referendum held the follow-ing year on fast-track naturalisation, a substantial proportion of its opponents, including prominent SVP members, built their campaign around Islam, rais-ing the spectre of a massive influx of Muslim foreigners applying for Swiss nationality.[44] Since its emergence in the political arena at canton level, the question of Islam has thus been intertwined with those of the state and reli-gious groups, immigration and naturalisation—all of which are, in turn, inter-twined in the SVP's national programme.

Conclusion

With the experience already acquired in drawing political attention to issues such as foreigners and asylum seekers, the SVP, the strongest Swiss party, has used its mobilisation powers to make the issue of Islam another weapon in its twenty-year battle to defend Christian values. It has thus employed religion in the definition of Swiss identity. While the SVP is the first major party to have included the fight against Islamisation in its platform, this does not represent a rediscovery of religious faith, but rather a successful attempt to politicise the presence of Islam in Switzerland. Above all, thanks to the SVP's support, a ban on the construction of minarets was adopted in 2009 as a constitutional principle for the first time in a Western democracy by a majority of Swiss voters. This was possible thanks to the specific opportunities provided by direct democracy in Switzerland, in particular popular initiatives, as well as a changing trend in public opinion concerning the role of religion in general and Islam in particular. In recent years, the SVP has continued to emphasise the threat posed by Islam, thus exploiting the turning point that occurred in the 2000s in Swiss politics. As had been the case with regard to the immigration issue, the SVP found itself at odds with the country's principal Churches—namely Protestant and Roman Catholic—which both considered a ban on minarets as contrary to the principle of religious freedom. Since the minaret ban, Islam has remained a salient issue in the Swiss political landscape. At national level, in late 2015 the referendum committee (co-chaired by SVP representatives) that had been responsible for the anti-minaret proposal launched a new popular initiative to introduce a ban in the Swiss Constitution on people covering or hiding their faces in public. However, Islamic State (IS) and other related questions have not appeared at the forefront of the SVP's agenda thus far. Rather, the party prefers to focus mainly on campaigns against immigration, asylum seekers and alleged EU interference. In this sense, the SVP's strategy continues to be influenced by its relations with the business community, which, in turn, is fearful of damaging Switzerland's image in Arab countries.

5

USING FAITH TO EXCLUDE

THE ROLE OF RELIGION IN DUTCH POPULISM

Stijn van Kessel[1]

Religion has played a crucial role in the formation of the Dutch party system, and party competition in the first decades after World War II was, to a considerable degree, still determined by the religious denomination of voters. Most religious voters were loyal to one of the three dominant 'confessional' parties: the large Catholic People's Party (KVP) or one of the two smaller Protestant parties (ARP and CHU).[2] Until the parliamentary election of 1963, the combined vote share of the three dominant confessional parties was around 50 per cent. Most secular voters, on the other hand, turned either to the Labour Party (PvdA), representing the working class, or the Liberal Party (VVD), representing the secular middle class. The fact that voting behaviour was rather predictable resulted from the fact that Dutch parties and the most significant religious and social groups—arguably with the exception of the secular middle class and the VVD—were closely aligned.[3] One aspect of this 'pillarisation' of society was that the electorate voted largely along traditional cleavage lines of religion and social class.

The dividing lines between the social groups gradually evaporated, in part due to the secularisation of society since the 1960s. Except for the secular middle class, the social background of the electorate continued to determine voting patterns quite predictably in the following decades, but by the turn of the twenty-first century the explanatory power of belonging to a traditional pillar had faded to a large extent.[4] What is more, as Dutch society became more secularised, the level of electoral support for the three dominant confessional parties began to decline. This provided an incentive for these parties to merge into the Christian Democratic Appeal (CDA) in 1980.

Although Dutch voters began to choose more freely, the traditional parties were hardly challenged by populist parties or politicians. During the twentieth century, political parties often associated with populism had intermittently managed to enter the Dutch lower house (*Tweede Kamer*), but were never very successful (see Table 5.1).[5] The Farmers' Party (Boerenpartij) entered parliament in 1963, but has never received more than 4.8 per cent of the vote. The ethno-nationalist xenophobic parties led by Hans Janmaat in the 1980s and 1990s (the Centre Party and Centre Democrats) never grew to play significant roles. Another populist party that emerged was the left-wing Socialist Party (SP—Socialistische Partij), a party with Maoist roots which could be described as a 'populist socialist' party in the 1990s.[6] However, the party toned down its populist, anti-establishment rhetoric to a considerable extent after the 1990s.[7]

It was only after the turn of the twenty-first century that a whole array of populist parties appeared on the Dutch political scene, though few came close to representation in the Dutch parliament. Two populist parties were clearly the most successful electorally: the Pim Fortuyn List (LPF—Lijst Pim Fortuyn)—although only for a short period of time—and Geert Wilders' Freedom Party (PVV—Partij voor de Vrijheid). In the parliamentary election of 15 May 2002, the party newly founded by maverick politician Pim Fortuyn, a columnist and former sociology professor, broke through with 17 per cent of the vote—an unprecedented result for a newcomer. Fortuyn himself did not witness the results of the 2002 parliamentary election; on 6 May, he was murdered by an environmental activist. The party's success was short-lived, not least due to continuous infighting after it joined a coalition government with the Liberals and the Christian Democrats. Mainly due to the organisational problems of the LPF, an early election was scheduled for 22 January 2003 in which the party that had aimed to represent the late Pim Fortuyn's ideas suffered a significant defeat. After the 2006 election, the party disappeared from the Dutch parliament altogether. At the same time, this election also marked the entrance of the populist, radical right Freedom Party, which was founded and has since been controlled by ex-Liberal MP Geert Wilders.[8] With 5.9 per cent of the vote, Wilders' success in this instance was still modest, but in the 2010 election his party won 15.5 per cent of the vote. After this election, the Freedom Party provided parliamentary support to the governing minority coalition formed between the Liberals and the Christian Democrats. In the early election of 2012, the Freedom Party was among the losers, but still received 10.1 per cent of the vote.

Table 5.1: Populist Parties and Seats Won in Elections for the Dutch Lower House

Party	Years in Parliament	Record vote share
Farmers Party (Boerenpartij)	1963–1981	4.8% (1967)
Centre Party (Centrumpartij)	1982–1986	2.5% (1994)
Centre Democrats (Centrumdemocraten)*	1989–1998	
Socialist Party (Socialistische Partij)**	1994 –present	16.6% (2006)
Livable Netherlands (Leefbaar Nederland)	2002–2003	1.6% (2002)
Pim Fortuyn List (Lijst Pim Fortuyn)	2002–2006	17% (2002)
Freedom Party (Partij voor de Vrijheid)	2006 –present	15.5% (2010)

Source: election data from http://www.verkiezingsuitslagen.nl
*In 1984, the Centre Party's leader and only MP, Hans Janmaat, split from the party but retained his seat. In 1989, Janmaat returned to parliament as leader of the Centre Democrats.
** It is questionable whether the Socialist Party can still be considered a populist party.

Over the years, populist parties have thus become a much stronger electoral force in the Netherlands, while the traditionally dominant position of the Christian Democratic parties has been eroded. As this chapter will show, it would be wrong to assume that populist parties have simply taken the Christian Democrats' role. Neither Pim Fortuyn nor Geert Wilders has explicitly appealed to Christian values. This is not to say, however, that religion has been absent from the discourse of Dutch populist parties—quite the contrary, in fact. However, it was not Christianity, but Islam, that featured prominently in Fortuyn's and Wilders' discourse. Instead of using religion as a means to conceive of the 'ordinary' people, the Dutch right-wing populist parties used it mainly as a means to identify those who did not belong to the 'heartland' to which they appealed.[9]

This chapter will focus firstly on the political programmes of both Pim Fortuyn and the Freedom Party of Geert Wilders, considering in particular the limited role of religion as a means for populists to conceive of Dutch culture and identity. Secondly, it will discuss the attention devoted to Islam in the programmes of populist politicians. Thirdly, the chapter will look at the relationship between the Freedom Party and Church authorities before finally outlining the (lack of) electoral potential for religious populism in the Netherlands.

'Liberal' instead of Religious Populism[10]

Pim Fortuyn railed above all against the 'Purple' coalitions that were formed between 1994 and 2002, including the 'blue' Liberals, the 'red' Social Democrats and the social liberals of the smaller D66 party. During this period, the Christian Democrats were excluded from government for the first time since 1918. After various failed attempts to build a political career via the traditional mainstream parties, Fortuyn became leader of the newly founded party Livable Netherlands (LN—Leefbar Nederland) in November 2001. He was expelled from this party by February 2002, following controversial statements in a newspaper interview (notably, Fortuyn stated that Islam could be perceived as a 'backward culture').[11] With only a few months to go before the parliamentary election in May, Fortuyn founded his own party, the Pim Fortuyn List (LPF). This party could immediately count on substantial support in the opinion polls, thereby eclipsing Fortuyn's old party, Livable Netherlands.

In his book (and, essentially, political programme) *The Shambles of Eight Years Purple*, Fortuyn stated that 'The Netherlands should become a real lively democracy of and for the ordinary people, and depart from the elite party democracy which we are currently acquainted with.'[12] In the official election manifesto it was argued that the 'Purple' coalitions had left the Netherlands with a rigid and self-satisfied political culture of appointed executives lacking creative or learning capacities.[13] Apart from the party's populist features, the LPF's more substantive political programme was eclectic.[14] Fortuyn promoted a free-market economy, took a tough line on law and order issues and stressed the need to cut red tape in the healthcare and education sectors. At the same time, his position on moral or cultural issues like drugs and traditional marriage was very liberal. However, it was Fortuyn's stance on immigration and the cultural integration of minorities that attracted the most controversy. According to the LPF manifesto, overcrowding in the Netherlands was leading to growing societal tensions.[15] The party deemed it necessary to resist the immigration of—often unemployed and unskilled—foreigners into the country. The party manifesto spoke further of problems caused by the social-cultural 'backwardness' of minority groups in society and related problems such as criminality and discrimination against women, especially in fundamentalist Islamic circles.

In his discourse, Fortuyn made a distinction between a native Dutch population (although by no means in an ethnic sense) and minorities whose customs did not conform to the Dutch way of life. The 2002 election manifesto stated that these minorities often arrived from countries untouched by the 'century-long Jewish-Christian-Humanist developments' that had occurred in Europe.[16] Aside from this—somewhat broad—conception of the religious and philosophical roots of European countries, Fortuyn did not truly use religion to define Dutch identity and values. Instead, he saw the Netherlands as a country of liberal Enlightenment values, and he was concerned about these being undermined.[17] The 2002 manifesto, for instance, explicitly expressed the view that all citizens had equal rights and duties, irrespective of race, gender, faith or sexual orientation.[18] Fortuyn's ideology was at odds with the idea of a diverse, multicultural society in which liberal principles were put at risk. In this sense, Fortuyn evoked an ostensibly liberal heartland, but was, so to speak, intolerant of intolerant minorities. Fortuyn himself was also hardly the embodiment of religious conservatism. For a start, he was openly homosexual, and quite explicit about his rather tempestuous love life. Van Holsteyn and Irwin further describe Fortuyn's lifestyle: 'Ferrari, Bentley with chauffeur, butler, two lap dogs, portraits of John F. Kennedy in his lavishly decorated Rotterdam home which he referred to as Palazzo di Pietro'.[19]

Following Fortuyn's murder, his party's subsequent unsuccessful record in government and its subsequent electoral decline, Geert Wilders' Freedom Party became the most successful new populist party. As an MP for the Liberal Party, Wilders had become increasingly critical of Islam, and he eventually broke with his party in September 2004 after a conflict with the parliamentary leader over the issue of Turkish EU membership—Wilders was very much against Turkish accession to the Union.[20] He formed his own one-man faction Groep Wilders (Wilders Group), and founded his Freedom Party (literally, 'Party for Freedom', PVV) in February 2006. In its early documents, the populist character of Wilders' party was already visible. In his 'declaration of independence' from the Liberal Party, for instance, Wilders declared: 'I do not want this country to be hijacked by an elite of cowardly and frightened people (from whichever party) any longer. [...] I therefore intend to challenge this elite on all fronts. I want to return this country to its citizens.'[21] Wilders expressed his contempt for the self-sustaining political system, which supposedly stood isolated from society and argued that 'politicians should no longer be deaf to the problems troubling ordinary people in every-day life'.[22]

While Fortuyn never explicitly portrayed the Dutch people as a homogeneous body,[23] Geert Wilders, from the end of the 2000s, constructed a more specific image of his 'heartland' of ordinary, hard-working Dutch people, epitomised by the fictional couple Henk and Ingrid. Wilders was also more explicitly patriotic than Pim Fortuyn, and increasingly used nationalistic discourse over time.[24] In the Freedom Party's manifestos, symbols such as the Netherlands' maritime past—the Dutch flag flying across the oceans for centuries—and the nation's dyke-building skills were used.[25] Symbols of Christianity, however, were absent from these patriotic conceptions of the Dutch heartland.

Nevertheless, and similarly to Fortuyn, Geert Wilders repeatedly referred to the 'Christian/Jewish/Humanistic' culture of the Netherlands; the Freedom Party even proposed a new Article 1 of the Constitution stating that this culture should remain dominant.[26] In the 2010 manifesto, 'Jewish-Christian and humanist values' were perceived to be fundamental to the Netherlands' success.[27] Both religious and secular citizens, it was further noted, could be proud of this.[28] References to Jewish, Christian or humanistic values were absent, however, from the Freedom Party's 2012 parliamentary election manifesto.

In terms of substantive policies, Wilders' initial programme was similar to Fortuyn's, but more radical concerning immigration and integration.[29] Wilders perceived Islam to be a violent 'ideology' and argued that Dutch culture had to be protected against the process of 'Islamisation'. The 2010 manifesto nevertheless argued that the PVV was not a single-issue party, as Islamisation allegedly touched upon a range of social issues: 'Economically it is a disaster, it damages the quality of our education, it undermines security on the streets, causes an exodus out of our cities, drives out Jewish and gay people, and flushes the century-long emancipation of women down the toilet.'[30] Similarly to Pim Fortuyn's message, as can be seen in this quote, the Freedom Party manifesto called for the preservation of Dutch liberal values threatened by the rise of Islam. Neither the LPF nor the PVV could thus be considered as examples of 'classical' extreme-right parties if we consider their organisational origins—both parties were essentially personal projects and shunned associations with extreme-right movements—or their political ideology.

Whether Wilders was a true liberal at heart is, however, a moot point. He worked together with conservative publicists Bart Jan Spruyt—who broke ties with the Freedom Party as early as 2006—and Paul Belien, who positioned himself strongly against Islam, but also against abortion and euthanasia.[31] In addition, Wilders built up links with various American neo-conservative think tanks.[32] Wilders' own ideology also contained some unmistakably conservative elements. The Freedom Party, it can be argued, presented a programme of 'militant civic nationalism'[33] characterised by a clear dislike of cultural diversity. The 2010 Freedom Party manifesto argued that the 'culture of the sixties' was to be abandoned, and that children at school should be taught a 'canon of Dutch history' with particular emphasis on the Netherlands' 'heroic national history'.[34] Somewhat analogously to Fortuyn's previous criticism of the 'left-wing Church', Wilders blamed progressive (left-wing) elites for undermining traditional norms and values. Furthermore, although Wilders presented himself as a defender of women and of gay rights, these issues were mainly discussed as part of Wilders' warnings against the threat of Islam. In its manifestos, the Freedom Party remained silent about moral-cultural issues such as euthanasia and abortion. When it (finally) expressed a position on the latter issue in March 2011, the Freedom Party parliamentary group actually favoured more restrictive legislation, when compared with the existing law.

It was not Christianity, however, that inspired Wilders' more conservative viewpoints. According to Koen Vossen, '[Wilders'] main objection to the progressive elite is what he terms their cultural and moral relativism, leading to a refusal to distinguish between superior and inferior cultures, as a result of which the West has become weakened and has not recognised the Islamic threat in time.'[35] As far as the role of religion in Wilders' discourse is concerned, negative references to Islam were clearly more dominant than positive references to traditional Christian norms and values.

Characterisation of the Religious 'Other'

Populist entrepreneurs in the Netherlands have not explicitly presented themselves as defenders of a 'good Christian' people. As clarified by the previous section, however, religion did play an important role in the discourses of both Pim Fortuyn and Geert Wilders. Both politicians pointed out the malign effects of the growing presence and influence of Islam in Dutch society, and it seems that Wilders' position on Islam has become more radical over the years.[36] By the time Wilders had founded his own party, much of his discourse revolved around this theme, and in early 2008, he attracted substantial controversy with his seventeen-minute anti-Islam film *Fitna*. Tensions reached their peak before the film was actually released; since its contents were unknown, there was widespread concern about the reactions it might provoke among the Muslim community. The film—the release of which triggered little societal unrest in the end—focused mainly on the violent and intolerant aspects of Islam and the threat of Islamisation in the Netherlands and beyond.

In its 2010 election manifesto, the Freedom Party went so far as to argue that 'Islam is predominantly a political ideology; a totalitarian doctrine aimed at dominance, violence and suppression'.[37] Islam was mainly associated with threats to culture, security and freedom of speech. The party claimed that many Muslims supported Sharia and that 'the Koran dictates behaviour which is incompatible with our *Rechtsstaat*, such as anti-Semitism, discrimination [against] women, killing infidels and [waging a] holy war until Islam has achieved world dominance'.[38] Wilders not only blamed the progressive elite for the decay of cultural norms and pride, but also for Islam's growing influence. The 2010 Freedom Party manifesto even spoke of an 'alliance' between the left-wing elite and Islam.[39] The PVV associated the dominance of 'mouldy left ideals' with 'the hated multicultural experiment' and its malign effects, and the manifesto concluded that 'Islam does not bring us cultural enrichment, but sharia-fatalism'.[40] In order to counter the process of Islamisation of Dutch society, the party for instance proposed to stop immigration from Islamic countries and the building of mosques, as well as banning the Koran and closing Islamic schools.

At the start of the decade, voicing concerns about immigration and the lack of social integration of the Muslim minority proved to be very effective electorally. Indeed, Fortuyn's success is generally linked to his hard line on the salient issues of immigration and integration, which at the time were insufficiently addressed by the major parties.[41] World-wide religiously motivated terrorist attacks and the murder in 2004 of the controversial filmmaker Theo van Gogh by an Islamic fundamentalist are likely to have bolstered concerns about Islam. After the demise of the Pim Fortuyn List, Geert Wilders filled the space on the radical right. The Freedom Party reached its electoral zenith in 2010, despite the fact that this election was fought more over the economic crisis and austerity measures than over the alleged Islamisation of society.[42]

In the parliamentary election campaign of 2012, the euro crisis and proposed austerity measures almost entirely eclipsed issues of immigration and integration.[43] In Wilders' campaign, Islam also played a relatively small role. In the televised debates, the Freedom Party leader mostly denounced

'Eurocrats', deceitful ouzo-drinking Greeks and Eastern European labourers threatening to take Dutch jobs. In previous years, Wilders had already adopted a Eurosceptic position, but now he went so far as to promote a Dutch exit from the European Union (EU) altogether. Yet despite the lack of focus on the issue, it would be wrong to suggest that Wilders had changed his mind about the influence of Islam in Dutch society. Although the Freedom Party prioritised 'Europe' to a greater extent than before, the statements concerning Islam, immigration and integration remained practically unchanged.[44] What is more, in an interview on 27 December 2012, Wilders announced that fighting Islam would be his priority again in the coming year.[45]

The Freedom Party has thus clearly continued to use Islam to distinguish between the native 'heartland' and the 'outsiders' threatening it. Indeed, events in the years following the 2012 election have provided Wilders with scope to revitalise his anti-Islamic discourse. The *Charlie Hebdo* shootings on 7 January 2015, for instance, were described by the PVV leader as an 'act of war against everything that we stand for: our freedom of speech, our freedom of expression, our freedom of press, by people inspired, once again, by Islam, by the Koran, by Muhammed'.[46] He furthermore criticised the political elites in Europe for ignoring the problem and for their lack of willingness to address the issue. Later that year, on 3 May, Wilders gave a keynote speech at the 'First Annual Muhammad Art Exhibit and Contest' in Garland, Texas, which featured cartoons satirising the Islamic prophet.[47] In addition, the advance of Islamic State (IS) in the Middle East, and the concomitant decision of European jihadists to join the battle (and possibly return home later) were portrayed by Wilders as severe security threats. The PVV leader expressed the view that it was best to let Dutch jihadists leave, strip them of their Dutch nationality and refuse them re-entry into the country.[48] Finally, Wilders also voiced concern about the surge in migration into Europe across the Mediterranean Sea from an anti-immigration as well as a security angle; on several occasions the populist politician picked up on reports that boats contained not only asylum seekers, but also IS fighters.[49]

Little Support from Religious Authorities

Since neither successful nor unsuccessful populist parties have made strong appeals for the preservation of traditional Christian values, it is unsurprising that there have been no official links between them and Church authorities. What is more, the populist parties could count on little religious backing.

Relevant data concerning Pim Fortuyn's short-lived party is lacking, but in a survey in the Protestant daily newspaper *Nederlands Dagblad*, Protestant Church leaders were asked about their own and their followers' views on Geert Wilders.[50] More than three-quarters of the 1,228 respondents agreed with the statement that 'a Christian cannot vote for the Freedom Party'. As regards their congregations' opinions, a third of the respondents thought there was some support for Wilders in their community. However, nine out of ten clergymen thought that there were not many, or just a few, Wilders-enthusiasts in their congregation. The former secretary-general of the Protestant Church of the Netherlands (PKN), Bas Plaisier, had denounced Geert Wilders' rhetoric on previous occasions. According to Plaisier, Wilders' philosophy was incompatible with the principles and message of the Church, since the politician failed to show respect for people of different faiths.[51]

Catholic Church authorities, too, have criticised the Freedom Party. Bishop Gerard de Korte, for example, argued that Wilders did call attention to genuine problems, but that his solutions were crude, and that his rhetoric divided people—something that he deemed irreconcilable with the Catholic social philosophy.[52] In a previous interview, the Bishop had stated that he was worried about the violent side of Islam, but that it was necessary to maintain an open dialogue, without hurting the feelings of Muslims in the way that Wilders did.[53] In an interview published in May 2009, Emeritus Bishop Tiny Muskens thought it was 'mean' that Wilders rallied people against Islam for political purposes, and that Dutch people were probably wise enough to vote for a different party.[54] Despite this, Muskens also expressed his own concerns about radical Islam.

Such concerns were certainly more widespread among the Dutch clergy. Although the ecumenical Council of Churches had described Wilders' short film *Fitna* as 'one-sided and provocative',[55] some priests reviewed the film more favourably, with one arguing that '[the] Koran and violence were inseparably linked to one another'.[56] Among the Protestant Church leaders in the *Nederland Dagblad* survey, furthermore, a quarter were concerned about the Islamisation of the Netherlands.[57] This rose to about 50 per cent of the respondents located in the Dutch 'bible belt'—despite the fact that this is an area with relatively few Muslim residents. On balance, however, Church authorities have been critical rather than supportive of Wilders' agenda, a response that was presumably felt by Wilders himself, who in March 2010 suggested that the Church should take a tougher line against Islam, instead of joining politicians in their political correctness.[58]

The fact that Churches were generally critical of Wilders was again evident on 23 March 2014, when the Protestant Church of the Netherlands organised an ecumenical service against racism.[59] Although the organisers stressed that the event did not constitute an 'anti-Wilders service', it was clearly a response to Wilders' remarks on the eve of the municipal elections of 19 March. The PVV leader had asked a crowd of supporters whether they wanted more or less of the Labour Party, more or less of the European Union and, most controversially, more or fewer Moroccans. After the audience shouted 'less, less, less' to all three, Wilders assured his supporters that his party would 'take care of that'.

Apart from the Church authorities, the Freedom Party also received criticism from other representatives of the more broadly defined Christian 'pillar'. Doekle Terpstra, a CDA member and former chairman of the Christian Trade Union CNV, has been particularly vocal in his critique of Wilders' polarising discourse, which he described in an op-ed article as 'a threat to a society in which toleration, hospitality and solidarity are core values'.[60] Prominent former Christian Democratic politicians also expressed their distaste for the Freedom Party's politics, particularly during the coalition formation process of 2010 (which resulted in a Liberal-Christian Democrat minority coalition with support from the Freedom Party). Among those who opposed the coalition because of Wilders' party's involvement were the former chairman of the Protestant ARP, Willem Aantjes, and former CDA minister, Cees Veerman. The acting CDA Justice Minister, Ernst Hirsch Ballin, also expressed his opposition, while acting Health Minister, Ab Klink, resigned as negotiator during the formation process—and gave up his seat in parliament—as he would not support any cooperation with the Freedom Party.

Although Wilders could count on little in the way of support from the Dutch Christian pillar, there is considerable evidence showing that the Freedom Party has relied on financial backing from conservative Christian and Jewish organisations in the United States.[61] Over the course of 2012, several former Freedom Party MPs provided insights concerning the party's funding sources (after resigning, disgruntled, it should be said). Hero Brinkman stated that the party received hundreds of thousands of euros from American donors, while Wim Kortenoeven confirmed that Wilders was very active in lobbying Jewish organisations for money.[62] Indeed, as well as conservative lobby groups, several Jewish organisations such as the Children of the Jewish Holocaust have openly admitted to sponsoring Wilders.[63]

The good relationship between Geert Wilders and sympathetic Jewish organisations goes further than merely sharing a common enemy in Islamic extremism. Wilders has said he feels a strong affinity with Judaism and the state of Israel, and has explained that his stay in Israel and travels through the Middle East as an adolescent (aged between seventeen and nineteen) contributed to shaping his ideas.[64] Other (former) Freedom Party MPs, such as Raymond de Roon and Wim Kortenoeven, shared Wilders' explicit pro-Israeli views or were active in Jewish interest organisations. Pro-Israeli sentiments were also clearly expressed in Freedom Party manifestos: 'For the Freedom Party the Jewish State has always been a beacon of hope, progress and western civilisation. The cheap Israel-bashing of the allied forces of Islam and the left should be countered on all fronts.'[65] With regard to the Israeli–Palestinian conflict, the Freedom Party stated that the Netherlands and the EU should not demand any further territorial concessions from Israel. The party also claimed the conflict had an ideological rather than a territorial character, and spoke of 'a conflict between the reason of the free West and the barbarism of the Islamic ideology'.[66]

The Freedom Party did not gain unanimous support from the Jewish community, however. Some American Jewish organisations, such as the Anti-Defamation League, have voiced their disapproval of the party on the basis of Wilders' intolerant message.[67] Jewish religious authorities in the Netherlands have not openly backed Wilders either. Similarly to various Christian Church leaders, Awraham Soetendorp, a prominent progressive Jewish Rabbi, even distanced himself strongly from Wilders' ideology on the grounds that the politician hurt people in their 'deepest being'.[68] What is more, several Jewish organisations and alleged sponsors of the Freedom Party reacted very negatively to the party's support for a ban on the ritual slaughter of animals.[69] In electoral terms, the results of a survey carried out by the Netherlands Interdisciplinary Demographic Institute in 2009 suggested that, despite Wilders' pro-Israeli stance, the Freedom Party could rely on the support of only 2 per cent of Jewish people in the Netherlands.[70]

The (Lack of) Electoral Scope for Religious Populism

From a purely electoral perspective, there appears to be little incentive for populists to place more emphasis on the Christian roots of Dutch society. The gradual decline of Christian Democracy as a dominant political tradition was noted earlier in this chapter. For most of the period between 1946 and 1967, the three confessional parties together controlled a majority of the seats in the Dutch Lower House. After the official merger of the three parties into the

CDA, the Christian Democrats' seat share dropped to forty-eight of the 150 seats in 1981. During the period of the 'Purple coalitions' (1994–2002), the Christian Democrats were out of office for the first time since 1918, but they did become the largest party in parliament again in the eight years that followed. In the parliamentary election of 2010, however, the party received just twenty-one seats, an all-time low at that point. In the early election of 2012, the CDA lost a further eight seats after receiving only 8.5 per cent of the vote, becoming the fifth party in parliament in terms of size. The (minor) gains made by the smaller Christian parties failed to compensate for the electoral misfortunes of the CDA, suggesting that the electoral scope for religiously inspired political platforms has decreased to a large extent. Although religion may still prove a good predictor of voting behaviour,[71] the absolute number of religious voters in the Netherlands has dwindled.[72] This has consequences for the traditionally dominant Christian Democrats and also for the smaller religious parties in the Netherlands. Despite the fact that their support levels have remained stable, the Christian Union (CU) and the Reformed Political Party (SGP), the two parties most clearly defined by their religious appeal, attract only a small percentage of the nationwide vote.[73]

Table 5.2: Answer to the Question: Are You Religious?

	Freedom Party (PVV) voters	Christian Democrat (CDA) voters	All respondents
Yes	39.8%	83.6%	47.9%
No	60.2%	16.4%	52.1%
N	241	262	2613

Source: Dutch Parliamentary Election Study (DPES) 2010.[74]
Note: only valid answers are included.

A close look at the Freedom Party's voters in the 2010 election further suggests that a more religious course would probably not hold much appeal for Geert Wilders' supporters (see Table 5.2). Data from the 2010 Dutch Parliamentary Election Study (DPES) suggest that about 40 per cent of Wilders' supporters were religious, a figure below the average of almost 50 per cent when all respondents are included. Among Christian Democrat voters, on the other hand, 83 per cent claimed to be religious. Data from the 2012 DPES survey indicate that these figures had essentially remained the same by the time of the following election.[75] Considering the overall low levels of religiosity among Freedom Party voters, most of Wilders' own supporters would probably not be overly impressed by a greater appeal to Christian values. Then again, one might suppose that 'religious populism' could appeal to more devout CDA supporters who are dissatisfied with the current state of political affairs, or concerned about the role of Islam in Dutch society.

Furthermore, even without an overt religious appeal, Wilders managed to attract a considerable number of voters who had previously opted for the Christian Democrats. According to a study undertaken by Van der Meer *et al.*, 10.4 per cent of those who voted for the CDA in 2006 switched to the Freedom Party four years later.[76] Of the eight largest parties in the Dutch Parliament, only the Liberals lost more voters to the Freedom Party (15.8 per cent of VVD voters switched to the PVV in 2010). The Freedom Party did particularly well in the traditionally Catholic province of Limburg in the south, which is also Wilders' home province.[77] This region was previously the heartland of the Catholic People's Party, and subsequently the CDA. While the Pim Fortuyn List also did well in this region in 2002, south Limburg could truly be seen as the Freedom Party's stronghold after the party broke through.

It has been alleged that certain theological or cultural differences between Catholics and Protestants (or even between different groups of Dutch Protestants) might explain why particular religious groups may be more (or less) inclined to share Wilders' monocultural conception of Dutch society.[78] It is questionable, however, whether Wilders' success in the traditionally Catholic south is related to the religious convictions of the voters living there. Results from a study conducted by Van der Brug *et al.* provide no reason to assume that Catholic voters are more likely than Protestant voters to support far-right parties.[79] Moreover, the Freedom Party has actually been relatively popular in some of the Protestant 'bible belt' areas in the Netherlands as well.[80] Van der Meer *et al.* showed that the PVV managed to attract a considerable share (9.1 per cent) of voters who had previously voted for the Christian Union, a party founded as the result of a merger between two Protestant parties.[81] A smaller share of Reformed Political Party (SGP) voters had made the switch to the Freedom Party, yet 17.4 per cent of those who voted SGP in 2010 had at some point expressed their intention to vote PVV in opinion polls conducted in the years prior to the 2010 election.[82]

Certainly not all Christian voters felt an affinity with the Freedom Party's programme. As well as (former) party representatives, many grassroots CDA members expressed their disapproval at the formation of the Liberal-Christian Democrat coalition, which relied on the parliamentary support of the Freedom Party. A significant share of Christian Democrat members who subscribed to values such as freedom of religion (and of religious education), hospitality towards asylum seekers and generosity towards the developing world were critical of Wilders' programme, which was at odds with these very values. About one-third of the members voted 'no' during a party congress in October 2010, which was held to decide on the Christian Democrats' participation in the minority coalition. Among the members of their Liberal coalition partner, the formation of the minority coalition caused much less of a debate.

Table 5.3: Probability of Future Vote for the Freedom Party

		1–3 (not likely)	4–7 (uncertain)	8–10 (likely)	N
2010	CDA voters	80.6%	13.8%	5.5%	253
	All non-PVV voters	71.7%	19.7%	8.6%	1904
2012	CDA voters	87.3%	10.8%	2.0%	102
	All non-PVV voters	78.0%	15.2%	6.9%	1339

Source: Dutch Parliamentary Election Study (DPES) 2010 and 2012.
Note: Respondents have been placed in the three categories by the author, and the labels represent the author's interpretation of the survey item values. Only valid answers are included.

Although the other two-thirds of the CDA members eventually endorsed the minority coalition, DPES data suggest that few of those who voted for the Christian Democrats in 2010 or 2012 were likely to make a future switch to the Freedom Party (see Table 5.3). Only 5.5 per cent of the CDA-voting respondents in 2010 thought it was likely that they would ever vote for the Freedom Party (providing an answer ranging between eight and ten on a ten-point scale). Less than 1 per cent of Christian Democrat voters surveyed thought they would 'certainly' vote for Wilders' party one day (giving an answer of ten). On the other hand, over 80 per cent thought it unlikely that they would ever vote for the Freedom Party, providing an answer ranging from one to three. At the same time, 59.3 per cent of Christian Democrat supporters indicated that they would 'never' vote for the Freedom Party (giving an answer of one). The data suggest that most Christian Democrat voters in 2010 were also less likely than other non-Freedom Party voters to support Wilders' party in the future. This may indicate that in the 2010 election Wilders had largely depleted the reservoir of former CDA voters willing to vote for the Freedom Party. What is more, compared with the 2010 data, CDA supporters in the parliamentary election of 2012 expressed an even lower likelihood of ever voting PVV.[83]

Although voters have switched from parties with a religious appeal to the populist radical right in the past, a substantial number of Christian voters disagree with Wilders' key policies concerning Islam, immigration and the developing world.[84] At the same time, it is highly questionable whether Wilders, or any populist party in general, would benefit from campaigning on the basis of an explicitly religious platform. After all, the Netherlands has become increasingly secularised,[85] a phenomenon illustrated by the gradual decline of the Christian Democratic party family.

Conclusion

Populist parties and entrepreneurs in contemporary Dutch politics have refrained from building an image of a religious 'heartland' and appealing to 'good Christian' people. This also applies to the most electorally successful populist parties: the Pim Fortuyn List and Geert Wilders' Freedom Party. Both Fortuyn and Wilders claimed to defend Dutch culture as shaped by liberal Enlightenment values, even though conservative elements could be found in the discourse of the latter politician in particular. Apart from referring to Jewish-Christian and humanist values, neither the Pim Fortuyn List nor the Freedom Party explicitly used religious symbols in their portrayal of Dutch identity.

Still, religion did play a prominent role in both of these populist political discourses. Rather than using religion to define those who belonged to the 'heartland' they appealed to, however, it was mainly employed as a means to identify the 'others', whose faith was considered to be incompatible with Dutch culture and values. Both Fortuyn and Wilders saw Islam—in terms of the immigration of Muslims, as well as their lack of social integration—as the main threat to Dutch culture. Whereas Fortuyn placed issues related to immigration and integration firmly on the political agenda in 2002, Wilders reaped electoral success on the basis of a harsher anti-Islamic discourse after Fortuyn's murder and his party's demise. Wilders' Islam-related rhetoric has certainly not softened in the years following the successful parliamentary election of 2010, although the populist radical right politician placed greater emphasis on his opposition to the EU in the early 2012 parliamentary election campaign. Events such as the *Charlie Hebdo* attacks and the rise of Islamic State in the Middle East gave new impetus to Wilders' anti-Islamic discourse in later years.

Despite some apparent concerns about (radical) Islam among the Dutch clergy, neither Fortuyn nor Wilders could rely on outspoken support from

Catholic or Protestant Church leaders. Instead, where Church officials commented on Geert Wilders' rhetoric, the remarks were mainly, although not exclusively, disapproving. Church leaders tended to criticise Wilders for offending Muslims with his harsh anti-Islamic criticism. There is sufficient reason to assume that neo-conservative and Jewish organisations, particularly from the United States, provided financial support to the Israel-friendly Freedom Party. At the national level, however, official ties between the Freedom Party and religious authorities have been lacking, and Wilders has also seemingly been unable to gain substantial electoral support from the Jewish community.

As far as the electoral scope for 'religious populism' is concerned, it is hard to see how a more explicit appeal to Christian values would pay off for Wilders, or indeed for any other populist party. The Freedom Party's share of the electorate in 2010 and 2012 largely consisted of non-religious voters, and although a substantial number of erstwhile Christian Democrat supporters voted for the Freedom Party in 2010, Wilders found it difficult to attract many more afterwards. Significant numbers of Christian Democrat members expressed their discontent with the Liberal-Christian Democrat minority government formed in the autumn of 2010, which relied on the Freedom Party's parliamentary support. Moreover, in view of the largely secularised nature of Dutch society and the diminished role of religion in Dutch electoral politics, it is unlikely that a religiously inspired discourse would greatly enhance the electoral fortunes of any populist party.

6

THE FRENCH NATIONAL FRONT

FROM CHRISTIAN IDENTITY TO *LAÏCITÉ*

Olivier Roy

The Front National (FN—National Front) was born as a neo-fascist movement, but has evolved, under the leadership of Marine Le Pen, the daughter of
its founder Jean-Marie Le Pen, into a more modern populist movement,
downplaying anti-Semitism, historical references to World War II and support
for traditional family values, in order to adopt a primarily anti-Islamic, anti-
establishment and anti-European stand. Although the party includes an ultra-
conservative Catholic wing, it never pushed for Christian values; the
neo-pagan component that was strong in the party at its birth slowly gave way
to a more modern secularist approach, where Christianity is defined in terms
of identity and not as a set of normative social and moral values. Moreover,
the FN turned during the electoral campaign for local elections in 2014 to a
vocal endorsement of *laïcité* (state secularity), which was the trademark of the
left during the twentieth century, and played down references to Christianity.
In a word, the party never endorsed Christianity as a religion, but skirted
around it by endorsing three overlapping positions: neo-paganism, neo-

Maurrasianism ('Catholicism as national identity, not as belief', which was a claim of Action Française, the monarchist movement led by Charles Maurras in the early twentieth century), and very recently *laïcité*, taking the concept from the hands of the left. But in all of these convoluted attitudes, the enemy remained the same: migrants, the majority of whom are composed of people with a Muslim background. Put simply, for the FN, *laïcité* offers a more appealing and fruitful tool with which to fight 'Islam' than a Christian religion whose practice is in steady decline. Indeed, opinion polls in 2015 placed *laïcité* as the most important republican value (ahead even of the universal right to vote).[1] In the 1970s and early 1980s the migrant was targeted first as a non-white ('Arab'), then as a non-Christian ('Muslim') and lastly as a 'religious fundamentalist'. Race, religion and secularism have been successively used to differently define the same 'other', but never to endorse Christianity as a religion or as a faith.

That could explain why the FN was not at the forefront of the campaign against the same-sex marriage law in 2013, and campaigned explicitly for the implementation of *laïcité* at school (no specific diet for religious exceptions) during the municipal elections of 2014.[2] In contrast the Church actively participated in the campaign against same-sex marriage, balancing the promotion of traditional 'family norms' as part of the anthropological identity of French society (thus reclaiming for itself the struggle around identity, which is the trademark of the populist right) and defending the recognition in the public sphere of religious norms and values, including Muslim symbols, with the risk of alienating secular public opinion. The relationship between conservative Catholics and the FN has thus always been ambivalent and shifting: they share the same discreet anti-Semitism, and a call for the promotion of the Christian identity of France against the newcomers (Muslims), but the former balk at the neo-pagan and/or secular references of the FN, while the Catholic hierarchy, despite the rise of its conservative wing, follows the historical reluctance of the French Catholic Church to be associated with the far right.

The FN was created in 1972 to bring together an array of splintered extreme-right formations that were sheltering former World War II *collaborateurs* (people who were involved in the Maréchal Pétain collaborationist regime during the Nazi occupation of France). For instance, founding figures included François Bousquet, a former volunteer in the SS Charlemagne Division, and François Brigneau, who joined the *Milice* (paramilitary units in charge of fighting the Resistance). This fascist group was followed by militants who were later involved in the underground movements opposing the coming independence of Algeria after 1960 (OAS—Organisation of the Secret Army), while a younger generation established violent radical groups in the late 1960s to fight the leftist students who took to the streets in May 1968. The FN thus united a whole spectrum of the French extreme right, ranging from neo-Nazis to Maurrasians, and from supporters of the OAS in Algeria (Roger Holeindre) to younger neo-fascists (Jean-Pierre Stirbois, and François Duprat, who was openly revisionist and anti-Semitic). Anti-Semitism, a trademark of the French extreme right, was pervasive in the party (Brigneau and Le Pen Snr have regularly been condemned by courts). The party strongly opposed the left (and the communists in particular) as well as the Gaullist right—De Gaulle was their arch villain because he was twice a 'traitor': in 1940, when he left occupied France for Britain, and in 1960, when he started negotiations on the independence of Algeria. The FN was thus created as a party of nostalgic fascists, who were not yet concerned by immigration and did not promote any kind of 'Christian identity' because they were more influenced by a neo-pagan imaginary exalting a pre-Christian Europe (Vikings and Celts). If they took the Celtic 'cross' as their emblem, it was more the Celtic dimension that attracted them: they were very critical of the post-Vatican II 'pacifism' of the Catholic Church. In the 1973 programme of the FN there is no reference to religion (or to *laïcité*). Further, the party was not really interested in participating in elections: the elitist and 'putschist' mentality of its hard-core members prevented the FN from reaching out to the ordinary people. The FN was not, in the beginning, a populist party, but a neo-fascist one; it was its forthcoming focus on immigration and its subsequent criticisms of the establishment (in other words, the major political parties) that would later place it in the category of populist movements.

The party stagnated as long as it was brooding over the past defeats of the extreme right with no focus on the critical issues of contemporary French society. This first stage ended around 1978, when the FN decided to focus on anti-immigration rather than on anti-communism. Two distinctive periods followed, corresponding to the successive leadership of the father, Jean-Marie Le Pen (1978–2011), and the daughter, Marine Le Pen (2011 onwards), the latter of whom strives to present the party as less ideological and more respectable. During the reign of Jean-Marie Le Pen, the party campaigned essentially against immigration; it entered the political scene as a troublemaker, rejecting all the dominant parties (lumped together by Jean-Marie Le Pen under the tag of 'the establishment') and contesting local elections but with no real aim of joining a governing coalition; during that period, the FN had both unexpected successes (in the 2002 presidential elections, when Le Pen finished in second position) and expected downfalls, but has always been able to bounce back after each defeat or crisis (splits or electoral disappointments). The most recent period, since Marine Le Pen succeeded her father in 2011, witnessed a definite turn: the avowedly populist party is now seeking respectability with the perspective of leading an electoral coalition with the conservative right. We will examine the party's attitude towards identity and religion during these two most recent stages.

The New Right and the Concept of Identity

The FN would have remained marginal had it not been joined around 1980 by members of what has been called the 'new right' (Gollnisch, Mégret, Chevallier, Le Gallou) just after it decided to put immigration at the core of its propaganda. The new members came from two recently created think tanks that were endeavouring to replace out-of-fashion fascist ideological references with more modern concepts in tune with contemporary debates in social sciences. The Club de l'Horloge (Le Gallou) and the Groupement de Recherche et d'Etudes pour la Civilisation Européenne (GRECE)—headed by Alain de Benoist, who did not join the FN—represented the intellectual laboratory of the new FN. In a premonitory 1978 article, de Benoist suggested that the right should read Antonio Gramsci, a Marxist intellectual, and make

Fig. 6.1: Presidential and European Parliament Results of the Front National, 1994–2014

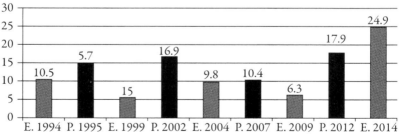

Note: Percentage results for European Parliament (E) elections are presented in grey columns and those for presidential (P) elections in black.

Source: NSD European election database (France): http://www.nsd.uib.no/european_election_database/country/france/

fighting the cultural hegemony of the left a priority.[3] Winning the cultural war (in fact, the war of 'representations' and ideas) was seen, according to Gramsci, as a precondition for accessing political power.[4]

These new thinkers replaced references to 'race' with the concept of 'culture' and 'ethnicity' as developed by anthropologists and social scientists. They downplayed the issue of racial superiority in favour of a differentialist approach in which cultures may be equal in dignity, but cannot mix. In short, they replaced racism with culturalism. They also shared the modern anthropological approach towards religion which proposes that religion is simply part of culture. De Benoist himself is a neo-pagan, not a Christian.[5] They see Christianity as a marker among others of Western culture, but not as its specific 'faith' or truth.

This change in the ideological framework of the party went along with the decision taken in 1978 to put immigration at the core of its political platform, renouncing the neo-fascists' references in favour of a contemporary populist approach. Populism here entails the party's construction of the 'people' against 'foreigners' (that is, immigrants) and against the betraying 'elites', called *l'établissement* by Jean-Marie Le Pen, who also coined the expression 'the gang of four' to attack the four main French political parties, all accused of favouring immigration and of making anti-racist laws to silence true 'patriots'. The slogan 'One million unemployed is one million migrants too many', which became the trademark of FN posters, appeared for the first time during the legislative elections of 1978; the formula was devised by François Duprat. Le Gallou subsequently forged the concept of 'national preference', meaning that social services and jobs should be provided only to French 'nationals'.

Opposition to immigration was at this point expressed in 'culturalist' and ethnic terms, and not yet in religious ones ('immigrants' and 'Arabs', not 'Muslims'). The FN preferred to refer to national identity rather than to Christian identity. Bruno Mégret set up the journal *Identité*, which explicitly presented immigration as a threat to national identity, rejecting the concept of 'integration' that was the basis of the other parties' approach towards the issue. In 1988, Pierre Vial, the leader of a neo-pagan movement and a white supremacist, joined the FN and later set up an organisation named *Terre et Peuple* (Land and People), a sign that the old racialist vision had not disappeared from the party, but was simply recast in more acceptable terms.

The National Front's first electoral breakthrough in local elections (Dreux in 1983) was achieved in a very secular constituency, where the issue of immigration was particularly salient: some 20 per cent of the population was composed of migrants, and the leftist mayor, Françoise Gaspard, took a militantly multiculturalist approach that triggered a backlash. The leading figure of the party in Dreux, Jean-Pierre Stirbois, came from the young neo-fascist generation, but adopted the party's new line, avoiding references to the history of the extreme right and concentrating on immigration.

The Entry of Catholic Fundamentalists into the FN

Interestingly enough, it was after the entry into the party of neo-pagan elements that a fundamentalist Catholic movement joined its ranks. This Catholic component did not come from the mainstream Church, but from the radical conservative wing that opposed the reforms introduced by the Second Vatican Council (1962–1963). Its members were close to the Fraternité Sacerdotale Saint Pie X (Sacerdotal Society of St Pius X), founded by the dissident bishop Mgr Lefebvre in 1970; the Fraternité lost its recognition by Rome in 1976 and Mgr Lefebvre was excommunicated in 1988. This conservative fringe refused to replace the Tridentine Mass in Latin with the modern version using vernacular languages and rejected modernism—that is, the reconciliation of the Enlightenment and faith—despite its rehabilitation by the new Vatican Council. Through their rejection of the legacy of the Enlightenment and the French Revolution, they thus sided with the extreme right. In 1977, a group of radicals forcibly occupied the Church of Saint-Nicolas de Chardonnet, which remains to this day the Paris headquarters of the traditionalist (or *intégriste*) Catholics and the place where all extreme-right political groups display their propaganda. For them *laïcité* and secularism are anathema; their hero is Pope Pius X (1835–1914) who imposed an anti-modernist oath on the clergy and, in the encyclical *Vehementer Nos*, rejected any compromise with the French law of 1905 separating Church and state. Although its opposition to Rome was based on ecclesiological, theological and ritual grounds rather than political ones, the Fraternité is clearly part of the extreme-right family: it shares its opposition to the Enlightenment and the French Revolution, to religious freedom, to the separation of Church and state, to reconciliation with the Jews (it rejected the suppression by the Council of the phrase *pro perfidis judaeis*, 'for the perfidious Jews', in an Easter prayer), to inter-faith dialogue in general and to Islam in particular, not to mention its support for right-wing dictatorships in Chile and Argentina.

The leader of this trend within the FN was Bernard Antony, the founder of AGRIF (Association Générale contre le Racisme et pour le Respect de l'Identité Française et Chrétienne); Antony joined the FN in 1984 and left it in 1999. Tensions were always strong between extreme conservative Catholics and the neo-pagan or secular components of the party, and Antony was never able to prevail over the paganist (and racialist) component headed by Alain Vial. Because of the inability of the FN to penetrate the milieu of mainstream conservative Catholics, Catholicism in the FN was hence represented by AGRIF. With the exception of some token individuals, Protestants, Jews and Muslims are not to be found among FN members (which does not mean that they are not present within the electorate, as shown by the breakthrough of the FN in Lutheran Protestant villages in Alsace or in the destitute neighbourhoods of Marseille during the 2014 local elections).[6]

The common denominator for both neo-pagans and traditionalist Catholics is their denunciation of the modernity produced by the French Revolution and the Enlightenment. As the name of AGRIF suggests, its adherents conceive religion in terms of identity; and although Antony sees it as the main component of French identity, for others it is one component among others. Nevertheless, the FN never aligned itself with the religious right and always played down religion in policy terms. One of the few borrowings from the Catholic conservative agenda was the strengthening of the party's position on abortion (the ban on abortion had been part of the lay conservative right's agenda since 1920, long before it became central to the Church's political agenda). While the FN's 1973 programme mentioned only restraining free abortion, the party later called for the repeal of the law of 1975 legalising abortion, but then reverted to its original position in 2011. The Christian fundamentalists never had the upper hand in the FN, which was more susceptible to the influence of the neo-pagans.

In parallel, Jean-Marie Le Pen, while chairing the FN, never adopted a 'crusader' approach towards the Middle East. He opposed immigration because he did not believe in assimilation or multiculturalism, but, as far as the Middle East was concerned, he was more in favour of Arab nationalist dictators than of Israel (a legacy of his not-so-veiled anti-Semitism). Le Pen supported Saddam Hussein during the two US wars; he went to Iraq to meet Saddam Hussein in November 1990 and opposed the decision to send French troops to fight to free Kuwait. In September 2013, he expressed his opposition to any intervention against Bashar al-Assad in Syria. Hence the anti-immigration stance was not connected, as it would be by other right-wing activists in France, with the idea of a geo-strategic confrontation between a Christian West and an Islamic Middle East. Israel was never defined by Jean-Marie Le

Pen as a Western bridgehead within a hostile Middle East, which explains why even the most strident anti-Arab French Jews almost never endorsed the FN and always saw it as being primarily anti-Semitic. (Conversely, a small fringe of right-wing French Muslims did consider joining, not necessarily the FN, but other factions within the extreme right; the Muslim organisation Fils de France joined the right-wing anti-Semitic leader Alain Soral in 2013.) The anti-Semitic strain, explicit in the 1980s—Le Pen has a history of making public anti-Semitic remarks or 'jokes' such as describing the Shoah or Holocaust as 'a detail of history')—remained often implicit in the 2000s (for instance, Marine Le Pen vowed to ban both the yarmulke and the veil but not Christian clerical garb). In short, there are two 'others' for the FN: Jews and Arabs, but Arabs have a legitimate place in which to live (the Middle East), while Jews are seen as cosmopolitan from the traditional anti-Semitic perspective. Neither Jean-Marie nor Marine Le Pen have visited Israel, while both have travelled to or spent holidays in Arab countries.

The paradox is that while Muslims replaced Jews as 'the enemy from within' (with the same arguments as in the 1930s, such as 'they don't assimilate, they put religion above citizenship, they have a dual loyalty'), this did not translate into a pro-Israel attitude for the FN as long as Jean-Marie Le Pen was in charge. Nevertheless, this position now appears to be changing with a new generation less influenced by the fascist legacy of the party. Hence, Marine Le Pen has indicated that she is seeking a rapprochement with Israel and the Jewish community, based on the common perception of Islam as a threat.[7]

The Celebration of Joan of Arc

Despite their cultural secularism, FN leaders have developed at length the notion of the Christian identity of France and found in Joan of Arc a good synthesis of what they consider such an identity to be. Jean-Marie Le Pen made Joan of Arc the iconic figure of French nationalism. The annual celebration of the Day of Joan of Arc has become a trademark of the FN since 1978, and embodies its conception of the role of religion. In 1988, the party decided to celebrate Joan of Arc Day on 1 May, the same date as 'Labour Day' when trade unions and leftist parties used to celebrate the working class. It was intended to oppose a symbolic 'blue' (the colour of the FN) but nevertheless non-aristocratic France (Joan was a shepherdess) against an alien 'red' France. However, the symbolism also embodies the subordination of religion to nationalism. The cult of Joan of Arc had little or no religious substance: Joan was extolled as a nationalist, not as a Christian figure. When Jean-Marie Le Pen mentioned her 'Christian trajectory', it was with the following commentary: 'As her divine model, she did not come to bring peace but a sword', an allusion to the biblical verse 'Do not suppose that I have come to bring peace to the earth, but a sword' (Matthew 10:34)—which is certainly not the favourite verse of the contemporary Church. Le Pen blamed the bishops of her time for having condemned her and never referred to her as a Christian saint, but as a patriotic warrior. The message is clear: the bishops could betray the nation, and the people do not need the advice of the bishops.[8]

By the same token, traditionalist Catholics of the far right also reject what they see as the 'demeaning' attitude of the Church when it asks for forgiveness or refers to humility, a consistent trait of Pope Francis, who is loathed by the extreme right because he is perceived as too progressive and too open on issues such as immigration and capitalism. They prefer to stress 'Christ King of Kings and Lord of Lords' instead of Jesus the poor and humble man.[9] In this sense, the far right does not subscribe to the teaching from Christ: 'whosoever shall smite thee on thy right cheek, turn to him the other also' (Matthew 5:39).

To sum up, all the components of the FN, whatever their beliefs and their conception of Christianity, have good reasons to denounce the Catholic Church as an institution, and more specifically the French bishops. The traditionalist Catholics blame them for approving the Second Vatican Council, the anti-communist hardliners for leaning towards leftist values, the neo-pagans for rejecting the 'true' roots of Western identity, and all of them join together in rejecting the Church's call for compassion towards poor migrants. Once again, Christianity is an identity marker in FN thinking, a component of French nationalism, but not a faith nor a set of values.

Such an attitude will by definition antagonise the Church, even if it experienced a 'turn to the right' from the early 1980s, coinciding both with the election of John Paul II as pope and François Mitterrand as the first socialist president of the French Republic. But if the Church always kept its distance from the FN, the common believer may well have a more complex relationship with the party's ideas.

The Church and the FN

Throughout the history of the French Republic, practising Catholics have tended to vote in large numbers for the right, or more precisely different 'rights'. However, after World War II they kept away from the extreme right, identified with pro-Nazi and neo-pagan trends. This remained true until recent years and the coming of a new generation, both in the FN and among Catholics, for whom the war is just history. Nevertheless, polls indicate that if church-going Catholics' votes slightly increased for the FN, it still remains a minority both among FN voters and among Catholic voters.[10] In essence, the Catholic vote for the FN is below that of the general population. This might be a consequence of both the party's neo-pagan overtones and its openly racist stance, on one hand, and of the disapproving attitude of the Church hierarchy towards the FN on the other. In fact, until 2015 the Catholic Church was always careful to keep its distance from the FN, although it never forbade believers to join it or vote for it (unlike the Church's condemnation of Action Française, another far-right group, in 1926). However, as we shall see later, some conservative bishops in 2015 have appeared to be trying to reach out to the new FN.

Until recently, the Church has always made it clear that the values defended by the FN were not Christian values. This position is explicit in the following comment about Jean-Marie Le Pen by Cardinal Barbarin of Lyon, who is himself seen as a conservative in the Church:

> M. Le Pen used to say: 'I prefer my daughter to my niece, my niece to my cousin, my cousin to my neighbour', or something like this. This is an exclusionary logic: push those for whom I have no or less interest away from me! The Bible, however, is inclusive. It always says: 'When you do this or that, take your wife and your children with you, and the foreigner who lives with you.' The biblical system pertains to a completely different logic.

This stance has been constantly repeated and made explicit not only by the bishops, but also by leading lay Catholic figures.[11] This, in turn, helps explains why, for three decades (1980–2010), the practising Catholic electorate voted less for the FN than did the rest of the population. However, when Marine Le Pen replaced her father, a new trend appeared: young practising Catholics tended to align more towards the party.[12]

This increase in voting for the FN among young Catholics has nothing to do with a growing emphasis on Christian values by the FN; on the contrary, under Marine Le Pen, references to *laïcité* became the dominant motto of the party. In its 2013 programme, the party made only very distant and occasional allusions to Christianity[13] while extensively invoking *laïcité*. The attraction of young Catholics to the FN thus seems more related to other phenomena, namely the fact that the FN has succeeded in its campaign of normalisation, embracing democracy and expelling members who make open racial slurs.

Although we lack data to substantiate this idea, the growth in support could also stem from a shift among many young Catholics from a value-based world vision to an identity conception of religion. This shift is exemplified by recent demonstrations by young Catholics against what they perceived as blasphemy (for instance, against *Piss Christ*, a photographic exhibit by the American artist Andres Serrano, in April 2011), leading to violence disapproved of by the Church. The movement Civitas, which seeks to abolish the separation of Church and state and declares France a Catholic country, is a good example of such new youth mobilisation among Catholics.[14] The FN found itself more in line with this new generation of Christians during the aftermath of the *Charlie Hebdo* attacks on 7 January 2015, even if it kept its distance from the huge movement of support for *Charlie Hebdo*, just as many conservative Catholics did. After all, the FN was a recurrent target of the satirical newspaper, as was the Catholic Church, and neither supported the right of blasphemy. Instead, the FN simply capitalised on fear of Islam, accentuated by the huge wave of refugees arriving in Europe during the summer.

The Church, while opposing the FN for its xenophobia, is more ambivalent on the issue of identity. Of course, the Church supports the idea that France has a Christian (and more specifically Catholic) identity, but strives to associate this identity with the defence of a set of Christian values that are meant to bring the French people back to religious practice. For the FN, meanwhile, Christian identity is not connected with Christian faith, religious practices and values. The complexity of the relationship between conservative practising Catholics and the FN came under the limelight when the former, supported by the Church, decided to launch a fully-fledged attack against the law legalising same-sex marriages. The *Manif pour Tous* (Demo for All) movement organised a huge street demonstration on 17 November 2012 to protest against a bill authorising same-sex marriage (voted into force by Parliament in May 2013). In the meantime, while still not supporting the proposed law, the FN decided to keep a low profile. The campaign waged by the Church insisted not on respecting 'God's laws' (unfeasible in secular France) but on denouncing the changes in the anthropological paradigm of society that would result from rejecting a biological basis for the definition of the family. In fact, the Church displayed a very classical Thomist position, arguing that there is a 'natural moral law' that reflects the 'Christian moral law', and that one does not need to be a believer to support and promote common norms and values. The FN, however, did not really join in the defence of traditional marriage. In fact, its growing youth constituency was more and more at odds with the traditionalist Christian milieu, even if more Catholics did join the FN.

The 'Bleu Marine' Front National and the Secularisation of Social Values

The FN, like all European populist parties, can only win elections if it reaches out to new generations outside the traditional extreme or conservative right constituency, particularly among educated youth and blue-collar workers. Neither of these groups are attracted by the usual nostalgic references produced by the extreme right (Pétain, the Algerian war, Christ as King and Lord, blood and soil, etc.). De Gaulle is for them either consigned to distant history or is still a hero. Anti-Semitism might not be dead but it is no longer the dominant identity-marker of the new extreme right: it has been replaced by Islamophobia. The electorate of the Marine Le Pen FN is younger, more modern on moral values, less politicised and more secular than the electorate of both Jean-Marie Le Pen and the conservative right. In terms of social values, it is more liberal too. A poll conducted in May 2013 shows that 36 per cent of FN sympathisers approve of same-sex marriage, compared to 25 per cent of sympathisers of the centre-right Union for a Popular Movement (UMP).[15] Moreover, to the dismay of the traditionalist wing of the party, Marine Le Pen has included several young gay people in her close political entourage.

The FN has consequently shifted from its conservative-traditional or neo-fascist stance to support for the Republic and for *laïcité*, two defining themes of the left during the twentieth century. As we saw, *laïcité* is the most popular identity marker of France in terms of public opinion. In his speech at the battlefield of Valmy on 20 September 2006, a landmark of leftist republican celebrations, Jean-Marie Le Pen extolled the Republic. Marine Le Pen put the defence of *laïcité* at the core of her programme as a way both to adapt to her new constituency and to reject Christian values that would contradict her anti-immigrant position.[16] In its policy statement for the local elections of 2014, the FN programme advocated putting *laïcité* at the core of its political project, blaming all the other parties for making too many concessions to all religious practices.[17]

Marine Le Pen's new FN no longer promoted Christian values and distanced itself somewhat from the moral conservatism of the party's former positions. It relaxed its position on abortion (no ban, but no social security reimbursement) and, by not openly joining the *Mariage pour Tous*, on homosexuality. Family values are no longer a central issue, and many of the FN's younger leaders are divorced, live in civil partnerships or are homosexual. Nonetheless, the FN did not relax its stance on immigration, identifying immigration with Islamisation, with the consequence that second and third generations will always remain the 'others' because they are Muslims.[18] The FN manifesto for Marine Le Pen's 2012 presidential campaign hence affirmed the rejection of 'mass immigration that unsettles our national identity and brings with it an increasingly visible Islamisation, and all sorts of demands. Communitarianism is a poison against national cohesion.'[19]

The shift from the migrant to the 'Muslim' is a consequence of the settlement of the first generations of migrant workers. Their grandchildren can no longer be seen as 'migrants', but they are still rejected in the name of identity and culture (explicit references to 'race' have disappeared from the FN's official statements). Marine Le Pen even suggested banning halal and kosher food from school canteens, and veils and yarmulkes from the country's streets, without mentioning the cassocks of Catholic priests, thus implicitly identifying Islam and Judaism as 'foreign' religions.[20] The paradox of the FN is that both *laïcité* and Christianity are presented as non-negotiable parts of the French identity. As Marine Le Pen put it:

> France is France. It has Christian roots. This is how it is. This is what makes its identity. It is *laïque* and we are attached to this identity. We won't allow the transformation of this identity.[21]

Christianity here is a matter of identity, not a matter of faith or religious observance. This Christianity should hence not be sub-contracted to the Church because the Church is too soft on immigration and too prone to form alliances with other faith communities. In other words, it is because Christianity is no longer a faith that it can give way to secularism. *Laïcité* was a key element of Marine Le Pen's campaign in the presidential elections of 2012, followed by an attack against 'Islamic fundamentalism', but without reference to other religions. This stance was repeated in a more explicit way during the 2014 campaign, where, for the first time, the FN endorsed the idea that religion should be kept in the private sphere (a position supported neither by the Church nor by the promoters of a Christian identity of France).[22]

Hence it is not at the level of values that the FN established a new bridge with practising Catholics, but rather within the debate on identity. The FN position, in fact, reflects a broader shift on the part of European populist movements vis-à-vis Christianity. They reject Christian values either because these values are too 'leftist' (charity and hospitality) or, on the contrary, because they are too conservative (moral positions on sexuality). Christianity is thus a matter of identity, not values. On this point there is both continuity and a rupture within the tradition of the extreme right. The disconnect between Christianity as faith and Christianity as culture was already entrenched in the Action Française of Charles Maurras during the 1920s: while promoting the Catholic identity of France (specifically against Jews, Protestants and Freemasons) Maurras referred to himself more as an 'agnostic' than as a true believer. This conceptual gap has been widened with the evolution of the FN, and it has gone hand-in-hand with another disconnect: on societal values (sexual freedom and the desacralisation of the traditional family) the new generation of FN militants and sympathisers are closer to mainstream society than to hardcore Christian believers.

An interesting consequence of this discrepancy is that the Catholic Church, more conservative than ever, preferred to go into battle against abortion and same-sex marriage under its own flag, or more precisely through front organisations with close connections to the Church. It would not make sense to analyse the relationship between the FN and the Church on a 'left-right' or 'liberal versus conservative' spectrum. But the relative success of the FN in the 2014 local elections has brought a new generation of activists, embodied by Marine Le Pen's niece, Marion Maréchal-Le Pen (born in 1989), whose support base is well rooted in the south-east of France. In contrast, Marine Le Pen's stronghold is in the far more secular north. A conspicuous invitation by a local bishop to Marion Maréchal-Le Pen to participate in a summer school in August 2015 triggered a wave of questions, first and foremost: is the Church changing its approach to the FN? Mgr Dominique Rey, Bishop of Toulon, who sent the invitation, made it clear that there is no agreement on many issues, but insisted that the FN is a legitimate actor on the French political scene, and that more and more Catholics are voting for it.[23] As a result, the Church has to follow its flock.

Bishop Rey, appointed by Pope John Paul II, is an avowed supporter of the 'Christian identity' of France and a member of the charismatic wing of the Church, which is reluctant to dilute Christian identity via inter-faith dialogue or opening-up to non-believers. More than indicating a change in the Church, this rapprochement signals both an increasing debate inside the Church (where many conservatives are openly critical of Pope Francis), the normalisation of the FN and a possible backlash inside the party against the ostensible pro-*laïcité* shift of Marine Le Pen. The significant success of the FN in the regional elections of November 2015 seems to have consolidated the gap between two opposed approaches to religion and morality. In the wake of the Paris attacks of November 2015, Marine Le Pen has insisted even more on the need to defend *laïcité* against the danger of Islamisation and radicalisation. Marion Maréchal Le Pen, by contrast, continues to emphasise her attachment to Catholic values, and has based part of her campaign on contesting same-sex marriage and public coverage for reproductive health for women.

Whatever the changing sensitivities in both the Church and the FN, they continue to differ as regards their very conception of what a religion is. The FN might be more liberal than the Church on certain issues (concerning sexual freedom) and more xenophobic on others (concerning immigration), but what is at stake are precisely the new boundaries between religion, identities, nation, culture and values. In fact—and this is a larger issue, both on the right and the left (with the concept of 'multiculturalism')—identity became the key word with which to deal with any kind of differences (racial, religious, linguistic or ethnic). What is new as regards the FN is its very recent shift from extolling the Christian identity of France in favour of a *laïque* identity. Whether this is a tactical move or a long-term evolution to adapt to a new sociological landscape remains to be seen.

7

RELIGION AND POPULISM IN BRITAIN

AN INFERTILE BREEDING GROUND?

Timothy Peace

Britain has seen significant growth in the number of populist parties competing in elections since the beginning of the new millennium. There is also an increasing tendency amongst such parties to focus on religious themes and issues. The question of Islam has become particularly salient, and Muslims are now firmly characterised by populist politicians as the 'religious other'. This is a trend that is mirrored across Europe among nativist parties of the right.[1] At the same time, the British case is also unique, as a left-leaning populist party that appeals directly to Muslim voters has existed since 2004. The use of such tactics has led to the election of candidates at both local and national levels, making the Respect Party a rare success story in a country where the radical left has always performed poorly. Nevertheless, this chapter will argue that populists in Britain struggle to gain support by using religion in their appeals to voters. The British National Party (BNP), which has done the most to exploit the issue of religion, is an electoral failure in comparison to its European counterparts. The UK Independence Party (UKIP) has fared much better, but does not place religion at the core of its message, which is firmly focused on the ills of the European Union (EU). In this chapter, I will firstly explain why politics and religion do not sit well together in the British context. I will then survey the populist landscape in Britain by providing an overview of the main populist parties of both the left and right. Through an analysis of their party websites and election manifestos, I will demonstrate how the issue of religion is invoked. Finally, I will analyse the relations between Church authorities and populists and how faith groups react to them.

Britain is one of the most secularised countries in Europe, which means that appeals to religious sympathies will always have diminishing returns. There are, of course, still established Churches in England and Scotland, but their political role is largely symbolic.[2] As Steve Bruce explains:

> the formal status of the established churches is no more a sign of their influence than the formal status of the monarch is a sign of her power. What matters is the strength of religious belief, and the vast majority of the citizens of the United Kingdom have little or no religion.[3]

Religion and religious representatives therefore play a small part in British political life, and faith has not historically been part of the political cleavage in the country.[4] There is no tradition of religious parties either, which could explain why the influence of both the established Churches and other denominations in political decision-making is marginal.[5] A 2012 poll indicated that the majority of British citizens who identify as Christians agree that religion should have no special influence upon public policy.[6] The irony of this situation is that religious groups are still seen as useful to politicians, and the positive values of faith for society are regularly extolled, much to the chagrin of humanist campaigners.[7] This positive focus on religion, at least at a local level, was continued by the Conservative Party-Liberal Democrat coalition government which took office in 2010. It created a Faith and Communities Ministry, the role of which is to 'work with religious and community leaders to promote faith, religious tolerance and stronger communities within the UK'.[8] In a speech to commemorate the four hundredth anniversary of the King James Bible, Prime Minister David Cameron declared that Britain was a Christian country and called for a revival of traditional Christian values to counter the 'moral collapse' evident in the summer 2011 riots.[9] He reiterated this stance in an article for the *Church Times* in April 2014, claiming that Britons should be 'more confident about our status as a Christian country'.[10]

Such pronouncements are largely superficial, though, as religious groups are not encouraged to shape national policy and religion is rarely raised in political debates. Invariably, when conflicts arise between faith-based and secular groups, the tendency of both judges and politicians has been to side with the latter. The February 2012 High Court ruling that prayers as part of town council meetings were not lawful is indicative of this trend.[11] A number of legal cases involving Christians have been a cause of concern for some prominent religious figures. The former Archbishop of Canterbury, Lord Carey, is one of those who believe that Christianity is being driven out of public life. In a submission to the European Court of Human Rights (ECtHR), he said that Britain was 'a country where Christians can be sacked for manifesting their faith, are vilified by state bodies, [and] are in fear of reprisal or even arrest for expressing their views on sexual ethics'.[12] The ECtHR did, in fact, uphold the UK courts' decision in January 2013 regarding the cases of four British Christians who claimed that they had suffered religious discrimination at work: *Eweida and others v United Kingdom*.[13] None of the mainstream political parties is involved in championing the causes of religious groups. In May 2013, the House of Commons voted to allow gay marriage in England and Wales with 366 votes in favour and 161 opposed, with religious voices largely excluded from the debate. While the mainstream parties might occasionally use populist language, there are a handful of smaller political parties that put this at the core of their appeal to voters, and it is these parties that will now be discussed in more detail.

The Respect Party

The Respect Party has been the most prominent recent populist party of the radical left in Britain. For Respect, 'the people' are not identified in terms of class, but simply as those who work hard but are exploited by the prevailing economic orthodoxy. The party's most high-profile personality is the former Labour MP George Galloway, who has often been described as a populist politician. Respect does not actively campaign on religious issues but has concentrated its efforts among a religiously defined segment of the electorate. It initially presented itself as the 'party for British Muslims' because of its ties to the anti-war movement and opposition to the wider war on terror. It also has used contacts connected with mosques and faith-based organisations to gain support in the local community.[14] The party campaigns among Muslims, selects them as candidates and stresses issues that they consider important, such as foreign policy. It is regularly accused of only representing Muslims but its official policy on religion is restricted to defending 'the religious and cultural expression of all faiths'.[15] Nevertheless, during election campaigns, Respect has been known to appeal to people's religious affiliations. During Galloway's election campaign in the Bradford West by-election of 2012, he sent out a letter in which he claimed that his Labour Party rival Imran Hussain was not a good Muslim, which was quoted in *The Guardian*: 'God KNOWS who is a Muslim. And he KNOWS who is not. Instinctively, so do you. Let me point out to all the Muslim brothers and sisters what I stand for', he wrote, giving a series of four reasons which included 'I, George Galloway, do not drink alcohol and never have. Ask yourself if the other candidate in this election can say that truthfully.'[16]

As well as receiving support from some religious leaders, Respect has also fought against the local political establishment, which was dominated by community elders, often from the same kinship network. Appealing to the values of Islam can be used as a reference point to oppose unjust and undemocratic practices that may be rooted in cultural rather than religious traditions. Frequent reference is made to foreign policy issues that are of concern to Muslim voters, particularly those who have grown up in Britain. The case of Respect illustrates that left-wing populists can also 'hijack religion', although it is worth noting that it has never included any reference to moral issues such as gay marriage, euthanasia or abortion in its election material. It may have scored some notable electoral victories, but these have been restricted to East London, Birmingham and Bradford, where there are significant Muslim communities. Nationwide, the most electorally successful populist parties are found on the right of the political spectrum, as demonstrated by Table 7.1, which shows results from recent European Parliament and general elections.

Table 7.1: Election Results of Populist Parties in Britain, 2004–2015 (Total Votes and Percentages)

Party	EP 2004	GE 2005	EP 2009	GE 2010	EP 2014	GE 2015
BNP	808,200 (4.9%)	192,745 (0.7%)	943,598 (6.3%)	564,321 (1.9%)	179,628 (1.14%)	1,667 (0.005%)
Respect	252,252 (1.5%)	68,094 (0.3%)	Did not stand	33,251 (0.1%)	Did not stand	9,989 (0.03%)
UKIP	2,650,768 (16.1%)	605,973 (2.2%)	2,498,226 (16.6%)	919,471 (3.1%)	4,351,204 (27.5%)	3,881,099 (12.6%)

Note: EP = European Parliament election; GE = general election.
Source: House of Commons Library.

UKIP

UKIP is a Eurosceptic party that was founded in 1993 to campaign for the UK's withdrawal from the European Union. Its breakthrough came in 1999 when it elected three MEPs, and it has always performed best at European Parliament (EP) elections, where British voters can signal their discontent about Europe, or indeed other issues, through a second order election. Proportional representation also ensures that they elect a number of candidates that is in line with the party's share of the vote. In the 2009 EP elections, UKIP came second to the Conservatives with 16.5 per cent of the vote and thirteen MEPs. The party went one better at the EP elections in 2014, when it came first with 27.5 per cent of the vote and twenty-four MEPs. The prominence of UKIP in British politics was confirmed when the voters of Clacton, and Rochester and Strood, elected UKIP candidates to become their MPs in late 2014. This occurred after two sitting Conservative members of the House of Commons defected to UKIP and subsequently won their seats again in the ensuing by-elections. Douglas Carswell then retained his seat in Clacton at the 2015 general election, with the first-past-the-post electoral system limiting the party to just one MP (although the party came second in 120 constituencies). UKIP has historically drawn its support from disaffected Conservatives and research has shown that many of those who vote for the party in EP elections do so strategically, and switch back to the Conservatives for general elections.[17] However, since 2011 it is evident that the party's support has grown to include former Labour voters in a range of constituencies.

The *raison d'être* of UKIP is the withdrawal of the United Kingdom from the European Union. Europe is seen to have taken sovereignty away from the British people but also, as Robert Ford and Matthew Goodwin put it, serves as 'a symbol of other problems in society and perceived threats to the nation: unresponsive and out-of-touch elites in Brussels and Westminster; a breakdown in respect for authority and British traditions; and, most importantly, the onset of mass immigration'.[18] UKIP links public fears about immigration to the EU as an institution. Therefore, British citizens are under threat from EU and human rights legislation as they have led to a loss of control over the UK's borders. It is argued that foreign criminals cannot be stopped from entering the country nor can they always be deported. The proposed solution to these problems is to remove the UK from the jurisdiction of the European Convention on Human Rights and the European Court of Justice, and to return control to the domestic legal system. The party's website describes the EU as 'only the biggest symptom of the real problem—the theft of our democracy by a powerful, remote political elite which has forgotten that it's here to serve the people'.[19] This leaves little doubt as to UKIP's populist credentials. Like many other populist parties, it favours the use of referendums and plebiscites to decide important issues. One of its key policies is the introduction of what it refers to as 'Direct Democracy', whereby 5 per cent of the national or local electorate can demand a binding referendum on any issue. A referendum on Britain's membership of the EU has been their key demand, something which Prime Minister David Cameron was eventually forced into promising, to take place in June 2016.

During the 7th European Parliament (2009–2014), UKIP was a leading member of the Eurosceptic 'Europe of Freedom and Democracy' (EFD) political group, which included other populist and xenophobic parties such as the Northern League (see Chapter 2), the Danish People's Party and the Finns Party (formerly known as the True Finns).[20] UKIP itself has been accused of racism, and David Cameron once described its supporters as 'closet racists'. Such allegations are flatly rejected by the party, which characterises itself as 'non-racist' in an attempt to disassociate itself from more extreme right-wing groups like the BNP.[21] However, xenophobia is correlated with UKIP support, particularly among its core voters rather than those who vote strategically.[22] The party's recent growth and increased prominence in political debate has led to a redoubling of efforts to dispel the idea that its policy on immigration is linked to racism.[23] These attempts were hampered by comments made by several of its candidates in the run-up to the 2014 EP elections, which were generally adjudged to be racist and offensive.[24] UKIP describes itself as a civic nationalist party, yet its rhetoric on immigration and issues of national identity has sometimes mirrored that of the more extreme parties. The party calls for an end to 'uncontrolled mass immigration' and for the safeguarding of British identity and culture. However, unlike many of the other parties in this volume, its focus is on immigration from other countries within the EU, particularly those from Central and Eastern Europe. There is no religious dimension when discussing migrants from countries such as Romania and Bulgaria. However, the conduct of Muslims in Britain has also been an issue for the party.

Under the brief leadership of Lord Pearson (2009–2010), UKIP linked its anti-immigration agenda with a particular focus on Muslims and Islam. Its 2010 manifesto stated that it would:

> Tackle extremist Islam by banning the burqa or veiled niqab in public buildings and certain private buildings. UKIP will deport radical preachers calling for violence or

the overthrow of democracy and reintroduce a proper Treason Act to prosecute British Citizens found guilty of attacks on the British people or armed forces. Religious school materials must not teach hatred of the western world and must be congruent with British values. Sharia courts must not override UK law.[25]

Lord Pearson invited Geert Wilders (leader of the Dutch Freedom Party—see Chapter 5) to show his controversial film *Fitna* at the House of Lords in March 2010, and other senior members of UKIP have declared their admiration for the Dutch politician. In a survey of UKIP general election candidates, 83 per cent agreed that they should campaign on Islamic extremism in the UK.[26] However, since Nigel Farage's return as leader of UKIP in November 2010, the party has been more careful to limit its characterisation of the religious 'other' to what it sees as radical Muslims and does not want to be associated with the more crude racism and Islamophobia espoused by many of its former European allies in the EFD. Occasionally its election candidates have strayed 'off message', for example when Steve Moxon, who was subsequently stripped of his candidacy, endorsed the reasoning of Norwegian mass murderer Anders Behring Breivik on his blog.[27] UKIP immigration spokesman Gerard Batten also courted controversy when he expressed a desire for British Muslims to sign a special code of conduct.[28] Party leader Nigel Farage distanced himself from these views explaining that this had never been official policy. The rise of the group calling itself the 'Islamic State' (IS) and revelations that some British Muslims have travelled to Syria to fight with them did encourage Farage to re-focus his party's attention on the issue of Islamic extremism. In a speech before a US audience, he blamed multiculturalism for the problem of Western Muslims joining IS: 'What we have done is, we have allowed, through a deliberate policy of multiculturalism, because we want to show the world what lovely people we are, and we have allowed different communities to develop a different culture within what ought to be a Judeo-Christian culture.'[29]

UKIP has made attempts to reach out to voters from ethnic and religious minorities, partly as a response to persistent claims that it is a racist party. In 2013 the party started visiting mosques, Hindu temples and Sikh gurdwaras.[30] This was facilitated by a prominent UKIP member of Pakistani descent, Amjad Bashir. He was subsequently selected to stand as a candidate during the 2014 EP elections and became an MEP for Yorkshire and the Humber as well as UKIP's official communities' spokesman.[31] The positive message about inclusion that Bashir's election represented was undermined by comments made during the election campaign by various UKIP candidates such as

Heino Vockrodt, who described Islam as a totalitarian ideology that is 'against everything modern Britain stands for'.[32] UKIP also angered Muslim and Jewish voters by backing the British Veterinary Association and the Royal Society for the Prevention of Cruelty to Animals (RSPCA) in calling for a ban on non-stun slaughter in early 2015.

UKIP does not conceive of the British people in terms of either ethnic or religious identities. However, it does believe in upholding the traditional institutions of the UK state. It therefore fully supports the monarchy and opposes the disestablishment of the Church of England. It also supported British Christians who had lost their jobs because they refused to remove their crucifixes. Leader Nigel Farage stated that UKIP:

> deplores the banning of anyone who wishes discreetly to wear some device which they have chosen to say something to the world about their identity and who they are. It appears that this Government wishes to drive Christianity from public life.[33]

Such support should be seen within the context of its strongly libertarian stance rather than specific support for a particular religion. On moral issues such as abortion or euthanasia, it avoids making pronouncements, and believes in Swiss-style referendums to allow the people to make their voice heard. It supported the concept of civil partnerships for same-sex couples but opposed the move to legislate for same-sex marriage. UKIP believes that Churches and other religious groups should be able to decide for themselves who they will and will not marry.[34] In February 2015 it emerged that an authorised group within the party called 'Christian Soldiers of UKIP' had criticised the Manchester Pride event in one of its newsletters. This led to calls for the party to cut ties with this group, although a UKIP spokesman was keen to stress that those in the group 'do not represent the party or its policies'.[35] This further illustrates how UKIP may wish to cultivate links with religious groups but will not let this damage the party's image. Religion is simply not a key part of UKIP's message and its stance on religious extremists is, in fact, very similar to that of the Conservative Party.

The BNP

The BNP is the most successful extreme-right party in the UK, although this success must be qualified: it has never made the same breakthrough that we have seen from similar parties featured in the other chapters of this volume, and is now unlikely to ever achieve comparable success. Like UKIP, the BNP has been severely hampered by the majoritarian 'first-past-the-post' electoral system. Its vote share in general elections increased between 2001, when it polled 47,129 votes, and 2010, when it took 564,331, but it never came close to electing an MP. Its best ever electoral result saw it receive 943,598 votes (6.2 per cent) in the 2009 EP elections where it elected two MEPs, one of whom was its former leader Nick Griffin. However, the BNP subsequently lost these seats in the 2014 EP elections, returning to just over 1 per cent of the vote, a trend that was confirmed in 2015, when the party received a paltry 1,667 votes at the 2015 general election.

Most experts classify the BNP as a neo-fascist party. When Griffin became leader in 1999, he modernised the BNP in an attempt to emulate other successful extreme-right populist parties in Europe, such as the Front National in France. There was a softening of the party's ideology, although this represented more of a recalibration of fascism than a fundamental break with the past.[36] Nonetheless, the BNP became more appealing to some voters who felt abandoned by the larger parties. The BNP's populism is rooted in portraying these 'old-gang' parties as a self-serving elite, who cannot appreciate the concerns of ordinary voters. In common with other populist parties, it makes a distinction between the 'virtuous people' and the 'corrupt elite', but its definition of 'the people' is restricted to white Britons who are referred to as the 'indigenous population'. This is spelled out clearly in its 2010 election manifesto, which states that being British is 'more than merely possessing a modern document known as a passport. It runs far deeper than that; it is to belong to a special chain of unique people who have the natural law right to remain a majority in their ancestral homeland.'[37] Similarly to UKIP, the BNP employs the populist rhetoric of the need to restore democracy and government to the people through various democratic innovations. The BNP is keen on the introduction of citizens' initiative referendums and on devolving power to the lowest level. Its local election manifesto in 2011 proposed giving 'local people' the right to call binding referendums on 'local issues', with only 12.5 per cent of the electorate required to trigger such a poll.[38] Here the term 'local' is clearly restricted to those whom the BNP considers to be ethnically British, who are contrasted with migrants and minorities.

Historically, the extreme right in Britain has not seen religion as a key part of its identity.[39] This contrasts with many of its European counterparts for whom a far-right Christian subculture formed an important element in the wider movement. There is no religious current within the BNP, and research has shown that those who vote BNP are less likely to be involved in civic and religious organisations, including Churches.[40] In recent years, however, the BNP has sought to invoke Christianity as part of Britain's cultural heritage and to attract older voters, who particularly lament the demise of this aspect in wider culture. Starting with the local elections in 2006, the BNP began to call for the re-introduction of morning assemblies based on Christian worship and the celebration of patron saints' days.[41] It is difficult for the BNP to define 'the people' as Christian, however, as this might include those whom they seek to exclude from the nation. For example, black-majority Churches are now an important part of the British religious landscape, particularly in London.[42] Instead, the BNP wants to see the return of a bygone age where cultural Christianity acts as a unifying element and moral compass. Calls for elements of this tradition to be restored are packaged as a 'commitment to the values of traditional Western Christianity, as a benchmark for a decent and civilised society'.[43] BNP members have also expressed dismay at the decline of Christianity, which they associate with the effects of immigration. As one member cited in Matthew Goodwin's study of the party said: 'We're not in a country that is British anymore, things are changing [...] What I want to see out there is my country, you know the way I knew it, as a Christian country.'[44]

Christianity, even if only in its cultural form, is also used in a deliberate way to provide a contrast to Islam, which the BNP and its supporters have interpreted as the main threat to the British way of life. Like many other European extremist parties, the BNP focuses its campaigns specifically on Muslims rather than ethnic minorities in general. As Hans-Georg Betz and Susi Meret note, 'the notion that Islam is not only a religion but a totalitarian ideology has become a central staple of the nativist right's case against Western Europe's Muslim community'.[45] In the wake of 11 September 2001, opposition to Islam inspired the BNP to set up an Ethnic Liaison Committee, which sought to attract South Asian Sikh voters who were in conflict with Muslims. This attempt to create internal tensions in South Asian communities in Britain was largely unsuccessful, but did point to a willingness to exploit religious sensitivities for electoral benefit. The party's 2005 general election manifesto claimed that it was not 'against Islam per se' but merely considered it as 'another foreign mindset whose adherents are welcome to do whatever it instructs them to do—in their own countries'.[46] This ambiguity was discarded two months after the general election when fifty-two people died in the London bombings of 7 July 2005. These atrocities and the subsequent attempted attacks on 21 July were the catalyst for the BNP to put Islam at the very heart of its campaigns and focus solely on Muslims as the ethnic and religious 'other'.[47] It billed the May 2006 local elections as a 'referendum on

Islam' and the strategy paid off as it achieved 19.2 per cent of the vote in the areas it contested and gained an extra thirty-three local councillors.[48] Its 2010 election manifesto stated that 'the historical record shows that Islam is by its very nature incompatible with modern secular western democracy'.[49]

Muslims are blamed by the party for a variety of social ills, from drug dealing to the sexual exploitation of minors.[50] BNP leaflets use emotive slogans such as 'Our children are not halal meat' and refer to 'Muslim paedophile gangs'. Halal meat itself has also been used by the BNP as a means to attack Muslims in more indirect ways. Using animal rights arguments, the party calls for ritual slaughter to be banned as a 'barbaric practice', and asserts that there should be no exceptions to such rules on religious grounds.[51] It also started to use iconography and language which harked back to historical battles between Christian Europe and the Muslim Orient. Party literature referred to the Battle of Tours, electoral material spoke of the need for a new crusade, and in 2010 the youth wing changed its name to BNP Crusaders to 'pay homage to our ancestors from the Middle Ages who saved Christian Europe from the onslaught of Islam'.[52]

The rise of the BNP in the first decade of the twenty-first century can certainly be correlated with an increase in anti-Muslim sentiment.[53] This has been more important than general feelings of hostility towards immigrants or even other settled ethnic minorities, although these trends have also benefited the BNP. There is a positive relationship between levels of BNP support and the presence of Muslim communities, so it comes as no surprise that the party has made breakthroughs in the Lancashire and Yorkshire towns that first attracted migrants from Pakistan in the 1950s and 1960s.[54] The BNP has been involved in local campaigns to halt the construction of mosques and demands that such buildings should be banned, along with wearing the burqa. These policies are described in its 2010 election manifesto under the heading of 'Counter Jihad: Confronting the Islamic Colonisation of Britain', which includes the foreign policy goal of 'striking a peace treaty with the Islamic world' in return for the halting of the Islamification (or what other European radical right populists call 'Islamisation') of Britain and the West.[55] This kind of proposal is evidence of the BNP's inability to present itself as a credible alternative to other parties. The BNP has been in freefall since the 2010 general and local elections, in which it lost twenty-six of its council seats, defeats followed by 'a period of internecine feuding and bloodletting'.[56] One of its MEPs, Andrew Brons, quit the party in 2012 to form the British Democratic Party, and other rival parties have also since been established, including Britain First, which looks set to continue with futile attempts to hijack religion (its activists have even begun handing out bibles in mosques).[57] Riven by factionalism and infighting over its finances, the BNP saw its leader Nick Griffin step down in July 2014, and he was subsequently expelled from the party in October of that year.

Faith Community Reactions to Populist Parties

How do the representatives of different faiths react to religion being used by populist parties? Of the parties discussed above, only the BNP has attempted to invoke Britain's Christian heritage, and this has prompted Churches to fight back. The BNP faced opposition from local faith groups as far back as 1993 when the party elected its first councillor.[58] From 2002 onwards, as the BNP became more successful, more senior Church figures came out to openly criticise the party and urged Christians to fight against it. Prior to the European elections in June 2004, a group of Church of England bishops in the West Midlands released a statement urging people to reject racism, stating that 'voting for or supporting a political party that offers racist policies is like spitting in the face of God'.[59] Catholic bishops in England and Wales joined their Church of England counterparts in issuing instructions to their congregations not to vote for the BNP. Other denominations also demonstrated their opposition to the BNP at this time. The Methodist Church launched an online information resource, 'Countering Political Extremism', and Church leaders in West Yorkshire across a variety of denominations signed a statement deploring the BNP's racist policies and calling on Christian people to use their vote against the party.[60] This opposition became increasingly vigorous from 2006 onwards, when the BNP started to portray itself as a party for Christians. In March of that year, the BNP launched a front group called the Christian Council of Britain, designed to rival the Muslim Council of Britain. Various Christian groups, including the ecumenical umbrella group Churches Together in Britain and Ireland (CTBI), issued statements condemning this move and distancing themselves from the new organisation. At a local level, many Church groups joined anti-fascist campaigners to oppose the BNP prior to the local elections in May 2006. Nick Griffin responded later that year with a BNP Christmas message in which he claimed that the Church of England had 'down-graded' Christmas. BNP representatives have been 'highly critical of what they allege is the "soft" liberalism of the established Church of England and its supposed naïve position regarding the threat of non-Christian religions, such as Islam, to British cultural identity'.[61]

The BNP has been unable to find a religious ally, which seriously compromises its message on Christian themes.[62] The 2008 London Assembly election provided the BNP with a genuine chance of electing a representative. This prompted a large grassroots campaign to oppose the party led by the anti-fascist campaigning group Hope Not Hate. Representatives of faith communities were an integral part of this campaign, as Steven Woodbridge explains:

> Church leaders of the various mainstream Christian denominations and other religious groups felt compelled to speak out publicly about the ways in which the BNP was deviously attempting to disguise its core extreme right political message on race and ethnicity in palpably religious clothes. A marked ideological and very public disagreement developed between the BNP and its critics over the relationship between religious values and political issues during the weeks immediately preceding the 2008 elections.[63]

The BNP won only one seat in the London Assembly, but this was seen as a major breakthrough at the time. Later that year, the BNP membership list, which included individuals claiming to be religious ministers, was leaked onto the internet.[64] This prompted the General Synod of the Church of England into voting overwhelmingly in favour of banning clergy from belonging to the party.[65] The BNP responded to the ban with an election poster featuring a portrait of Jesus and his words from the Gospel of John, 'If they have persecuted me, they will also persecute you' (see Fig. 7.1). Dr Rowan Williams, then Archbishop of Canterbury, and Dr John Sentamu, Archbishop of York, released a statement prior to the 2009 EP elections advising people not to vote for the BNP. It stated that 'Christians have been deeply disturbed by the conscious adoption by the BNP of the language of our faith when the effect of those policies is not to promote those values but to foster fear and division within communities, especially between people of different faiths or racial background.'[66] This represented a significant step for the Church hierarchy, which would normally refuse to pronounce on such issues because of the risk of being viewed as interfering in the electoral process. Nick Griffin lamented this situation, claiming:

> We've got to be nice to them but the Church of England wants to be nasty to the BNP. I think it is bizarre. We think that our vote and our support is now sufficient that it's time the Church of England grew up and decided to sit down and talk with us about the issues that we're getting across to our supporters.[67]

Unsurprisingly, no such offer has been forthcoming.

Conclusion

This chapter has demonstrated that Britain represents an infertile breeding ground for populists wishing to use religion to advance their cause. UKIP, the

Fig. 7.1: BNP Poster for the 2009 European Elections

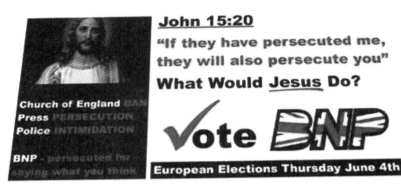

most successful populist party, draws its support from those who reject the influence of the EU. While it has supported Christians who have been involved in court battles, it does not use explicit appeals to religious voters. It attracts votes from citizens who are alarmed about immigration, but Islamophobia is not significantly associated with UKIP support.[68] Its official criticism of the 'religious other' is limited to 'extremist Muslims'. The BNP, on the other hand, is cruder in its depiction of Muslims and actively seeks support from those who see them as a threat to the British way of life. Most religious voters, however, reject the politics and policies of the BNP, and faith communities regularly unite to oppose the party. The threat of the BNP to British democracy has been widely exaggerated in the past and one must not lose sight of the fact that it has never had a member elected to the UK parliament. The Respect Party is unique in Europe as a party that appeals explicitly to Muslim voters, but it too has been weakened by defections and resignations, most notably that of its founder, Salma Yaqoob, who quit in September 2012. George Galloway also lost his Bradford parliamentary seat in 2015. It is unlikely that we will see a recovery from either the BNP or Respect in the near future, but populist parties will remain a regular feature of the British political landscape. Despite its leader, Nigel Farage, failing to win a seat in the 2015 general election, UKIP is in its strongest position since the party's foundation. It is set to play a key role during the debate on Britain's membership of the EU in the lead up to the referendum. Nevertheless, as things stand, it will remain difficult for any party in British politics—populist or not—to successfully mobilise on religious issues.

8

DEFENDERS OF THE CROSS

POPULIST POLITICS AND RELIGION IN POST-COMMUNIST POLAND

Ben Stanley

The politics of religious identity was of major importance to Poland's 'populist turn' of 2005–2007 and to the reorientation of the country's nascent party system thereafter. Populism relies not only on the identification of an antagonistic relationship between the elite and the people; it also posits a moral dichotomy between an inauthentic, illegitimate and corrupt elite on the one hand, and an authentic, legitimate and honest people on the other.[1] The success of populism depends on the ability of political entrepreneurs to appeal to voters on the basis of this dichotomy. Religions have a number of attributes that make them powerful tools of populist mobilisation. They express and communicate a clear distinction between good and evil, which corresponds with the moral dichotomy at the heart of populism. They create and perpetuate communities on the basis of emotional ties and rituals. They often possess institutional structures that furnish the means and motivation for grassroots organisation.

While religion alone does not account for why populism became an important factor in Polish party politics, the appeal to an inward-looking and nation-centric brand of Catholicism was one of its leading characteristics. This chapter explains how religion and the politics of religious identity and values interacted with populism, and with what consequences. The first section briefly outlines the emergence of Polish populism in the second decade of transition. The second section focuses on the case of the League of Polish Families (LPR—Liga Polskich Rodzin), a party embodying the values and worldview of a 'closed' form of Catholicism that was in conflict not only with the forces of atheism but also a liberal, 'open' strand of Catholicism. The third section turns to the case of Law and Justice (PiS—Prawo i Sprawiedliwość), a party that exploited the strategic advantages of religious populism to entrench its position in the party system. Both case studies examine the ways in which these parties invoked religious values and identities to construct both sides of populism's moral dichotomy between the good people and the evil elite, and the relationships between these parties and the Catholic Church in Poland. The final section turns to an analysis of the relevance of religious populism for Polish voters.

The Emergence of Polish Populism after 2001

During the first decade of transition, Polish populists either led noisy but ultimately irrelevant political movements or eked out an existence on the fringes of mainstream parties. Political competition was driven by attitudes to the past rather than the present. The 'regime divide' between successors to the Communist Party and successors to the opposition Solidarity movement informed patterns of voting and coalition formation, and the competitive divide between these two camps seemed set to deepen into a 'post-communist cleavage' that linked voting behaviour with distinct social groups, partisan identities and ideological attitudes.[2] However, from 2001 onwards, this divide was superseded by 'a new political agenda that appealed to the "anxieties of transition".'[3]

Self-Defence (SO—Samoobrona), a party which originated in agrarian protest movements at the beginning of the 1990s, captured the souring of the public mood at the end of that decade, broadening its appeal to incorporate the interests of small-town and urban 'transition losers' on both sides of the regime divide. SO came closer than any relevant Polish party of the post-communist era to 'pure' populism, largely subordinating programmatic consistency to the maintenance of a classically populist 'us versus them' discourse,[4] which focused on the rejection of the Round Table agreement of 1989 and the political elites that emerged in its wake. The anti-liberal economic profile of the party was more clearly articulated than its stances on matters of identity and morality, and it continued to espouse a decidedly ambiguous attitude to religion and the role of the clergy in public life. As such, it is ancillary to the present discussion.

Table 8.1: Parties' Vote Percentage and Seat Share, 2001

Party	% vote	Seats	Change
SLD-UP	41.04	216	+52
PO	12.68	65	–
SO	10.20	53	–
PiS	9.50	44	–
PSL	8.93	42	+15
LPR	7.87	38	–

Source: Państwowa Komisja Wyborcza (n.d.).

If the rise of 'economic anger' at the politics of transition brought SO into parliament, the emergence of the clerical-nationalist LPR was driven by the 'cultural anger' associated with the ascendance of liberal values and their entrenchment in the 1997 Constitution. LPR combined a populist discourse similar to that deployed by SO with a radical right-wing ideology.[5] Given the centrality of religious values and identity both to its populist discourse and the programmatically substantive elements of its ideological appeal, it can be regarded as the most consistently 'religious populist' of the parties under discussion. However, the greatest beneficiary of religious populism was not the party that most consistently expounded its message, but the party which most adroitly employed it in the service of a broader political strategy: the conservative, statist and strongly anti-communist Law and Justice (PiS). Initially, PiS took a rather ambiguous stance on the politics of religion, and was very critical of the disruptive tactics of the populists. SO and LPR returned the hostility in kind, portraying PiS as part of the political mainstream. However, after Poland's 'populist turn' during 2006 and 2007, when all three of the aforementioned parties participated in government, PiS replaced SO as the representative of the economically disenfranchised, LPR as the representative of alienated religious traditionalists, and both parties as the most skilled practitioner of populist rhetoric.

The League of Polish Families: Clerical Right-Wing Nationalism

The religious populism of LPR emerged from the attempt to revive pre-communist clerical-nationalist movements within a post-communist context of elite-led rapid modernisation, in light of the experiences of the Church under communism. The party was not bound together by anti-communist sentiments and organisational ties, but rather drew together various small parties and associations of Catholic-nationalist provenance. Its leading element was the National Party (SN—Stronnictwo Narodowe), which dated back to the inter-war Polish Second Republic, when it served as the party-political wing of the National Democracy (*Endecja*) movement led by Roman Dmowski. Dmowski's conception of the relationship between Church, nation and state concisely expresses the ethos of the Catholic-nationalist movement in Poland:

> The Polish state is a Catholic state [...] because our state is a nation state, and the nation is a Catholic nation. [...] While the law of the state guarantees freedom to all confessions, the dominant religion, the principles of which direct state legislation, is the Catholic religion, and the Catholic Church is the representative of the religious in the functions of state.[6]

This fusion of Polish ethnic identity and statehood with Catholicism placed the 'Pole-Catholic' (*Polak-katolik*) atop a hierarchy of the ethnic groups that populated Poland in the inter-war years, serving in particular to emphasise the otherness of Poland's Jewish population and justify anti-Semitic policies.[7]

After the genocide and ethnic cleansing of World War II and the border shifts that followed, Poland was characterised by much greater ethnic homogeneity. The *Polak-katolik* concept gained a broader character in the communist era, connoting a 'real' Polishness, the authenticity and legitimacy of which contrasted with the illegitimacy of Soviet-imposed political elites. Although the Church's relationship with the regime and with opposition movements was more complex than myth suggests, the overtly religious character of Solidarity, the vocal support expressed for it by Pope John Paul II and the brutal treatment meted out to Solidarity-sympathising pastors demonstrated to the public that the Church was on the side of the opposition.

The Church entered the post-communist era possessing substantial moral capital, which it sought to parlay into political influence. Expecting the Polish state to be 'democratic in form, but Christian in content',[8] it engaged in a number of skirmishes with liberal modernisers over sensitive areas of policy such as education, regulation of the media and abortion. This conflict came to a head during the drafting and ratification of Poland's 1997 Constitution, which sought to accommodate Christian sentiment while retaining an essentially liberal character, but failed to placate those who sought to entrench a privileged role for Catholic values and institutions.[9]

However, the divide between liberal reformers and the Church was not the only politically salient distinction from a religious perspective. The swift decomposition of the opposition camp into a multitude of parties, movements and ideological tendencies exposed and intensified the differences between distinct currents of Polish Catholicism. The discourse of an authentic and morally pure popular majority opposed to an inauthentic and morally compromised elite could be adapted to incorporate a new set of villains. While economic populists concentrated on demonising the authors of liberal economic reforms, religious populists adapted the *Polak-katolik* discourse to fit an 'us versus them' divide that not only distinguished liberals and believers, but also different camps of believers.

While there were numerous philosophical currents in the Polish Catholic Church, the split between 'open' and 'closed' Catholicism became the most politically significant of them. 'Open Catholicism' (*Katoliczym otwarty*) was characterised by 'acceptance of the basic values of modernity, with freedom to the fore', a critical attitude to a mass-based popularisation of religion which is superficial and empty of profound belief, and opposition to those who reject Christian universality in favour of a nation-based religious experience.[10] This ethos was formulated through direct—and often explicit—rejection of its opposite: 'closed Catholicism' (*Katolicyzm zamknięty*), whose advocates opposed the idea that the era of democracy should lead to a flourishing of religious freedom, and tasked the Church with resisting 'the eradication of the Catholic identity of the Polish nation' by protecting it from the corrosive influence of modern Western civilisation.[11]

While some political parties of the early 1990s offered a platform based on the precepts of closed Catholicism, its most influential exposition emerged from a source outside of party politics: the Catholic-nationalist media empire centred around Radio Maryja and headed by the charismatic Redemptorist priest Father Tadeusz Rydzyk. It was Rydzyk's patronage that brought LPR together prior to the 2001 election, and in order to understand the populist and programmatic appeal of the party it is necessary to appreciate the nature of the Radio Maryja movement.

Founded in 1991, Radio Maryja lends its imprimatur to a set of institutions distinct from those of mainstream Polish society: *inter alia*, a newspaper, a television station, a university and an educational foundation. The radio station and associated institutions run in large part on the basis of volunteer labour, and provide a focal point for the spontaneous grassroots initiatives of its listeners, such as local prayer circles, protests and pilgrimages to holy sites. As Burdziej observes, these organisations permit 'less privileged members of society [...] to maintain social ties and create networks of social interaction outside the direct influence of the state'.[12] Much of Radio Maryja's content is politically neutral, consisting of regular broadcasts of prayers, catechism and masses. However, it has developed a reputation as a mouthpiece for traditionalist clericalism, national chauvinism and xenophobia. A detailed analysis of its main discussion programme, 'Unfinished Conversations' (*Rozmowy niedokończone*), found the content of the station's 'opinion-forming' broadcasts to be broader and more nuanced than Radio Maryja's reputation suggested. Nevertheless, the station clearly articulates a worldview that binds religious belief to national identity and patriotic sentiment, makes tendentious use of historical narratives to support this worldview and—at the very least—tolerates the expression of anti-Semitic and anti-German sentiments in the context of defending the honour of the Polish nation.[13]

These findings serve as an apt summary of the ideological profile of LPR. The party updated the ethno-nationalist concerns of the *Endecja* movement to the context of post-communist transition, basing its appeal on the need to defend the integrity of the *Polak-katolik* nation state from the internal and external threats of imitative liberal modernisation. LPR explicitly rooted its ideological principles in 'the traditional moral order of the Nation, with a fundamental role for Christianity, its ethics and system of values'.[14] With the integrity of the nation threatened by the 'dogmas of globalisation and international integration' on which the politics of transition were founded, LPR advocated fundamental political, economic and social reforms 'rooted in the culture and tradition of Christianity and natural law'.[15] This resulted in a political programme that advocated a principled, 'hard' Euroscepticism and egoistic pursuit of national interests, an uncompromising defence of Christian sexual ethics and the promotion of traditional values and patriotic attitudes, and a concept of economic organisation based on the exclusion of foreign capital, protectionism and autarchy.[16]

The populist element of LPR's political appeal was informed by the worldview of closed Catholicism, which, as Gowin observes, is dominated by the perception of a Manichaean divide between good and evil, a black and white depiction of historical events which emphasises the suffering experienced by the Polish nation and a penchant for characterising various purported enemies of Christianity such as communists, Masons, neo-pagans, social-liberals and Jews as 'branches of a wider, global network of connections'.[17]

LPR's identification with the intellectual traditions of the *Endecja* linked it with a conspiratorial version of history, according to which Jews, Masons and Germans were responsible for the woes of the *Polak-katolik*. Roman Giertych, who became party leader after an initial power struggle, attempted to distance LPR from the anti-Semitism of the *Endecja*, declaring that if Dmowski were alive today, he would not be accepted as a member of LPR.[18] However, the party was unable to escape being tainted by anti-Semitic attitudes, particularly in light of its association with the notorious youth organisation All-Polish Youth (MW—Młodzież Wszechpolska). As late as 2005, this movement explicitly committed itself to 'the economic and political isolation of Jews and their restriction, as far as possible, in number'.[19] This goal reflected the character of the original MW, a violent, nationalist and anti-Semitic youth organisation of the inter-war era. The revived MW—of which Giertych himself was the first leader—propagated anti-Semitism and organised events with the involvement of extreme nationalists.[20] Many of the most prominent young LPR politicians and activists came up through the ranks of the movement.

The attitude of LPR to Jews was linked to a broader diagnosis of 'external' threats. Here, LPR's antipathy to the European Union was of particular relevance: its Eurosceptic stance was informed not only by negative expectations about the likely economic and cultural impact, but also by the conviction that European integration was another iteration of a recurrent foreign conspiracy to deprive the Polish nation of its sovereignty. In a Radio Maryja interview in 2002, a prominent LPR deputy, Zygmunt Wrzodak, gave a clear articulation of the party's concerns, declaring that 'the European Union is controlled by Freemasonry', and motivated by the aim of 'empower[ing] [...] a global Jewish nation and a European German nation'.[21]

If the *Polak-katolik* nation was under threat from without, it also faced threats from within. At its broadest, the domestic enemy was identified with those who advocated a 'cosmopolitan liberalism [...] which undermines Christian principles for making sense of the world',[22] or who 'systematically' sought to 'demythologise' Polish history by drawing attention to events which did not fit a positive and patriotic narrative.[23] In particular, the party focused on the role allegedly played by homosexuals and feminists in destabilising the natural order upon which the nation was founded. Homosexuals were condemned not only for demanding acceptance of their 'abnormal' behaviour, but also for infecting society—and in particular the Polish family—with the bacillus of moral relativism. Feminists were responsible for propagating a 'false justification of social engineering' in the form of support for abortion, cohabitation, childlessness and irresponsible sexual relations, and thereby encouraging the demographic decline of the Polish nation.[24]

Against this panoply of enemies, LPR's vision of 'the people' was essentially rather simple. The 'traditionally understood Polish family' constituted 'the elementary unit of the life of the nation'[25] and served as the repository of authentic *Polak-katolik* values and identities. 'True Poles' were those who upheld the virtues of 'pro-family, pro-natal, religious and patriotic' values against the anti-Polish values advanced by Poland's enemies.[26]

Ideologically and temperamentally, LPR was straightforwardly compatible with closed Catholicism. However, this is not to imply that it appealed only to a narrow element of the Church. The Radio Maryja movement enjoyed substantial support from within the Church hierarchy, even if the controversial nature of the movement dissuaded some more moderate clerics from voicing their approval openly. LPR maintained close contacts with conservative members of the clergy, such as Father Henryk Jankowski, a former Solidarity priest later banned from preaching sermons for making anti-Semitic remarks, yet sympathy for the party was not confined only to radical circles. For the first few years of its existence, LPR was the only party which unambiguously prioritised the interests and values of the Catholic Church in its ideological pronouncements and its political activity. It was therefore not in the interests of the Church to take too critical a stance. Individual clerics who disapproved of the ethos of closed Catholicism, such as Archbishops Tadeusz Gocłowski and Józef Życiński, often made negative references to LPR in the media which were duly reciprocated by the party. Yet, the episcopate as a whole rarely spoke out against LPR, and then only in the context of individual initiatives such as the deeply controversial lustration (decommunisation) project the party prepared in 2005.[27] At the same time, LPR's relationship with Radio Maryja soured as Giertych sought to assert his prerogatives as leader of the party, refusing to be steered by Rydzyk.[28] From 2005 onwards, the Radio Maryja movement was openly critical of many of LPR's actions, with Giertych later alleging that this was motivated by Rydzyk's desire to curry favour with more powerful politicians.[29]

Law and Justice: Strategic Uses of Religious Populism

If LPR's religious populism emerged from an ideologically consistent current of clerical nationalism with clear historical antecedents, PiS' embrace of the politics of religion and the discourse of populism was more strategic in character. In the first few years of its existence, PiS did not espouse a strongly religious message. Indeed, party leader Jarosław Kaczyński had demonstrated a clear aversion to a surfeit of clericalism in the appeals of political parties; in the early 1990s he dubbed the Catholic-nationalist Christian-National Union 'the shortest route to the de-Christianisation of Poland'.[30] Moreover, in the first years of its existence, PiS was regarded as a mainstream party. This is not to say that its turn towards populism was inexplicable in retrospect. The Centre Accord (PC—Porozumienie Centrum), an early 1990s precursor to PiS in terms of its ideology and personnel, was a vehicle for leader Jarosław Kaczyński's diagnosis of the pathologies of the post-communist transition elite. Prior to the 2001 elections, PiS gained momentum as a result of the popularity of Jarosław's twin brother Lech, whose short but uncompromising stint as minister of justice in 2000 reinforced the image of a party unafraid to take on the establishment. However, amid the consternation of liberal elites at the emergence of SO and LPR, reaction to PiS' electoral success in 2001 was relatively muted.

The 2001–2005 parliamentary term was characterised by a mood of political radicalism, with the incumbent post-communist government struggling simultaneously to deal with an economic downturn, the travails of accession to the European Union and significant allegations of corruption. It was PiS, rather than SO and LPR, which benefited most from this atmosphere. The dynamic of the dual parliamentary and presidential elections of 2005 created incentives for PiS to distinguish itself from the liberal-conservative post-Solidarity party Civic Platform (PO—Platforma Obywatelska) by articulating a distinctly anti-liberal electoral appeal.[31] Exploiting popular concerns about the impact of further market reforms, PiS contrasted its 'solidaristic' economic stance with the orthodox liberalism espoused by PO. The deepening of the politics of religious identity was a logical corollary of the turn towards economic anti-liberalism.

Prior to the elections, PiS issued the document 'A Catholic Poland in a Christian Europe', which placed the party's main programme in the context of religious values and the defence of Poland's Catholic identity. It declared that Christian values 'embrace [...] our activity [...] in all dimensions—from the material and fiscal rights of the family to the institutional bases of moral order', and committed the party to the defence of these institutions against the 'new threats' of liberal rights and freedoms which 'attack values, structures and institutions inherited from generations past'.[32] Immediately prior to the election campaign, PiS' presidential candidate Lech Kaczyński banned a gay rights parade in his capacity as mayor of Warsaw. Subsequently, Kaczyński sent a letter to the rectors of churches in a number of major towns and cities which expanded on his actions as a defender of Catholic values and gave his commitment as president—and that of PiS as a governing party—to take continued action against threats to Catholic morality and religious freedoms.[33] In an interview for a Catholic weekly, Kaczyński further declared that 'there are no differences between my basic values and those of Radio Maryja'.[34]

These overtures were not lost on Father Rydzyk, whose priority was to 'sink the Platform' (*zatopić Platformę*). Disenchanted with LPR's leadership and the failure of the party to increase its support, he extended his endorsement to PiS. The subsequent course of events justified this decision. After the breakdown of PiS-PO coalition talks and a period of minority government, PiS entered into a 'stabilisation pact' and ultimately a formal coalition with SO and LPR. The formation of this 'exotic threesome'[35] surprised observers of Polish politics. Although mainstream parties had failed to erect a *cordon sanitaire* to exclude these radicals from participation in political life, it was generally assumed that no party would regard them as worthy coalition partners. However, Jarosław Kaczyński was unwilling to pass up an opportunity to advance his party's reform agenda, particularly since Lech Kaczyński's victory in the presidential race removed an important veto point.

Table 8.2: Parties' Vote Percentage and Seat Share, 2005

Party	% vote	Seats	Change
PiS	26.99	155	111
PO	24.14	133	68
SO	11.41	56	3
SLD	11.31	55	−161
LPR	7.97	34	−4
PSL	6.96	25	−17

Source: Państwowa Komisja Wyborcza (n.d.).

In retrospect, the formation of this coalition seems logical from the perspectives of ideological coherence and the political strategy of its senior member. Each of the coalition parties rejected the legitimacy of the institutions and political elites of Poland's post-1989 Third Republic, and contested the liberal orthodox politics of transition. SO concentrated for the most part on opposition to economic reforms, LPR railed against the impact of

Westernisation on religiosity and traditional morality and PiS focused in broader terms on the nature and consequences of the compact upon which the new regime was founded. These currents came together in a coalition agreement that outlined an ambitious programme for the creation of a 'Fourth Republic'. It embraced four key topics: the reform of the state, the pursuit of a more assertive foreign policy, moral and cultural renewal and a more socially sensitive economic policy.[36]

PiS' turn towards populism began in earnest with Jarosław Kaczyński's defence of the coalition agreement to parliament. The reform programme was couched in classic populist terms as the means to remove an elite network (*układ*) from public life so that order could be restored 'in the interests of ordinary people, ordinary Poles'.[37] The coalition's attempts to implement its policies drew it into repeated conflict with liberal-democratic institutions—in particular the Constitutional Court, which stymied key elements of the coalition's legislative programme—while the political elites of the Third Republic joined forces to discredit the government at home and abroad. Polish politics became increasingly meta-political in character, with questions about the legitimacy of political elites and the nature and conduct of politics coming to the fore. With politics increasingly conducted in an emotional and moralistic register and the junior coalition parties increasingly mutinous, the divide between PiS and other parties deepened and widened to the point of apparent insuperability.

PiS' populism grew out of the rhetorical soil prepared for them by their radical predecessors. It was not sufficient that political opponents be criticised for their incompetence or corruption; they must also be condemned for their inauthenticity and anti-Polishness. However, as a party aspiring to capture a wide range of voters from the centre ground to the Catholic-nationalist right, PiS could not rely on the blunt and rather unsophisticated yoking of ethnicity and religiosity that LPR employed. Rather, PiS' references to Catholic identity and values served a broader 'politics of history' (*polityka historyczna*); an attempt to restore national prestige by portraying Poland and the Poles as 'key players of modern history' and giving due weight to their contributions and suffering.[38] This narrative linked 'real Polishness' with traditions of resistance to foreign occupation and repression, focusing in particular on the moral legacies of the 1944 Warsaw Uprising and the Solidarity movement. The emphasis on proud defeat rather than cynical compromise chimed with the recurrent metaphor of Poland as 'Christ of Nations' (*Polska Chrystusem Narodów*), a conception of national identity which emphasises Poland's suffering at the hands of other countries and its redemptive rebirth.

The narrative of a Poland of heroic and incorruptible resisters versus unpatriotic collaborators was an element of Kaczyński's rhetorical repertoire that predated his interest in the politics of religious identity. However, the majoritarian character of Polish Catholicism was compatible with this narrative. Kaczyński averred that Catholicism constituted 'the only general system of values'[39] available to Poles, and spoke of his suspicion of 'initiatives which are not the authentic emanations of social movements'.[40] In so doing, he distinguished between those 'real Poles' who lived in accordance with values that had the weight of tradition behind them, and those who sought to undermine those values.

From 2005 onwards, PiS' attacks on leading figures of the Third Republic were deliberately provocative: they were a 'mendacious elite' (*łże-elita*); a group of 'pseudo-intellectuals' (*wykształciuchy*); a 'front for the defence of criminals' (*front obrony przestępców*). This rhetorical escalation of hostilities was increasingly characterised by attempts at the delegitimation of specific individuals by reference to their political genealogy, with the ideological convictions and political affiliations of fathers and forefathers an infallible guide to those of their descendants. However, in contrast to LPR, the party eschewed direct references to religious belief when criticising the elite. The party leadership remained particularly sensitive to the possibility that they might be accused of perpetuating the anti-Semitic tropes associated with LPR and the Radio Maryja movement. Where LPR's religious populism was direct and explicit, PiS' was diffuse and allusive. In one of the defining speeches of his premiership, held before a crowd of pilgrims at the holy site of Jasna Góra in the presence of Father Rydzyk, Jarosław Kaczyński stated his 'full conviction and belief' that 'today, Poland is here' (*tu jest Polska*).[41] This phrase, which would become a recurrent slogan of PiS rallies in the years to follow, was innocuous at face value but rich in implicit meaning. It confirmed that PiS spoke for the pious and principled *Polak-katolik* whose interests and values were legitimate and whose voice was authentic.

Although PiS appealed to religious sentiment, the party's relationship with the Church remained ambiguous. It found apt expression in Jarosław Kaczyński's declaration that 'personally, I tend to sympathise with an open Church, although that leaves open the question of what [this concept] means'.[42] This ambiguity was clear in the relationship of PiS with the Radio Maryja movement, which was guided by mutual interests and mutual benefits. PiS offered Father Rydzyk a means by which his organisation could pursue and protect its expanding commercial interests, which ranged from setting up a digital television station to exploiting geothermal energy. In return, Rydzyk offered PiS congenial media outlets, with many PiS politicians invited to participate in sympathetic discussions of the party's policies and outlook. The grassroots network that emerged around Rydzyk's media empire also ensured the successful organisation of numerous well-attended PiS protests and rallies. During PiS' term in office, Radio Maryja and assorted nationalist movements staged several counter-marches against protests at the politics of the coalition government, and, after the fall of the coalition, engaged in protests against the new government.

Table 8.3: Parties' Vote Percentage and Seat Share, 2007

Party	% vote	Seats	Change
PO	41.51	209	+76
PiS	32.11	166	+11
LiD	13.15	53	−2
PSL	8.91	31	+6
SO	1.53	0	−56
LPR	1.30	0	−34

Source: Państwowa Komisja Wyborcza (n.d.).
Notes: SLD ran as the major party of the Left and Democrats (LiD—Lewica i Demokracji) electoral coalition. The LiD figure under 'Change' refers to the statistic for SLD in 2005.

The relationship between PiS and Radio Maryja was not solely one of convenience; a substantial faction of the party was genuinely committed to the pursuit of a Catholic-nationalist legislative agenda. Aware of the dangers of alienating moderate sympathisers on the conservative centre-right, Kaczyński fought against the perception that PiS was hostage to Radio Maryja. The coalition did not always legislate in accordance with Rydzyk's preferences, with PiS often acting to rein in the more radical intentions of LPR and its own pro-clerical faction. Where the interests of Radio Maryja clashed with PiS' key priorities, they gave preference to those priorities. As president, Lech Kaczyński blocked the ingress of Archbishop Stanisław Wielgus to the archdiocese of Warsaw after revelations of Wielgus' cooperation with the Communist secret services. This action was consistent with the party's uncompromising anti-communist stance, but Rydzyk took to the airwaves of Radio Maryja to declare himself 'very disappointed' with the 'Bolshevik methods' used by PiS against a respected cleric.[43] Tensions were further inflamed by PiS' support for the Lisbon Treaty, and came to a head over a constitutional amendment proposed by PiS deputies that protected the right to life from the moment of conception. In spite of the origins of this motion, Jarosław Kaczyński refused to endorse it, and it failed to pass. After President Lech Kaczyński's wife Maria signed an appeal expressing opposition to a more restrictive abortion law, Rydzyk was secretly recorded describing her as 'a witch', who should 'allow herself to be euthanised'.[44]

Nevertheless, these incidents did not dissuade PiS from deepening its cooperation with the Radio Maryja movement, particularly in the aftermath of the April 2010 air disaster at Smoleńsk, which claimed the lives of the presidential couple and dozens of other prominent figures. In the days after the tragedy, a wooden cross was erected outside the Presidential Palace as a focal point for mourners. When the new President Bronisław Komorowski announced its removal, a Committee for the Defence of the Cross was formed, with Radio Maryja broadcasting appeals to its listeners to resist its removal by 'bellicose leftists'.[45] This standoff, which echoed an earlier conflict concerning the removal of crosses from the immediate vicinity of the former concentration camp of Auschwitz-Birkenau in the late 1990s,[46] escalated into a series of confrontations between the two sides, mostly verbal but occasionally physical. Although PiS initially distanced itself from overt politicisation of the Smoleńsk tragedy, it increasingly came to support and identify with the 'defenders'. In turn, Radio Maryja lent support to PiS' demand for a re-investigation of the causes of the disaster, and helped to disseminate a version of events steeped in conspiracy theories.

Religious populism has remained a significant element of Polish political discourse, with political issues—particularly, but not exclusively, those pertaining to questions of personal and collective morality—often discussed in terms redolent of populism's distinction between an evil elite and a morally pure people. This was particularly evident during the public debate over the government's attempts to regulate *in vitro* fertilisation during the 2011–2015 parliamentary term. Moral disagreements over this legislation spilled over into divisive rhetoric. Supporters of a complete ban described those who sought to regulate the procedure and make it easier to obtain as emissaries of the 'civilisation of death',[47] with the Episcopacy indicating that priests should refuse to give communion to politicians who had voted in favour of the bill. At the same time, supporters of a liberal *in vitro* law sought to portray their opponents as a fearful and anti-progressive 'hicksville' (*ciemnogród*) whose views were at odds with Poland's trajectory of development.[48]

Another potential area of conflict arose in mid-2015 with the emergence of the Syrian refugee crisis. While the issue of immigration has tended to be much less salient in post-communist countries than in Western Europe, the European Union's plan for member states to share the intake of refugees proved controversial. Several prominent opposition politicians called for the government to accept only Christian refugees, since giving asylum to Muslim refugees would risk 'spreading the plague of terrorism'.[49] The issue remained relatively minor, given the small numbers of immigrants proposed. However, the arguments it prompted provided a foretaste of the potential for rising levels of immigration to stimulate religious populism in the future, with good, virtuous and easier-to-integrate Christians counterpoised with the threatening bacillus of Islam.

Appealing to the People? Religious Populism and Attitudes to Political Parties

By adopting and transcending the populist discourse of their minor partners, PiS rendered SO and LPR electorally irrelevant by the time the coalition fell in late 2007. From 2007 onwards, the regime divide lapsed into a moribund state, as the post-Solidarity PO formed a government with the post-communist Polish Peasant Party (PSL—Polskie Stronnictwo Ludowe). PiS was the major party of opposition, a status boosted by the presidency of Lech Kaczyński. President Kaczyński's openly intransigent and obstructive attitude to the PO-PSL government's policy initiatives, and his ambition to pursue an independent foreign policy, ensured that the new line of division ran through the executive as well as the legislature, deepening the enmity between the two camps. The Smoleńsk disaster and its aftermath entrenched this divide.

Table 8.4: Parties' Vote Percentage and Seat Share, 2011

Party	% vote	Seats	Change
PO	39.18	207	−2
PiS	29.89	157	−9
RP	10.02	40	40
PSL	8.36	28	−3
SLD	8.24	27	−26

Source: Państwowa Komisja Wyborcza (n.d.).

PiS' strategic deployment of populism played a significant role in redefining patterns of elite competition, and its religious component was of particular importance in helping PiS to couch the new divide in terms of authenticity and legitimacy. However, ascertaining the demand-side impact of elite-level shifts in the party system was a more difficult task. In the case of Poland, it was additionally complicated by the fact that the most important divide lay not between believers and non-believers, but between cohorts of believers who differed, not in the object of their belief, but in their attitudes towards the writ of religious authority in the private lives of citizens and in the public sphere. Statistics belied the common observation that Poland was secularising rapidly in the post-communist era. According to survey data collected between 1998 and 2009, the vast majority of Poles (around 90 per cent) continued to identify themselves as 'believing' or 'deeply believing', with the proportion of declared atheists rarely exceeding 5 per cent of the population.[50] Official figures collected by the Statistical Institute of the Catholic Church between 1992 and 2010 suggested a moderate decline in the proportion of parishioners attending church on Sundays (*dominicantes*) from 47 per cent in 1992 to 41 per cent in 2010, and some fluctuation in the proportion of parishioners taking communion (*communicantes*).[51]

The divide between closed and open Catholicism mapped onto an emergent sociological divide between 'Poland A' and 'Poland B': a Poland of those who had benefited from transition, and a Poland of those who had—at least in a relative sense—lost out. The old, those living in small towns and villages, those of lower educational attainment, those in the lower income quartile, the unemployed, the retired and those receiving invalidity benefit were increasingly more likely to state that the post-1989 reforms had negatively affected them.[52] While the inhabitants of Poland A were more likely to couch their faith in private and individualistic terms, inhabitants of Poland B were characterised by a collectivist and Church-centric conception of their religious beliefs.[53]

Inhabitants of Poland B were more likely to listen regularly to Radio Maryja.[54] Analyses of the characteristics and voting habits of Radio Maryja listeners indicate that the notion of Father Rydzyk's followers as a 'disciplined army' was somewhat exaggerated.[55] Radio Maryja may have influenced its followers to participate in elections: in both 2008 and 2011 they were slightly more likely than the rest of society to have participated in the preceding parliamentary and presidential elections.[56] However, this participation did not translate into unanimous support for the object of Rydzyk's favours.[57] In any case, with a large majority of the Polish population (85 per cent in 2011) declaring that they never listened to Radio Maryja,[58] the widening difference between Radio Maryja listeners and the rest of society was not in itself evidence that religious divides were politically influential.

Analysis of religious populism's impact on party preferences is hampered by the difficulty of applying typical survey instruments in the Polish case. Two aspects of religious identity, 'belonging' (institutionalised religion) and 'believing' (spirituality),[59] are usually operationalised by measures of self-assessment of spiritual beliefs and frequency of attendance at church services. However, while very few Poles identify themselves as atheist and non-practising, figures on actual church attendance indicate that there are many Poles for whom religious observance is of little importance. On the other hand, the ranks of the particularly devout may not in fact differ all that significantly from the cohort of 'ordinary believers' with respect to the way in which their religiosity influences their political choices. Surveys rarely ask respondents to declare the extent to which their political choices are motivated by religious 'belonging' and 'believing'. They also rarely ask questions directly intended to measure populist attitudes.

While not perfect on these counts, the post-election survey conducted by the Polish General Election Study in 2011 provides some data that goes beyond the standard variables on religiosity. Table 8.5 (see Appendix) presents the results of Poisson models that regress respondents' attitudes to all relevant political parties on four sets of variables: standard socio-demographic controls, broad ideological dimensions, religious identities and attitudes, and attitudes redolent of populism. For reasons of space and relevance, only the full models are presented. Instead of actual voting behaviour, the dependent variable is attitudes to political parties. These variables give an impression of how cohorts of voters approach the party system as a constellation of ideologically distinct parties, independently of non-ideological factors that might influence the casting of a vote, such as party size or strategic considerations.

The results suggest that, for all the importance of religious populism to the demand-side divide, it had only a limited influence on the structure of party-political preferences. On standard measures of religiosity, there were almost no statistically significant differences between the two major parties PiS and PO: it was the anti-clerical Palikot Movement (RP—Ruch Palikota) that attracted the sympathies of infrequent churchgoers. Where attitudes to the Church were concerned, the difference was more marked. Two aspects of the relationship between the Church and the political process proved particularly controversial in the post-communist era: the involvement of the Church in the legislative process, and priests instructing their congregation how to vote.

Positive attitudes toward these phenomena were associated with higher levels of support for PiS, while negative attitudes were associated with higher levels of support for PO. However, populist attitudes had very little influence. Those who discerned a clear divide between good and evil in politics had slightly more positive attitudes to PiS, but aside from that, populism played no discernible role in differentiating between preferences for one party or another. While more detailed surveys are necessary to explore the impact of religious populism on the demand side of Polish politics, there is insufficient evidence from the available data to suggest that the divide between 'open' and 'closed' Catholicism is particularly important for the Polish voter.

Conclusion

PiS' adroit exploitation of the political potential of religious identity and values—hitherto only realised in part by LPR—made a significant contribution to the reshaping of the relationships between political parties by bringing the divide between 'open' and 'closed' Catholicism into the mainstream of party politics. However, the extent to which the Polish party system has consolidated around this new line of competition remains a matter of dispute. Gwiazda regarded it as 'quasi-institutionalized' by 2007,[60] with political elites playing a crucial role in stabilising both parties themselves (through the more efficient enforcement of party discipline) and the relationships between them (through the politicisation of key political cleavages). However, Millard took a distinctly more sceptical stance on this stability, arguing that public distrust of political parties, Polish voters' history of electoral volatility and 'the tenuous nature of the links between parties and their supporters' cast doubt on the wisdom of ruling out further realignments.[61]

On the evidence presented here, while the politics of religious populism has been important in shaping Polish politics at the supply side, it is not unambiguously reflected in the preferences of voters. Party-system consolidation remains susceptible to the vicissitudes of electoral behaviour, and in the broader sweep of Polish party-system building the turn to religious populism may yet prove an ephemeral one. While it might be tempting to interpret the emergence of the anti-clerical RP in 2011 as a deepening of the religious divide, the party's strident atheism and secularism cut across the prevailing distinction between open and closed Catholicism, disturbing the dominant pattern of competition. RP has also faded badly during its four years in parliament, and its future as a single party is in doubt. Meanwhile, PO is far from united on a number of questions of potential relevance to a renaissance of populist Catholicism. The relationship between the liberal leadership of PO and the party's sizeable conservative faction has grown increasingly fractious, with clear divisions over moral issues such as *in vitro* fertilisation, abortion and gay rights.

It is also unclear what role religious populism will play in the political discourse of its key adherent, PiS. The strategy of party leader Jarosław Kaczyński has been to gain the support of conservatives in the Church hierarchy while avoiding becoming their political instrument. Bearing in mind the incentive that exists for the party to gain support by projecting a more moderate image to centrist floating voters, the philosophical divide between open and closed forms of Catholicism is unlikely to become an unambiguous dividing line between non-populist and populist parties. Issues of the role of the Church in public life and the centrality of Catholic morality to policymaking will continue to be areas of significant controversy, but while religious populism played a substantial role in changing the nature of Polish party competition, its legacy—and its future—remains an uncertain one.

Appendix

Table 8.5: The Impact of Religiosity and Populism on Attitudes to Political Parties

	Like RP	Like PiS	Like SLD	Like PO	Like PSL
2.gender	−0.176'''	0.013	−0.004	0.020	−0.001
2.resid	0.019	−0.052	−0.087'	0.072'	−0.080'
3.resid	0.093	−0.119'	−0.106''	0.071'	−0.151'''
2.educ	−0.121'	−0.049	−0.005	−0.013	−0.055
3.educ	0.029	−0.160'	0.096'	0.063	0.003
Age	−0.019'''	0.000	0.001	0.002'	0.004'''
hincome	−0.009	−0.060'	−0.052'	0.054''	0.002
Leftrt	−0.066'''	0.072'''	−0.078'''	0.006	−0.005
Sollib	0.023'	−0.054'''	0.008	0.036'''	0.008
1.relig	−0.075	−0.011	−0.032	−0.202'	0.016
2.relig	0.119	−0.148	−0.038	−0.016	−0.017
4.relig	−0.102	0.101	−0.069	−0.043	−0.017
1.partic	0.078	−0.099	−0.001	0.026	−0.235'
2.partic	0.257''	−0.110	0.050	−0.008	−0.101
3.partic	0.157''	−0.128''	0.059	0.026	0.015
5.partic	−0.768''	0.021	−0.206	−0.080	0.022
crspub	−0.238''	0.026	−0.103	−0.034	−0.041

Relles	−0.287***	0.226*	−0.060	−0.010	−0.008
reloath	−0.101	0.307*	0.070	0.020	0.135*
Prsttv	−0.027	0.034	−0.077*	0.031	0.004
chlegis	−0.219***	0.349***	−0.060	−0.130***	0.046
prvote	−0.070	0.197***	−0.057	−0.243***	0.022
gdevil	0.001	−0.024*	−0.005	−0.000	0.007
minopin	0.011	−0.000	−0.013	−0.008	−0.002
disfree	−0.012	−0.005	−0.020*	−0.006	−0.011
_cons	3.647***	−0.211	2.678***	1.398***	1.095***
N	1919	1919	1919	1919	1919

Source: author's own calculations on the basis of the dataset provided by Polskie Generalne Studium Wyborcze (2011).
Notes: all models are Poisson regressions with robust standard errors, using multiple imputation of missing data (m=10).

9

'THE GOD OF HUNGARIANS'

RELIGION AND RIGHT-WING POPULISM IN HUNGARY

Zoltán Ádám and *András Bozóki*

A magyarok istenére esküszünk,
hogy rabok tovább nem leszünk!
'We swear on the God of Hungarians
that we won't stay as slaves any more!'

Sándor Petőfi, *Nemzeti dal* (National Song), 1848

Religious interventions into politics and the role of the Church in shaping policy decisions and even political strategies have long represented an important topic for academic research.[1] In this chapter, however, we argue that the relationship between populism and religion in Hungary is not particularly strong, and only contextually significant. The traditional Christian Churches— Catholic and Hungarian Calvinist—provide a societal basis for right-wing populist parties, with the latter making religious references to signal their traditional social values and identification with the societal mainstream. Yet, as Hungary is not a particularly religious society, and most people ignore all

129

Churches, right-wing populist parties make sure that they are not hijacked by religious thinking or controlled by any Church.

Right-wing populism does not necessarily contain an important religious element, as, for instance, the Dutch case demonstrates.[2] In a secular country like Hungary, in fact, right-wing populist parties could refrain from making significant recourse to appeals to religious identity. Yet, even under such structural conditions, right-wing parties tend to refer to religious values and to seek religious legitimation, as we will show in the case of two Hungarian right-wing populist parties. In this sense, a link between right-wing populism and religion has been created in Hungarian politics over the past twenty-five years, which in fact follows longstanding historical traditions. Meanwhile, left-wing parties are associated with the communist past, which promoted a secular ideology. The divide between leftist and anti-communist forces thus basically refers to the classic secular versus confessional cleavage.[3]

In this chapter, we will first discuss the role of right-wing populism in Hungary and its dominance of the country's political landscape since the end of the 2000s. Second, we will examine the role of religion in the formation of the politics of the governing right-wing Fidesz party and its far-right opposition, the Movement for a Better Hungary (Jobbik Magyarországért Mozgalom—usually known simply as Jobbik). In so doing, we will compare their usage of religious references in competitive party politics.[4] Third, we will analyse the role of religion in Hungarian society and politics, arguing that—despite its longstanding historical roots—it remains comparatively limited.

The Populist Takeover of Hungary

The rise and consolidation of right-wing populist and extreme nationalist movements across Europe has puzzled democratic theorists and observers alike as a trend that would seem to be incompatible with the purportedly liberal democracies in which they are taking root. In the nearly three decades since the collapse of communism in the former Soviet bloc, countries in East Central Europe have struggled to create a democratic legacy and propel their societies towards democratic futures. Although the Round Table Talks of 1989 led to a democratic arrangement and non-violent transition from communism to a market economy and democracy in Hungary,[5] many Hungarians have become disillusioned by their post-transition situation. A sense has arisen that democracy was 'stolen' from Hungarians and that a new transformation must be undertaken if the country is to be truly vindicated from centuries of indignity under various imperial powers and then many decades of communism. Hence, according to a 2009 Pew Research report, 77 per cent of Hungarian respondents were frustrated with the way Hungarian democracy had worked during the 1991–2009 period, and 91 per cent of Hungarians thought that the country was not on the right track.[6] Approval of democracy in Hungary immediately following the fall of communism was 74 per cent, whereas by 2009 this figure had fallen eighteen percentage points to 56 per cent.[7]

At the June 2009 European Parliament (EP) elections, the right-wing Fidesz party gained 56 per cent of popular votes, while the far-right Jobbik received 15 per cent. In the following year's general election, Fidesz received 53 per cent, while Jobbik obtained 17 per cent, representing a noteworthy increase in radical right-wing representation in Hungarian elections. Due to the dominance of single mandate districts, Fidesz's electoral victory was transformed into a two-thirds parliamentary supermajority. Left-wing and centrist parties together gained fewer than 20 per cent of parliamentary seats. The full takeover by the right was thus completed politically, ideologically and culturally, and an openly anti-liberal regime was established.[8] Using its two-thirds parliamentary majority, Fidesz altered the entire constitutional system. Not only did the party introduce a new Constitution, but it changed electoral rules and fundamental laws regulating the relationship between government bodies and between the government and the citizenry.[9] The new Orbán regime, named after Prime Minister Viktor Orbán, proved to be very flexible in several ways but constantly moved in an authoritarian direction. At the beginning, it was a majoritarian democracy, but it subsequently became an illiberal, populist one. Moreover, since the 2014 general elections, it has been an increasingly autocratic hybrid regime.

This authoritarian turn was carried out by the two-thirds parliamentary majority, without any meaningful concession to the opposition and without a referendum or any other institutionalised form of popular approval for the new Fundamental Law that replaced the 1989 Constitution. Precisely because of this, some observers have argued that the Fundamental Law suffers from a critical lack of legitimacy, and hence will be relatively easy to modify by a future liberal democratic majority.[10] However, perhaps the most shocking aspect of the Fidesz takeover from a liberal democratic viewpoint has been the fact that even this restricted legitimacy seems to possess a seemingly larger, more extensive, popular political appeal than the pre-2010 liberal democratic regime did.

Fig. 9.1: Share of Votes for Party Lists (as Percentage of Total Votes)

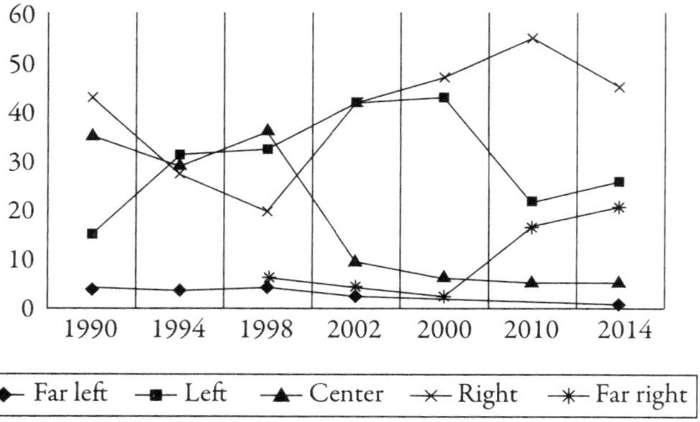

Source: National Election Office.

Notes: far-left: Hungarian Socialist Worker's Party/Worker's Party (1990–2002; 2014: 0.6 per cent); left: Hungarian Social Democratic Party (1990), Hungarian Socialist Party (1990–2014); centre: Agrarian Alliance (1990–1994), Centre Party (2002), Fidesz (1990–1998), LMP (2010–2014), Alliance of Free Democrats (1990–2006), Entrepreneurs' Party (1990); right: Fidesz (2002–2014), Independent Smallholders' Party (1990–2002), Christian Democratic People's Party (1990–1998), Hungarian Democratic Forum (1990–1998, 2006–2010), far-right: Hungarian Justice and Life Party (1998–2006), Jobbik (2010–2014).

Fidesz

Founded in 1988 during the mobilisation of radical liberal student activists, Fidesz has undergone a profound ideological and policy shift since the mid-1990s. Led by Viktor Orbán and his college friends, Fidesz entered the national political arena as a fresh, young, alternative liberal party in 1989–1990. Its name was an abbreviation of Federation of Young Democrats (Fiatal Demokraták Szövetsége), and the party espoused an anti-clerical political stance. In the mid-1990s it took a right-wing turn and gradually transformed itself into the leading centre-right party. It developed an essentially traditional right-wing political stance, one that includes reservations about liberal democracy and Western influence in Hungarian internal affairs. Though the evolution of Fidesz was nuanced and complex, the party has consistently and conspicuously adopted increasingly nationalistic policy stances as it rose to power.[11]

Already at the turn of the millennium, when Orbán was prime minister for the first time (1998–2002), his government pursued ideologically driven policies such as the creation of a 'Civic Hungary'. It also sought to enlist the conservative cultural elite as a political ally, so that Fidesz could claim to be the political representative of the traditional 'Christian-national middle classes' that played a dominant role in inter-war Hungary.[12] In order for his party to become the leading force of the right, Orbán needed historical and cultural symbols, and had to eliminate his right-wing rivals, the traditional agrarian Independent Smallholders' Party (FKGP—Független Kisgazdapárt) and the 'old school', anti-Semitic and far-right Hungarian Justice and Life Party (MIÉP—Magyar Igazság és Élet Pártja).[13] Although the turn from anti-clericalism to an openly positive stance towards religion never played a very important role in the history of Fidesz, Orbán himself regularly participated in the festive Catholic processions known as *Szent Jobb Körmenet*, held on the anniversary of the foundation of the Hungarian state (20 August). He started openly to identify his own political camp with 'the Nation' and to cast his opponents as serving 'foreign interests'.

'We need to win only once but with a big margin,' Orbán infamously said in 2007 after having lost two general elections in a row in 2002 and 2006. He knew that Fidesz could transform the entire constitutional system via a two-thirds parliamentary majority, and thus fulfil the anti-liberal agenda that the traditional right had been nurturing since the regime change of 1989. Using an enormous amount of public financial resources, constraining opposition parties' access to national media and manipulating electoral rules, Fidesz has won all national and European Parliament elections with huge margins since 2010. It has built a centralised and personalised political system in which Orbán plays the role of a populist leader, based on his personal charisma, unchallenged both within and outside his party. The 'national Christian' political identity of Fidesz has played an instrumental role but conveyed no substantial religious content. When Hungary was admitted to the European Union (EU) in 2004, Fidesz joined the centre-right, conservative grouping of the European Parliament, the European People's Party (EPP). However, religion has not been a significant part of Fidesz's identity and policies, not even after it embraced a nationalist-populist stance on most policy issues. Hence, a recently published semi-official history of Fidesz did not even discuss the role of religion in the formation of party ideology.[14]

Jobbik

Fidesz's overwhelming political dominance in recent years has been based on its capacity to describe social reality in its own terms, ideologically unchallenged by the left. However, since the end of the 2000s, Fidesz has been increasingly challenged by its far-right opponent, Jobbik. Founded in 2002 via a conservative university movement, Jobbik describes itself as a

> principled, conservative and radically patriotic Christian party. Its fundamental purpose is protecting Hungarian values and interests. It stands up against the ever more blatant efforts to eradicate the nation as the foundation of human community.[15]

Jobbik's ideology is that of a right-wing, radical party 'whose core element is a myth of a homogeneous nation, a romantic and populist ultra-nationalism directed against the concept of liberal and pluralistic democracy and its underlying principles of individualism and universalism'.[16] In addition to this nationalist rhetoric, Jobbik has an underlying economic appeal that blames globalisation for Hungary's troubles. The party has been clear about its radical far-right nationalism from the beginning. It arose from relative obscurity[17] by harnessing deeply held anti-Roma sentiment following the countryside lynching of a non-Roma teacher by a group of Roma in a remote north-east Hungarian village in October 2006. Jobbik uses its ideology to address what it calls 'gypsy crime', an issue the party portrays as the fundamental problem in Hungarian society. Its solution is to establish jobs, education and vocational training in addition to harsher punitive sentences. Jobbik has thus managed to establish itself as a radical, nationalist and blatantly anti-Roma party that believes in law and order as the solution to the issue of 'gypsy crime'.

In addition to its evocation of rampant Roma criminality, Jobbik gained further notoriety—and followers—with the formation of a paramilitary force. The August 2007 founding ceremony in Budapest of the Hungarian Guard (*Magyar Gárda*) caused further concern among those alarmed by the burgeoning radical right in the country. Gábor Vona, chairman of Jobbik and a co-founder of the Guard, stated: 'The Hungarian Guard has been set up in order to carry out the real change of regime from communism and to rescue Hungarians.'[18] This theme of 'rescuing Hungarians' is consistent with Jobbik's self-conception as the saviour of Hungary and the radical redeemer of what its members consider a failed transition. One of the most prominently displayed pledges in Jobbik's manifesto on the party's official website is the '[completion of] the change of the political system' and 'creating a more just society than the current one'.[19] In 2008, the 650-member Guard wore black uniforms inspired by traditional Hungarian national dress with the ancient Árpád banner as their symbol. The symbolism seemed obvious: a homage to Mussolini, if not Hitler, and to the fusion of race, state and national unity. The Árpád stripes are a part of Hungary's coat of arms, but are now associated with the far right, as the Nazi-inspired Arrow Cross regime, which ruled the country in the winter of 1944–1945, incorporated the stripes into its flag.

While there are certainly true believers in Jobbik's nationalist ideology, the party has really only been able to grow in an environment where the population is radicalised, not by nationalism or racism but by anger at the economic and political situation. In this sense, the far right in Hungary is not to be confused with the radical parties that exist in Western Europe, for the far right in Central Europe differs from its Western counterparts in its choice of enemies. As an *Economist* article put it: 'In the West it thrives on immigrant-bashing. In the East it dwells on more atavistic grievances: ethnic minorities, old territorial disputes [...] and, naturally, Jews. Hatred of the Roma has become a defining issue. Everywhere economic anxiety is exploited. Even a decade of growth has left plenty of poor and disaffected people. Many hark back to an era when the state protected them from crude market forces. This produces a far right that likes nationalization and dislikes the market.'[20]

The Role of Religion in Hungarian Right-Wing Populism

The new Fundamental Law adopted in 2011 was the result of a unilateral governmental process, which did not reflect a national consensus. It was approved by Fidesz MPs only, and is therefore often called the Fidesz Constitution. Although the Fundamental Law kept several portions of the 1989 Constitution, it represents a clear break with its spirit.[21] It lumps individual freedoms together with communal interests, not valuing individual freedoms in their own right. Moreover, rights are not separated from duties, and the latter are derived from Christian worldviews. The Fundamental Law refers to Hungary as a country based on Christian values. Although it formally maintains the form of governance as a republic (in one sentence only), it changes the official name of the country from 'the Republic of Hungary' to simply 'Hungary'. The text increases the role of religion, traditions and so-called 'national values'. It speaks of a unified nation, yet certain social minorities are not mentioned with the same degree of importance. In its definition of equality before the law, it mentions gender, ethnicity and religion, but it does not extend this to legal protection against discrimination based on sexual orientation.

In contrast to the 1989–1990 democratic constitution, the Fundamental Law of 2011 serves as the expression of a secularised national religious belief system: a sort of paganised, provincial, particularistic understanding of the universalistic spirit of Christianity. It is a vow in which Hungarians are meant to list all of their sources of pride and hope and pledge to join hands and build a better future, parallel to Orbán's 'System of National Cooperation', announced immediately after the 2010 general elections by the new Parliament. The political fusion of nationalism and Christianity is clearly presented in the preamble to the Fidesz Constitution: 'We recognise the role of Christianity in preserving nationhood.'[22] The signing of the Fundamental Law by the President of the Republic took place on the first anniversary of the electoral victory of Fidesz, which happened to be Easter Monday, 25 April 2011, a date symbolising the alleged rise of Hungarian Christianity and statehood, and drawing a bizarre parallel between the resurrection of Jesus and the new Fidesz Constitution.[23]

Fidesz uses religious symbols in an eclectic way in which references to Christianity are often mentioned together with pre-Christian pagan traditions. This refers to the idea of 'two Hungaries': the Western Christian version and its Eastern, pagan and tribal counterpart. When Orbán talks about the reunification of the Hungarian nation, he means that he intends to build bridges between the two camps. He aims to 'Christianise' pagan traditions— or paganise Christianity to accommodate the needs of the Hungarian right— when he brings together seemingly incompatible religious symbols. In his speeches, the Holy Crown of St Stephen, the first Hungarian king, can easily appear side-by-side with the mythical Turul bird, a symbol of ancient Hungarians. The concept of political nationhood has thus given way to the ethnic idea of national consciousness. On inaugurating the monument of 'National Togetherness', Viktor Orbán voiced his conviction that the Turul bird is the ancient image into which the Hungarians are born:

> From the moment of our births, our seven tribes enter into an alliance, our St-King Stephen establishes a state, our armies suffer a defeat at the Battle of Mohács, and the Turul bird is the symbol of national identity of the living, the deceased and the yet-to-be-born Hungarians.[24]

Orbán conjectures that, like a family, the nation also has a natural home— in Hungary's case, the Carpathian Basin—where the state-organised world of work produces order and security, and where one's status in the hierarchy defines authority. The legitimacy of the government and the Fundamental Law is not only based on democratic approval, but is approved by God, and features the spirit of Hungarians represented by the Turul. These concepts have replaced an earlier public discourse whose central categories were liberal democracy, market economy, pluralism, inalienable human rights, the republic, an elected political community and cultural diversity.

As Éva Balogh observes, Orbán's references to nation, nationalism and Christianity are abundant. Orbán claims that 'Christian culture is the unifying force of the nation', it gives 'the inner essence and meaning of the state [...] that's why we declare that Hungary will either be Christian or not at all.' He has also asserted that Hungarians are Europeans, not because Hungary is geographically part of Europe, but again 'because we are Christians'.[25] Both Fidesz and Jobbik politicians believe in the homogenised and ethnicised concept of culture, both use religion as complementary to nationalist ideology and both prefer a strongman's rule to liberal democracy. Both parties use or support discriminatory policies against the Roma minority, and both display a claustrophobic approach to foreigners. They differ, however, as regards their position on the Islamophobia-anti-Semitism axis: Fidesz is openly Islamophobic but it rejects anti-Semitism, while Jobbik is anti-Semitic and openly anti-Roma.

Jobbik members and voters have exhibited blatant anti-Semitism[26] and the party has been criticised for its members' intentionally intimidating stance towards the country's significant Roma population, as well as for its paramilitary wing in the Guard. It has led the charge to restore Hungary to its former glory, utilising old national symbols and foundational myths to construct the image of a unified, homogeneous, Christian nation that must retrieve what has been taken by centuries of foreign domination, communist rule and a weak post-transition democratic state. Pirro identifies Jobbik by its clericalism, by its irredentism, by its social-nationalist economic programme and by its anti-Roma, anti-corruption and anti-EU stances.[27] From its early documents, it is clear that the party believes that 'national morality can only be based on the strengthening of the teachings of Christ', and Jobbik promotes the spiritual recovery of the Hungarian people. This is to be achieved by returning to traditional communities (the family, the Churches and the nation).[28]

As self-described 'Christians', Jobbik politicians have consistently taken a pro-Arab stance against the Jews and the state of Israel, underlining the alleged similarities between the situation of the Palestinian people in Israel and of Hungarians in Europe. Anti-Semitism thus overrides Islamophobia within the party. In 2012, for instance, Csanád Szegedi, an influential Jobbik politician and former member of the European Parliament, had to leave the party after he discovered his Jewish origins.[29] On the other hand, a former leader of the

Hungarian Guard, the paramilitary organisation closely connected to Jobbik, was active in helping Syrian refugees to enter Hungary in 2015. This is, of course, another point that distances Jobbik from the far-right parties of Western Europe, for the party has displayed relative openness to Islam. Its leader, Gábor Vona, embraced a new Eastern alliance for Hungary (instead of the North Atlantic one) based on neo-Turanism,[30] a historical ideology 'that aspires to the unification of the "Uralo-Altaic" race, including the Turks of Turkey, the Turkic peoples of Central Asia, Tatars, Hungarians, the aboriginal tribes in Siberia and even distant Mongolians, Manchus, Koreans and Japanese'.[31] Some Jobbik politicians thus claim that their party stands out among the European radical right-wing parties through its close relationship with Islam.[32] This reinforces our observation that anti-Semitism is the glue that connects the parallel pro-Islam and pro-Christian stance of the party.

Jobbik has thus been vehemently pro-Christian (even installing crosses in several Budapest squares). However, while it enjoys the support of certain members of both the Catholic and the Calvinist Church—the two largest Hungarian religious congregations—neither Church in general approves of Jobbik. Despite its manifestly Christian self-identification, Jobbik is seen by many clerics as representing an essentially pagan, anti-Christian cultural tradition.

Religion and Populism in Hungarian Society

Despite all of the differences discussed above, Fidesz and Jobbik are not real political enemies. Rather, their convergences in ideology and policy have opened up a space for the far right in the Hungarian political mainstream. As Jobbik has ventured further into the political mainstream and boosted its core constituency, Fidesz has adopted policies further to the right in an effort to strengthen its position on the right and consolidate its power under the auspices of a strongly nationalist populism.[33] This political space has opened up an opportunity for Fidesz to adopt increasingly illiberal policies while maintaining its political dominance and a parliamentary supermajority.[34] In a sense, the political centre shifted further to the right, polarising left and right and making it more difficult for political moderates to appeal to the majority of the electorate. Due to this shift, we can say that Hungary not only has an extreme-right party, but an 'extreme centre'.

From our perspective in this chapter, the most important question is whether the politicisation of religion has played a significant role in this further shift to the right. Our short answer is no. Hungarian right-wing pop-

Fig. 9.2: Percentage of Respondents Attending Religious Services other than Weddings or Funerals at Least Once a Week

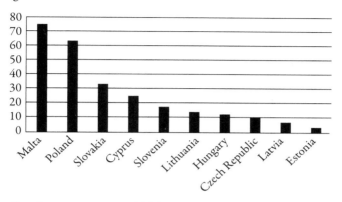

Source: Eurobarometer, spring 2004.

ulism, enacted by Fidesz and Jobbik in an increasingly similar ideological fashion, has used limited religious references in the post-1989 era. The most important reason for this, we would argue, is the limited role of the Churches and religion in Hungarian society.

Although Hungary is certainly not an extremely atheistic society, a clear majority refuses to join Churches and to participate in institutionalised religious activities. This is a relatively recent development, dating back to the post-World War II period in which Hungary went through a process of urbanisation and industrialisation while Churches were severely repressed by the communist regime. Although a revival of churchgoing has taken place since 1989, a large part of society still distances itself from Churches and religious references. Hence, for a political party, appearing to be overly religious may alienate a substantial part of the electorate. In fact, while József Torgyán's FKGP renewed the historic party slogan of 'God, Fatherland, Family' in the 1990s, Christianity itself played a limited role even in its relatively old-fashioned right-wing populism.[35] As representatives of current right-wing populism, neither Fidesz nor Jobbik defines itself in terms of religious identity, although in their respective party manifestos both claim to be 'Christian'. However, Christianity in this context signifies a degree of social conservatism and traditional nationalism rather than any substantive religious reference. Research proves that Jobbik's pro-Christian stance simply indicates that the party should be interpreted as 'non-Jewish'.[36] By using this discourse, Jobbik simply creates an identifiable reference to its anti-Semitism. In fact, despite Jobbik's self-definition as a Christian party, Jobbik voters are the least religious citizens in Hungary.

Table 9.1: Answers to the Question 'How Religious Are You?' Among Voters of Parliamentary Parties (Percentage of the Particular Party's Total Electorate)

	'religious, and I follow the guidance of the Church'	'religious in my own way'	'not religious'	'cannot tell whether I am religious or not'	Refuse to answer	Total
Fidesz-KDNP	22	51	22	5	1	100
Jobbik	6	43	41	9	1	100
MSZP	15	57	21	7	1	100
LMP	4	51	35	9	1	100

Source: Political Capital Institute research, Budapest, 2012.

Although followers of Churches seem to represent the highest share among Fidesz voters, their ratio is a mere 22 per cent, followed by 15 per cent among Socialist voters. Again, Church members represent a conspicuously low figure of 6 per cent among Jobbik voters. At the same time, explicitly non-religious people represent the highest share among Jobbik voters (41 per cent), and their share, interestingly, is lower among Socialist voters (21 per cent) than among the Fidesz electorate (22 per cent). Fidesz has probably been the preferred political party of Christian Churches since at least the beginning of the 2000s, and Prime Minister Orbán has identified himself as a Christian believer on numerous occasions. Fidesz has also formed a strategic alliance with the Christian Democratic People's Party (KDNP), historically a dominantly Catholic party, since 2002. As part of this agreement, the KDNP receives enough seats to form its own parliamentary faction and is also allocated a generous number of government positions when the parties are in power. In exchange, the KDNP has effectively given up its separate political identity and become a Fidesz satellite, endorsing its 'Christianity' by its mere name.

Although certainly not disliked by the Catholic Church, Fidesz probably has closer ties to the Calvinist Church, Hungary's second largest congregation. Orbán himself is a Calvinist and one of his closest political confidants, Zoltán Balog (minister of human resources), was a Calvinist pastor before becoming a professional politician. Orbán likes to attend religious ceremonies and to deliver semi-public speeches in churches. Correspondingly, Fidesz's relationship with the Churches is friendly but not strongly institutionalised. However, Christianity in general serves as a broad ideological reference, and this reference becomes more concrete at some politically prominent moments. For instance, in the new Memorial to the German Occupation of 1944–45 on Szabadság tér, a central square in Budapest, Hungary is represented as Archangel Gabriel being attacked by the German imperial eagle. This is a highly controversial new memorial that seeks to modify public discourse on Hungary's role in World War II, depicting the country as a victim rather than a perpetrator. In this context, Hungary is represented by the Archangel, providing an obviously religious reference for national identity politics. Nevertheless, Fidesz generally refrains from advocating hard-core religious ideas that may alienate people. We explain this by the fact that Fidesz is a large umbrella organisation, 'the party of power', and its voters typically do not nurture strong religious identities. Therefore, while using religion to justify its populist policies, Fidesz must also strike a delicate balance.

Jobbik does not appear to be a representative of religious interests either. In contrast to other right-wing populist parties of the region, such as Law and Justice (PiS) in Poland, it does not cast itself as the protagonist of religious values. Rather, it sometimes seems to nurture pagan affiliations, cultivating a longstanding relationship between far-right or Nazi political culture and pre-Christian paganism. However, just like Fidesz, Jobbik also has its own direct

Fig. 9.3: Share of Religious Congregations in Hungary (Percentage of the Total Population)

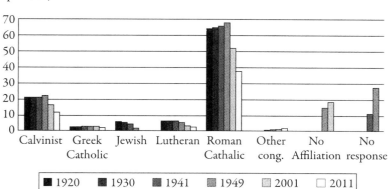

Source: Hungarian Central Statistical Office, Census data.

links to the Calvinist Church, with one of Budapest's most prominent pastors, Lóránt Hegedűs, being an explicit supporter, while his wife, another Calvinist pastor by profession, is a Jobbik MP. The particular congregation run by Hegedűs is located on Szabadság tér in Budapest, about fifty metres from the Memorial to the German Occupation. On the staircase of the church, on private property but facing the square, is a bust of Admiral Horthy, governor of Hungary from 1920 to 1944, a far-right political icon.[37] This is how religious ideas and (semi-)public religious spaces meet radical right politics in present-day Hungary: typically they do not themselves create political identities, but both Fidesz and Jobbik use them as references to secure their positions and enhance their legitimacy as protagonists of the illiberal, right-wing political cause.

However, the relationship between right-wing populism and religion can also be interpreted in another way. Just as in other dominantly secular European countries such as the Netherlands,[38] in which the state has been firmly detached institutionally from any Churches, populism itself can be seen as playing a semi-religious role. In the particular Hungarian context, this is a highly nationalistic surrogate-religion in which the nation itself becomes a sacred entity and the process of national identification carries religious attributes. Admittedly, from a serious religious perspective, such an approach represents a kind of worldly paganism, and as such should be dismissed on truly religious grounds. Nonetheless, this kind of surrogate religion is able to draw a sizeable crowd of followers in Hungary, as well as in other countries. However, this has little to do with actual religious beliefs, even if populism uses religion in general, and Christianity in particular, as a source of legitimacy and political endorsement.

Interestingly, Judaism can also play a similar politically instrumental role. Fidesz has sought to establish a special relationship with the Orthodox Jewish community (although relations between Reform Judaism and Fidesz are less friendly). Jobbik, as a representative of the anti-Semitic radical right, has not, of course, sought a friendly relationship with any factions of Judaism. Nonetheless, even the leader of Jobbik has met Orthodox Rabbis publicly. In a sense, this is not very difficult to explain: Orthodox Judaism is socially conservative, internally closed and politically indifferent enough to be appreciated even by some on the radical right. Jobbik's leaders can accept living together with Jews as long as the latter nurture their collective identity as a religion and do not come out of the 'ghetto'.

At the same time, the three large historical Christian Churches—the Catholics, the Calvinists and the Lutherans—are now responsible for administering an increasing number of publicly funded education and healthcare services. This makes institutional relations between Churches and secular authorities increasingly vital for both sides: Church-run schools, hospitals and even universities are quite generously financed by the state but, in exchange, they need to fulfil certain government criteria. Another effect of the institutionalised participation of Churches in everyday life is the incorporation of religious studies into the national curriculum of elementary schools that the Fidesz government introduced from 2013.[39]

Finally, we should note that Fidesz in government has insisted on approving Church statuses on political grounds. In a high-profile case, the Fidesz government in 2012 introduced a restrictive regime of registering Churches, making it the prerogative of Parliament to recognise a religious community as a Church. However, both the Constitutional Court (in 2013) and the European Court of Human Rights (in 2014) adjudged the new provisions to be unacceptable, forcing Parliament to repeatedly revise the legislation. The new provisions obviously sought to extend government control and to differentiate between 'accepted' and 'non-accepted' Churches. In this way, the ruling Fidesz party attempted to alter the relationship between Church and state, and to strengthen the strategic alliance between the government and the politically preferred, large, historically grounded Christian Churches.[40]

The Presentation of the Ethnic 'Other' during the Refugee Crisis

The refugee crisis of 2015 brought the deep hostility of the populist right towards non-mainstream cultural patterns and multiculturalism to the surface. Orbán saw in it the opportunity to improve his approval ratings after a number of corruption scandals and a showdown with his long-time business ally and government-preferred oligarch Lajos Simicska.[41] Taking the initiative, Orbán used tough rhetoric on immigration that culminated in an aggressive campaign against immigrants on billboards, proclaiming (in Hungarian) statements such as 'If you come to Hungary you must respect our laws' or 'If you come to Hungary you cannot take the Hungarians' jobs'. These statements were government communications, using the official Hungarian coat-of-arms, and were formally part of the 'national consultation on immigration and terrorism'.

Fidesz, as always, acted instrumentally: its goal was to change course and regain the support of hundreds of thousands of voters who had abandoned the party for Jobbik. The underlying strategy was to reinforce the concept of ethnic nationalism in the context of the refugee crisis, identifying the ethnically constructed Hungarian nation as an 'in-group' (politically represented and defended by the government) against the 'out-group' of immigrants and the EU, which has called on Hungary to accept a small amount of migrants. The division between the in-group and the out-group is based upon ethnicity rather than religion, although it contains references to Europe as a Christian entity, in contrast to the predominantly non-Christian migrants. However, neither government officials nor Christian Churches made any distinction between Christian and Muslim refugees, and the large Christian Churches typically refused to participate in aid efforts for refugees provided by NGOs and volunteers.

Cardinal Péter Erdő, head of the Hungarian Roman Catholic Church, even said that providing shelter for refugees would constitute an act of people trafficking, while the Hungarian Catholic Bishops' Conference declared: 'it is with the knowledge of the depth of this historical situation that we express our concern for the fate of our Middle Eastern Christian brethren. At the same time, we must emphasise that it is the state's right and responsibility to defend its citizens.'[42] The implication was that the protection of 'the people' (that is, Hungarian citizens) was a government responsibility, and that the Church must respect the laws of the state, regardless of humanitarian needs.[43] By expressing such views, the Hungarian Catholic Church went against the statements of Pope Francis, and acted as a national organisation loyal to the government before the Vatican. Christianity, as an organised set of principles in the Hungarian refugee crisis, did not play any discernible role in either the state or Church authorities' actions.[44] This can once again be explained by the fact that Hungary is not a particularly religious country and Christianity as a religion plays a limited role even in the integration of the right-wing electorate.

Nonetheless, Christianity as a cultural identity and historical narrative is part of Fidesz's identity politics. Orbán has made it clear that the Christian-national idea is a political creed which he wishes to apply to the whole of Europe.[45] The refugee crisis provided him with an excellent opportunity to promote this theme, and Orbán wasted no time in reinforcing his identity politics, delivering a number of mobilising speeches and statements amidst the crisis. For example, when speaking in the European Parliament in May 2015, he said:

> We [Hungarians] are a frank and open people, and we are speaking our mind when we say loud and clear that we Hungarians would like to keep Europe for the Europeans, and we also wish to keep Hungary as a Hungarian country. Both of these goals of ours are legitimate, and I am convinced that both of them are fully in harmony with the core values of Europe and the intentions of the founders of the European Union.[46]

Immigration also ranked high among the topics addressed by Orbán in his 2015 speech at the Bálványos summer open university and student camp, where he usually sets out his ideological visions in a regional context.[47] A year earlier at Bálványos, Orbán had announced his intention to build an illiberal state. This time he positioned himself as the defender of European values and interests against the uncontrolled flow of non-European immigrants. As Cas Mudde argues, Orbán delivered 'the most significant radical right speech in Europe of the past decades', making the radical right agenda his government's official stance and proposing its adoption by Europe.[48] As he said:

> The question now is not merely what kind of Europe we Hungarians would like to live in, but whether Europe as we now know it will survive at all. Our answer is clear: we would like Europe to remain the continent of Europeans. [...] We can say we want it, because it depends only on us: we want to preserve Hungary as a Hungarian country.

While Fidesz has its own extreme-right opposition (Jobbik), it has itself become a radical right-wing populist party over the past decade. It no longer matters whether Fidesz believes in what it says or whether its pronouncements are just intended to compete with Jobbik. The reality is that Fidesz's policies reflect a radical right agenda, including the concept of illiberal democracy and a crackdown on left-leaning media and NGOs, as well as the claim that Hungary and Europe need to be saved from the inflow of immigrants.[49]

Representing a strongly majoritarian and illiberal view of the political order, Fidesz believes that social and political minorities should respect the primacy of majority views and adapt their behaviour accordingly. As a radical ethno-nationalist party, Jobbik, in turn, is against the assimilationist policies of classic nationalism. Its leadership is comprised of ethnic separatists who reject the politics of inclusion, regardless of the origin of 'the other' (Syrian or Afghan refugees, Jews or Roma). Their views are perhaps best depicted by Péter Boross, a former prime minister of Hungary and former advisor to Viktor Orbán, who is equally close to Fidesz and Jobbik. In an August 2015 interview, Boross blamed the United States for the rise of refugees coming to Europe and the crisis in the Middle East. He criticised the Americans for maintaining universalistic principles like democracy and God, instead of accepting local democracies and local gods. As he said:

> Rome was wise back then. They left the conquered provinces in peace and officially adopted some of their gods in Rome. Washington does the opposite. It wants to impose its own God, Democracy, on the conquered countries.[50]

As an influential figure in shaping the ideas of the Hungarian right, Boross suggests that each nation has a right to create its own state, and political regime (whether it is democracy or autocracy seems to be of secondary importance), and also to choose its own God. While he wants to defend Europe, he displays strong anti-EU sentiments. For him, any supranational entity which bases itself upon general principles beyond the nation state (a universalistic approach to democracy, human rights and Christianity) is wrong. Mass migration is interpreted by him as not a cultural but a biological and genetic problem, which cannot be solved by the classic nationalist means of assimilation. Boross' views embrace ethnic nationalism in its crudest form:

> Today nobody dares to say that immigration is not a problem of culture and civilisation, but an ethnic problem. At the same time millions of people speaking different languages and with a different skin color are arriving to Europe. [...] Cultural integration has not yielded anything good. Unfortunately, if this has not been a successful process in the case of the gypsies living with us, then there is not much chance that this is possible with the hordes of Muslims crossing the green border. [...] The European Union should not be thinking in terms of its own refugee quota system, but in forming its own armed forces.[51]

In this militaristic approach, 'national Christianity' is contrasted with the mainstream, universal form of Christianity as a religion of love. It is also contrasted with the Gods of the refugees, deemed unacceptable in Europe. In Hungary, ethno-nationalism provides a sufficient basis for political identification as a type of surrogate-religion. While Fidesz interprets Christianity within the framework of nationalism, Jobbik frames it as part of its nationalism and anti-Semitism. God is not presented as a symbol of universal religious identity, as understood in the New Testament or explained in the speeches of Pope Francis, but as 'the God of Hungarians', in its particularistic, tribal, paganised, political understanding. In this sense, Hungarian right-wing populism does not have to rely on religious affiliations and does not place a particular emphasis on mobilising them: they are part of its fundamentally nationalist and authoritarian worldview[52] without any substantive religious references.

Conclusion

Hungarian right-wing populists, in both Fidesz and Jobbik, attribute a limited role to religious identities when providing answers to the question of 'who are we?'[53] Although religion in general—and Christianity in particular—serves as an important reference point that right-wing populists use instrumentally, neither their electorate's expectations nor their organisational self-interest allow for an extensive role for Christianity and/or religious authorities in their policy formation.[54] Christianity therefore plays a secondary role in political identification, although it remains a primary attribute for the KDNP (Fidesz's small religious satellite party).

Relations between Church authorities and right-wing populist parties and politicians are generally friendly but not overly close. The Churches—especially the Catholic Church—view the semi-pagan practices of some far-right communities with deep suspicion. Yet, as the role of the large historical Christian Churches is becoming increasingly institutionalised in public education, healthcare and even in higher education, the interdependence between Churches and the right-wing government is also increasing. The conspicuous silence of the Catholic and Hungarian Protestant Churches on burning social and political issues in Hungary can be explained by their increasing institutional power, as legislated for by Fidesz and supported by Jobbik.

At the same time, the Fidesz government has created a new situation by exerting open political influence on the recognition of Churches. Religious communities and heads of Churches must take this into consideration, and may feel compelled to adjust their political strategies accordingly.

Although religion plays a limited role in Hungarian right-wing populism, we have argued that populism itself can be understood as a nationalistic surrogate religion. It functions as an organising principle of worldviews, providing a quasi-religious status for the nation as a collective identity, to which individuals are meant to be subordinated. Populist leaders themselves embody this collective identity, exercising illiberal, institutionally unconstrained governance. Hungary's Viktor Orbán is perhaps the closest approximation to this type of political leadership in contemporary EU politics. He is operating in a hybrid regime within the European Union where democratic institutions are facades of non-democratic practices, and where two populist radical right-wing parties compete for power, mesmerising the qualified majority of voters.

10

THE TEA PARTY AND RELIGION

BETWEEN RELIGIOUS AND HISTORICAL
FUNDAMENTALISM

Nadia Marzouki

While Christian identity has long been regarded as important in US political competition and discourse, the decade following the attacks of 11 September 2001 in particular saw this concept emphasised in the context of global anxieties about the place of Muslims in the West. One of the key actors in the promotion of the juxtaposition between 'good, American' Christians and 'bad, other' Muslims has been the Tea Party, a movement that owes its notoriety to its significant impact on the midterm elections of 2 November 2010. Two years after Barack Obama's election, and while the Republican Party was experiencing a drop in popularity, Republicans won a majority in the Chamber of Representatives with sixty-three additional seats. This unforeseen success was due to large-scale Tea Party mobilisation against Democrats. Tea Party supporters made up 41 per cent of the electorate, and 86 per cent of them voted for Republican House candidates, according to exit polls.

This unexpected outcome brought the importance of a new political player in the American political landscape to the fore. Clearly drawing on populist rhetoric, the Tea Party (TP) is not a political party. Alternately described as a space for radical reinvention of democratic politics and grassroots activism, or as the latest and loudest expression of the longstanding rightward transformation of the Republican Party,[1] the TP[2] is more adequately understood as a broad social movement fighting for tax reductions and a small government. As such, it revivifies a long tradition of engagement with right-wing religious figures within the Republican Party (from Pat Robertson and Pat Buchanan through to George Bush Jr. and Sarah Palin). Yet the Tea Party is not a new embodiment of the Moral Majority,[3] nor a simple instrument of the Christian right. More specifically, the TP's success is based on a loose coalition of three groups of actors,[4] namely grassroots associations, right-wing media such as Fox News (or radio anchors such as Sean Hannity) and anti-tax foundations[5] such as Americans for Prosperity and FreedomWorks. Notwithstanding this internal diversity, the defence of America's supposedly threatened Christian identity has become a major theme of Tea Party rhetoric. Warnings against the danger of the alleged Islamisation of the nation represent an essential corollary to support for America's Christian identity. True, the rejection of Islam is by no means the Tea Party's main driver, but it is a recurring theme for the movement's major figures. This chapter seeks to understand how anti-Islamic sentiments materialise in the rhetoric and the actions of TP supporters and leaders, and how the endorsement of this anti-Islamic discourse translates into an understanding of the 'good' Christian people.

The first section will present those persons who make up the TP and discuss what they seek to achieve, while section two will show how TP leaders define the 'good people' as Christian and American. In the third section, the chapter will examine the various expressions of the TP's antagonistic attitude towards Islam. The fourth section will focus on the anti-Sharia movement in order to illustrate the impact of the TP's vision of 'the other' on policy and legislation. After underlining the ambivalent relationship between the TP and Church leaders in section five, the chapter's conclusion will suggest that the TP project is based on an idea of religion centred on the nation and its history.

Who Are the Tea Party, and What Do They Want?

The Tea Party's origins go back to the organisation of the 234th anniversary of the original Boston Tea Party in December 2007, when supporters of Ron

Paul[6] launched a fundraising operation for his 2008 'Campaign for Liberty'. Editorialist Rick Santelli's performance on 19 February 2009 on CNBC[7]— two days after President Obama passed the American Recovery and Reinvestment Act—is generally referred to as the event which gave rise to the Tea Party. From the Chicago Stock Exchange, Santelli launched a violent attack against the Obama government and its policy, which sought to help middle-class families pay their mortgages.[8]

Beyond their anti-tax and anti-government common cause, TP activists and supporters hold very different views as far as moral and social values are concerned. While some are morally conservative, others defend libertarian points of view in relation to economics, but also with regard to abortion, gay marriage and religious freedom. Regardless of this disparity, Islam and Muslims have been built up as embodiments of everything that threatens and weakens the good American people and the self-righteous common man.

Demographics and Organisation

TP members constitute a rather homogeneous group in demographic terms. Members and supporters of TP grassroots associations are typically white men and women, over the age of fifty, from the middle or upper-middle classes. Retirees and 'stay-at-home moms' played an important role in the birth of the movement. A study conducted by the Institute for Research and Education on Human Rights (IREHR)[9] distinguishes three levels of TP support: 16 per cent of the general adult population defines itself as supporting the TP; a couple of million are activists who regularly attend meetings; and 250,000 members have officially registered on the websites of one of the six main TP national organisations (namely, FreedomWorks Tea Party, the 1776 Tea Party, ResistNet, Tea Party Nation, Tea Party Patriots and the Tea Party Express).[10] The level of coherence among the various Tea Party organisations should not be exaggerated. Although it would be more accurate to speak of 'Tea Parties', here we will use the expression 'Tea Party' to refer to all such groups for the sake of conciseness. It is also important to distinguish between grassroots activists and organisations and what is referred to as 'astroturf'—major anti-tax advocacy groups such as Americans for Prosperity.

The People and their Opportunist Representative

The TP project is structured around the four key elements of populist discourse described in the first chapter of this volume: the 'people', 'elites', 'democracy' and the 'others'. They claim to seek to restore a virtuous democracy that is both respectful of the will of the people and true to the original meaning of the Constitution. They define the future of America against the threat represented by a series of 'others' (those who are not considered to be 'good people'): Muslims, immigrants and black people. Major political and social events are recast as 'crises', which serves to create a sense of emergency among the public. The construction of mosques, the reform of the healthcare system, upheavals in the Middle East and debates about immigration are amongst the events and issues that have been cited as evidence of a deep crisis and imminent danger.

Although the TP's success in the 2010 midterm elections was largely unanticipated, it is necessary to qualify the novelty of its claims and rhetoric. The TP continues a long tradition of anti-tax movements based on conflict between those who 'produce wealth' and so-called 'free riders'.[11] In 1973, the Tax Rebellion Committee of Los Angeles, led by Robert Lyon, organised demonstrations against taxes, during which protesters wearing revolutionary costumes threw tea bags around, in memory of the 1773 Boston revolt.[12] The TP's populist rhetoric also echoes a long tradition of political persuasion that has informed different progressive and reactionary movements and parties throughout American history, such as the People's Party in 1892, the Women's Christian Temperance Union (1873) and the anti-civil rights movement in the 1950s and 1960s.[13] Despite the different objectives defended by each of these movements, all drew upon similar modes of persuasion. Hofstadter argues that 'it has been our fate as a nation not to have ideologies but to be one'.[14] Indeed, in the discourse of populist leaders, definitions of the people, or of the fundamental values of the nation, are often notoriously vague. But it is precisely this lack of clarity that accounts for the persuasiveness of populist discourse.

Religious Affiliations

A 2010 survey by the Pew Research Center for the People & the Press and the Pew Forum on Religion & Public Life[15] showed the different ways in which TP members and supporters relate to religion. Most people who define themselves as part of the Christian right claim that they support the TP, but the contrary is not necessarily true. Forty-six per cent of TP supporters say they have never heard of the Christian right, and 11 per cent say that they disagree with the views of the Christian right. Most of them criticise liberal and secular values: 64 per cent are opposed to same-sex marriage, and 59 per cent to abortion. A small minority, however, advocate for a libertarian approach to both economic and moral issues and defend rights to abortion and gay marriage. Although 48 per cent of white evangelicals say that they have no opinion on the movement, or that they have never heard of it, it is within this group that the TP finds the most support. Thirty-three per cent of white Catholics and 30 per cent of white mainline Protestants agree with the TP. In contrast, only 15 per cent of Jews agree with it and 49 per cent disagree with it. Sixty-seven per cent of atheists and agnostics reject the movement. Thirty-seven per cent of black Protestants who have heard of the TP disagree with the movement, and only 7 per cent agree with it. Scholars have shown that the support of right-wing Evangelical networks has played a key role in the success of the Tea Party. As early as the summer of 2009, a confederation of religious right groups created the Freedom Federation and issued a 'Declaration of American Values', in which it promoted the same anti-tax view as the TP. Peter Montgomery[16] has described how a number of politicians, religious leaders and opinion makers such as Senator Jim De Mint, Sarah Palin, Ralph Reed and Glenn Beck have reinforced the collaboration between the Evangelical right and the TP. However, this partnership is not without its tensions and rivalries, due to concern among some Evangelical leaders and members over the strong presence of a libertarian trend in the TP. This is why Montgomery describes the relationship between the two as that of 'frenemies with benefits'.

'America is a Christian Nation'

TP activists and politicians like to present themselves as defenders of the good American people, and often define these people as 'Christian', or 'Judeo-Christian'. Confederate battle flags with slogans such as 'America is a Christian nation' have been seen at numerous TP demonstrations. In an article entitled 'An Ardent Plea', Karen Pack, the leader of the Wood County TP (Ohio), who is also listed as an official supporter of Thom Robb's Knights of the Ku Klux Klan,[17] stated that 'there is no separation of church and state'. She contended that 'there are people at work today who hate our God, despise our Country and will stop at nothing to destroy both Christianity and the USA'.[18]

At the Tea Party Nation convention held in Nashville in February 2010, the Southern Baptist Pastor Rick Scarborough, leader of the Judeo-Christian Council for Constitutional Restoration, organised a workshop to outline the religious identity of the nation. Bishop E.W. Jackson also attended the convention. Bishop Jackson is the founder of STAND (Staying True to America's

National Destiny), which is described as 'a national grassroots organization of Americans dedicated to preserving our Judeo-Christian History and Values'.[19] The evening keynote speech was delivered by Joseph Farah, editor in chief of the conservative website WorldNetDaily and the most vocal actor in questioning the president's citizenship.

This combination of Christian nationalism and fierce opposition to Obama's person and policy has had a profound impact upon the discourse of a number of prominent GOP figures such as Sarah Palin. Governor of Alaska from 2006 to 2009, she was the nominee for vice-president alongside Senator John McCain during the 2008 presidential campaign. She publicly defended the ideas of the TP in 2008, as well as during the midterm campaign of 2010 and the presidential campaign of 2012. Palin has made multiple speeches and media appearances in which she has expressed her attachment to Christian values and symbols. In May 2010, on Bill O'Reilly's TV show (*Fox News*), she condemned those who had criticised the National Day of Prayer, and warned the public against the threat of those who want to 'revisit and rewrite history' and to deny the fact that American law is based on Judeo-Christian beliefs.[20]

According to Palin and her supporters in the TP, Christianity needs to be defended against Islam but also against the threat of secular liberalism and atheism. In December 2013, she directed her criticism against the hijacking of Christmas by atheists who, according to her, were trying to separate the holiday from its Christian meaning.[21] In November 2013, in an interview on CNN, she suggested that Pope Francis sounded too liberal to her, referring to a declaration made by the pope in September 2013 in which he had warned Catholics of the danger of focusing only on 'small-minded rules' about abortion and gay marriage.[22]

Similarly, Rush Limbaugh, a famous radio anchor and editorialist who supports the TP, blamed the pope for criticising capitalism, and contended that Jesus was a capitalist.[23] In other words, the attachment to Christianity in the discourse of TP leaders and supporters is focused on the defence of nationalist symbols, conservative values and a capitalist/libertarian view of economy. As such, it departs from the numerous trends within Christianity that defend social justice and international solidarity, and that value faith over symbols. Julie Ingersoll[24] argues that the TP's endorsement of Christianity is based on Christian Reconstructionism,[25] a fundamentalist, conservative movement that supports the idea of a theocratic government, whereby very limited powers have been delegated to government by God, as well as a libertarian interpretation of capitalism. Tea Party senators expressed closely related views at the 'kick-off meeting' of Ralph Reed's Faith and Freedom Coalition in June 2013. Rand Paul (Kentucky), Ron Johnson (Wisconsin), Mike Lee (Utah) and Marco Rubio (Florida) argued that a war on Christianity had been launched by liberal elites, and that the Christian foundations of the US Constitution had been wrongly forgotten.[26] At the September 2010 conference of the Faith and Freedom Coalition, Ralph Reed contended that 'people have the right and duty to overthrow that government, by force if necessary'. The rationale for such an argument is that God granted the government limited sovereignty, and thus individuals can reclaim their rights if the government tries to infringe their religious freedom.[27]

Islam: a Threat to the Good (Judeo-)Christian People

For most TP leaders and supporters, Islam embodies the numerous threats that challenge the permanence of this tradition, and Muslims, whether 'moderate' or 'radical', are all seen as enemies of the American people. Mark Williams, the first chairman of the Tea Party Express,[28] argued that 'the story involves lots of bisexual men who are oddly homophobic and a psychotic paedophile, who coughed up this twisted and violent ideology during seizures in the desert, augmented by an inbred paranoia and an imposed ignorance acquired and reinforced over the centuries'.[29]

Anti-Islamic rhetoric is not specific to the TP, and is popular among gatherings and activists who do not always explicitly identify themselves as TP members or supporters. It is very difficult to determine with precision the extent of the Tea Party's responsibility for each event or declaration that celebrates a rejection of Islam. However, a number of studies have shown that, while anti-Islamic arguments became increasingly common in the public debate in the years following the attacks of 11 September 2001, the year 2010 marked a clear increase in the numbers of controversies around mosque constructions, of court trials concerning Muslims' religious freedom and of hate crimes against Muslims.[30] This suggests that while Islamophobic speech and acts existed long before the birth of the various Tea Parties, the TP's success has undoubtedly played an important role in the spreading and normalisation of Islamophobic statements and acts. In places where some of the population had already mobilised against Islam, TP activists tended to rally to their cause. For example, in Murfreesboro, a small town in Tennessee, a heated controversy began in June 2010 when some inhabitants rejected the zoning commission's decision to authorise the construction of a mosque. Lou Ann Zelenik, a

Tea Party candidate in the midterm elections of November 2010, immediately joined the anti-mosque camp in order to take advantage of the local population's frustration and fear. In Florida, the Fort Lauderdale Tea Party played a central role in organising a protest that aimed to shut down a mosque, even though the city commissioner, Lesa Peerman, defended the rights of the community who used the mosque. O'Neal Dozier, the leader of the protest, is a member of the board of Ralph Reed's Faith and Freedom Coalition, and the editor of a journal entitled *Judeo-Christian View*.

More specifically, the TP's Islam-bashing takes two main forms: the denunciation of 'stealth jihad', and warnings against the Muslim Brotherhood-Obama 'syndicate'. TP supporters consider all the symbols and rituals of American Muslims to constitute evidence of a secret plan to subvert American society. Mosques are defined as breeding camps for terrorism, headscarves as symbols of conquest and halal food as an attempt to infect the citizenry. Controversies have broken out in Texas and Florida about textbooks that supposedly grant too much space to Islamic history. In the summer of 2013, a group of parents protested against the use of a world history textbook that included a thirty-six page chapter on Islam. Representative Ritch Workman criticised the one-sidedness of the textbook and viewed the lack of interest in Christianity as personally 'offensive'.

Pamela Geller, one of the fiercest opponents of the construction of the Islamic Community Center in New York and co-founder, with Robert Spencer, of the Stop Islamization of America (SIOA) platform, participated in numerous demonstrations organised by Tea Parties. SIOA, her blog (called *Atlas Shrugs*) and her third organisation, the Freedom Defense Initiative, are all listed as official 'partner' organisations of the ResistNet Tea Party faction. In June 2011, she spoke at a rally organised by the Tea Party Patriots in Fort Lauderdale, Florida, where she declared: 'The stealth jihad is very real. [...] It is a covert operation, although increasingly more brazen under Obama.'[31] Geller also played an important role in spreading the idea that Obama is not an American-born citizen and went so far as to suggest that he was the illegitimate child of Malcolm X. According to the NewsCorpsWatch website, Geller's blog contains 267 posts on the theme 'Muslim in the White House?'[32]

The battle against Islam is also closely associated with criticism of Barack Obama.[33] The election of the first African-American president gave TP discourse a specific direction. Islam-bashing has become a necessary ingredient in a project that aims to question the loyalty, the nationality and the background of the American president. For many TP activists who question whether Obama is actually American[34] and contend that he is a Muslim, Islamophobia and 'birtherism' go hand-in-hand. Somewhat ironically, Obama is at once described as an Islamist, with links to the Muslim Brotherhood, and as a socialist, influenced by a European, secular-liberal worldview. TP activists have seized upon any opportunity to express their anti-Islamic and anti-Obama views in a single message. In April 2013, the Tea Party Nation, a group that the Southern Poverty Law Center considers a hate group,[35] blamed Obama's kindness towards Muslims for the Boston marathon attacks. A Texas Republican, Louie Gohmert, declared on a conservative radio show that the investigations into the Boston bombings had been hindered by Obama's ties to the Muslim Brotherhood.[36] Gohmert alleged that 'this administration has so many Muslim Brotherhood members that have influence that they just are making wrong decisions for America'.[37]

In the summer of 2012, Gohmert supported Representative Michele Bachman, a notorious TP figure, in her witch-hunt against members of the administration who were supposedly tied to the Muslim Brotherhood. Bachman accused Huma Abedin, an advisor to Secretary of State Hillary Clinton, of helping the Muslim Brotherhood to infiltrate the administration. Leading Republican figures, such as John McCain, Marco Rubio and John Boehner, firmly condemned these allegations and warned against a return to McCarthyism. However, a number of politicians, lawyers and media personalities close to the TP helped to spread Bachman's alarmist theories.[38]

Excess and buffoonery are key ingredients of the TP's rhetoric, and form part of its strategy concerning most topics in general, and in relation to Islam in particular. The 'X-ray plot' is one illustration (among many) of the level of absurdity that the Islamophobic actions of some TP activists can attain.[39] In June 2013, two men from upstate New York were arrested and charged for building an X-ray device that was supposed to serve as a weapon with which to kill Muslims. The initiator of the plan, Glendon Scott Crawford, a mechanic working for General Electric, was a member of the United Northern and Southern Knights of the Ku Klux Klan, a member of a local chapter of the Tea Party Patriots called Americans Demanding Liberty and Freedom, and a member of FreedomWorks.

Although this type of enterprise clearly diverges from the liberal ideal of a civil public debate where everyone 'agrees to disagree', the paranoid rationality upon which it rests is far from a new phenomenon in American political history. The rejection of Islam draws upon a long discursive tradition of scapegoating religious and cultural minorities. Freemasons, Jews, Catholics and

Mormons have all successively been perceived as groups plotting against American culture or the American Constitution. Self-righteous indignation and prophetic alarmism represent key ingredients of this paranoid style: unveiling the conspiracy and revealing the true face of the plotters is of the utmost importance to the survival of the nation. Concern for nuance or ambiguity would be unacceptable; it would be a sign of weakness, and would denote assent to the deceptive reasoning of the wicked elite in power. More specifically, the TP's anti-Islamic discourse recalls anti-Catholic arguments that have been prominent in American history since the nineteenth century. In the same way as American Muslims' loyalty to America is often called into question, Catholic Americans used to be considered foreign agents, whose allegiance to the pope was essentially incompatible with their integration into the American nation.[40]

The Anti-Sharia Movement

The TP's populist vision of the Christian identity of the American people has not merely been apparent in the normalisation of anti-Islamic rhetoric in the public sphere. More concretely, it also manifested itself in the legislative battle that began in 2010 to ban references to Sharia from American courthouses and legislatures. On July 2010, a conference given by Newt Gingrich, a former speaker in the House of Representatives (1995–1999), and a political consultant for different right-wing think tanks at the American Enterprise Institute, marked the birth of the anti-Sharia movement. In his speech, entitled 'America at risk, the war with no name', Gingrich defined Sharia as a threat to the survival of the US Constitution, and proposed the adoption of a federal law banning reference to Sharia law in the US. The theme of the Sharia threat was immediately appropriated by a significant number of conservative pundits, think tanks, experts, bloggers and activists. In 2010, the Center for Security Policy, a right-wing think tank led by Frank Gaffney (a former deputy under-secretary of defence during Ronald Reagan's presidency) published a lengthy report, *Shariah: the Threat to America*.[41] Other players have since jumped on the anti-Sharia bandwagon, including the American Public Policy Alliance and the American Center for Law and Justice, two conservative lobbies of lawyers, along with think tanks such as the Ethics and Public Policy Center and grassroots organisations such as Brigitte Gabriel's ACT for America.

In the midterm elections of November 2010 in the state of Oklahoma, voters were presented with state question 755, soon relabeled the 'Save our state amendment', which proposed to include the following provision in the state's Constitution: 'The courts shall not look to the legal precepts of other nations or cultures. Specifically, the courts shall not consider international law or Sharia Law.' The two authors of the amendment, State Senator Rex Duncan and Representative Mike Reynolds, both members of the GOP, explained this project as a pre-emptive strike. In an interview on MSNBC, Rex Duncan declared, 'this is a war for the survival of America. It's a cultural war.'

On 2 November 2010, 70 per cent of Oklahoma voters approved the proposed amendment. Muneer Awaad, the director of the local chapter of the Council on American Islamic Relations, sued the electoral board and demanded the annulation of the certification of the amendment due to its unconstitutional targeting of Islam. The certification of the amendment was ultimately rejected by the Court of Appeal in January 2012 but this legal decision did not mark the end of the anti-Sharia movement. Learning from the mistakes made by the Oklahoma legislators, the American Public Policy Alliance (APPA) proposed a new model of legislation, entitled American Laws for American Courts (ALAC), in which the phrase 'Islamic law' was replaced by the apparently more neutral 'foreign law'.

Proponents of ALAC not only call for the defence of the Judeo-Christian tradition against Islam, but also insist on the need for the people to reclaim their right to defend the Constitution against the negative influence of Islam, and indeed international law. In other words, the replacement of 'Islamic' or 'Sharia law' with the more neutral 'foreign law' is not merely a rhetorical strategy to avoid accusations of Islamophobia. It expresses a worldview that combines popular constitutionalism, Islamophobia and a rejection of international law. The anti-Sharia movement weaves together three objectives: resistance against the Islamist threat, the struggle against the liberal 'juristocracy' and an affirmation of the superiority of the American nation above and beyond the international world order.[42] In 2011 and 2012, seventy-eight bills or amendments of this type were introduced in the legislatures of twenty-nine states and in the US Congress. Sixty-two of these bills were based on ALAC model legislation, and seventy-three were introduced by Republicans. By the early 2010s, such bills had been signed into law in Arizona, Kansas, South Dakota, Tennessee, Oklahoma and Louisiana.

At grassroots level, TP media outlets and organisations played a central role in publicising the anti-Sharia movement. The Arizona Freedom Alliance, a small TP group dedicated to sharing information, warned against the dangers of Sharia and insisted on the fact that 'America was founded on Judeo-

Christian Principles'.[43] The Williams Tea Party (Arizona) also published articles explaining that Sharia is opposed to the US Constitution. In July 2012, Ted Cruz, the then TP Senate candidate, contended that 'Sharia Law is an enormous problem'.[44] In Tennessee, Carol Swain, a professor of political science at Vanderbilt University and TP supporter, endorsed an early version of the anti-Sharia bill that equated support for Sharia with material support for terrorism.[45] In South Dakota, former representative Phil Jensen, a TP supporter, justified the need for anti-Sharia laws on account of the fact that too many 'American women' marry 'Muslim men'.[46] As for Representative Carl Gatto, a TP supporter from Alaska, he explained the need for anti-Sharia laws by describing the threat that Muslim immigrants represent to the survival of American culture.[47]

In some rare instances, the anti-Sharia project stirred controversy within Tea Parties themselves. For example, in Tennessee, the initial bill proposed by Bill Ketron was rejected by some TP supporters, who were more attached to libertarian principles than to conservative values. This debate even led to the creation of a Muslim Tea Party by Will Coley, a thirty-one-year-old Tennessean, Muslim convert and TP activist.[48] Notwithstanding these few exceptions, TP politicians, activists and supporters largely endorsed and participated in the anti-Sharia movement.

The Ambivalent Relationship between Religious Leaders and TP Supporters

There is some degree of overlap between the rhetoric of the TP and that of the US Christian Zionist movement. Media figures such as Glenn Beck, who supports the TP project, have also argued in favour of strengthening US support for Israel. In August 2012, Beck organised a 'Restoring Courage' rally in Israel that was modelled on a previous rally ('Restoring Honor') that he had organised in Washington in August 2011. Initiatives such as Beck's trip to Israel met with little enthusiasm, either from American Jewish leaders, who have traditionally been closer to the Democrats, or from Orthodox rabbis, who consider the philo-Semitism of the Christian right as a suspicious strategy that aims to convert Israeli Jews to Evangelical Christianity. Moreover, the reference to the Judeo-Christian tradition co-exists with statements that are openly racist and anti-Semitic. For example, Dale Robertson, a former naval officer, chairman of the 1776 Tea Party and host of the *Tea Party Radio Hour* radio programme, invited Martin Red Beckman, an activist notorious for his anti-Semitic and pro-militia views, to appear on his show. Robertson also endorsed Pastor John Weaver from Fitzgerald, Georgia, who is closely linked with neo-Confederate groups preaching the Christian identity canon. This doctrine is based on a theology that considers Jews to be a satanic force and black people as inferior to humans, and praises white people as the descendants of the Tribes of Israel. Drawing upon the theology of British Israelism, it describes America as the Promised Land. The participation of the Council of Conservative Citizens (CCC) in many Tea Parties has also contributed to the spread of anti-Semitic rhetoric among rank and file activists. The largest white nationalist organisation in the country, the CCC argues that the US should be a solely white Christian nation.

The ambivalence of TP activists towards Judaism was made visible, for example, in the speech delivered on 23 October 2013 by E.W. Jackson, a Republican TP candidate for the governorship of Virginia. After declaring that all religions but Christianity were 'false religions', he felt compelled to add, when confronted by Jews: 'I'm a Christian. I'm a believer in the Lord Jesus Christ. Of course, like every Christian, I believe that he's the only way. But we understand that Christianity came out of Judaism. We have deep and profound respect for Judaism. We do not view Judaism as a false religion. I can't say that about everything. But that is true of Judaism.'[49] Notwithstanding these religious considerations, politically speaking, the TP project, with its emphasis on small government and conservative values, does not appeal to the majority of the Jewish American electorate.[50] In an interview with the *Jerusalem Post*, Rabbi David Saperstein, the head of the Washington office of the Religious Action Center of Reform Judaism, argued that TP attacks on government and its 'high identification with Christian conservatives would alienate Jewish voters already wary of the movement'.[51]

More generally, the TP has elicited contrasting responses from, and has enjoyed varying relations with, Church authorities. Opposition to the contraceptive mandate[52] in the name of religious liberty provided the TP and religious authorities with a common platform. Glenn Beck was one of the most vocal opponents of the contraceptive mandate and has attempted to build a trans-faith coalition against secularism. He met with Church leaders such as Cardinal Timothy Dolan, and created the 'We Are All Catholics Now' movement. With this slogan he encouraged the public to call upon their senators to rally support for the 'Blunt Conscience Protection Amendment'. He met with Evangelical leaders such as Dr James Dobson, John Hagee, James Robison and Billy Graham. Glenn Beck also approached Israel's then Chief Rabbi, Yona Metzger, as well as Rabbi Marc Schneier, high-ranking officials from the Eastern

Orthodox community, Coptic Christians from the Middle East and others. In February 2012, Beck went to Rome to meet clergy from the Vatican and to organise an international Tea Party, as part of his efforts to initiate a worldwide coalition against secularism, an initiative supported by FreedomWorks.

However, the TP's radical stance on Obama's health reform plan and on matters of taxes and finance did not please all religious organisations. In late 2013, the US Conference of Catholic Bishops condemned the GOP's plan in relation to national debt. As early as July 2011, a group of seventy Catholic priests, nuns, theologians and social justice leaders from Ohio urged the Republican Speaker, John Boehner, to distance himself from the TP. They issued the following statement:

> As one of the most powerful Catholics in Congress, you are now faced with a monumental choice. You can heed the consistent moral calls from Catholic leaders who have urged lawmakers to decrease our debt fairly and protect the most vulnerable, or you can yield to growing political pressure from Tea Party Republicans willing to accept catastrophic default for the first time in our nation's history.

The letter's authors urged Boehner 'to reject the reckless path urged by many Tea Party leaders in Congress'.[53] Sojourners, a Christian social justice organisation, also lobbied against the TP agenda on budget cuts. Sojourners' supporters sent a massive number of emails to Congress and argued that 'Scriptures teach that God is especially concerned with how the decisions of the politically powarful effect the poor and vulnerable (Isaiah 10)'.[54]

A Religion of History and the Nation

Ultimately, the TP's rejection of Islam and its promotion of the ideal of Christian America do not stem from a coherent theological worldview. The fact that Islam embodies the dangerous 'other' does not transform the TP project into a programme of theological warfare. To engage in such a conflict would imply that the adversary was seen as a religion that is theologically sound. Most TP supporters, however, refuse to consider Islam as a religion, arguing *ad nauseam* that it is a political ideology or a military code. Similarly, when they refer to Christianity, they almost never mention specific doctrinal aspects or values (such as sincerity or generosity). In that respect, they are very similar to European right-wing populists. Christianity is essentially associated with a national identity, history and territory.

For TP activists, the defence of Christianity is inseparable from a defence of history—of the heritage of the founding fathers and of the Constitution.

Although biblical references abound in the TP's rhetoric, the party has essentially developed a religion based on the foundation of the United States. Its members see the Constitution, like the Bible, not as a source of values and principles that can be interpreted differently over time, but rather as a sacred symbol of the nation. The populism of TP activists not only translates into calls for an unmediated relationship between the people and the government, but also into an attachment to a literalist, unmediated relation to America's history. Historian Jill Lepore defines TP members as historical fundamentalists, and their discourse as anti-historical: 'Antihistory has no patience for ambiguity, self-doubt and introspection.' The TP project, Lepore argues, 'subscribes to a set of assumptions about the relationship between the past and the present, stricter, even, than the strictest form of originalism, a set of assumptions that, conflating originalism, evangelicalism, and heritage tourism, amounts to a variety of fundamentalism'.[55]

TP activists revere the Constitution with the same fervour as they do the Bible. Constitution study groups have been formed throughout the country, modelled on Bible Schools. The TP's discourse on history and politics echoes some themes that have been developed since the 1960s within the most conservative trends of Mormonism. One of the most popular readings in these groups is *The Five Thousand Year Leap*, written in 1981 by W. Cleon Skousen.[56] A Mormon political and constitutional theorist, closely linked to the John Birch Society, Skousen explains the founding of the United States in biblical terms. He argues that the Founding Fathers, when writing the Constitution, drew their main inspiration from the Bible. This divine inspiration enabled the United States to accomplish in 200 years what could normally only be achieved in 5000 years.[57] While his book was largely ignored until 2010, it has since gained new popularity thanks to the publicity generated by Mormon Fox News anchor, Glenn Beck. He, like Skousen, advocates a return to a literalist reading of the Constitution as a solution to what he describes as the current state of moral, social and economic decay.

The work of the Utah-based painter Jon McNaughton, also a Mormon, is another illustration of the overlap between populist arguments and the Christian imaginary in the TP. His painting entitled *One Nation Under God* has become the TP's quasi-official banner. In the painting, Jesus, who is holding the Constitution, is surrounded by 'good' Americans including Ronald Reagan, Abigail Adams, a farmer, a policeman, a mother and a student holding Skousen's book. To Jesus' left stand all the 'bad' Americans: a journalist, a professor holding Charles Darwin's book *On the Origin of Species* and a Supreme Court judge.

When the Fringe Becomes Mainstream

The rise of the Islamic State (IS) and the globalisation of the spectacle of terror (including kidnappings, beheadings, the destruction of ancient sites in Syria and Iraq, and the persecution of Christian minorities) have produced three principal effects. First, they have reinforced the belief of many TP activists in the righteousness of their fight against Islam. Second, they have endowed more legitimacy to the Islamophobic discourse of politicians and intellectuals close to the TP. Third, they have facilitated the quick reintroduction into the public sphere of the notion that there is no essential difference between Islam and Islamism, and that there is something fundamentally wrong with Islam. The title of Glenn Beck's last publication illustrates this shift: *It IS About Islam, Exposing the Truth About ISIS, Al Qaeda, Iran, and the Caliphate.*[58] Ironically, IS extremists and TP Islamophobes share the same objective: spreading the idea that there is no difference between IS and Islam. The IS strategy of publicising horror and spreading terror, combined with the TP's interest in echoing horrific scenes of beheadings and destruction, have seriously challenged efforts made by civil society organisations to establish a more civil and courteous discussion about Islam, based on the distinction between American Islam and violence. While the rise of IS has not changed the views of the TP, it has created a context in which it has become easier for the TP's view on Islam to spread from the fringes to the mainstream.[59]

The first months of the campaign for the Republican primary elections in the second half of 2015 show that it is increasingly acceptable for public figures in the United States to make derogatory comments about Islam and Muslims. For example, on 20 September 2015 Republican presidential candidate Ben Carson, supported by TP activists, said he 'would not advocate that we put a Muslim in charge of this nation', causing a new controversy about the inclusion of American Muslims in the definition of the nation and the interpretation of the Constitution (Article VI, Clause 3 forbids a religious test for public office).[60] Republican candidate and billionaire businessman Donald Trump has used the IS attacks to reinforce his anti-Muslim populist rhetoric and appeal to the supporters of the TP. After the Paris attacks of 13 November 2015, he argued for the construction of a comprehensive database tracking all Muslims present in the US. On 8 December, six days after the shootings in San Bernardino, he proposed to ban all Muslims from entry into the US. Contrary to Trump's previous provocative statements, this declaration triggered a backlash from other Republican candidates such as Jeb Bush and Lindsey Graham, who described Trump as a 'race-baiting, xenophobic religious bigot'.[61] Notwithstanding these salutary critiques, the amount of public and media attention attracted by the provocative statements of Carson and Trump about Islam indicates the extent to which TP populist rhetoric has become acceptable in the mainstream.

The Paris attacks on 7 January and 13 November 2015 have also fuelled the Islamophobic rhetoric of the TP. The TP's response to the attacks has provided evidence of a continuing process of standardisation and globalisation of disputes about Islam in the West, and the increased interconnectedness of violence occurring in the West and in the Middle East. In May 2015, in response to the Paris attacks, Pamela Geller decided to organise a cartoon contest in Garland, Texas, consisting of drawings of the Prophet Muhammad. Geert Wilders, the prominent anti-Islam leader in the Netherlands (see Chapter 5), attended the event. Two gunmen, suspected of being IS sympathisers, opened fire during the event, shot a security guard and were then shot by police officers. On 28 May, hundreds of armed bikers staged an anti-Islam rally outside a mosque in Phoenix, Arizona, to retaliate against the two gunmen. These events show how the violence of each extremist side feeds the violence of the other.

Conclusion

Through a study of the Tea Party's discourse and initiatives in relation to Christianity, Islam, the US Constitution and American politics, this chapter has argued that TP leaders and supporters have actually articulated their own religion rather than hijacking another religion. Despite their best efforts to present themselves as defenders of a good Christian people, their activity cannot be described solely as an attempt to use religious values to serve a political agenda. The TP project is distinguished by the promotion of a fundamentalist reading of history and the Constitution, and of sentiments of self-righteousness and outrage. According to the TP's rationale, the locus of power is in the righteous self and the righteous people.[62] The TP has contributed to the normalisation of a particular style of political expression, mixing parody (costumes) with anger and inversion rituals. Like right-wing populist parties in Europe, the TP emphasises the cultivation of emotions of outrage and self-righteousness to a far greater extent than it does the learning of values associated with religious traditions (such as social justice, family and fairness). While the question of the exact durability and extent of the impact of the TP on the broader American political debate remains to be measured, it is clear that the TP's emotional rhetoric about Islam has successfully shifted from the fringe to the mainstream. It has lowered the standard of the kind of public speech concerning Islam that is acceptable. A Gallup poll of October 2015 suggests a significant decrease in general support for the TP, down from 32 per cent in November 2010 to 17 per cent in October 2015.[63] However, the rhetoric used by Republican candidates such as Ben Carson and Donald Trump to describe Islam and American Muslims, and their politicisation of religious identities, suggest that the ideas and strategies proposed by the TP are more than an episodic phenomenon.

11

'WE ARE ALSO THE (CHOSEN) PEOPLE, YOU ARE NOT'

THE CASE OF SHAS' POPULISM

Dani Filc

Populism may be considered a modern phenomenon that sees the people as the source of truth and legitimate power,[1] against the claim that God is the ultimate source of both. However, the study of populism shows that, in several cases, there are strong links between religion and populist movements. Unlike the Christian and Muslim forms of populism, the link between the Jewish religion and populism in Israel does not require mediation between religion's universal and populism's particular claims, since for Jewish orthodoxy there is an absolute correspondence between Judaism as a religion and the Jewish people.

Populism is prevalent in Israeli politics because conflict concerning the inclusion/exclusion of subordinate social groups has marked Israeli society since its inception. Such conflict stems from the interplay of three factors: the aforementioned correspondence between the Jewish religion and the religious definition of the Jewish people; confrontation with the indigenous Palestinian population; and the ongoing colonial situation in the Occupied Territories.

There are persistent conflicts surrounding the inclusion/exclusion of different social groups, among them, Mizrahim (the name given in Israel to Jews who immigrated to Israel from Arab-majority countries), Israeli Arabs and immigrants from the former USSR. In a divided society, the signifier 'people' has become a major reference point for the constitution of political identity, and populism a central feature of the political system.

The present chapter looks at the Shas party in Israel as a case study of the links between religion and populism in contemporary Israel. Shas is an ultra-orthodox Mizrahi party. Being a populist party, Shas perceives the socio-political world as divided into 'we the people' (the Jewish people, understood as a religious community, with the subordinate Mizrahim as its core—the 'true' people) and the 'other' (the elites, mainly the secular Israeli Ashkenazi Jews who immigrated from Poland and Russia, and non-Jews as a whole, but mainly foreign workers, refugees and asylum seekers). The chapter will begin by briefly describing the emergence and development of Shas. Then an explanation will be given as to why Shas can be considered a populist movement. The final two sections will discuss the inclusive and exclusionary characteristics of Shas' populism, elaborating on the dialectic between inclusion and exclusion.

History

Shas began as a relatively small party representing ultra-orthodox Sephardic Jews, and has evolved into a populist party that puts forward radical claims for the inclusion of Mizrahim, together with an exclusionary stance towards non-Jews stemming from an orthodox interpretation of Judaism.

Shas was created in Jerusalem in 1983 as a municipal party. It emerged as a reaction to the exclusion and segregation of Mizrahim within the closed ultra-orthodox world. Nonetheless, since its inception, its growth has also been fuelled by anger at the exclusion and marginalisation of Mizrahim in Israeli society as a whole. Within the ultra-orthodox world, exclusion took various forms. Only a few among the Mizrahim were admitted to the most prestigious Yeshivot (religious schools), and they were not allowed to study the sacred texts in their own languages. They were compelled to adopt Ashkenazi rituals, forms of prayer and exegesis. Ultra-orthodox Mizrahim had to behave according to the Ashkenazi rabbis' rulings, which were more rigorous and harsh than the Sephardic tradition. Finally, they were excluded from the direction of religious institutions and were barred from elective posts within Agudat Israel, which was then the only party representing ultra-orthodox Jews. Women suffered even more. Ultra-orthodox women are banned from studying the sacred texts, but while Ashkenazi women could become teachers, Mizrahi women were only allowed to acquire limited skills.[2]

Shas' founders were ultra-orthodox Mizrahim who wished to present an alternative to an existing model that resulted in their exclusion and marginalisation. Its first organiser was Rabbi Nissim Zehev, headmaster of a Mizrahi religious school in Jerusalem. Zehev's efforts to develop an independent ultra-orthodox Mizrahi educational institution were repeatedly frustrated by his lack of political power. He therefore concluded that the only way in which ultra-orthodox Mizrahim would be able to develop their communities and interests was to create an autonomous political organisation.[3] He joined forces with two other Mizrahi rabbis, Yakov Cohen and Shlomo Dayan, and they created a new party: Shas (the Association of Sephardic Torah Keepers). This party enjoyed unexpected results in the election, winning 125,000 votes and three representatives in the city council.

Shas' performance in Jerusalem, as well as the relative success of two similar lists in the cities of Bnei Brak and Tiberias, was the catalyst for the consolidation of a nationwide organisation. As Shas developed into a national party, Rabbi Ovadia Yosef (Israel's Sephardic head rabbi between 1973 and 1983) and Aryeh Deri replaced the original leaders. Their joint leadership would result in Shas becoming one of Israel's most important political parties in the 1990s.

Shas participated in national elections for the first time 1984, winning four seats. Interestingly, Shas did not just receive votes from ultra-orthodox Mizrahim who had previously voted for Agudat Israel, but also from Mizrahim who had voted for other parties in previous elections. From this point onwards, Shas would develop as a complex party, combining an ultra-orthodox core of supporters, leadership and ideology with features of a populist party, addressing the exclusion of all Mizrahim. This twofold and parallel configuration was reflected in the joint leadership of Ovadia Yosef (the religious authority) and Aryeh Deri (the political leader) but is chiefly expressed by the party's two central goals: 'Restoring the Crown—of the Torah—to its Ancient Glory', and advancing social justice.[4] The first goal is not just a religious one; it also has a 'socio-political' reading. As Yakov Yadgar states, 'For Rabbi Yosef [...] the call to 'Restore the Crown to its Ancient Glory' is a [religious] matter [...] for the Mizrahi masses. [...] 'Restoring the Crown to its Ancient Glory' is first and foremost an ethnic matter, raising the status and stature of the Mizrahi identity and culture in Israel.'[5] Even its religious vision expresses the party's dual nature. It blends elements of 'high', more abstract, religion with those of popular religion, such as blessings and amulets. Finally, this dual nature was reflected in the composition of its constituency, which comprises an ultra-orthodox core and a traditionalist periphery. Shas appeals mostly to those excluded according to both ethno-cultural and class parameters. The bulk of its voters are traditionalist, lower-class Mizrahim, and support for the party declines with affluence.[6]

Shas' growth was striking. In the 1988 and 1992 elections it won six seats; in 1996, ten; and in 1999, seventeen, becoming Israel's third party (see Table 11.1). The second Intifada and the centrality of the Israeli-Palestinian conflict combined with Aryeh Deri's withdrawal from the party leadership (following his indictment for bribery) to significantly reduce the party's electoral support. In 2009 and 2013 it won eleven seats. At the 2015 elections, however, it lost four seats, following Ovadia Yosef's death and a split in the party.

Table 11.1: Shas' Results in National Elections

Year	Percentage of total votes
1984	3.1
1988	4.7
1992	4.9
1996	8.5
1999	13.0
2003	8.2
2006	9.5
2009	8.5
2013	8.8
2015	5.7

Shas' Populism

The idea of the people is pivotal to the Shas worldview. Like all inclusive populist movements, Shas emphasises the conception of the people both as the nation as a whole and as plebeians. This conception is qualified by the fact that for Shas, the Jewish people and the Jewish religion are one and the same. There is no national existence outside religion; for Shas supporters, a secular Jew is an oxymoron. Thus, any claim put forward in the name of the people is a claim put forward in the name of the Jewish religion. When Shas states that its main goal is the welfare of the people, this welfare has a necessary religious facet: 'restor[ing] the Crown to its Ancient Glory for all the classes, groups and communities that make our people, especially the poor classes'.[7]

Shas considers Israel to be the state of the Jewish people, characterised in accordance with the religious matrilineal definition, and aspires 'to reunite all remote and excluded Jews'.[8] In the party's own view, 'Shas is made up of the needed, the middle classes and the people as a whole', and contrary to other parties which care only for their sectoral interests, 'we must take care of all [the people]'.[9] In the 2009 election campaign, Eli Yishai, Shas chairperson at the time, defined himself as 'the head of the movement that represents the plebeian'.[10]

In fact, Shas builds what Ernesto Laclau calls a chain of equivalences[11] between three different signifiers, namely the Jewish people, Mizrahim and religious Sephardic Jews. As Kamil contends, Shas aims 'to redefine a Zionist ideology based on secular elements into an ideology that is based only on the Sephardic interpretation of Judaism, the Sephardic *minhag*'.[12] Quoting a Sephardic rabbi, Shlomo Benizri (a former Shas leading politician) has said, 'Israel is a nation only through the Torah'.[13] In this redefinition of Zionist ideology, Shas is committed to halting a process that, in its members' view, is producing a shift from 'being a people without a state to being a state without a people'.[14]

Shas' populism is built around three Manichean oppositions represented in the 'us and them' dichotomy: Sephardic religious versus secular Jews, Mizrahim versus Ashkenazim and Jews versus non-Jews. Like all populist movements, Shas is anti-elitist, and since its inception its darts have been aimed at the secular Ashkenazi elite. Shas' anti-elitism has a religious and a broader, political nature. It condemns both ultra-orthodox Ashkenazim for their discrimination against Mizrahi students and rabbis, and the secular Ashkenazi elite for the exclusion and marginalisation of Mizrahi Jews. Shas' anti-elitism does not aim to equate Mizrahim with the dominant elites, but to make Mizrahim the core of Israelness, a core built on a religious/national worldview and on religious/national values.

This challenge takes two forms, namely constructing a historical narrative that defies the dominant one, and offering an alternative to the elites' cultural domination. Like all Shas leaders, Ovadia Yosef spoke in Mizrahi Hebrew, which serves 'as a label for lower class stereotyping'.[15] In this way, he contests the 'Israeli Hebrew dictated by the Ashkenazi elites and defined as standard speech'. Shas 'consciously chooses to challenge the dominant hierarchic system by turning "street Hebrew" into a legitimate form of speech'.[16]

A clear manifestation of Shas' anti-elitism was its attack on the judiciary and judges as being part of the anti-Mizrahi elites. This attack began when several members of Shas' core leadership were investigated and indicted for misuse of public funds in the early 1990s, and reached its peak with Aryeh Deri's investigation and indictment. Deri and Shas saw the investigation, the trial and the indictment as an elite plot to bring down the most popular Mizrahi leader and to harm Shas. In their view, the prosecution and indictment were due to the elites' fear of Shas' strength as a Mizrahi anti-elitist movement.

Shas transformed its leader's investigation and trial into an indictment of the Ashkenazi establishment, and especially of the judicial and media elites. This anti-elite campaign ranged from mass demonstrations to a videotape (entitled *I Accuse*, aping the famous essay by Emile Zola) that presented the judges as members of the socio-economic elite. It showed, for example, the neighbourhoods and homes where they lived, comparing them with Deri's humble residence. The phrase 'I accuse' became Shas' slogan in the 1999 elections. Ten years later, in a blog written for the 2009 election campaign, Eli Yishai attacked Kadima's leader and then Foreign Minister Tzipi Livni for her elitist and ethno-centric views. He accused Kadima's leaders of creating 'a climate of racism and hubris, in reaction to their panic. They savagely attack us in the name of a "clean culture", "white" and pure.'[17] In the 2015 election campaign, Shas presented itself as the champion of the transparent people, the poor and the marginalised, opposing them to the affluent middle classes.[18]

The specific characteristics of Jewish national identity (the lack of a common territorial basis, the correspondence between national and religious belonging) produce a special kind of nativism, where the 'natives' are not the inhabitants of the territory but the members of the religious group. Shas' nativism is thus expressed in the belief that non-Jewish immigrants (such as migrant workers or asylum seekers) 'are fundamentally threatening to the homogeneous nation-state'.[19]

Shas' vision of the political, of democracy and of politics is profoundly anti-liberal. In accordance with traditional religious views, its leaders do not believe in the separation of spheres—personal and political, state and civil society, state and Church. In its own way, the ultra-orthodox party sees the personal as political. The movement's political aims will be achieved first and foremost through changes in individual behaviour, that is, by 'returning to one's roots', to Sephardic religious values and conduct.[20] These values are strongly differentiated from, and even in opposition to, those of secular modern liberalism. Shas has led, and still leads, a movement of *hazarah bitshuvah*, repenting and readopting the religious values and way of life which have been abandoned with modernisation. This process of individual, family and community change is a key political goal, and there are several institutions funded by the movement which have the aim of bringing individuals back to the religious world.[21]

Shas strongly opposes the liberal separation between the public sphere and individual religion. In line with ancient Jewish theocracy, its members believe that religion is an inseparable part of the public sphere. The source of political authority is transcendental and was embodied in the figure of Rabbi Ovadia Yosef. State institutions, therefore, should be subordinate to religious authority. Nonetheless, subordination should not be achieved through imposition, but through education and persuasion, transforming the religious way of life into the will of the majority.

Shas members do not share the liberal democratic conception of a neutral state and a pluralistic society where the state's task is to ensure that everyone is able to pursue his or her conception of the good. They firmly believe in the centrality of the community (which is both religious and political), in the need to define and build a common good, in the need to stimulate the development of civic (which in this case is religious) virtue and in the state's role in ensuring that every individual achieves a good life.

In an article discussing youth violence, Rabbi Hayim Ammsalem, a former Shas member of the Knesset, asserts that:

> specialists [...] claim that like every animal, every human being has violent impulses. They contend that we must take these impulses into account. That means, I am an egotist, I only care about myself, you only care about yourself. Let's find ways of co-existence, otherwise we both lose [...] we are the disciples of Moshe Rabbenu, we know that man was created in God's image. We do not want to tame our bad impulses, but to increase our good ones. The real solution is education toward humility, modesty, readiness to concede to others, lack of greed, consideration toward our fellowmen and women, respect for our parents, respect for our friends.[22]

This argument sets republican contentions about civic virtue against a Hobbesian view of society, or rather, against Adam Smith's assertion that we must build on our fellowmen's selfishness and not on their compassion.

As we have seen above, Shas is even more distrustful vis-à-vis the judicial power, and firmly opposes the concept of judicial review, which is central to the liberal conception of democracy. In his blog for the 2009 elections, Eli Yishai stated that the '"juridification" of Israeli society, and the belief that every governmental decision can be brought to the Supreme Court, represent an unbearable obstacle for the state when promoting economic policies for the people's benefit'.[23]

Shas shares an anti-party, anti-politics attitude with many populist movements. Populist movements tend to perceive their own practices as different from routine, corrupt parliamentary politics. Populist leaders see themselves, and are seen by their supporters, as 'non-political' political leaders. Even when they participate in political life and struggles, they do not really belong; they are outsiders. Shas' strategy in its first electoral campaign was to portray the party as a political movement that was anti-partisan and anti-establishment. One of its main messages was that since Menahem Begin (the last populist leader) politics and political leaders had become corrupt. The targets were the party's two main political rivals: Agudat Israel (the party of ultra-orthodox Jews who emigrated from Europe) and Tami (a less orthodox, Mizrahi religious party). Shas claimed that Agudat Israel was 'a corrupt party, for they discriminated and still discriminate against Mizrahim. Tami is corrupt because their leaders appropriated monies that were intended for the traditionalist and religious public.'[24]

The demand to 'Restore the Crown (of the Torah) to its Ancient Glory', which expresses the core of Shas' political vision, reflects the dual interpretation of the historical process that characterises the populist worldview. The phrase considers the past as a glorious and lost era, but relies on political agency as the means to bring it back, embodying the Manichean populist division of the world into 'us' and 'them'—the ancient glory was lost because of them, and our actions will bring it back. This understanding of history is significantly different from both the mainstream Zionist and the Ashkenazi ultra-orthodox worldviews. The classic Zionist view of history is a modernist one. The convergence of the Jewish people in the land of Israel signifies redemption from a dark past, and the goal is to build a new, modern Judaism, free from diasporic oppression. For Shas, the Diaspora years were flourishing years of glory, and it is modernism, and its embodiment in secular European Zionism, that is responsible for the 'fall'. For ultra-orthodox Ashkenazim, by contrast, Jewish history is a story of continuous degeneration that started after the glorious days of the Sanhedrin and the Temple. The most each generation can hope to achieve is slowing down the pace of decline. Only the coming of the Messiah, not political agency, will restore past glory. Shas, however, considers that education and social agency can bring back the glorious days when the Sephardic interpretation of the sacred texts prevailed.

Ovadia Yosef's style of command was in keeping with the centaur-like nature of populist leaders—he was both different from his supporters and yet was 'one of us'. On the one hand, in his weekly sermons Yosef used folksy language and a 'common' style—'street talk'.[25] His homilies addressed not only Yeshiva students, but also 'plasterers, construction workers and wall painters'.[26] On the other hand, as the most important Sephardic rabbi, he was special, different from common men, unique in his generation. In the Jewish religion, there is no hierarchical Church, but several different communities under the leadership of one or more rabbis. As stated above, one of the motives of the emergence of Shas was to 'free' ultra-orthodox Mizrahi from the tutelage of Ashkenazi rabbis, and to consolidate the leadership of Mizrahi rabbis, especially Rabbi Ovadia Yosef. Until Aryeh Deri abandoned political life (in the wake of his indictment), Shas had a dual leadership. Ovadia Yosef was the spiritual inspiration and the father figure; Aryeh Deri, the political strategist and the more 'revolutionary' figure.[27] With Deri's withdrawal, however, Ovadia Yosef came to embody both forms of leadership until his death in October 2013. According to police sources, some 800,000 people attended his burial, the greatest number in the history of Israel, furnishing proof of his popularity.

To facilitate interaction between the leader and his supporters, Shas makes use of electronic media and the internet. Yosef's sermons were broadcast by several of the party's radio stations and by its satellite TV station, and are still posted on the web. However, mass rallies where people could meet directly with Ovadia Yosef were an important part of Shas culture. They have grown to be pivotal to its electoral campaigns since 1988, and combine 'music, introductory speeches, popular humour, and a homily given by the Rabbi Ovadia Yosef'.[28] More than a year after his death, Ovadia Yosef still played a central role in Shas' campaign for the 2015 elections.

In sum, we can see that Shas shares all the main motives and organisational characteristics of populist movements. However, it is less clear whether the party belongs to the inclusive populism sub-family or to the exclusionary one. Indeed, when it began, the party combined radical claims for the inclusion of Mizrahim with exclusionary policies, while during the years in which Eli Yishai replaced Aryeh Deri it emphasised populist religious exclusionary traits.[29]

Shas as a Populist Inclusive Movement

The party aims to 'restore' the prominence of excluded Mizrahim and puts forward inclusive steps with regard to this project's symbolic, political and material dimensions. Shas' attempt to symbolically include Mizrahim entails a radical challenge to the prevailing symbolic framework. Shas does not aspire to be part of mainstream Israelness, which was constituted by secular European Zionism. Its leaders hope to replace the latter's worldview, culture and societal organisation with a model of Israelness rooted in the Sephardic ultra-orthodox worldview. Shas' goal is not a Eurocentric melting pot but 'an alternative way, in which all Jews of Israel, both Ashkenazim and Sephardim, can be unified under the Crown of the Torah as it is interpreted in Sephardic Judaism'.[30]

Symbolic inclusion has been one of the party's main explicit goals since its creation. Nissim Zehev, one of its founders, explained that party members chose to call themselves the Keepers of the Torah and not the Sons of the Torah because the latter term is applied only to Yeshiva scholars. For this reason, 'it does not include the common people, and they would have felt alienated. We did not want them to feel that we came from above.'[31] The paramount message at Shas' first meeting was that the new party should help Mizrahim to become an important part of society and become relevant within social and political institutions. Speakers at early meetings asserted that, until then, the political leadership had treated them in a patronising way. 'From now on we want to lead our community according to our traditions, our leaders and our culture.'[32] Rabbi Shlomo Dayan, another of Shas' founders, claimed that their aim was 'to stand by the Sephardic Jews and work toward their progress both concerning Torah learning and social class and status'.[33]

Shas' account of its own history emphasises its role in the symbolic inclusion of Mizrahim:

> The Shas national movement was created in 1984 by the convention of Torah's wise men under the presidency of [...] Rabbi Ovadia Yosef in order to enhance the honour and glory of Sephardic Judaism and provide a proper answer to the discrimination of Sephardic Jews and to the on-going damages imposed on the poor classes.[34]

As is clear from this claim, symbolic inclusion has two facets that are analytically distinct, but are one and the same in practice. The first is religious—the Sephardic religious view vis-à-vis the dominant Ashkenazi ultra-orthodox conception. The second is cultural—Mizrahi culture as part of Israelness. Shas' leader, Rabbi Ovadia Yosef, aimed to transform Yosef Karo's old Sephardic interpretation of the sacred texts—which he deems the authentic, 'native' interpretation—into the dominant interpretation in present-day Israel. For Ovadia Yosef, the central goal was 'to rewrite the codex of *halachic* law [...] according to which the binding religious practice [...] is the Sephardic practice [...]'.[35] Shas' cultural, religious and political institutions are part of this effort, a 'religious revolution' in its members' words.[36] This programme has two main aspects. One is the creation of an erudite corpus of religious interpretation and of a network of Yeshivot and schools, based on the Sephardic interpretation of religion (an interpretation which is not accepted by ultra-orthodox Ashkenazi rabbis, who consider it less rigorous than theirs). The other aspect is the propagation of popular, ultra-orthodox Mizrahi religion through rabbinical homilies, lectures and talks, summer camps, subsidised weekends for families, radio programmes, amulets, popular literature and so on.[37]

The second facet is the legitimisation of the Mizrahi traditional worldview as a core component of Israelness. This goal is grounded in the claim that Jewishness, rather than (secular) Israeli values or attitudes (such as those put forward by parties like the Labour Party, 'There is a Future', Meretz or the Communist Party), must be the gateway to participation in Israeli society.[38] The dual nature of the claim to symbolic inclusion also entails legitimising Mizrahim's demand to be part of the power structure. In 1994 Aryeh Deri clearly stated that his plan was 'to be part of the government [...] we do not want to be a metastasis of their government. Rather, we want to be partners in a revolution whereby we will become part of the government [...] not only with regard to religious but also to social and other issues'.[39] In the first interview he gave after leaving prison, Deri voiced his challenge to the dominant secular Ashkenazi view of Israelness:

> They claim that they are Israelness. They took over Israelness, they want to be the ones who determine the agenda for being Israeli. They want to decide what an Israeli has to look like, and anyone who does not adhere to their style and standards is not a 'true' Israeli; he is a fanatic, a Mizrahi, a fool. They have an arrogant urge to patronise us, to despise our culture and education [...] and they are a minority. Through the rule of law they define every standard: moral, religious, secular, cultural. [...] They want to be alone. This [is] isolationism, they want to be a Western island in the Middle East.[40]

When asked by the interviewer what alternative there was to being a Western island in the Middle East, Deri answered,

> A people. The Jewish people. With our Torah, with our culture. Of course, with all the modern improvements we can have. But why should I be ashamed of being Mizrahi? Have we contributed less than they have to our tradition? Which tradition did they bring here, the ills of American culture? I am proud of our ancestors, of their devotion, of their modesty. I am proud of my grandmother, simple and naïve. For them, this means being primitive. Mizrahi nobleness, our open heart, our naivety, they all emerge from our goodness.[41]

The Shas leadership was well aware of the importance of political institutional inclusion. As described earlier, Nissim Zehev and his partners saw this inclusion as the main reason for the creation of an autonomous party. They knew that the only way to overcome symbolic and material exclusion was to penetrate the centres of institutional power. Ovadia Yosef shared this perception. He was acutely aware of the consequences of the lack of an educational network. He was also aware that the courts' composition revealed the almost absolute prevalence of the dominant social group (secular Ashkenazi Jews), resulting in 'discrimination against members of groups not represented among the judges'.[42] Long before the emergence of Shas, Yosef wrote in relation to religious courts that 'the leaders of the people must include at least one Sephardic judge [...] in each court, especially if there are many Sephardic Jews under that jurisdiction, to avoid mistakes'.[43] Through Shas, Mizrahim have become a new and autonomous political subject that provides a solid institutional structure. This new subject has brought about the unprecedented inclusion of Mizrahim in the entire political field, both nationally and locally.

Shas' approach to material inclusion is limited and full of contradictions. In analysing it, we must take into account three different aspects, namely its rhetoric, state policies and material inclusion through civil society organisations. Shas' declaration of principles concerning socio-economic policies is similar to that of traditional social-democratic parties. As we saw above, Shas considers social justice as one of its two main goals. In its economic chapter, the party declares its opposition to the 'adoption of the values of globalisation, free competition, and privatisation of welfare institutions and services as sacred'. Shas believes that such all-embracing values represent a 'threat to the country's character, and damage the Jewish values of equality, charity, compassion, and mutual responsibility'.[44] As a consequence, 'economic inequalities grew, as did unemployment and poverty [...] and social solidarity weakened'.[45] Shas supports a 'social economy' aiming to achieve the 'just distribution of wealth, national resources and opportunities', based on programmes for poverty reduction and full employment.[46] For Shas, the right to work is 'a basic right that the government must guarantee to every citizen', and it 'must include the right to decent wages and working conditions'. Thus, Shas aims to increase the minimum monthly wage to US$1,250 (a 25 per cent increase), to eliminate employment through manpower firms and to end outsourcing by government agencies and departments. However, in Shas' vision, such rights are limited to Jewish workers. Shas supports strict limitations on the admission of non-Jewish migrant workers to Israel, as discussed below, denying migrants the very right that the party considers 'a basic right'.

Shas supports a welfare state 'grounded on the values of equality, social justice and communitarian solidarity', which places the needs of the lower classes high on the national agenda, ensuring basic services to low-income families, and increasing family and old-age allowances.[47] In the 2006 electoral campaign, Yishai defined Shas' goal as 'the fight against social apartheid'.[48] Michael Abizdir, the party's campaign advisor, contended that 'the campaign's central theme, bringing back the child allowance [...] did the job. We reached groups that had not voted for us in the past. Shas stuck with the people, and this opens possibilities for future growth. We showed the Rabbi's [Ovadia Yosef] tears, how he hurts for every hungry kid.'[49] The 2009 election campaign followed this line and Shas presented itself, in a time of economic crisis and uncertainty, as an alternative to the model in which the government is unresponsive to the people's pleas and needs; as a movement that sees care for the needy as one of its main goals. With Aryeh Deri's return to the party leadership, Shas emphasised its inclusionary approach to an even greater extent. As mentioned above, Shas built its 2015 election campaign on the opposition between the marginalised and the affluent. In a campaign in which the elected prime minister emphasised the threats posed to Israel by Islam State (IS), Iran and Islamic fundamentalism, Shas dealt only with the opposition between excluded Jews and the elites and affluent sectors.[50]

Summing up, we can see that, at least rhetorically, Shas' socio-economic vision is quite inclusive. It is based on social solidarity and a certain degree of redistribution of wealth. However, Shas was a part of the government during twenty-one of its twenty-four years of existence, a period in which Israel underwent a transition to a neo-liberal/post-Fordist model. As a key member of the government coalition, Shas was a fundamental partner in the neo-liberalisation process. Although the party claims that its participation in government was conditional on the implementation of measures such as the increase in transference payments, and that it opposed regressive measures such as charging VAT on fruit and vegetables or 'across the board' budget cuts, Shas was *de facto* a full, albeit reluctant, partner in the overall neo-liberal transition.[51]

In considering Shas' inclusive approach to the socio-economic sphere, we must also take into account the role of its civil society organisations, since the party puts an emphasis on the establishment of an independent educational system, synagogues and *Mikvaot* (ritual baths), and organisations for the rehabilitation of delinquents and drug addicts, and for improving housing.[52] The party runs organisations that provide food for the needy and organises after-school educational activities for children and teenagers. Through its civil society organisations, maintained mainly by state financial support, Shas implements inclusive social policies.[53]

Shas as an Exclusionary Populist Movement

Notwithstanding the inclusive characteristics described above, Shas also functions as an exclusionary populist movement, because the ultra-orthodox definition of Judaism is inherently exclusionary. Its definition of the Jews as the chosen people and its narrow, biological understanding of Jewish belonging (you are a Jew only if you are born to a Jewish mother)[54] combine to produce a narrow, ethno-centric approach to social life. Similarly to other exclusionary populist movements, theirs is a Manichean approach that divides the world into 'the good [Jewish] people' and the dangerous or evil 'others', which for Shas, whose nativism is of a religious character, are the secular liberal elites that threaten the (religious) Jewish character of the state, and non-Jews. The secular elites threaten the people since they undermine the absolute correlation between people and religion. Non-Jews in Israel are seen as a threat to the people because they embody the danger of assimilation and loss of religious/national purity.[55] Thus Shas directs its attacks mainly against migrant workers and particularly against African asylum seekers who, since the late 2000s, have arrived in Israel via the Sinai desert.

Refugees, asylum seekers and migrant workers represent a threat to the homogeneity of the people by their very presence as different, as non-Jews. Since Shas sees an absolute correspondence between nation and religion, migrant workers and asylum seekers represent not a 'theological' threat but an existential one. They should leave Israel not because they profess a different religion, but because they are 'other'. As Rabbi Moshe Shafir (a Shas advocate) has written in the party's newspaper, by their very presence they represent the threat of assimilation, 'a threat to the institution of marriage, to the decent family'.[56] According to this view, Shas supports welfare chauvinism, according to which asylum seekers should be denied access to basic social rights, such as the right to work and the right to health care services. Shas considers the right to work as limited almost entirely to Jews (and, as discussed below, to Israeli Arabs also). Migrant workers may come only in limited numbers and for relatively short periods, and asylum seekers should be sent back to their countries of origin. The complex interplay of inclusion and exclusion is also illustrated by one of Eli Yishai's decisions as minister of industry and trade. The ministry issued a regulation establishing that industries and services should prepare themselves for a total ban on migrant worker employment. However, until its implementation, employers were to pay these workers a minimum monthly wage of NIS2,000.[57]

As is the case in many Western European exclusionary populist parties, one of Shas' main prescriptions to deal with unemployment is to 'get rid of' migrant workers. Shas leaders have headed a crusade against them. As minister of internal affairs, Yishai supported the reclusion and deportation of asylum seekers. This endeavour reached almost absurd extremes, such as the letter sent by Yishai to the producer of *A Star is Born* (the Israeli version of the TV show *American Idol*). The letter asked the producer not to include migrant workers' children in the programme:

> I was astonished to learn that the producers of the program *A Star is Born* asked the NGO Migrant Workers Hot Line to find migrant workers' children over 17. Granting [the migrant worker population] an official position in Israel changes the nature of the Jewish state, and I see it as a mortal blow to [Israel's] foundation as the state of the Jewish people. [...] Investing resources in foreign workers' children conveys to Israeli youth that priorities have changed in Israeli society, and that once again young Israelis are negatively affected because of rating considerations. It is a pity that the program's producers are imitating the political decisions that granted permanent residency to migrant workers' children while neglecting Israel's own children.[58]

Shas' exclusionary aspects were strongly emphasised after Yishai became its chairperson. Its 2009 election campaign was based on three main promises: 'making Israel stronger' and protecting Jerusalem as its eternal, unified capital (meaning the continuation of the colonial project in the Occupied Territories); making Israel 'more Jewish' (meaning more religious, but also deepening the exclusion of non-Jews); and making Israel 'more social and more compassionate' (a compassion limited to Jews, and in a more restricted way to Israeli Arabs).[59]

Yishai's attacks on migrant workers, and particularly on asylum seekers, became very similar to those of the most virulent leaders of European radical right-wing populist parties. As minister of internal affairs in charge of immigration policy (2009–2013), he declared that he would 'keep fighting until we send the last of the "infiltrators" [the pejorative name chosen by the Israeli right to refer to asylum seekers] back to their countries of origin'.[60] In a radio interview, he claimed that he would do 'anything in order for the state not to fall apart, because if [...] we receive hundreds of thousands of "infiltrators" that will be the end of the state of Israel'.[61]

Immigrants from the former USSR are another target of Shas' xenophobia.[62] These immigrants, who arrived in Israel in large numbers during the

1990s, are also considered as a dangerous 'other'. They are mostly secular, and a significant percentage of them are not Jews according to the ultra-orthodox view; a combination which makes them a threat to the 'true people'. For example, in the 2013 elections, Aryeh Deri attacked the fusion between the prime minister's Likud party and Yisrael Beiteinu ('Israel is Our Home')—a party led by Avigdor Lieberman, an immigrant from the former USSR, and supported mostly by immigrants from the former USSR—claiming that Likud had been conquered by 'the white and the Russians who humiliate the Mizrahi ministers'.[63] Moreover, in one of its TV advertisements, Shas depicted immigrants from the former USSR as non-Jews who, through fake conversions, threaten to corrupt the pure Mizrahim.[64]

Interestingly, while non-Jews as a whole are not considered as belonging to the people, Shas' approach to Israeli Arabs is more nuanced, and different from the clearly exclusionary and xenophobic approach of the populist exclusionary party Israel is Our Home. On the one hand, particularly under Yishai's leadership, Shas has adopted extreme positions, opposing not only an end to the Occupation and recognition of the Palestinians' right to national self-determination, but also any step towards an eventual Israeli retreat from the Occupied Palestinian Territories (OPT). On the other hand, Ovadia Yosef was the only major orthodox or ultra-orthodox religious figure who declared that, under certain circumstances, retreating from the OPT would be acceptable. Moreover, Shas' religious leadership engages in theological discussions and confrontations with other branches of Judaism (not only with the ultra-orthodox Askenazi view, but also with religious Zionism and especially with the conservative and reformist currents), but does not initiate theological confrontations with Islam. This particular approach to Arabs is also ambivalent vis-à-vis Israeli Arabs. On the one hand, Shas members have been very active in their opposition to mixed neighbourhoods.[65] On the other, with his return to the party leadership in 2013, Deri proclaimed there to be a community of interests between Mizrahi Jews and Israeli Arabs. During the 2013 electoral campaign, Deri invited Israeli Arabs to consider Shas as their political home, adding that '[...] unfortunately most Israeli Arabs live in deprivation [...] we are the party that cares for people like them. Israeli Arabs want to preserve their tradition, and we [Mizrahim] want to preserve ours.'[66]

Conclusions: The Complex Dynamics between Inclusion and Exclusion

Religion has played both an inclusive and an exclusionary role in the case of Shas. Shas was from its beginnings a religious party, with no roots and no links to proto-fascists or neo-fascist movements or parties. When it began, Shas emerged as a populist inclusive movement in which the Sephardic religious worldview represented the ground for claims for inclusion. Shas reached out to the Sephardic economic lower classes 'by stressing a message of Jewish unity rooted in religious values'.[67]

However, the specific characteristics of the ultra-orthodox religious view produced tensions between claims for inclusion, based on broadening the borders of 'the people', and the exclusionary consequences of the ultra-orthodox conflation between the boundaries of the Jewish people and those of the Jewish religion, which resulted in the emphasis being placed on the latter. The demand to restore the Crown's ancient glory was an inclusionary claim when posed in opposition to what was then the—mostly secular—Ashkenazi establishment. Religion, however, became an instrument of exclusionary populism, grounding 'religious nativism'.

It is important to note, however, that the dialectic between inclusion and exclusion makes Shas less exclusionary than other orthodox and ultra-orthodox parties, a characteristic that has been strengthened with Deri's return as party chairman.[68] As Kopelowitz notes, Shas' 'emphasis on outreach [...] mediates and softens the potential extremism of centralized rabbinical authority in the religious movement'.[69] In a society like Israel, which is characterised by a multi-layered structure of different degrees of inclusion and exclusion, Shas plays an inclusive role for Mizrahim, while adopting extreme exclusionary and xenophobic rhetoric and policies towards the non-Jew 'other', mainly embodied by African asylum seekers.

12

BEYOND POPULISM

THE CONSERVATIVE RIGHT, THE COURTS, THE CHURCHES AND THE CONCEPT OF A CHRISTIAN EUROPE

Olivier Roy

This book has examined the manner in which right-wing populist parties in a series of Western democracies have used religion in recent decades to define a good 'people' whose identity and traditions are alleged to be under siege from liberal elites and dangerous 'others'. European societies are marked by varying forms of state regulation of religion and very different historical relationships between religion and politics; each of the different populist parties has a specific history and a specific relationship with religion. Some are the offspring of a fascist tradition, predating World War II (France, Austria), while others have emerged in recent decades mobilising on a mixture of themes such as anti-immigration and anti-European integration (the Netherlands, Hungary, Italy). What all right-wing populists share is the fact that they are anti-Muslim. Indeed, the opposition to Islam, identified with immigration, is the main *raison d'être* for some. All, except Shas, of course, stress—to very varying degrees—the Christian identity of their country. The only difference is their attitude towards secularism: most European populist parties are secularist and pay lip service to Christianity as an identity, not as a faith or a set of religious values (the exception being Poland for Europe, and Shas and the Tea Party for Israel and the United States). Put simply, most of these parties are Christian largely to the extent that they reject Islam.

Right-wing populist parties usually see Islam as part of a global threat. Hence, the Freiheitliche Partei Österreichs (FPÖ—Austrian Freedom Party), the Italian Lega Nord (LN—Northern League), the French Front National (FN—National Front), the Dutch Partij voor de Vrijheid (PVV—Party for Freedom) and UKIP in Great Britain have all claimed that the Christian identity of European nations is being threatened by a potentially deadly combination of pro-globalisation national/supranational liberal elites on the one hand, and, on the other, by an aggressive process of Islamisation. While the latter claim seeks to exploit national immigration trends in many countries, it is also clearly linked to the international replacement of the communist 'red threat' with the 'Islamic threat' as the main physical and ideological 'enemy' of Western civilisation. As such, Islam is not only portrayed as a serious danger to the identity and values of the people, but also to their very physical wellbeing. The events of 9/11, of course, presented an excellent opportunity for populist mobilisation on these themes, and most right-wing populists in the West have duly grabbed it with both hands.

For the populist parties discussed in this book, we have seen that religion matters first and foremost as a marker of identity, enabling them to distinguish between the good 'us' and the bad 'them'. Most populists tend to be secular themselves, and do not consider Christianity as a faith, but rather as an identity. They place Christendom above Christianity. We have also seen that, when evoking the Christian identities of their nations, populist leaders tend to refer to symbols such as the cross, rather than to theological dogma. While this reference to Christian symbols has become an important part of right-wing populist discourse, we have also noted that these parties do not all define the 'good people' as Christian to the same extent. For example, the FN defines the good 'people' who need to be defended as both secular and Catholic (*catholaïque*), while in Britain, Switzerland and the Netherlands, 'the people' are understood as mostly secular, albeit with undeniable Christian roots. In Poland and Italy, the situation is different again, as 'the people' are very clearly conceived of as solely Catholic, and in Israel as solely Jewish. In Hungary, right-wing populist parties associate the celebration of the Christian roots of the nation with nostalgia for pre-Christian paganism.

Whereas the exact level of Christian religiosity that populists assign to the people varies, their rejection of Islam is perfectly consistent and unambiguous. Or, to put it another way, while the populists we examine may have different notions of 'us', there is wide agreement about what constitutes the principal 'them' (Islam and persons of that faith). Thus, with the exception of the Israeli Shas party (which does not primarily target Islam), all populist parties examined in this volume see Islam either as a dangerous, backwards, conquering religion, or even as a fake religion that is in fact nothing less than a political and military code of conquest. This is why 'Islamisation', more than 'Islam' or 'Muslim', is the key religious watchword for many populist leaders, who warn their followers against the imminent threat of Muslims taking over Western society, law and institutions, and denounce the loss of Western identity and power.

As mentioned already, the demonisation and rejection of Islam is also very much connected to the issue of immigration. In this sense, it represents a reaction to a basic and crucial question: how should Western societies react to the arrival of non-Christian 'others'? This, of course, is an extremely wide and complex issue, which goes well beyond the scope of our book, but what we can say here is that the populists discussed in the preceding chapters have undoubtedly stepped into a gap opened up by the increasing presence of non-Christians in their societies, by processes of economic and cultural globalisation and by the failure of national and international political elites to offer clear, fact-based responses and considered arguments in order to counter some of the more outrageous populist claims. Indeed, although mainstream parties usually denigrate populists, they do not always denigrate populist arguments to the same degree. Rather, they seek either to avoid the subject or to re-propose watered-down versions of populist arguments in order to garner electoral gains.

2015 has certainly marked a watershed in the mainstreaming of populist arguments. The two terrorist attacks in France and the sudden massive influx of Syrian refugees into Europe have triggered a very significant anti-Islam and anti-migrant backlash across Europe. What is particularly interesting from our perspective is that part of the Catholic clergy sided openly with the anti-immigration movements, motivated by fear of the so-called 'Islamisation' of Europe and by references to the plight of the Middle Eastern Christians. These tensions culminated after Pope Francis launched a passionate appeal to host the Syrian refugees. Not surprisingly, as the chapters by McDonnell on Italy and Hadj-Abdou on Austria discuss, the Italian Northern League and the Austrian Freedom Party rejected this position in very strong terms. Similarly, as the chapters by Stanley on Poland and Ádám and Bozóki on Hungary note, several governments in Central and Eastern Europe insisted that they wanted only to host Christian refugees (thus playing, once again, on the idea that Muslims are not easily integrated into Western democracies). But Pope Francis's appeal also stirred mixed feelings inside the Church. For example, the Polish clergy rejected it in the name of preserving Polish Catholic identity. Indeed, the October 2015 electoral victory of Law and Justice, a populist and strongly pro-Catholic party, may have been facilitated to some degree by the debate on Syrian refugees (especially since the incumbent government had accepted the European Commission's requested refugee quota. It also seems that Geert Wilders steep rise in the Dutch opinion polls in late 2015 was closely linked to the refugee crisis.

A further event exacerbating tensions and providing fuel for the populist fire occurred on the final day of 2015, when hundreds of attacks on women in Cologne were wrongly attributed to new Syrian refugees (although details are still vague at the time of writing, the attacks were apparently perpetrated mostly by recent North African migrants). Their behaviour was, quite oddly, attributed to 'Islamic culture', instead of a more classically Mediterranean macho attitude. The subtext was that, unlike Arab males, European males neither grope nor rape women, because they have a Christian culture. The consequence was to concentrate the public debate even more on the meaning of 'Christian identity' and thereby to attract a bigger part of the Christian constituency to populist movements. Tougher measures against Islam as a religion became not only popular among secular milieus (which of course is not new), but even more acceptable for Christians. As a result, the line of division between staunch secularists and Christian conservatives is being blurred, thanks to their common opposition to Islam. The 2015 refugee crisis has thus provided yet another rallying point for anti-Islamic appeals and has served as a 'common cause' for politicians at international level—from Matteo Salvini in Italy to Geert Wilders in the Netherlands to Donald Trump in the United States.

In fact, the cases examined in this book point to an increasing standardisation and formatting of populist arguments about both Islam and Christianity across Western countries. For example, Nadia Marzouki's discussion of the Tea Party's rhetoric on Islamisation and its involvement in anti-Sharia movements shows how arguments made by Western European populists have become prominent in the US debate concerning Islam. What is particularly interesting is that this parallel formatting of populist discourses about Islam on both sides of the Atlantic has taken place notwithstanding a key structural difference: in the US (unlike Western Europe), Islam is not inextricably linked to the issue of immigration. Rather, when cast as a 'problem issue' in the US, immigration tends to refer to the arrival of people from Latin America (who are mostly Catholic). Here, of course, we must also factor in the impact of 9/11 on US politics and views of Islam—something which we also find among Western European populists.

Beyond these and other important commonalities, the book also notes differences in how the anti-Islamic agenda of right-wing populist parties expresses itself. In Switzerland, the SVP threw its weight behind the anti-minaret initiative (gaining a major success through the referendum victory on that issue), but it has not done likewise with anti-burqa proposals. In the United States, the populist pushback against Islamisation has mainly translated into campaigns to protect the US Constitution and American law from the supposed danger of an increased influence of Sharia law. In Austria, the Netherlands and Italy, mosques as physical spaces (alleged also to serve as meeting places for extremists) have represented a key target for populists, who present themselves as at the forefront of efforts to defend the values, identity and territorial integrity of local communities. Meanwhile, in France, the FN has sought to foment and exploit the ongoing debate in that country about the wearing of headscarves in schools and burqas in public spaces.

The cases of the Shas party and the Liga Polskich Rodzin (LPR—League of Polish Families) offer interesting counterpoints to the others discussed in this book. The rhetoric of Shas does not focus on the Islamic threat. Rather, it is centred on the relationship between Mizrahi, Sephardic and Ashkenazi Jews. The party's critique of the hegemony of Ashkenazi Jews over Israeli politics is closely linked to a critique of European Zionism and American influence, and certainly does not praise the West. Another distinctive feature of the Shas platform is its insistence not so much on the exclusion of the bad 'other', but on the need to include Mizrahi and Sephardic Jews (that is, 'us') among the wider recognised 'good people' who make up the Jewish community. Islam also occupies a very limited space in the discourse of Polish populist parties, which advocate the strengthening of the Catholic aspect of their national identity. Instead, their main targets are liberals and unbelievers, Freemasons, Jews, feminists and homosexuals.

Another important question raised by the analyses in this book concerns the relationship between Christian Churches and populist parties. At a very superficial level, they could even be seen as fighting similar battles. Most notably, both populist movements and Church authorities describe Europe as

'Christian', and point to the continuing importance of this. However, when we look more closely, we quickly find that they mean quite different things. As the chapters in this volume have shown, populists speak of identity and Churches speak of faith. Of course, populists are not alone in their appeals to religious identity. The concept of 'Christian identity' is now used far and wide within European politics and many secular conservative political leaders like David Cameron and Nicolas Sarkozy have also spoken of Christian nations or a Christian Europe—an idea that has been supported by judgments of European courts such as the European Court of Human Rights.

The 'hijacking' of religion by the populist parties opens a wider range of questions: to what extent can they impose their vision of religion on the 'legitimate owners' of religion that are the Christian Churches and, in particular, the Catholic Church? The latter, in contrast to the Protestant Churches, which are usually divided along national lines and unable or unwilling to speak in the name of 'Christianity', is eager not to have the 'voice of the Church' confiscated or manipulated by lay movements, even when they claim to be Christian. This issue is important because only the Church can effectively dismiss the populist reference to (and use of) Christianity, something that neither social-democratic nor liberal parties can do. The simple expression of a 'Christian voice' can force right-wing populist movements to make explicit their relationship to Christianity, and, by consequence, their relationship to secularism. It is therefore important to look at what the Church says about the Christian identity of Europe, and how it does or does not object to the use of religion by populist parties. And, of course, it is a complicated issue, because, if the Church is adamant about defining religion first as a faith and a values system, it is more ambivalent about the concept of 'Christian identity'. Any prospective approach to the use of religion by populist parties should take into consideration the other side of the coin: what does the Church say about religion and identity?

But the issue is not just about the debate between the Church and the populists: firstly, there is no genuine debate in the strict sense of the term, given that both sides avoid debating publicly together and it is only among right-wing Christian groups that there is such a debate; secondly, the debate has now extended beyond the 'populist vs churches' debate on who owns the copyright on religion. The courts have also had their say on the underlying argument: is religion foremost a faith or just an identity? So the last, and probably the most important, issue is: to what extent have right-wing populist conceptions of religious identity spread beyond their usual constituency and how much have they been legitimised by courts and parliaments?

Reference by politicians to the Christian identity of Europe, and to the Christian identity of the European Union, is in fact a recent historical development. The founding fathers of the European integration process—many of whom were devout Catholics (Jean Monnet, Robert Schumann, Alcide De Gasperi)—never mentioned any Christian roots, values or identity for their new European construction. Indeed, none of the Western European Christian Democratic parties pushed for such a reference, despite the fact that they had an explicit reference to Christianity in their names and in their programmes. Of course, this omission might simply have occurred because such an identity was obvious to them. However, it might also be at least in part because they came into existence in order to bypass the stalemate between a conservative Catholicism (which longed for an alliance between the Throne and the Altar) and a staunchly secularist republican movement. Certainly, for its part, the Catholic Church had become aware by the end of the nineteenth century that this rift could bring many European countries to the verge of civil war.

Moreover, no other political or ecclesiastical representatives endorsed the idea of a 'Christian' Europe. Protestant leaders in Catholic countries preferred to support the secularisation of the state, while northern Protestant Churches were involved in national debates about the establishment of the national Church (in the UK, Denmark, Sweden and Norway), or about disentangling religion and politics. In either case, they were not engaged in discussions or claims regarding a European religious identity. On this point, we should not forget that, of the six first members of the European Economic Community (EEC), four were majority Catholic—France, Italy, Belgium and Luxembourg—and only two were majority Protestant: the Netherlands and West Germany. As for the extreme right (fascist or neo-Nazi), what remained of this political tradition at the time of the Treaty of Rome was still deeply rooted in a pagan anti-clericalism, and did not support the concept of a Christian Europe during this period. As for the left, it stressed secularism and the separation of Church and state, and, as such, was automatically opposed to the very idea of a Christian Europe.

Obviously, the political landscape has changed enormously since the end of the 1980s. Christian democracy is in decline and has been replaced by parties that are more conservative but also more secular (this is true even of the German Christian Democrats, who have kept their name, but not their spirit). Further, as we have discussed extensively in this book, a new wave of right-wing populist movements has emerged, and has proven far more resilient than most commentators would have expected, either via a shift on the part of traditional extreme right parties (like the FN), through the transformation of right-wing conservative parties like the Schweizerische Volkspartei (SVP—Swiss People's Party), or through the creation of totally new parties such as the UK Independence Party (UKIP), the Dansk Folkeparti (DF—Danish People's Party) the PVV, the LN, and so on.

Most of these populists (whether new or transformed) accept key principles of secularism, even if some like the LN in Italy pay lip service to Christianity (but not to the Church). In short, the influence of Christian Churches on politics is in decline everywhere, including in countries with a traditionally strong and influential Catholic Church (for example, Poland and Ireland). Nevertheless, the more secular the European political scene becomes, the more vocal are the calls to reclaim Europe's 'Christian roots'. This reference to the Christian identity of Europe started with right-wing populist movements, but that discourse has slowly pervaded a part of the new conservative right and of the political establishment. For example, during the early years of the last decade, some members of the Europe People's Party (the conservative centre-right group in the European Parliament) lobbied alongside right-wing populists to have a specific reference to Europe's Judeo-Christian roots included in the Preamble to the proposed European Constitution. Indeed, mainstream party leaders like Cameron, Merkel and Sarkozy have all spoken at times about the Christian identity of their specific countries, or of Europe generally. However, while Christian Democratic parties in previous decades used to made explicit references to Christian principles (the social doctrine of the Church, for instance, as far as relations between workers and employers were concerned), the new conservatives have taken a more distant approach towards the established Churches and have not refrained from criticising them on occasion. The increase in the number of references to the Christian identity of Europe is hence paradoxically accompanied by the widening of the distance between the Christian Churches and the political establishment, as well as to the decrease in explicit references to the doctrines and values of these Churches.

Beyond the conservative and centre-right party political establishment, the reference to Europe's Christian identity has also been endorsed by the courts in cases when they have found themselves confronted with claims concerning either the equality of religions or the neutrality of public spaces. For instance, the European Court of Human Rights (ECHR) upheld the right of Italian schools to display the crucifix in classrooms, branding it a symbol of Italian culture and not a tool of proselytising.[1] By the same token, it endorsed the right of the Swiss authorities to ban Muslim civil servants from wearing headscarves. Similarly, a German court supported the decision of a school to ban the wearing of headscarves by Muslim pupils, yet did not object to the presence of Christian symbols in the classroom. In so doing, it referred to the Constitution of Baden-Württemberg, which mentions Christianity.[2] The court thus used the concept of a 'lead culture' (*Leitkultur*), without defining it. In 2004, after protracted appeals, the government of Baden-Württemberg enacted a law that banned teachers from displaying religious signs, except for the 'exhibition of Christian or Western educational and cultural values or traditions'.[3] Furthermore, without mentioning Christianity, the campaign in Switzerland to introduce a ban on the construction of new minarets explicitly defined them as symbols of a 'foreign culture'.[4] In these cases, the courts gave a legal basis to a new concept of 'religious freedom' by acting according to the underlying principle that the prevalence of a dominant Christian identity or culture (*Leitkultur*) does not impinge on the freedom of religion of other citizens, but instead merely expresses a collective historical and cultural fact.

The fundamental idea informing such views (expressed both by courts and political actors) is that the display of Christian symbols (like the cross) and the ban on some Muslim symbols (like minarets or veils) in public spaces do not stand in opposition to freedom of religion, because Christian symbols do not denote religious practices, and are culturally European. In contrast, Muslim symbols are held to be culturally alien and explicitly religious (thus amounting to proselytising). Christianity is therefore *de facto* defined as culture, not as faith. After all, if it were defined as faith, then the display of such symbols would amount to proselytising. This, in turn, would mean that it would have to be seen as infringing on both the separation of Church and State and on the right 'not to believe', or to have a different faith. In short, despite the continuous populist criticisms of elites (and especially of non-elected elites such as judges), many recent court decisions actually condone the populist view of Christianity in Europe—that it is a culture and an identity, but not necessarily a faith.

This distinction, which we could also term as one between 'belonging' and 'believing', is important. It has always existed (the sociology of religion distinguishes between 'nominal believers' and 'churchgoers'), but the new element is that it is presented by the courts as almost antagonistic: the crucifix 'only' represents belonging (a cultural symbol), and does not imply 'believing', because, if it did, it would amount to proselytising, which would be an infringement upon the religious freedom of non-Catholics. Thus, the only legal way (within the context of the framework of the European constitutions and treaties, and of the Universal Declaration of Human Rights) to defend the presence of Christian religious symbols and to ban those of other faiths is to define Christianity as a culture, and not a religion. This, however, conflicts with another trend, which is pervasive not only in Europe, but in the West generally: the divorce between culture and religion. The 'true' believers (whether traditional, or born again, charismatic or converts, Evangelical Protestants or charismatic Catholics) do not tend to recognise the dominant culture as 'Christian', even nominally. Hence, the gap between sociological Christians and churchgoers is growing, and many believers consider their churches more as 'faith communities'—composed only of believers like them—and no longer as wider territorial parishes where people can choose their level of participation.[5] Put simply, hard-core believers see Christianity as a faith more than as a culture, and in any case, do not consider the dominant culture to be Christian.

This discussion is, of course, linked to one of the major contemporary questions facing the Christian Churches: what is the connection between Christian identity and Christian values in Europe? The Catholic Church is explicit on this point: Europe is Christian, but by letting a secular culture become dominant, it has betrayed its Christian nature. As Pope John Paul II put it during his speech at Le Bourget during his first official visit to France in June 1980: 'France, elder daughter of the Church, did you keep the promises of your baptism?'[6] Or, as the then Cardinal Ratzinger stated in a 2004 interview: 'Europe is a cultural continent, not a geographical one. It is its culture that gives it a common identity. The roots that have formed it, that have permitted the formation of this continent, are those of Christianity.'[7] Later, as Pope Benedict XVI, he declared at a COMECE (Commission of the Bishops' Conferences of the European Community) meeting on 24 March 2007 that Europe was on the verge of apostasy to the point of 'doubting of its own identity'.[8] The key point for the Catholic Church is thus that a Christian identity without a Christian faith does not make sense, that identity is a consequence of faith; of course, there could be a kind of 'secularisation' of Christian values, but a culture that relies on values antagonistic to Christian values is not a Christian identity, but is 'apostasy'.

It is clear that for Pope Benedict this identity is not just cultural, but is linked to respect of Catholic norms and values, especially those concerning 'life' and 'the family' (the rejection of abortion, gay marriage, euthanasia, medically assisted procreation and so on). By the same token, the Church does not see the crucifix merely as a 'national' symbol (as the logic of the court decisions discussed above and those of many right-wing populists suggest).

Indeed, the Church in various countries has opposed the use of the crucifix as a purely nationalist and xenophobic symbol. For example, Cardinal Christoph Schönborn, Archbishop of Vienna, criticised the FPÖ in 2009 for including the cross on election campaign posters and argued that the party was exploiting the symbol in order to fight other religions, rather than expressing *Feindesliebe* (love for one's enemy), which is a core Christian value.[9]

Simply put, there is a contradiction for the Catholic Church between the dominant secular values of Europe and its Christian identity (as claimed by politicians). In the Church's eyes, identity is not just a tag, and so it must have content. Such content should be based on Christian norms and values, even if this does not exclude other legacies (Greek philosophy, the Enlightenment, etc.). As we have seen in the preceding chapters, this is not what right-wing populist movements, and an increasing number of mainstream conservative parties, call 'the Christian identity of Europe'. After all, despite their rhetoric about 'Christian Europe', most European populist movements—and many conservative rightists—have endorsed at least some modern liberal cultural values. Indeed, this is one of the two major differences between right-wing European populist movements and the US Tea Party: the former are not opposed to a strong state and they do not push for politics to be an expression of conservative religious values.

In fact, '1968 values', which were long a feature of the left, have slowly become tolerated (and taken on board) by both the conservative and the populist right. Many of these parties, while still expressing qualms about sexual freedom, the accessibility of abortion, easy divorce, second families and the increasing rights granted to gay people, have come to show a lukewarm acceptance (or at least a less confrontational attitude) towards these changes. Although many baulked at same-sex marriage, some have endorsed gay civil unions (such as UKIP and the FN). Indeed, the PVV in the Netherlands has endorsed gay marriage, and Pim Fortuyn, leader of the Lijst Pim Fortuyn (LPF—Pim Fortuyn List), was himself openly gay. Moreover, irrespective of the specific policies of populist movements, their constituency is often more 'progressive' in terms of norms than their conservative counterparts. This is because—with some exceptions—populist party voters are usually younger than those of centre-right and conservative parties. For example, although agreement with the legality of same-sex marriage is still a minority view amongst the FN electorate, it is growing, and already exceeds support levels among voters of the conservative Union pour un Mouvement Populaire (UMP—Union for Popular Movement).[10] This difference may also be explained by the fact that practising Catholics in most countries tend to vote for populist movements much less than they do for the conservative right. Thus, the populist electorate is further removed from the cultural influence of the Church than the mainstream conservative electorate.

If views on sexuality represent a key point of difference on which populist parties are more liberal than the Catholic Church, immigration is one topic where the opposite is the case. In fact, populists often criticise the supposedly soft position of the Church on migrants, as well as its dialogue with Muslim communities. Indeed, on this issue, they accuse the Church of siding with the 'irresponsible do-gooders' of the left. For example, as McDonnell shows in Chapter 2, the Lega Nord in Italy strongly rebuked the then Archbishop of Milan, Dionigi Tettamanzi, because he opposed the expulsion of migrants, and sought to maintain a dialogue with Muslims (including supporting their right to a new place of worship in the city).[11] By the same token, senior Church figures have explicitly condemned many of the 'values' promoted by right-wing populists (such as xenophobia, welfare chauvinism and the rejection of cooperation concerning aid in the developing world). This, of course, is because the populist separation of society into the 'good' people and the 'bad' others (who do not deserve help from the people) contradicts a basic tenet of Christianity: 'love thy neighbour'.

As shown in this book's studies of Switzerland, the Netherlands and the United States, mainstream Protestant Churches have kept their distance from right-wing populist parties. During the anti-minaret campaign spearheaded by the SVP, the Swiss Federation of Evangelical Churches refused to accept the reductive view that the minaret is a symbol of conquest, and instead insisted that minarets should be seen as an expression of belief, and, as such, worthy of respect (see Chapter 4). In the case of the Netherlands, Stijn Van Kessel mentions how, according to a 2010 survey, more than three-quarters of the 1,228 Protestant Church leaders in the country agreed that 'a Christian cannot vote for the PVV'. Finally, in the US, the leaders of mainstream Protestant Churches tend to promote inclusivity, and do not support Islamophobia. That said, the story regarding conservative Evangelical and Catholic leaders in the US is different. As shown by Marzouki in Chapter 10, some right-wing Evangelical leaders have fully endorsed the discourse of the Tea Party concerning the Islamic threat and the need to re-enact the golden age of the Founding Fathers. For these Evangelical leaders and their followers, insistence on faith does not encompass an ecumenical message of charity towards foreigners and inter-faith dialogue. On the contrary, they place great emphasis on the dichotomy between 'the good religion' of the good people—namely Protestantism—and Islam, which is treated as a false religion based on bad laws, rigid rituals and superstitions.[12] Despite their emphasis on Protestantism as 'the true religion' of the chosen American people, right-wing Evangelical leaders who support the Tea Party share with Catholics a common concern for the promotion of Public Christianity, a strong presence of Christianity and its symbols in public life. In fact, since 2008 some Tea Party Republicans have participated in the creation of a trans-faith coalition against secularism and there has been a concurrent rise of 'Evangelical Catholics' within the Republican Party.[13] This suggests that, while mainstream Protestant Churches continue not to endorse the Tea Party, the religious nationalism of the latter has been able to bring together right-wing Evangelical and Catholic leaders.

The above discussions raise the question: if the Christian identity claimed by right-wing populists is not Christian, then what is it and what purpose does it serve? Christian identity for populists is strongly linked to a romanticised idea about how things once were. It promotes an idealised and ahistorical notion of a harmonious community life that existed before the elites and bad 'others' began to endanger the prosperity, rights and wellbeing of the good people. The reference to Christian identity also serves a strategic purpose, of course: it is essentially a means to render Islam foreign and incompatible with integration into the community.[14] In other words, the European right advocates a Christian identity for Europe not because it wants to promote Christianity, but because it wants to fight Islam and the increased presence within European societies of Muslims, or what the Front National calls 'the Islamisation of Europe'. The first goal of this anti-Islam campaign is the 'reconquering' of the 'public space', and there have been a number of 'victories' in this sense in recent years. There are bans on headscarves and other signs of religious affiliation in schools (in France); there are bans on the burqa and the niqab in the streets (in France and Belgium); there are concerted efforts to block the construction of mosques (throughout Europe) and of minarets (in Switzerland). The pushback against Islam also concerns the human body, for example through campaigns to prohibit circumcision and halal food in Norway.

Although populists claim to be defending 'Christian identity', we can see quite clearly that the values they put forward to counteract supposedly threatening Islamic values are not Christian at all. For example, the hijab is said to offend women's rights; circumcision infringes children's rights; ritual slaughter is against animals' rights, etc. Hence, right-wing populists offer a paradoxical message: in order to defend the Christian identity of the people (and, more widely, of Europe), they promote 'progressive' values, which the Church itself does not support, and which can easily appeal to leftists and liberals. Indeed, in their opposition to Islam, populists in fact contribute to the secularisation of Europe. That said, populists adopt entirely different views on similar issues where Islam is not involved: for example, they are usually reluctant to extend the definition of rape and sexual violence and they defend fox hunting in Britain and bull-fighting in Spain and southern France.

De facto, therefore, the populist strategy is to stress both a Christian identity and the secularisation of the public space. On this point, it is worth noting that if the aim is to expel Islam from the public space, then secularism has more appeal than promoting Christianity. There are two main reasons for this: first, the younger section of the electorate is more individualistic and liberal; whether young people favour the right or left, they do not usually want harsher laws on sexual practices and they are culturally more secular than Christian. Second, for their part, many Christian clerical elites are reluctant to build an interfaith religious coalition to fight against an increasingly aggressive continent-wide process of secularisation. This is precisely because they still believe in the Christian identity of Europe, and they are therefore not ready to 'share' the religious field with non-Christian faiths. For example, there is a tension within the Catholic Church between two trends; on the one hand, it opposes the ban on religious symbols at school (for example, the French Church disagreed with the banning of the Muslim veil from schools). On the other hand, it deplores the fact that the visibility of Islam may exceed that of Christianity (as seen by the attitudes of some members of the clergy to the increasing number of mosques). Hence many in the Church reluctantly endorse a secularisation drive that targets Islam first, even if it means less visibility for all religions. We also find similar tensions among other faiths: for example, while French Chief Rabbi Joseph Sitruk opposed the law banning religious symbols from school, another French rabbi, Michel Serfaty, supported the ban on religious symbols from a private kindergarten, even though this also entailed prohibiting pupils from wearing the yarmulke.[15]

There are thus two collateral victims (sometimes consenting, sometimes opposing) of this new push for a forced secularisation: Jews and practising Christians. Jews come under attack because some of their religious practices are similar to those of Muslims: most notably, circumcision (challenged in Norway and Germany) and ritual slaughter of animals. In France, Marine Le Pen of the FN has called for banning of both the hijab and the yarmulke (but not the priest's cassock) in public places. In this respect, the defence of

Europe's Christian identity has taken on an especially ugly quality: so much for the 'Judeo-Christian roots' of European culture, as once again, the Jews of Europe are made to feel like foreigners. In Hungary, while Fidesz rejects anti-Semitism, Jobbik is openly anti-Semitic. This does not contradict the fact that many right-wing populist parties have adopted a pro-Israeli stance (following, perhaps, the logic of 'the enemy of my main enemy is my friend'). They therefore support Israel in its fight against Muslim Arabs, but they do not support the rights of European Jews. For populists, Israel is the place for the Jews, while in Europe they must conform to the dominant local culture.

Many of the arguments deployed against Islam are thus precisely those that are used against a certain form of conservative Christianity: feminism and gay rights have never been endorsed by the Catholic Church. Moreover, the campaign to extend the secularisation process to new parts of the public sphere (schools, streets, private business), and to promote 'liberal' values (defined as 'European' values), is pushing Europe closer to a French-style *laïcité* and away from the multiculturalist approach endorsed by the British Conservative Party in the 1990s. This campaign is being pursued at the expense of all religions, and brings the process of secularisation to new levels. To promote a purely cultural Christian identity for Europe, and to further secularise the public space in order to contain Islam, is, in the end, in contradiction with what the Christian Churches are trying to defend: a post-secular society, where religious symbols and values are part of the common society. Or, to put it another way, depriving religious symbols such as the crucifix of their spiritual content and turning them into cultural symbols (as the courts and politicians have done) serves to detach them from faith and religious practices.

What then is left for the 'Christian identity' of Europe from the perspective of the Christian Churches? How can the Churches regain religion? In this sense, the two pontificates of John Paul II and Benedict XVI have been 'reconquering' missions. They excluded any religious coalition with Muslims, stressing the 'Christian identity' of Europe, and interfaith dialogue sank to its lowest ebb since Vatican II. Without compromising with populists (but also without always confronting them), the Church tried to 'raise the flag'—or perhaps we should say 'the cross'—by promoting Christian values and norms in the public sphere and defending non-negotiable norms. However, these initiatives were predicated on the hope of a new spiritual dynamic occurring within the Church, driven by a new generation of believers and priests that could regain part of the ground lost to secularisation. Such initiatives also required finding common ground between secular and religious values, based on the Habermasian concept of the translation of religious norms into secular values. French bishops thus spoke of a 'common anthropological ground' for defining society. These efforts failed, however, and the Church had to resort to a more defensive attitude, defending the 'clerical exception' (the right to be exempted from complying with legal norms it strongly opposes). It has done so with only a mixed degree of success. The challenge for Pope Francis is therefore to redefine the relationship between identity and religion. Moreover, the decisive shift of the global Catholic Church's centre of gravity from Europe to Africa, Asia and Latin America points to the fact that Europe is now a mission land which has to be 're-converted' to Christianity.[16]

As for Protestantism, the new proselytising is largely being accomplished by Pentecostals and Evangelicals, who have made significant breakthroughs among migrants in Europe. By definition, they do not see Europe as an identity, both because they emphasise faith and conversion and because they are truly universalist in their outlook. They reject Islam, not as an alien culture, but as a 'false' religion. In this sense, like the Catholic Church, they cannot endorse the populist vision of 'belonging' without believing. In fact, it is interesting to note on this point that according to a 2010 poll, only 5 per cent of French Evangelicals vote for the FN,[17] as opposed to 38 per cent of traditional Lutherans in Alsace who do so.[18] It thus seems to be the case that the more the individual insists on 'faith' versus 'identity', the less likely he or she is to vote for populists. Finally, we should note here that many Muslim believers also push for the disconnection of faith and culture: they preach and pray in European languages, build mosques according to local architectural criteria and try to organise themselves on a congregational model, in Muslim 'parishes'. So, just as right-wing populists try to 'externalise' Islam by casting it as a 'foreign' culture, Muslim believers are contemporaneously seeking to adapt to a secularised society by insisting on the purely religious dimension of Islam. The populist narrative (a Christian Europe threatened by a foreign religion and culture) is therefore, in reality, increasingly disconnected from contemporary societal changes in Europe.

In conclusion, we can say that Europe is now a continent where nobody owns religion, but where many—including right-wing populists—'rent' it. There are no major 'religious' or Church-affiliated political parties in Europe, and political decision-making is increasingly independent from religion. In this sense, secularisation has won. However, references to religion are still commonplace. This is probably due to the fact that the issue of 'identity' has in recent decades risen to the top of political debate. In particular, this concerns identity in the sense of 'us' and the 'other', a sheer boundary sign, a negative identity defined by exclusion. Religion for many politicians—and right-wing populists in particular—has thus been transformed into a purely nominal marker of identity, without any positive content, and certainly not concomitant with traditional values based on theology and spirituality (such as charity, to name but one). In the wake of the Paris attacks on 13 November 2015 and the deaths of 130 civilians, the recasting of Christianity as an identity marker that allows for a clear distinction between the West and the Muslim world will likely spread beyond right-wing populists and become more mainstream. Politicians from across parties in France and the US have responded to those attacks by emphasising the necessity of a 'war' to defend the Western values and lifestyle that are alternately defined as 'Christian' and 'secular'. The challenge now for the Churches is to re-affirm their spiritual message as a universal message, without allowing it to create new boundaries. In other words, religious leaders need to find ways to stress their values and identities without adding further fuel to the populist fire.

NOTES

1. POPULISM AND RELIGION

1. The LL would later merge with similar northern Italian movements to form the Lega Nord (LN—Northern League).
2. See the discussion of populism in the introductory chapter of Albertazzi, Daniele, and McDonnell, Duncan, *Populists in Power*, London: Routledge, 2015.
3. Mudde, Cas, *Populist Radical Right Parties in Europe*, New York: Cambridge University Press, 2007, p. 296.
4. Regarding media uses of the term, see Bale, Tim, van Kessel, Stijn, and Taggart, Paul, 'Thrown Around with Abandon? Popular Understandings of Populism as Conveyed by the Print Media: A UK Case Study', *Acta Politica* 46(2) (2011), pp. 111–31; McDonnell, Duncan, 'Abbott, Rudd and de Blasio: Many Things, But Not Populists', *The Conversation*, 19 September 2013, https://theconversation.com/abbott-rudd-and-de-blasio-many-things-but-not-populists-18390, accessed 25 August 2014.
5. See Mudde, Cas, and Kaltwasser, Cristóbal, 'Populism', in Freeden, Michael, Sargent, Lyman Tower, and Stears, Marc (eds), *The Oxford Handbook of Political Ideologies*, Oxford: Oxford University Press, 2013.
6. Canovan, Margaret, *Populism*, New York: Harcourt Brace Jovanovich, 1981, p. 294.
7. Mudde, Cas, 'The Populist Zeitgeist', *Government and Opposition* 39(4) (2004), pp. 541–63, 544.
8. See the introductory chapter in Albertazzi and McDonnell, *op. cit.*
9. See Mudde 2007, *op. cit.*; Stanley, Ben, 'The Thin Ideology of Populism', *Journal of Political Ideologies* 13(1) (2008), pp. 95–110.
10. Betz, Hans-Georg, and Johnson, Carol, 'Against the Current—Stemming the Tide: The Nostalgic Ideology of the Contemporary Radical Populist Right', *Journal of Political Ideologies* 9(3) (2004), pp. 311–27, 323.

11. See the discussion in Albertazzi, Daniele, and McDonnell, Duncan, 'Introduction: The Sceptre and the Spectre', in Albertazzi, Daniele, and McDonnell, Duncan (eds), *Twenty-First Century Populism: The Spectre of Western European Democracy*, Basingstoke: Palgrave Macmillan, 2008, pp. 4–5.

12. Panizza, Francisco, 'Introduction: Populism and the Mirror of Democracy' in Panizza, Francisco (ed.), *Populism and the Mirror of Democracy*, London: Verso, 2005, p. 23.

13. Bauman, Zygmunt, *Community. Seeking Safety in an Insecure World*, Cambridge: Polity Press, 2001, p. 12.

14. Taggart, Paul, *Populism*, Buckingham: Open University Press, 2000, p. 95.

15. Roy, Olivier, 'The Closing of the Right's Mind', *New York Times*, 4 June 2014.

16. http://theconversation.com/across-europes-schools-push-for-national-values-is-infringing-religious-freedoms-27833, accessed 27 July 2014.

17. The fear of intoxication of the minds of future generations was very prominent in the June 2014 controversy about the so-called Trojan horse of Islamism implanted in Birmingham schools. See http://www.theguardian.com/education/2014/jun/09/trojan-horse-row-birmingham-schools-special-measures-ofsted, accessed 27 July 2014.

18. Ben-Porat, Guy, *Between State and Synagogue: The Secularization of Contemporary Israel*, Cambridge: Cambridge University Press, 2013.

19. To be clear, we use the term 'secularised' in a descriptive and non-normative way to acknowledge the importance of phenomena such as the gap between declared religious practice and actual practice, the individualisation of faith, the disconnection between religion and culture, the pluralisation of the religious offer and the emergence of new religious movements. Such features are present, to varying degrees, in all the countries studied in this book.

20. For the US case, see Movsesian, Mark L., 'Defining Religion in American Law: Psychic Sophie and the Rise of the Nones', EUI working paper, RSCAS 2014/19, Robert Schuman Centre for Advanced Studies, ReligioWest. For Poland, see Ramet, Sabrina, 'The Catholic Church in Post-Communist Poland: Polarization, Privatization, and Decline in Influence', in Ramet, Sabrina (ed.), *Religion and Politics in Post-Socialist Central and Southeastern Europe. Challenges since 1989*, Basingstoke: Palgrave Macmillan, 2014.

21. Inherited from Action Française, a monarchist movement led by Charles Maurras in the early twentieth century.

2. THE LEGA NORD: THE NEW SAVIOUR OF NORTHERN ITALY

1. Destro, Adriana, 'A New Era and New Themes in Italian Politics: The Case of Padania', *Journal of Modern Italian Studies* 2(3) (1997), pp. 358–77.

2. Betz, Hans-Georg, and Meret, Susi, 'Revisiting Lepanto: the Political Mobilization

against Islam in Contemporary Western Europe', *Patterns of Prejudice* 43(3–4) (2009), pp. 313–34.

3. Albertazzi, Daniele, and McDonnell, Duncan, 'The Lega Nord Back in Government', *West European Politics* 33(6) (2010), pp. 1318–40.

4. Diamanti, Ilvo, 'Lega Nord: un Partito per le Periferie', in Ginsborg, Paul (ed.), *Stato dell'Italia*, Milan: il Saggiatore, 2009, p. 672.

5. Lucardie, Paul, 'Prophets, Purifiers and Prolocutors: Towards a Theory on the Emergence of New Parties', *Party Politics* 6(2) (2000), p. 177.

6. Spektorowski, Alberto, 'Ethnoregionalism: The Intellectual New Right and the Lega Nord', *The Global Review of Ethnopolitics* 2(3) (2003), pp. 55–70.

7. Tarchi, Marco, *L'italia populista: Dal qualunquismo ai girotondi*, Bologna: il Mulino, 2003, p. 151.

8. Tambini, Damian, *Nationalism in Italian Politics: The Stories of the Northern League, 1980–2000*, London: Routledge, 2001, p. 105.

9. Ignazi, Piero, *Extreme Right Parties in Western Europe*, Oxford: Oxford University Press, 2006, p. 54.

10. Tarchi, *op. cit.*, p. 144.

11. Biorcio, Roberto, *La Padania promessa: La storia, le idee e la logica d'azione della Lega Nord*, Milan: il Saggiatore, 1997, p. 198.

12. Stavrakakis, Yannis, 'Antinomies of Formalism: Laclau's Theory of Populism and the Lessons from Religious Populism in Greece', *Journal of Political Ideologies* 9(2) (2004), p. 264.

13. McDonnell, Duncan, 'A Weekend in Padania: Regionalist Populism and the Lega Nord', *Politics* 26(2) (2006), pp. 126–32.

14. All quotes from *La Padania* are cited in McDonnell, *op. cit.*, pp. 130–1.

15. Destro, *op. cit.*, pp. 365–6.

16. Cited in Guolo, Renzo, *Chi impugna la croce? Lega e Chiesa*, Rome: Laterza (Kindle edition), 2009, pp. 279–80.

17. Rosaspina, Elisabetta, 'Un rito celtico per le prime nozze padane', *Corriere della Sera*, 21 September 1998.

18. Albertazzi, Daniele, and McDonnell, Duncan, 'The Lega Nord in the Second Berlusconi Government: In a League of its Own', *West European Politics* 28(2) (2005), pp. 952–72.

19. Massetti, Emanuele, 'Mainstream Parties and the Politics of Immigration in Italy: A Structural Advantage for the Right or a Missed Opportunity for the Left?', *Acta Politica* 50(4) (2015), pp. 486–505, 491.

20. *La Repubblica*, 6 March 2006.

21. McDonnell, *op. cit.*, p. 130.

22. Betz, Hans-Georg, and Johnson, Carol, 'Against the current—stemming the tide: the nostalgic ideology of the contemporary radical populist right', *Journal of Political Ideologies* 9(3) (2004), p. 318.

23. McDonnell, *op. cit.*, p. 129.

24. Saint-Blancat, Chantal, and Schmidt di Friedberg, Ottavia, 'Why are Mosques a Problem? Local Politics and Fear of Islam in Northern Italy', *Journal of Ethnic and Migration Studies* 31(6) (2005), p. 1101.

25. *Ibid.*

26. Giannatasio, Maurizio, 'Bossi: abbiamo chiuso la moschea di Milano', *Corriere della Sera*, 5 July 2008.

27. *Ibid.*

28. Dazzi, Zita, 'La Lega Nord attacca Tettamanzi', *La Repubblica*, 5 September 2010.

29. Berizzi, Paolo, 'La Lega assapora la rivincita e prepara la crociata in Padania', *La Repubblica*, 4 March 2006.

30. *La Repubblica*, 17 February 2006. Although there is doubt about what exactly was on Calderoli's T-shirt, many media outlets reported that it was one of the twelve cartoons featuring Muhammad published by the Danish newspaper *Jyllands-Posten* on 30 September 2005. Considered blasphemous by some, these cartoons provoked strong protests in a series of Muslim countries around the world.

31. Ozzano, Luca, and Giorgi, Alberta, 'The Debate on the Crucifix in Public Spaces in Twenty-First Century Italy', *Mediterranean Politics* 18(2) (2013), p. 264.

32. *Ibid.*, p. 263.

33. *Ibid.*, pp. 267–70. This decision was subsequently overturned on appeal in March 2011.

34. Lega Nord, *Scuola Quadri Politica*, 2012, p. 168. The European Convention was established at the end of 2001 in order to devise a draft Constitution for the EU. On 18 July 2003, it produced its 'Draft Treaty establishing a Constitution for Europe'. See: http://european-convention.eu.int/EN/bienvenue/bienvenue2352.html?lang=EN, accessed 10 December 2015.

35. Lega Nord, *La Costituzione europea e le radici cristiane*, 2003.

36. Lega Nord 2012 *op. cit.*, p. 169.

37. *Ibid.*

38. *Ibid.*, p. 351.

39. Lega Nord, *Proposte e Obiettivi*, 2009, p. 38.

40. Lega Nord 2012 *op. cit.*, p. 353.

41. Tgcom24, 'Salvini Shock: "Milioni di musulmani pronti a sgozzare in nome dell'Islam"', tgcom24.mediaset.it/mondo/speciale-attacco-charlie-hebdo/salvini-shock-milioni-di-musulmani-pronti-a-sgozzare-in-nome-dell-islam-_2088784-201502a.shtm, 10 January 2015, accessed 11 December 2015.

42. *La Repubblica*, 'Bossi promette alla Lega "Trionferemo Alle Elezioni"', 9 December 1989.

43. Cavalera, Fabio, 'Bossi: questo Papa fa politica per Roma', *Corriere della Sera*, 17 August 1997. The IOR (Istituto per le Opere di Religione) is more commonly known as the Vatican Bank. It and its president in the 1980s, Archbishop Paul

Marcinkus, were caught up in a series of scandals involving Italian Masonic lodges and the Mafia.

44. Pace, Enzo, 'La questione nazionale fra Lega e Chiesa cattolica', *Il Mulino* no. 5, September–October 1997, pp. 857–64.

45. Massetti, *op. cit.*, p. 498; see also Ozzano and Giorgi, *op. cit.* on the importance of these issues for the Church in the second half of the decade.

46. Massetti, *op. cit.*, p. 498.

47. Vecchi, Gian Guido, 'Fisichella: l'intervento dei vescovi era necessario', *Corriere della Sera*, 30 March 2010.

48. Biffi, Giacomo, 'La città di San Petronio nel terzo millennio', 12 September 2000 pastoral letter, point 44, http://www.toscanaoggi.it/Documenti/Altri-episcopati/Card.-Biffi-La-citta-di-San-Petronio-nel-terzo-millennio-12–09–2000, accessed 15 March 2014.

49. *Ibid.*, point 50.

50. Dazzi, Zita, and Monestiroli, Teresa, 'La Padania attacca Tettamanzi', *La Repubblica*, 7 December 2009.

51. Della Frattina, Giannino, 'Ma c'è chi approfitta di Francesco per le proprie squallide battaglie', *Il Giornale*, 8 July 2013.

52. *Il Fatto Quotidiano*, 'Migranti, Papa: "Perdono per chi chiude porte". Salvini: "Non abbiamo bisogno"', http://www.ilfattoquotidiano.it/2015/06/17/migranti-il-papa-perdono-per-chiude-le-porte-salvini-non-abbiamo-bisogno/1787505/, 17 June 2015, accessed 10 December 2015.

53. *La Repubblica*, 'Le polemiche sui campi rom, Salvini rivela: "Facebook mi ha sospeso per la parola zingari"', 9 April 2015, http://milano.repubblica.it/cronaca/2015/04/09/news/milano_salvini_dopo_le_polemiche_sui_campi_rom_ho_usato_la_parola_zingari_facebook_mi_ha_sospeso_-111501066/, accessed 10 December 2015.

54. *La Repubblica*, 'Galantino (Cei): "Contro i migranti piazzisti da 4 soldi". Salvini: "Chi difende invasione o non capisce o ci guadagna"', 10 August 2015, http://www.repubblica.it/vaticano/2015/08/10/news/immigrati_galantino_cei_contro_loro_piazzisti_da_4_soldi_-120738402/?ref=search, accessed 10 December 2015.

55. Massetti, *op. cit.*, p. 491.

3. THE 'RELIGIOUS CONVERSION' OF THE AUSTRIAN FREEDOM PARTY

1. In 2005 the FPÖ was replaced in coalition by the BZÖ, a splinter party of the FPÖ. The BZÖ remained in government until 2007.

2. After Haider's death, the party leadership was taken over by Josef Bucher.

3. In Austria, people who abandon their Church membership are officially registered

by the State; according to the Austrian Law on Church Contributions, adult members of the Catholic, Protestant and Old Catholic Churches are liable for contributions. The collection of payment is regulated internally by the Churches, but non-payment of contributions may be the subject of civil court action (Potz, Richard, 'State and Church in Austria', in Robbers, Gerhard (ed.), *State and Church in the European Union*, Baden-Baden: Nomos, 2005, p. 412). In order to abandon one's Church membership and thus cease to be liable for contributions, it is necessary to hand in a declaration to the Austrian public authority in charge, which then notifies the relevant parish. See Segal, Jérôme, and Mansfield, Ian, 'Contention and Discontent Surrounding Religion in Noughties' Austria', *Austrian Studies* 19 (2011), pp. 52–67, 58.

4. ORF, 'Deutlicher Rückgang: 58.603 Kirchenaustritte 2011', http://religionv1. orf.at/projekt03/news/1201/ne120110_statistik_fr.htm, accessed 9 October 2012.

5. Polak, Regina, and Schachinger, Christoph, 'Stabil in Veränderung: Konfessionsnahe Religiosität in Europa' in Polak, Regina (ed.), *Zukunft. Werte. Europa: Die Europäische Wertestudie 1990–2010: Österreich im Vergleich*, Vienna: Böhlau, 2011, p. 197.

6. Luther, Kurt Richard, 'The Revival of the Radical Right: The Austrian Parliamentary Election of 2008', Working Paper 29, Keele European Parties Research Unit, 2008.

7. Helms, Ludger, 'Right-wing Populist Parties in Austria and Switzerland: A Comparative Analysis of Electoral Support and Conditions of Success', *West European Politics* 20(2) (1997), p. 39.

8. Weiss, Gilbert, 'A.E.I.O.U.—Austria Europe Imago, Onus, Unio?' in af Malmborg, Mikael, and Strath, Bo (eds), *Meanings of Europe*, Oxford: Berg, 2000, p. 266.

9. *Ibid.*

10. *Ibid.*

11. Morrow, Duncan, 'Jörg Haider and the New FPÖ: Beyond the Democratic Pale?', in Hainsworth, Paul (ed.) *The Politics of the Extreme Right: From the Margins to the Mainstream*, London: Pinter, 2000, p. 4.

12. Luther, Kurt Richard, 'Die Freiheitliche Partei Österreichs (FPÖ) und das Bündnis Zukunft Österreichs (BZÖ)', Working Paper 22, Keele European Parties Research Unit, 2005, p. 3.

13. Frischenschlager, Friedhelm, 'Das Verhältnis der FPÖ zu den Kirchen', in *Österreichisches Jahrbuch für Politik 1983*, Wien: ÖVP Bildungsakademie, 1984, p. 379.

14. *Ibid.*

15. *Ibid.*

16. *Ibid.*

17. Brückmüller, Ernst, 'Die Entwicklung des Österreichbewusstseins', in Kriechbaumer, Robert (ed.), *Österreichische Nationalgeschichte nach 1945. Die Spiegel der*

Erinnerung: Die Sicht von innen, Volume 1, Wien/Köln/Weimar: Böhlau, 1998, p. 16.

18. Perchinig, Bernhard, 'Ein langsamer Weg nach Europa. Österreichische (Arbeits) migrations- und Integrationspolitik seit 1945', in Leibnitz Institut für Sozial-wissenschaften/Bundesamt für Migration und Flüchtlinge (ed.), *Sozialwissen-schaftlicher Fachinformationsdienst (SoFid) 2010/1, Migration und ethnische Minderheiten*, Mannheim: GESIS, 2010, p. 19.

19. Plasser, Fritz, and Ulram, Peter A., 1992, cited in Wodak, Ruth, 'Austria and Its New East Central European Minorities. The Discourses of Racism', in Kürti, Laszlo, and Langmann, Juliet (eds), *Beyond Borders. Remaking Cultural Identities in the New East and Central Europe*, Boulder: Westview Press, 1997.

20. Frölich-Steffen, Susanne, 'Die Identitätspolitik der FPÖ: Vom Deutschnationalismus zum Österreich-Patriotismus', *Österreichische Zeitschrift für Politikwissenschaft* (ÖZP) 33(3) (2004), p. 286.

21. Frölich-Steffen, *op. cit.*

22. Heinisch, Reinhard, *Populism, Proporz, Pariah: Austria Turns Right: Austrian Political Change, its Causes and Repercussions*, New York: Nova Science, 2002, p. 128.

23. 'Was wir brauchen, ist eine klare Rückbesinnung auf jene Werte und Tugenden, die im Wohlfahrtsstaat- und Wachstumstaumel in die Vergangenheit abgescho-ben wurden. Ich meine Werte wie Fleiß, Leistungswille, Arbeitsmoral, Disziplin und Ordnung. Ich meine Tugenden wie Bescheidenheit, Gemeinsinn, Sparsamkeit und Anstand', Haider, Jörg, 'Österreich-Erklärung zur Nationalratswahl 1994', 1994, p. 43.

24. For example, 'Interview mit Jörg Haider', *Berliner Tagesspiegel*, 11 June 2000: 'Ich bin sozusagen eine Symbolfigur für den zivilen Widerstand gegen das Establishment in Österreich und Europa geworden [...] Aber nicht jeder kann zur Symbolfigur werden. Ich bin auserkoren.'

25. See also Pelinka, Anton, 'Die FPÖ in der vergleichenden Parteienforschung. Zur typologischen Einordnung der Freiheitlichen Partei Österreichs', *Österreichische Zeitschrift für Politikwissenschaft* (ÖZP) 31(3) (2002), p. 285.

26. Albertazzi, Daniele, and McDonnell, Duncan, *Twenty-First Century Populism. The Spectre of Western European Democracy*, London: Palgrave Macmillan, 2008, p. 16.

27. FPÖ, 'Das Parteiprogramm der Freiheitlichen Partei Österreichs', 1997, chapter 5, art. 2.5.

28. *Ibid.*, chapter 5, art. 1.1.

29. *Ibid.*, chapter 5, art. 2.3.

30. *Ibid.*, chapter 5, art. 2.2.

31. *Ibid.*, chapter 5, art. 2.

32. Gingrich, Andre, 'A man for all seasons. An anthropological perspective on pub-

lic representatives and cultural politics of the Austrian Freedom Party' in Wodak, Ruth, and Pelinka, Anton, *The Haider Phenomenon in Austria*, New Brunswick and London: Transaction Publishers, 2002, p. 89.

33. 'FPÖ auf antiklerikalen Kurs. "Ehre, Freiheit, Vaterland statt Armut, Keuschheit, Gehorsam"', *Der Standard*, 8 August 1997.

34. Meijer, David, *FPÖ und Christentum. Zwischen Gegnerschaft und Vereinnahmung*, Master's thesis, University of Vienna, 2012, p. 91.

35. Luther, *op. cit.*, p. 388.

36. Luther, *op. cit.*, p. 379.

37. Haider, Jörg, 1995, cited in Heinisch, *op. cit.*, p. 126.

38. Hödl, Klaus, 'Islamophobia in Austria: The Recent Emergence of Anti-Muslim Sentiments in the Country'. *Journal of Muslim Minority Affairs* 30(4) (2010), p. 446

39. 'FP-Sichrovsky: Religionsfreiheit muß in Österreich garantiert werden', OTS0051, 11 October 2001.

40. Hadj-Abdou, Leila, Rosenberger, Sieglinde, Saharso, Sawitri, and Siim, Birte, 'The Limits of Populism. Accommodative Headscarf Policies in Austria, Denmark, and the Netherlands', in Rosenberger, Sieglinde, and Sauer, Birgit (eds), *Politics, Religion and Gender. Framing and Regulating the Veil*, Oxford: Routledge, 2012, pp. 132–49.

41. See also Rosenberger, Sieglinde, and Hadj-Abdou, Leila, 'Islam at Issue. Anti-Islamic Mobilization of the Extreme-Right in Austria', in Mammone, Andrea, Godin, Emmanuel, and Jenkins, Brian (eds), *Varieties of Right-wing Extremism in Europe*, New York: Routledge, 2012, pp. 149–63.

42. 'Verantwortung für Österreich—im Herzen Europas', Government Declaration, 3 February 2000.

43. Friesl, Christian, Polak, Regina, and Hamachers-Zuba, Ursula (eds), *Die Österreicherinnen. Wertewandel 1990–2008*, Vienna: Czernin Verlag, 2009, p. 265.

44. See, for example, FPÖ, 'Wir und der Islam. Freiheitliche Positionen zur Religionsfreiheit, zur islamischen Welt und zur Problematik des ZuwanderungsIslam in Europa', Vienna, 22 January 2008.

45. Wodak, Ruth, and Köhler, Katharina, 'Wer oder was ist "fremd"? Diskurshistorische Analyse fremdenfeindlicher Rhetorik in Österreich', SWS-Rundschau 50(1) (2010), p. 40.

46. See Adamson, Fiona, Triadafilopoulos, Triadfilos, and Zolberg, Aristide, 'The Limits of the Liberal State: Migration, Identity and Belonging in Europe'. *Journal of Ethnic and Migration Studies* 37(6) (2011), pp. 843–59.

47. In line with this position, in 2007 the FPÖ even launched an association named SOS-Abendland (SOS-West) aiming to save Western cultures and customs.

48. Rosenberger and Hadj-Abdou, *op. cit.*

49. See Zúquete, José Pedro, 'The European Extreme-Right and Islam: New Directions?' *Journal of Political Ideologies* 13(3) (2008), pp. 321–44.

50. See http://www.womenagainstislamisation.org/ and http://www.citiesagainstis-lamisation.org/, accessed 17 July 2013.

51. 'FPÖ: Strache und Wilders warnen vor Islamisierung Europas', OTS0128, 27 March 2015.

52. See http://www.releur.eu/index.html, accessed 17 July 2013. The numbers refer to the seventh parliamentary term, and a total of 2,390 parliamentary questions from Austrian MEPs analysed, of which seventy-five questions in total were related to religion.

53. Mourão Permoser, Julia, 'Between Privatization and Politicization: Assessing the "Return of Religion" in the Attitudes of Austrian MEPs', workshop report, 'Religion at the European Parliament' research project, unpublished, p. 20, www.releur.eu/index.html, accessed 1 November 2013.

54. Mourão Permoser, *op. cit.*

55. Zuser, Peter, 'Die Konstruktion der Ausländerfrage in Österreich. Eine Analyse des öffentlichen Diskurses 1990', Working Papers no. 35, Institute for Advanced Studies Vienna, 1996, p. 46.

56. Groll, Verena, 'Die Wahrnehmung von Migration und WählerInnen mit Migrationshintergrund durch die österreichischen Parteien', Master's thesis, University of Vienna, 2010, p. 107.

57. 'Christlich Freiheitliche Plattform für ein freies Europa souveräner Völker, Über uns', CFP, 2012, http://www.cfp.co.at/index.php/ueber-uns, accessed 8 October 2012.

58. 'Österreich nimmt 1000 weitere syrische Flüchtlinge auf. FPÖ-Generalsekretär Harald Vilimsky fordert, dass verfolgte Christen bevorzugt werden', *Die Presse*, 20 April 2014.

59. 'HC Strache: Terror-Camps—Grenzkontrollen zum Schutz vor IS dringlicher denn je', OTS0079, 22 July 2015.

60. El Tayeb, Fatima, *European Others. Queering Ethnicity in Postnational Europe*, Minnesota: Minnesota University Press, 2011.

61. Scharsach, Hans-Henning, *Strache. Im braunen Sumpf*, Vienna: Kremayr & Scheriau, 2012, p. 283.

62. Zulehner, Paul, 'Über die religiöse Verbuntung Österreichs', *Die Presse*, 3 June 2011.

63. If one considers the additional third of the Austrian population who, although less militantly, also identify as 'Cultural Christians' (Zulehner, *op. cit.*), then the potential number of voters that could successfully be mobilised in one way or another by anti-Islamic positions is even larger.

64. Burchianti, Flora, and Itcaina, Xabier, 'Between Hospitality and Competition. The Catholic Church and Immigration in Spain' in Haynes, Jeffrey, and Hennig, Anja (eds), *Religious Actors in the Public Sphere: Means, Objectives and Effects*, London/New York: Routledge, 2011, pp. 57–76.

65. Meijer, *op. cit.*, p. 83.

66. Cited in Heinisch, *op. cit.*, p. 111.

67. Cited in Meijer, *op. cit.*, p. 78.

68. Meijer, *op. cit.*, p. 105.

69. See, for example, Haider, Jörg, 'Grundsätzliches zum Verhältnis FPÖ und katholische Kirche', in Wilhelm, Michael and Wuthe, Paul (eds), *Parteien und Katholische Kirche im Gespräch*, Graz/Vienna: Verlag Zeitpunkt, p. 38.

70. Haider 1999, *op. cit.*

71. 'Ökumenischer Rat der Kirchen kritisiert FPÖ', *Kleine Zeitung*, 5 May 2009, http://www.kleinezeitung.at, accessed 9 October 2012.

72. ORF, 'Kirchliche Kritik an FPÖ-Wahlplakaten', 12 August 2013, http://religion.orf.at/stories/2597798/, accessed 22 April 2014.

73. ORF, 'Asyl: Strache attackiert Schönborn', 17 January 2013, http://wien.orf.at, accessed 15 July 2013.

74. 'SOS-Abendland: "Sind entsetzt über Werteverfall in der Europäischen Union"', FPÖ, 4 November 2009, www.fpoe.at, accessed 2 July 2013.

75. Mourão Permoser, *op. cit.*, p. 20.

76. 'Das Kreuz wurde von mir niemals als Kampfinstrument verwendet, sondern als ein Symbol der Erlösung und Befreiung—und darum geht's uns im kulturellen Sinn.' 'Strache: Gegenschlag gegen Kirche', OTS0361, 19 May 2009.

77. News.at, 'Nach Strache-Sager zur Fristenlösung: Heftige Kritik der ÖVP, der SPÖ & den Grünen', 13 January 2006, www.news.at, accessed 12 July 2013.

78. FPÖ, 'Handbuch freiheitlicher Politik', Vienna, 2013, p. 160.

79. FPÖ 2013, *op. cit.*

80. FPÖ 2013, *op. cit.*, p. 103.

81. Scharsach, *op. cit.*, p. 53.

82. *Ibid.*, p. 53 *et seq.*

83. FPÖ, 'Parteiprogramm'der Freiheitlichen Partei Österreichs', 2011, chapter 2.

84. *Ibid.*

85. *Ibid.*

86. Lentin, Alana, and Titley, Gavan, *The Crises of Multiculturalism: Racism in a Neoliberal Age*, London: Zed Books, 2011, p. 35.

4. POPULISM AND ISLAM IN SWITZERLAND: THE ROLE OF THE SWISS PEOPLE'S PARTY

1. Switzerland is one of the countries where direct democracy (including legislative referendums and constitutional initiatives) is used most (see Kobach, Kris William, *The Referendum: Direct Democracy in Switzerland*, Aldershot: Dartmouth, 1993). Through constitutional (or popular) initiatives, citizens' committees and political parties may propose a modification of the Constitution at any time. Once 100,000 signatures by Swiss citizens have been collected, the proposal is submitted to a

popular nationwide vote. If it gains a majority, the proposal is directly implemented in the federal Constitution.

2. Mazzoleni, Oscar, *Nationalisme et populisme en Suisse. La radicalisation de la 'nouvelle' UDC*, Lausanne: Presses polytechniques et universitaires romandes, 2008, pp. 61–84; Skenderovic, Damir, 'Campagnes et agenda politiques. La transformation de l'Union démocratique du centre', in Mazzoleni, Oscar, and Rayner, Hervé (eds), *Les partis politiques en Suisse. Traditions et renouvellements*, Paris: Michel Houdiard Editeur, 2009, pp. 378–409; Mazzoleni, Oscar, 'Between Opposition and Government. The Swiss People's Party', in Grabow, Karsten, and Hartleb, Florian (eds), *Exposing the Demagogues. Right-wing and National Populists in Europe*, Brussels: CES-KAS, 2013, pp. 237–60.

3. Mazzoleni, Oscar, 'Between Centralisation and Nationalisation: The Case of the Swiss People's Party', in Pallaver, Günther, and Wagemann, Claudius (eds), *Challenges for Alpine Parties. Strategies of Political Parties for Identity and Territory in the Alpine Regions*, Innsbruck/Vienna/Bozen: Studien Verlag, 2012, pp. 17–33.

4. Mazzoleni, Oscar, and Skenderovic, Damir, 'The rise and impact of the Swiss People's Party: Challenging the rules of governance in Switzerland', in Delwit, Pascal, and Poirier, Philippe (eds), *Droites nouvelles et pouvoir en Europe/The New Right-wing Parties and Power in Europe*, Brussels: Editions de l'Université de Bruxelles, 2007, pp. 85–115; Burgos, Elie, Mazzoleni, Oscar, and Rayner, Hervé, *La Formule Magique: conflits et consensus partisans dans l'élection du Conseil Fédéral*, Lausanne: Presses Polytechniques et Universitaires Romandes, 2011, p. 51 *et seq.*

5. Mazzoleni 2008, *op. cit.*, pp. 28–39.

6. Mazzoleni 2008, *op. cit.*, chapter 1.

7. SVP, *SVP—The Party for Switzerland. Party Programme 2011–2015*, Bern, 2011; SVP, *SVP—The Party for Switzerland. Party Programme 2015–2019*, Bern, 2015.

8. SVP 2011, *op. cit.*, p. 121; SVP 2015, *op. cit.*, p. 90.

9. Roy, Olivier, *La Sainte ignorance. Le temps de la religion sans culture*, Paris: Seuil, 2008, pp. 61–3, 125 *et seq.*

10. SVP 2011, *op. cit.*, p. 121; see also the same in SVP 2015, *op. cit.*, p. 92.

11. SVP 2015, *op. cit.*, p. 91.

12. *Ibid.*

13. See Gianni, Matteo, *Vie musulmane en Suisse. Profils identitaires, demandes et perceptions des musulmans en Suisse. Rapport réalisé par le Groupe de Recherche sur l'Islam en Suisse*, Bern: Commission Fédérale pour les Questions de Migration, 2010, p. 12 *et seq.*

14. SVP 2015, *op. cit.*, p. 92.

15. *Ibid.*, p. 122.

16. SVP 2011, *op. cit.*, p. 121.

17. *Ibid.*, p. 122.

18. In a press release dated 21 February 2009, the national SVP stated: 'The growth

of Islamisation in our country must be stopped. The popular initiative lodged by the Egerkingen Committee is a first step in the right direction. The SVP parliamentary group has therefore decided unanimously to support it.' On 25 September 2009 the SVP national Assembly of Delegates voted almost unanimously to confirm this support (288 votes in favour, three against, three abstentions).

19. The website at www.minarette.ch, accessed 30 October 2012, sets out details of the initiative and its supporters.

20. See, for instance, Müller, Felix, and Tanner, Mathias, 'Muslime, Minarette und die Minarett-Initiative in der Schweiz: Grundlagen', in Tanner, Mathias *et al.* (eds), *Streit um das Minarett. Zusammenleben in der religiös pluralistischen Gesellschaft,* Zurich: Theologischer Verlag, 2009, pp. 21–44.

21. Niggli, Peter, and Frischknecht, Jürg, *Rechte Seilschaften. Wie die 'unheimlichen Patrioten' den Zusammenbruch des Kommunismus meisterten,* Zurich: Woz im Rotpunktverlag, 1998; Skenderovic, Damir, *The Radical Right in Switzerland: Continuity and Change, 1945–2000,* New York: Berghahn, 2009.

22. Huntington, Samuel P., *The Clash of Civilizations and the Remaking of World Order,* New York: Simon and Schuster, 1996.

23. Niggli and Frischknecht, *op. cit.,* p. 567 *et seq.*

24. 'Il minareto e il suo significato', 2009, www.minarette.ch, accessed 30 October 2012.

25. 'Wir schlafen noch. Europa befindet sich im Krieg mit dem Islam'. Waber, Christian, 'Facts', *Schweizer Nachrichten* 20 (2007), p. 26.

26. Swiss Bishops' Conference, 'L'initiative contre la construction de minarets', press release, 9 September 2009, http://www.eveques.ch, accessed 27 October 2012.

27. Swiss Federation of Jewish Communities, 'Pas de loi d'exception. Non à l'interdiction des minarets', press release, 28 October 2009.

28. 'Maurer und Spuhler gegen Minarett-Verbot. Warnung vor Boykotten', *Sontagszeitung,* 25 October 2009.

29. Christmann, Anna, Danaci, Deniz, and Krömler, Oliver, 'Ein Sonderfall? Das Stimmverhalten bei der Minarettverbots-Initiative im Vergleich zu andern Abstimmungen und Sachfragen', in Vatter, Adrian (ed.), *Vom Schächt- zum Minarettverbot. Religiöse Minderheiten in der direkten Demokratie,* Zurich: NZZ Verlag, 2011, pp. 171–90.

30. Behloul, Samuel M., 'Religion und Religionzugehörigkeit im Spannungfeld von normativer Exklusion und Zivilgesellschaftlichem Bekenntnis. Islam und Muslime als öffentliches Thema in der Schweiz', in Allenbach, Birgit and Sökefeld, Martin (eds), *Muslime in der Schweiz,* Zurich: Seismo, 2010, pp. 43–65.

31. Baumann, Martin, and Stolz, Jörg, 'Vielfalt der Religionen. Risiken und Chancen des Zusammenlebens', in Baumann, Martin, and Stolz Jörg (eds), *Eine Schweiz— viele Religionen. Risiken und Chancen des Zusammenleben,* Bielefeld: Transcript Verlag, 2007, p. 358 *et seq.*

32. Cesari, Jocelyne, 'Islam, Secularism and Multiculturalism After 9/11: A

Transatlantic Comparison', in Cesari, Jocelyne, and McLoughlin, Séan (eds), *European Muslims and the Secular State*, Aldershot: Ashgate, 2005, pp. 39–54.

33. See Imhof, Kurt, and Ettinger, Patrik, 'Religionen in der Medienvermittelten Öffentichkeit der Schweiz', in Baumann and Stolz (eds), *op. cit.*, pp. 284–300.

34. Dolezal, Martin, Helbling, Marc, and Hutter, Swen, 'Debating Islam in Austria, Germany and Switzerland: Ethnic Citizenship, Church-State Relations and Right-Wing Populism', *West European Politics* 33(2) (2010), p. 184.

35. In August 2012, the city of Geneva invoked the 'law on external worship' to prohibit a Catholic event.

36. Berger, Peter L. (ed.), *The Desecularization of the World: Resurgent Religion and World Politics*, Michigan: Eerdmans, 1999.

37. Campiche, Roland J., *Les deux visages de la religion. Fascination et désenchantement*, Geneva: Labor et Fides, 2004, p. 181 *et seq.*

38. Imhof and Ettinger, *op. cit.*, p. 293.

39. Altermatt, Urs, 'Die Christlichdemokratische Volkspartei der Schweiz, 1945–1999', in Veen, Hans-Joachim (ed.), *Christlich-demokratische und konservative Parteien in Westeuropa*, Munich: Schöningh, 2000, pp. 37–118.

40. 'Un non clair à l'initiative anti-minarets', press release, 20 October 2009, www.pdc.ch, accessed 30 October 2012.

41. *Background paper on Switzerland's vote on Minarets*, Report of the Federation of Swiss Protestant Churches, Bern, 2010, p. 2.

42. Wälti, Carole, 'Minaret vote was a "lesson in civic spirit"', Swissinfo.ch, 16 December 2009, accessed 29 November 2012.

43. Windisch, Uli, *Suisse-immigrés. Quarante ans de débats 1960–2001*, Lausanne/Paris: L'Age d'Homme, 2002.

44. Behloul, Samuel Martin, 'Discours Total! Le débat sur l'Islam en Suisse et le positionnement de l'Islam comme religion publique', in Schneuwly Purdie, Mallory, Gianni, Matteo, and Magali, Jenny (eds), *Musulmans d'aujourd'hui. Identités plurielles en Suisse*, Geneva: Labor et Fides, 2009, pp. 59–60; Clavien, Gaëtan, 'Médias et discours islamophobe: au croisement du dicible et du recevable', in Schneuwly Purdie *et al.* (eds), *op. cit.*, pp. 95–109.

5. USING FAITH TO EXCLUDE: THE ROLE OF RELIGION IN DUTCH POPULISM

1. I would like to thank the Alexander von Humboldt Foundation for its support during the later stages of the work on this chapter.

2. See Andeweg, Rudy, and Irwin, Galen, *Governance and Politics of the Netherlands*, 3rd ed., Basingstoke: Palgrave Macmillan, 2009.

3. See Lijphart, Arend, *The Politics of Accommodation: Pluralism and Democracy in the Netherlands*, 2nd ed., Berkeley: University of California Press, 1975.

4. Andeweg and Irwin, *op. cit.*, p. 112.

5. See Lucardie, Paul, and Voerman, Gerrit, *Populisten in de Polder*, Amsterdam: Boom, 2012.

6. March, Luke, *Radical Left Parties in Europe*, Oxford: Routledge, 2011, pp. 128–33.

7. For this reason, the party will be excluded from the analysis in this chapter. Religion never played a role in the ideology of the SP in any case. See de Lange, Sarah, and Rooduijn, Matthijs, 'Een populistische Zeitgeist in Nederland? Een inhoudsanalyse van de verkiezingsprogramma's van populistische en gevestigde politieke partijen', in Andeweg, Rudy, and Thomassen, Jacques (eds), *Democratie Doorgelicht, het functioneren van de Nederlandse democratie*, Leiden: Leiden University Press, 2011, pp. 319–34; see also Lucardie and Voerman, *op. cit.*, pp. 64–9.

8. See de Lange, Sarah, and Art, David, 'Fortuyn versus Wilders: An Agency-Based Approach to Radical Right Party Building', *West European Politics* 34(6) (2011), pp. 1229–49.

9. See Taggart, Paul, *Populism*, Buckingham and Philadelphia: Open University Press, 2000.

10. Quotes from Dutch sources in this chapter have been translated from Dutch into English by the author.

11. Poorthuis, Frank, and Wansink, Hans, 'Pim Fortuyn op herhaling: "De islam is een achterlijke cultuur"', *Volkskrant*, 9 February 2002, http://www.volkskrant.nl/vk/nl/2824/Politiek/article/detail/611698/2002/02/09/De-islam-is-een-achterlijke-cultuur.dhtml, accessed 25 October 2012.

12. Fortuyn, Pim, *De Puinhopen van acht jaar paars. Een genadeloze analyse van de collectieve sector en aanbevelingen voor een krachtig herstelprogramma*, Uithoorn-Rotterdam: Karakter Uitgevers-Speakers Academy, 2002, p. 186.

13. LPF, *Lijst Pim Fortuyn. Zakelijk met een hart* (Pim Fortuyn List parliamentary election manifesto 2002), in Documentatiecentrum Nederlandse politieke partijen, 2002, p. 1, http://dnpp.eldoc.ub.rug.nl/FILES/root/programmas/vp-per-partij/lpf/lpf02.pdf, accessed 19 July 2011.

14. Lucardie, Paul, 'The Netherlands: Populism versus Pillarization', in Albertazzi, Daniele, and McDonnell, Duncan (eds), *Twenty-First Century Populism. The Spectre of Western European Democracy*, Basingstoke: Palgrave Macmillan, 2008, pp. 151–65.

15. LPF, *op. cit.*, p. 5.

16. *Ibid.*

17. Akkerman, Tjitske, 'Anti-immigration Parties and the Defence of Liberal Values: The Exceptional Case of the List Pim Fortuyn', *Journal of Political Ideologies* 10(3) (2005), pp. 337–54.

18. LPF, *op. cit.*, p. 5.

19. Van Holsteyn, Joop and Irwin, Galen, 'Never a Dull Moment: Pim Fortuyn and

the Dutch Parliamentary Election of 2002', *West European Politics* 26(2) (2003), p. 44.

20. Lucardie and Voerman, *op. cit.*, pp. 153–4.
21. Wilders, Geert, *Groep Wilders. Onafhankelijkheidsverklaring*, party document, Groep Wilders, The Hague, 2005, p. 2.
22. Wilders, *op. cit.*, p. 16.
23. Lucardie and Voerman, *op. cit.*, pp. 114–5.
24. Vossen, Koen, 'Classifying Wilders: The Ideological Development of Geert Wilders and His Party for Freedom', *Politics* 31(3) (2011), pp. 179–89.
25. PVV, Partij voor de Vrijheid: *De agenda van hoop en optimisme. Een tijd om te kiezen*, Partij voor de Vrijheid parliamentary election manifesto, 2010, p. 6. The less successful populist entrepreneur Rita Verdonk, a former immigration minister for the Liberal Party, similarly made reference to 'good old' Dutch habits, such as eating herring and pickles (these items were on display during a party conference).
26. PVV, *op. cit.*, p. 35; PVV, *Verkiezingspamflet*, Partij voor de Vrijheid parliamentary election manifesto, 2006.
27. PVV 2010, *op. cit.*, p. 6.
28. *Ibid.*, p. 33.
29. Keman, Hans, and Pennings, Paul, 'Oude en nieuwe conflictdimensies in de Nederlandse politiek na 1989: een vergelijkende analyse', in Andeweg, Rudy, and Thomassen, Jacques (eds), *Democratie Doorgelicht, het functioneren van de Nederlandse democratie*, Leiden: Leiden University Press, 2011, pp. 247–66.
30. PVV 2010, *op. cit.*, p. 6.
31. Van de Griend, 'Wilders' diepe denker uit België', *Vrij Nederland*, 22 September 2010, http://www.vn.nl/Archief/Politiek/Artikel-Politiek/Wilders-diepe-denker-uit-Belgie.htm, accessed 6 March 2013.
32. Vossen, *op. cit.*, p. 182.
33. Vossen, Koen, 'Populism in the Netherlands after Fortuyn: Rita Verdonk and Geert Wilders Compared', *Perspectives on European Politics and Society* 11(1) (2010), p. 22.
34. PVV 2010, *op. cit.*, p. 33.
35. Vossen 2010, *op. cit.*, p. 27.
36. See Vossen 2011, *op. cit.* As a consequence of his controversial anti-Islam statements, Wilders has received numerous death threats. The PVV leader has required constant police protection, and security measures have greatly restricted Wilders' personal freedom.
37. PVV 2010, *op. cit.*, p. 13.
38. *Ibid.*, p. 13.
39. *Ibid*, p. 6.
40. *Ibid.*

41. See, for example, Van Holsteyn, Joop, Irwin, Galen, and den Ridder, Josje, 'In the Eye of the Beholder: The Perception of the List Pim Fortuyn and the Parliamentary Elections of 2002', *Acta Politica* 38(1) (2003), pp. 69–87; Aarts, Kees, and Thomassen, Jacques, 'Dutch Voters and the Changing Party Space 1989–2006', *Acta Politica* 43(2–3) (2008), pp. 203–34; Van Kessel, Stijn, *Populist Parties in Europe. Agents of Discontent?*, Basingstoke: Palgrave Macmillan, 2015.

42. Van Kessel, Stijn, 'The Dutch General Election of June 2010', European Parties Elections and Referendums Network, Election Briefing Paper no. 54, 2010.

43. See Van Kessel, Stijn, and Hollander, Saskia, 'Europe and the Dutch Parliamentary Election, September 2012', European Parties Elections and Referendums Network, Election Briefing Paper, no. 71, 2012.

44. PVV, *Hún Brussel, óns Nederland*, Partij voor de Vrijheid parliamentary election manifesto, 2012.

45. NOS, 'Wilders: aanpak islam prioriteit 2013', 27 December 2012, http://nos.nl/artikel/455673-wildersaanpak-islam-prioriteit-2013.html, accessed 9 March 2012.

46. Sun News Network, 'Geert Wilders on the Islamic terror attacks on Charlie Hebdo cartoonists', 8 February 2015, https://www.youtube.com/watch?v=vzDCeWNObBo, accessed 25 May 2015.

47. The event would feature in the news primarily due to the attack by two gunmen, allegedly operating on behalf of IS, which left both assailants dead and one security officer wounded.

48. Wilders, Geert, 'Inbreng Geert Wilders bij terreurdebat', 11 February 2015, http://www.pvv.nl/index.php/36-fj-related/geert-wilders/8168-inbreng-geert-wilders-bij-debat-over-inzet-en-capaciteit-in-de-veiligheidsketen.html, accessed 25 May 2015.

49. See, for instance, Wilders, Geert, 'Speech Geert Wilders for US Congressmen, Washington DC, Conservative Opportunity Society', 29 April 2015, http://www.pvv.nl/index.php/36-fj-related/geert-wilders/8324-speech-geert-wilders-for-us-congressmen-washington-dc-conservative-opportunity-society-29-april-2015.html, accessed 25 May 2015.

50. Gillissen, Daniël, and Houtman, Wim, 'PVV-aanhang in kerken blijft beperkt', *Nederlands Dagblad*, 26 February 2010, http://www.nd.nl/artikelen/2010/februari/25/-christen-kan-geen-wilders-stemmen-, accessed 22 October 2012.

51. IKON, 'Plaisier: denkbeelden Wilders onverenigbaar met kerk', 5 April 2008, http://www.kerknieuws.nl/nieuws.asp?oId=12863, accessed 11 October 2012.

52. *Trouw*, 'Bisschop De Korte: Wilders drijft mensen uiteen', 29 June 2012, http://www.trouw.nl/tr/nl/5009/Archief/archief/article/detail/3278827/2012/06/29/Bisschop-De-Korte-Wilders-drijft-mensen-uiteen.dhtml, accessed 22 October 2012.

53. RKK, 'Bisschop vraagt Wilders om fatsoen', 29 February 2008, http://www.rkk.nl/actualiteit/2008/detail_objectID666796_FJaar2008.html, accessed 11 October 2012.

54. Weseman, Pauline, 'Muskens: "Wilders misbruikt angstgevoelens in crisistijd"', *Nieuwwij*, 1 May 2009, http://www.nieuwwij.nl/index.php?pageID=13& messageID=2187, accessed 11 October 2012.

55. IKON, 'Raad van Kerken: "Fitna is eenzijdig en provocerend"', 27 March 2008, http://www.kerknieuws.nl/nieuws.asp?oId=12815, accessed 11 October 2012.

56. RKK, 'Brabantse priesters steunen Wilders', 9 April 2008, http://www.rkk.nl/ actualiteit/2008/detail_objectID668982_FJaar2008.html, accessed 11 October 2012.

57. Gillissen and Houtman, *op. cit.*

58. *Parool*, 'Wilders wil dat kerken kiezen tegen de Islam', 23 March 2010, http:// www.parool.nl/parool/nl/224/BINNENLAND/article/ detail/285523/2010/03/23/Wilders-wil-dat-kerken-kiezen-tegen-de-Islam. dhtml, accessed 22 October 2012.

59. De Wever, Robin, '"Een kerkdienst tegen Wilders? Zo moet je het niet zien"', *Trouw*, 21 March 2014, http://www.trouw.nl/tr/nl/5091/Religie/article/ detail/3620085/2014/03/21/Een-kerkdienst-tegen-Wilders-Zo-moet-je-het-niet-zien.dhtml, accessed 27 May 2015.

60. Terpstra, Doekle, '"Nee" tegen kwade boodschap Wilders', *Trouw*, 30 November 2007, http://www.trouw.nl/tr/nl/4324/Nieuws/article/detail/1369213/2007/ 11/30/rsquo-Nee-rsquo-tegen-kwade-boodschap-Wilders-opinie.dhtml, accessed 9 March 2013.

61. Political parties in the Netherlands are not obliged to publicise sources of external funding, and Wilders has always refused to do so. A parliamentary bill was put forward in January 2012 with the aim of increasing the transparency of party financing. At the time of writing, this bill is being processed by the Dutch Senate. See Vossen 2011, *op. cit.*, p. 182; Vuijst, Freke, 'Op zoek naar dollars', *Vrij Nederland*, 13 June 2009, http://www.vn.nl/Meer-dossiers/Wilders-en-de-PVV/Artikel-Wilders/Op-zoek-naar-dollars.htm, accessed 9 March 2013; De Wever, Robin, 'Wilders' joodse, christelijke en anti-islamitische geldschieters', *Trouw*, 3 July 2012, http://www.trouw.nl/tr/nl/5091/Religie/article/detail/3281078/2012/07/03/ Wilders-joodse-christelijke-en-anti-islamitische-geldschieters.dhtml, accessed 22 October 2012.

62. De Wever 2012, *op. cit.*

63. *Ibid.*

64. Vossen 2011, *op. cit.*, p. 181.

65. PVV 2012, *op. cit.*, p. 47.

66. PVV 2010, *op. cit.*, p. 41.

67. Vuijst, *op. cit.*; De Wever 2012, *op. cit.*

68. RKK, 'Rabbijn Soetendorp: kerken moeten zich mengen in Wilders-debat', 20 January 2008, http://www.rkk.nl/actualiteit/2008/detail_objectID663067_ FJaar2008.html, accessed 13 October 2012.

69. See Sanders, Charles, 'Joodse sponsors woest op Wilders', *Telegraaf*, 21 August

2012, http://www.telegraaf.nl/binnenland/verkiezingen2012/12796867/__
Sponsors_woest_op_Wilders__.html, accessed 25 October 2012. Remarkably,
Wilders' party is also known for its animal-friendly policies, mainly associated
with the ideas of MP Dion Graus.

70. CIDI, 'Mythe ontzenuwd: Joden stemmen amper PVV', 4 June 2010, http://www.
cidi.nl/Nieuwsberichten-in-2010/-Mythe-ontzenuwd-Joden-stemmen-amper-
PVV.html, accessed 25 October 2012.

71. See Van der Brug, Wouter, Hobolt, Sara, and de Vreese, Claes, 'Religion and Party
Choice in Europe', *West European Politics* 32(6) (2009), pp. 1266–83.

72. Andeweg and Irwin, *op. cit.*, pp. 111–12.

73. The Christian Union won 3.1 per cent of the vote in the 2012 parliamentary election; the Reformed Political Party's vote share was 2.1 per cent.

74. Van der Kolk, Henk, Aarts, Kees, and Tillie, Jean, *Dutch Parliamentary Election
Study 2010*, The Hague: DANS, 2012.

75. Van der Kolk, Henk, Tillie, Jean, van Erkel, Patrick, van der Velden, Mariken, and
Damstra, Alyt, *Dutch Parliamentary Election Study 2012*, The Hague: DANS,
2013.

76. Van der Meer, Tom, Lubbe, Rozemarijn, van Elsas, Erika, Elff, Martin, and van der
Brug, Wouter, 'Bounded Volatility in the Dutch Electoral Battlefield: A Panel
Study on the Structure of Changing Vote Intentions in the Netherlands during
2006–2010', *Acta Politica* 47(4) (2012), pp. 333–55.

77. De Jong, Ron, van der Kolk, Henk, and Voerman, Gerrit, *Verkiezingen op de kaart,
1848–2010. Tweede Kamerverkiezingen vanuit geografisch perspectief*, Utrecht:
Matrijs, 2011.

78. See Klei, Ewout, and Lemm, Jeffrey, 'Een nieuwe Messias? Christenen en het fenomeen Geert Wilders', *Liberaal Reveil*, Decembernummer, 16 December 2010,
Den Haag: Teldersstichting.

79. Van der Brug *et al.*, *op. cit.*, pp. 1277–8.

80. Hakkenes, Emiel, 'De tweede christelijke partij van Nederland', *Trouw*,
26 November 2009, http://www.trouw.nl/tr/nl/4324/Nieuws/article/detail/
1179389/2009/11/26/De-tweede-christelijke-partij-van-Nederland.dhtml,
accessed 25 October 2012.

81. Van der Meer *et al.*, *op. cit.*, p. 12.

82. *Ibid.*, p. 13.

83. A study by Immerzeel *et al.* has furthermore shown that besides more moderate
religious voters orthodox Protestant believers were more likely to vote for a
Christian party (the SGP) than for the populist radical right. See Immerzeel, Tim,
Jaspers, Eva, and Lubbers, Marcel, 'Religion as Catalyst or Restraint of Radical
Right Voting?' *West European Politics* 36(5) (2013), pp. 946–68.

84. See van Kersbergen, Kees, and Krouwel, André, 'A Double-Edged Sword! The

Dutch Centre-Right and the "Foreigners Issue"', *Journal of European Public Policy* 15(3) (2008), pp. 399–400.

85. See Andeweg and Irwin, *op. cit.*, pp. 111–12.

6. THE FRENCH NATIONAL FRONT: FROM CHRISTIAN IDENTITY TO *LAÏCITÉ*

1. IFOP opinion poll (8 February 2015): *laïcité* is put at the top of republican values by 46 per cent of French respondents, universal suffrage comes second with 36 per cent), http://www.ifop.fr/?option=com_publication&type=poll&id=2929, accessed 10 December 2015. A previous opinion poll in February 2005 (CSA), found that *laïcité* is 'an essential component of the French identity' for 75 per cent of the sample, http://www.csa.eu/multimedia/data/sondages/data2005/opi2005 0203c.htm, accessed 10 December 2015.

2. Interview at the French broadcast station RTL, 4 April 2014, http://tempsreel. nouvelobs.com/video/20140404.OBS2693/marine-le-pen-ne-veut-plus-de-menus-sans-porc-dans-les-cantines.html, accessed 10 December 2015.

3. Benoist, Alain de, 'Gramsci et la conquête du pouvoir culturel', *Le Figaro Magazine*, 11/12 March 1978.

4. Amselle, Jean-Loup, *Les nouveaux rouges-bruns. Le racisme qui vient*, Paris: Éditions Lignes, 2014.

5. On the paganist perspective, see the interview with Alain de Benoist in *Terre et Peuple*, Lyon, September 2001.

6. Schwengler, Bernard, *Le vote Front National: L'Alsace: un cas particulier? Sociologie d'un vote complexe*, Strasbourg: Éditions Oberlin, 2003.

7. On the occasion of a visit to New York in April 2015, she ostensibly shook hands with former Israeli Prime Minister Ehud Barak and had a meeting with the Jewish European Parliament in Strasbourg (8 July 2015), followed by a kosher meal (while the ban on ritual slaughtering is still on the FN agenda).

8. 'Comme son divin modèle, elle ne venait pas apporter la paix mais l'épée': speech of Jean-Marie Le Pen for the 600th anniversary of Joan of Arc's birthday, http://www.frontnational.com/2012/01/discours-de-jean-marie-le-pen-lors-de-la-celebration-du-600eme-anniversaire-de-la-naissance-de-jeanne-darc/, accessed 10 December 2015.

9. A recent example is the criticism of Pope Francis by Abbot Christian Bouchacourt, a member of the Fraternité Sacerdotale Saint Pie X, who blames the pontiff for his neglect of the rites, glamour and protocol of the Church in favour of simplicity and poverty; he also criticises the Church for its call for dialogue with Muslims. Jesus is regularly referred to in this article as 'Lord' and 'King'. See Bouchacourt, Christian, 'Une nouvelle ère?' *TradiNews*, 29 April 2013, http://tradinews.blogspot.fr/2013/04/abbe-christian-bouchacourt-fsspx-une.html?utm_source=feedburner

&utm_medium=feed&utm_campaign=Feed:+Tradinews+(TradiNews), accessed 10 December 2015.

10. A poll conducted in 2013 and published by the French Catholic magazine *La Vie* shows that 8 per cent of church-going Catholics claimed to be willing to vote for the FN, in contrast with 13 per cent of the general French population. Http://www.lavie.fr/medias/les-catholiques-mois-attires-par-le-fn-que-la-moyenne-des-francais-04–12–2013–47318_73.php, accessed 11 December 2015.

11. For example, the French rightist MP Étienne Pinte wrote a book with a parish priest, Jacques Turck, attacking the FN: *Extrême droite: pourquoi les chrétiens ne peuvent pas se taire*, Paris: Éditions de l'Atelier, 2012.

12. Fourquet, Jerôme, 'Présidentielle 2012: l'analyse du vote catholique par l'Ifop', *Famille Chrétienne*, 23 April 2012, http://www.libertepolitique.com/Actualite/Decryptage/Presidentielle-2012-l-analyse-du-vote-catholique-par-l-Ifop, accessed 11 December 2015.

13. For instance, a policy of including churches among the buildings that should be rehabilitated as part of the 'national patrimony', http://www.frontnational.com/le-projet-de-marine-le-pen/avenir-de-la-nation/culture/, accessed 11 December 2015.

14. http://www.civitas-institut.com/, accessed 11 December 2015.

15. IFOP, *Les Français et les manifestations sur le mariage et l'adoption pour les couples de même sexe après le vote de la loi*, FD/EP, no. 111316, May 2013.

16. In an interview for a Catholic journal, she stated that the Catholic priests should not meddle in politics: http://www.lavie.fr/hebdo/2011/3433/marine-le-pen-les-cures-devraient-rester-dans-leur-sacristie-15–06–2011–17717_231.php, accessed 11 December 2015. The defence of *laïcité* also reveals some ambivalence as she considers the Church as too pro-migrant and rejects the humanist values that the Church articulates in defence of migrants (charity, hospitality, etc.). The Italian Lega Nord holds the same position in regard to the Catholic Church (see Chapter 2).

17. http://www.frontnational.com/le-projet-de-marine-le-pen/refondation-republicaine/laicite/, accessed 11 December 2015.

18. Alduy, Cécile and Wahnich, Stéphane, *Marine Le Pen prise aux mots, décryptage du nouveau discours frontiste?* Paris: Le Seuil, 2015.

19. 'La laïcité: une valeur au cœur du projet républicain', http://www.frontnational.com/le-projet-de-marine-le-pen/refondation-republicaine/laicite/, accessed 11 December 2015.

20. L'Express, http://www.lexpress.fr/actualite/politique/marine-le-pen-veut-interdire-le-voile-et-la-kippa-dans-la-rue_1164264.html, accessed 11 December 2015.

21. Le Parisien, http://www.leparisien.fr/election-presidentielle-2012/marine-le-pen-donne-sa-definition-d-une-france-laique-28–01–2011–1247059.php, accessed 11 December 2015.

22. See http://www.frontnational.com/le-projet-de-marine-le-pen/refondation-republicaine/laicite/, accessed 11 December 2015.
23. 'Avec l'invitation de Marion Maréchal-Le Pen, l'évêque du Var brise un tabou', *L'Express*, 27 August 2015.

7. RELIGION AND POPULISM IN BRITAIN: AN INFERTILE BREEDING GROUND?

1. Betz, Hans-Georg, and Meret, Susi, 'Revisiting Lepanto: the Political Mobilization against Islam in Contemporary Western Europe', *Patterns of Prejudice*, 43(3–4) (2009), pp. 313–34.
2. The Episcopal Church of England is the established Church of the United Kingdom and its Parliament. The Presbyterian Church of Scotland is the national Church in Scotland and has a special statutory relationship with the UK Parliament and the Queen, although she is not the supreme governor of the Church of Scotland as she is of the Church of England. The Church of England provides major functions for the state and the monarchy itself is an institution that is religiously legitimated by that Church and thereby the state (see Bonney, Norman, 'Established Religion, Parliamentary Devolution and New State Religion in the UK', *Parliamentary Affairs*, 66(2) (2013), pp. 425–42.
3. Bruce, Steve, *Politics and Religion in the United Kingdom*, London: Routledge, 2012, p. 30.
4. It should be noted that this chapter is dedicated to Great Britain and therefore excludes Northern Ireland, where the sectarian cleavage continues to dominate the political agenda. When speaking of 'Britain', this includes all countries that make up Great Britain, but the focus is on England as this is where populist parties have had most success.
5. The Archbishop of Canterbury is an important figure who is expected to make interventions in public debate, albeit from a non-partisan standpoint. However, his views do not carry comparable political weight to pronouncements by the Catholic Church in a country such as Italy.
6. This Ipsos MORI poll was conducted among UK adults who said they were recorded as Christian in the 2011 Census. Fifty-nine per cent of the population in England and Wales selected this option, although it is acknowledged that the number of 'census Christians' does not reflect the number that actually regularly attend church on Sunday (see Bruce, *op. cit.*). The results therefore reflect the British population as a whole, rather than committed Christians who regularly attend church. http://www.ipsos-mori.com/researchpublications/researcharchive/2921/Religious-and-Social-Attitudes-of-UK-Christians-in-2011.aspx, accessed 19 April 2016.
7. This is a tendency that emerged with the Labour government of Tony Blair, which was very much influenced by the work of Robert Putnam. Religious groups were

seen as an important source of 'social capital' and could be a replacement for the state in terms of the provision of social action programmes along with charities and other social entrepreneurs.

8. See https://www.gov.uk/government/ministers/senior-minister-of-state-and-minister-for-faith-and-communities, accessed 19 April 2016.

9. BBC, 'David Cameron says the UK is a Christian country', *BBC News*, http://www.bbc.co.uk/news/uk-politics-16224394, last accessed 13 September 2013.

10. BBC, 'Stand up for our Christianity, David Cameron tells UK', BBC News, http://www.bbc.co.uk/news/uk-politics-27053112, last accessed 22 May 2014.

11. This action was brought against Bideford Town Council in Devon by the National Secular Society.

12. Bingham, John, 'Britain's Christians are being vilified, warns Lord Carey', *The Daily Telegraph*, http://www.telegraph.co.uk/news/religion/9203953/Britains-Christians-are-being-vilified-warns-Lord-Carey.html, last accessed 13 September 2013.

13. The court ruled in favour of Nadia Eweida, a British Airways employee who had been told to remove a gold cross. However, this was only a symbolic victory as the company had already decided to change its uniform policy back in 2007 after negative publicity surrounding the issue. See Hill, Mark, 'Religious Symbolism and Conscientious Objection in the Workplace: An Evaluation of Strasbourg's Judgment in Eweida and others v United Kingdom', *Ecclesiastical Law Journal*, 15(2) (2013), pp. 191–203.

14. Peace, Timothy, 'Muslims and Electoral Politics in Britain: The Case of Respect', in Nielsen, Jorgen (ed.) *Muslims and Political Participation in Europe*, Edinburgh: Edinburgh University Press, 2013, pp. 426–54.

15. Peace, *op. cit.*

16. Pidd, Helen, 'George Galloway hails "Bradford spring" as Labour licks its wounds', *The Guardian*, http://www.theguardian.com/politics/2012/mar/30/george-galloway-bradford-spring-labour, last accessed 13 September 2013.

17. Ford, Robert, Goodwin, Matthew, and Cutts, David, 'Strategic Eurosceptics and Polite Xenophobes: Support for the UK Independence Party (UKIP) in the 2009 European Parliament Elections', *European Journal of Political Research*, 51(2) (2012), pp. 204–34.

18. Ford, Robert, and Goodwin, Matthew, *Revolt on the Right: Explaining Support for the Radical Right in Britain*. London: Routledge, 2014, p. 146.

19. http://www.ukip.org/page/ukip-history, last accessed 13 September 2013.

20. Membership of this group was often a source of embarrassment for the party. After the 2014 European elections the party helped to set up the Europe of Freedom and Direct Democracy group, which includes the Five Star Movement as the Italian representative rather than the Northern League.

21. Lynch, Philip, Whitaker, Richard, and Loomes, Gemma, 'The UK Independence

Party: Understanding a Niche Party's Strategy, Candidates and Supporters', *Parliamentary Affairs*, 65(4) (2012), pp. 733–57.

22. Ford and Goodwin, *op. cit.*

23. A 2013 election broadcast featured a number of ethnic minority actors and party leader Nigel Farage reassuring potential voters that 'we're not against people from other countries but common sense dictates that we should not have a total open door to the whole of Eastern Europe.' UKIP, 'Party Election Broadcast: Common Sense on Immigration', UKIP, http://www.youtube.com/watch?v=Zt9uDZF24x8, last accessed 11 September 2013.

24. Hasan, Mehdi, 'The Great UKIP Racism Debate—Debunking the Six Main Myths', *The Huffington Post*, http://www.huffingtonpost.co.uk/mehdi-hasan/ukip-racism-myths_b_5271986.html?utm_hp_ref=uk, last accessed 22 May 2014.

25. UKIP, *UKIP Manifesto April 2010: Empowering the People*. Newton Abbot: United Kingdom Independence Party, 2010.

26. Lynch *et al.*, *op. cit.*

27. Wainwright, Martin, 'Sheffield UKIP candidate sacked over Breivik comments', *The Guardian*, http://www.guardian.co.uk/uk/the-northerner/2012/may/02/ukip-steve-moxon-whistleblower-home-office-beverley-hughes, last accessed 13 September 2013.

28. Mason, Rowena, 'Ukip MEP says British Muslims should sign charter rejecting violence', *The Guardian*, http://www.theguardian.com/politics/2014/feb/04/ukip-mep-gerard-batten-muslims-sign-charter-rejecting-violence, last accessed 22 May 2014.

29. Mason, Rowena, 'Nigel Farage: UK mosques have been infiltrated by hate preachers', *The Guardian*, http://www.theguardian.com/politics/2015/feb/26/nigel-farage-uk-mosques-have-been-infiltrated-by-hate-preachers, last accessed 5 March 2015.

30. Neiyyar, Dil, 'UKIP holds meetings to win over British Asians', BBC News, http://www.bbc.co.uk/news/uk-politics-24175687, last accessed 22 May 2014.

31. Bashir defected to the Conservatives in January 2015.

32. 'Heino Vockrodt Is Yet Another Ukip Candidate In Outrageous Anti-Muslim Rant', *The Huffington Post UK*, http://www.huffingtonpost.co.uk/2014/05/15/heino-vockrodt-ukip-musli_n_5329311.html, last accessed 22 May 2014.

33. http://www.ukip.org/content/latest-news/2759-decision-over-show-of-faith-bizarre, last accessed 13 September 2013.

34. UKIP explains this policy with reference to the ECHR: 'We believe that, given the current nature of the European Court of Human Rights' attitude to such matters, there is a very strong likelihood that the Court at Strasbourg will [...] order the United Kingdom to introduce laws which will force Churches to marry gay people according to their rites, rituals and customs.' http://www.ukip.org/index.php/issues/policy-pages/same-sex-marriage

35. Mason, Rowena, 'Ukip urged to cut ties with Christian group over gay "depravity" comments', *The Guardian*, http://www.theguardian.com/politics/2015/feb/03/christian-soldiers-ukip-gay-depravity, last accessed 5 March 2015.

36. Copsey, Nigel, 'Changing Course or Changing Clothes? Reflections on the Ideological Evolution of the British National Party 1999–2006', *Patterns of Prejudice* 41(1) (2007), pp. 61–82.

37. BNP, *Democracy, Freedom, Culture and Identity: British National Party General Elections Manifesto 2010*, Welshpool: British National Party, 2010.

38. BNP, *Putting Local People First: Local Election Manifesto 2011*, Turriff: British National Party, 2011.

39. Traditionally its followers were more likely to be interested in Norse mythology than Christianity.

40. Goodwin, Matthew, *New British Fascism: Rise of the British National Party*, London: Routledge, 2011, p. 107.

41. Mammone, Andrea, and Peace, Timothy, 'Cross-National Ideology in Local Elections: The Case of Azione Sociale and the British National Party', in Mammone *et al.* (eds), *Mapping the Extreme Right in Contemporary Europe: From Local to Transnational*, London: Routledge, 2012.

42. In the 2010 general election campaign, Nick Griffin was standing in the constituency of Barking in East London. Anti-fascist campaigners tried to win the support of black Christians and so the BNP 'went through the local electoral register for African names and sent a letter to black Christians accusing Labour of undermining Christian values, of promoting ungodly lifestyles and encouraging the spread of Islam.' See Copsey, Nigel, 'Sustaining a Mortal Blow? The British National Party and the 2010 General and Local Elections', *Patterns of Prejudice*, 46(1) (2012) pp. 16–39.

43. BNP (2010), *op. cit.*

44. BNP member 'Peter' quoted in Goodwin, *op. cit.*, p. 146.

45. Betz and Meret, *op. cit.*, p. 320.

46. BNP, *Rebuilding British Democracy: British National Party General Election 2005 Manifesto*, Welshpool: British National Party, 2005.

47. Wood, Chris, and Finlay, Mick, 'British National Party Representations of Muslims in the Month after the London Bombings: Homogeneity, Threat, and the Conspiracy Tradition', *British Journal of Social Psychology*, 47(4) (2008), pp. 707–26.

48. Mammone and Peace, *op. cit.*

49. BNP 2010, *op. cit.*

50. Court cases involving men of Pakistani origin convicted of sex offences against children have been seized upon by the BNP and other groups like the English Defence League (EDL) and framed as a Muslim problem. The BNP has been campaigning on this issue since at least 2004 when Nick Griffin was filmed under-

cover making a speech about it in Keighley, where he later stood as a candidate in the 2005 general election.

51. Such a ban would naturally also affect the Jewish community, although anti-Semitism now plays a minor role in the BNP's appeals to voters, with occasional references to the 'Zionist lobby'. When its founder John Tyndall led the BNP, it was known for its rabid anti-Semitism and obsession with Jewish conspiracies. Nick Griffin himself co-authored a publication on such conspiracies, entitled *Who are the Mind-Benders?* (see Copsey, Nigel, *Contemporary British Fascism: The British National Party and the Quest for Legitimacy*, Basingstoke: Palgrave Macmillan, 2004). Yet by 2004 the BNP was putting forward its first Jewish candidate and later began to campaign in predominantly Jewish areas to exploit potential enmity with Muslims. See Taylor, Matthew, 'BNP seeks to bury antisemitism and gain Jewish votes in Islamophobic campaign', *The Guardian*, http://www.guardian.co.uk/politics/2008/apr/10/thefarright.race, last accessed 13 September 2013.

52. Goodwin, *op. cit.*, p. 87.

53. Field, Clive, 'Islamophobia in Contemporary Britain: The Evidence of the Opinion Polls, 1988–2006', *Islam and Christian-Muslim Relations*, 18(4) (2007), pp. 447–77.

54. These two regions were revealed to have the highest numbers of BNP members, and membership has been shown to be correlated with the presence of South Asian Muslims, while the presence of non-Muslim South Asians has no significant effect (see Goodwin, *op. cit.*, p. 128). This highlights the specifically anti-Muslim nature of BNP support. The BNP has tailored its discourse to suit this mood while remaining a racial nationalist party opposed to all minorities and dedicated to the preservation of a white Britain.

55. BNP 2010, *op. cit.*

56. Copsey (2012), *op. cit.*, p. 17.

57. Brown, Jonathan, 'Far-right activists hand out Bibles outside mosques in Bradford', *The Independent*, http://www.independent.co.uk/news/uk/home-news/farright-activists-hand-out-bibles-outside-mosques-in-bradford-9352271.html, last accessed 22 May 2014.

58. Goodwin, *op. cit.*

59. BBC, 'Racist voters "spitting at God"', BBC News, 2004, http://news.bbc.co.uk/1/hi/england/west_midlands/3756201.stm, last accessed 13 September 2013.

60. Ekklesia, 'BNP hits back against churches', *Ekklesia*, 2004, http://www.ekklesia.co.uk/content/news_syndication/article_040428bnpchc.shtml, last accessed 13 September 2013.

61. Woodbridge, Steven, 'Christian Credentials? The Role of Religion in British National Party Ideology', *Journal for the Study of Radicalism*, 4(1) (2010), p. 26.

62. Its attempts to appeal to Christian voters became increasingly desperate. In 2007, it was reported that the party was attempting to build links with anti-abortion

activists in order to appeal to Catholics in Northern Ireland. However, this jarred with the traditional image of the party supporting the Unionist cause. Nick Griffin claimed that he wanted to reach across the sectarian divide in Northern Ireland and Scotland and that the BNP was no longer an 'Orange party'. See McDonald, Henry, 'BNP seeks anti-abortion Catholic votes', *The Observer*, http://www.guardian.co.uk/uk/2007/mar/04/thefarright.otherparties, last accessed 13 September 2013.

63. Woodbridge, *op. cit.*, p. 45.
64. This list provided details of BNP members including their names, phone numbers and home addresses. Five names appeared with the title of 'Reverend', although only one of these persons could be found in *Crockford's Clerical Directory*.
65. Butt, Riazat, 'Church of England votes to ban BNP clergy', *The Guardian*, http://www.guardian.co.uk/politics/2009/feb/10/general-synod-bnp-vote, last accessed 13 September 2013.
66. The full statement and others dealing with the BNP can be viewed on the Church of England website: http://www.churchofengland.org/our-views/home-and-community-affairs/community-urban-affairs/countering-racist-politics/what-has-the-church-said.aspx, last accessed 12 September 2013.
67. BBC, 'BNP rejects church boycott call', *BBC News*, 2009, http://news.bbc.co.uk/1/hi/uk_politics/8066000.stm, last accessed 13 September 2013.
68. Ford *et al.*, *op. cit.*

8. DEFENDERS OF THE CROSS: POPULIST POLITICS AND RELIGION IN POST-COMMUNIST POLAND

1. In line with the discussion in the first chapter by Marzouki and McDonnell, I employ a non-normative definition of populism as a 'thin ideology' which is ideological in that it expresses a distinct and internally coherent 'map' of the political, but 'thin' in its focus on broad normative principles and ontological matters rather than the detail of policy. See Stanley, Ben, 'The Thin Ideology of Populism', *Journal of Political Ideologies* 13(1) (2008), p. 102, for a full exposition of this definition.
2. Grabowska, Mirosława, *Podział Postkomunistyczny: Społeczne Podstawy Polityki w Polsce Po 1989 Roku*, Warsaw: Scholar, 2004.
3. Millard, Frances, 'Poland's Politics and the Travails of Transition After 2001: The 2005 Elections', *Europe-Asia Studies* 58(7) (2006), p. 1007.
4. Wojtas, Kinga, 'Poland', in Havlík, Vlastimil (ed.), *Populist Political Parties in East-Central Europe*, Brno: MUNI Press, 2012, p. 169.
5. Wojtas, *op. cit.*, pp. 170–1, argues that LPR should not be defined as a populist party because its profile is clearly radical right in character. However, as the majority of its practical manifestations demonstrate, populism is primarily combinatorial in character rather than a 'standalone' ideology. LPR's ideological profile fulfils each of the criteria specified by Mudde's 'maximum definition' of a populist

radical right party: nativism, authoritarianism and populism (Mudde, Cas, *Populist Radical Right Parties in Europe*, Cambridge: Cambridge University Press, 2007, p. 22).

6. Dmowski, Roman, *Kościół, Naród i Państwo*, Wrocław: Wydawnictwo NORTOM, 2000, pp. 26–7.

7. Zubrzycki, Genevieve, *The Crosses of Auschwitz: Nationalism and Religion in Post-Communist Poland*, new edition, Chicago: University of Chicago Press, 2006, pp. 57–9.

8. Gowin, Jarosław, *Kościół Po Komunizmie*, Kraków: Wydawnictwo Znak, 1995, p. 73.

9. See Senator Alicja Grześkowiak's remarks on the first point of order, 24 February 1997, as given by the official stenographic transcript of the Sejm. Sejm Rzeczypospolitej Polskiej, 'Sprawozdanie Stenograficzne z Posiedzeń Sejmu RP II Kadencji', 1997, http://orka2.sejm.gov.pl/Debata2.nsf, accessed 3 August 2012.

10. Gowin, *op. cit.*, pp. 242–3.

11. *Ibid*, pp. 250–3.

12. Burdziej, Stanisław, 'Radio Maryja a społeczeństwo obywatelskie', *Znak*, issue 640, 2008, pp. 17–28.

13. Krzemiński, Ireneusz, 'Radio Maryja i Jego Przekaz. Analiza Treści Wybranych Audycji "Rozmowy Niedokończone" z Sierpnia 2007 Roku', in *Czego nas uczy Radio Maryja?*, Warsaw: Wydawnictwo Akademickie i Profesjonalne, 2009, pp. 119, 121–2, 126–8.

14. Liga Polskich Rodzin, 'Skrót Programu Gospodarczego', in Słodkowska, Inka and Dolbakowska, Magdalena (eds), *Wybory 2005: Partie i ich programy*, Warsaw, 2006, p. 66.

15. Liga Polskich Rodzin *op. cit.*, p. 67.

16. *Ibid*, pp. 68–76.

17. Gowin, *op. cit.*, pp. 250–3.

18. Wroński, Paweł, 'Dmowskiego Do Ligi Bym Nie Przyjął' (interview with Roman Giertych), *Gazeta.pl*, http://serwisy.gazeta.pl/wyborcza/1,68586,3484547.html, accessed 12 September 2013.

19. Jędrzejczak, Aleksandra, 'Młodzież Wszech Stanowisk', *Przekrój* 26 (2006).

20. See Pankowski, Rafal, *The Populist Radical Right in Poland: The Patriots*, Oxford: Routledge, 2011, pp. 116–9, for an extensive discussion of this group's activities.

21. Cited in Pankowski, *op. cit.*, p. 121.

22. Ryba, Mieczysław, 'O Przełom Cywilizacyjny w Europie i w Polsce', in Jacyna-Onyszkiewicz, Zbigniew (ed.), *Ku odnowie Polski*, Warsaw: Liga Polskich Rodzin, 2005, p. 85.

23. Polak, Bogusław, 'W Sprawie Wychowania Patriotycznego Młodych Polaków i Wyzwań Dla Historyków. Kilka Uwag i Propozycji', in Jacyna-Onyszkiewicz, *op. cit.*, p. 171.

24. Hajdukiewicz, Lech, 'Uwarunkowania Demograficzno-społeczne Rozwoju Polski', in Jacyna-Onyszkiewicz, *op. cit.*, p. 31.

25. Liga Polskich Rodzin, *op. cit.*, p. 68.

26. Hajdukiewicz, *op. cit.*, p. 31.

27. Zając, Marek, 'Między Zdradą Judasza i Drzemką w Ogrójcu', *Tygodnik Powszechny*, 4 (2005).

28. Pankowski, *op. cit.*, p. 124.

29. Giertych, Roman, 'List Romana Giertycha Do Przełożonego Ojca Rydzyka', *Gazeta.pl*, http://wyborcza.pl/1,75478,13186919,List_Romana_Giertycha_do_przelozonego_ojca_Rydzyka.html, accessed 10 September 2013.

30. Cited in Załuska, Wojciech, 'Dlaczego Jarosław Kaczyński Zaprzyjaźnił Się z Ojcem Rydzykiem?', *Gazeta Wyborcza*, 2005.

31. See Szczerbiak, Aleks, '"Social Poland" Defeats "Liberal Poland"? The September–October 2005 Polish Parliamentary and Presidential Elections', *Journal of Communist Studies and Transition Politics* 23(2) (2007), pp. 203–32, for a comprehensive account of these elections and their consequences for the party system.

32. Prawo i Sprawiedliwość, *Polska Katolicka w Chrześćijańskiej Europie*, Warsaw: Komitet Wyborczy Prawo i Sprawiedliwość, 2005, pp. 7–9.

33. Wiśniewska, Katarzyna, 'Lech Kaczyński Wysłał Proboszczom List', *Gazeta Wyborcza*, 2005.

34. Kucharczak, Przemysław, and Stopka, Artur, 'Na Pewno Jestem Patriotą' (interview with Lech Kaczyński), *Gość Niedzielny*, 40, 2005.

35. Paradowska, Janina, 'Tercet Egzotyczny', *Polityka* 19 (2006), p. 2553.

36. Prawo i Sprawiedliwość, Samoobrona Rzeczypospolitej Polskiej, and Narodowe Koło Parlamentarne, *Koalicyjna Deklaracja Programowa 'Solidarne Państwo' z 27 Kwietnia 2006 R., Załącznik Nr.1, Cele i Zadania Rządu Koalicyjnego w Latach 2006–2009*, 2006, http://www.pis.org.pl/download.php?g=mmedia&f=zalacznik_nr_1.pdf, accessed 13 September 2013.

37. Jarosław Kaczyński, cited in (Sejm stenographic transcript, term 5, session 10, day 3, 12 May 2006) Sejm Rzeczypospolitej Polskiej, 'Sprawozdanie Stenograficzne z Posiedzeń Sejmu RP V Kadencji', 2007, http://orka2.sejm.gov.pl/Debata5.nsf, accessed 4 January 2012.

38. Nijakowski, Lech, *Polska Polityki Pamięci: Esej Socjologiczny*, Warsaw: Wydawnictwo Akademickie i Profesjonalne, 2008, p. 198.

39. *Gazeta.pl*, 'Kaczyński: Ich Zwycięstwo Będzie Nowym 13 Grudnia 1981 Roku', http://wiadomosci.gazeta.pl/wiadomosci/1,114873,4511730.html, accessed 1 December 2012.

40. Janicki, Mariusz, and Władyka, Wiesław, *Cień Wielkiego Brata: Ideologia i Praktyka IV RP*, Warsaw: POLITYKA Spółdzielnia Pracy, 2007, p. 134.

41. Mamoń, Marek, 'Tu Jest Polska Kaczyńskiego', *Gazeta Wyborcza*, 2007.

42. Karnowski, Michał, and Zaremba, Piotr, *O Dwóch Takich... Alfabet Braci Kaczyńskich*, Kraków: Wydawnictwo M, 2006, p. 286.

43. *Radiomaryja.pl*, 'O. Rydzyk o PiS-ie i Szambie' (transcript of broadcast by Radio Maryja, 8 March 2007), http://www.radiomaryja.pl.eu.org/nagrania/20070308-rydzyk/20070308-rydzyk.html, accessed 4 April 2013.

44. *Gazeta.pl.*, 'Co Powiedział O. Rydzyk?—Zapis Nagrań', http://wiadomosci.gazeta.pl/kraj/1,34308,4300292.html, accessed 1 December 2012.

45. Hołub, Jacek, 'Radio Maryja Mobilizuje: "Bojówki Lewicowe Chcą Zabrać Krzyż"', *Gazeta Wyborcza*, 2010, http://wyborcza.pl/Polityka/1,103835,8231658,Radio_Maryja_mobilizuje__Bojowki_lewicowe_chca_zabrac.html, accessed 13 February 2012.

46. See Zubrzycki, *op. cit.* for a comprehensive analysis of this controversy and its social and historical context.

47. *Gazeta.pl*, '"Ustawa o in vitro to zwycięstwo wolności", "prezydent po stronie ludzi". A prawica dalej swoje: "Komorowski za cywilizacją śmierci"', 2015, http://wyborcza.pl/1,75478,18403640,komentarze-po-podpisaniu-ustawy-o-in-vitro-prezydent-wybral.html, accessed 9 August 2015.

48. Grochal, Renata, 'Ciemnogród w polskiej polityce trzyma się mocno', *wyborcza.pl*, 2015, http://wyborcza.pl/politykaekstra/1,147093,18359428,ciemnogrod-w-polskiej-polityce-trzyma-sie-mocno.html, accessed 9 August 2015.

49. Jarosław Gowin, cited in *wPolityce.pl*, 'Gowin w Radiu Kraków o imigrantach: Przyjmijmy chrześcijan, ale nie muzułmanów. "Wystarczą setki tysięcy niezasymilowanych, żeby rozosić zarazę terroryzmu"', 2015, http://wpolityce.pl/polityka/259191-gowin-w-radiu-krakow-o-imigrantach-przyjmijmy-chrzescijan-ale-nie-muzulmanow-wystarcza-setki-tysiecy-niezasymilowanych-zeby-roznosic-zaraze-terroryzmu, accessed 10 August 2015.

50. See CBOS, *Wiara i Religijność Polaków Dwadzieścia Lat Po Rozpoczęciu Przemian Ustrojowych*, Warsaw: Centrum Badania Opinii Społecznej, 2009, p. 5, Fig. 3.

51. Instytut Statystyki Kościoła Katolickiego, 'Dominicantes 1992–2010—Wykresy', http://www.iskk.pl/kosciolnaswiecie/75-dominicantes.html, accessed 11 December 2012.

52. Czapiński, Janusz, 'Stosunek Do Przemian Systemowych i Ocena Ich Wpływu Na Życie Badanych', in Czapiński, Janusz, and Panek, Janusz (eds), *Diagnoza Społeczna 2005: Warunki i jakość życia Polaków*, Warsaw: Wyższa Szkoła Finansów i Zarządzania w Warszawie, 2006, p. 184.

53. CBOS, *Religijność Polaków Na Przełomie Wieków*. Warsaw: Centrum Badania Opinii Społecznej, 2001, pp. 11–12.

54. CBOS, *Dwadzieścia Lat Radia Maryja*, Warsaw: Centrum Badania Opinii Społecznej, 2011, pp. 3–5.

55. CBOS 2011, *op. cit.*; CBOS, *Słuchacze Radia Maryja*, Warsaw: Centrum Badania Opinii Społecznej, 2008.

56. CBOS 2008, *op. cit.*, p. 6; CBOS 2011, *op. cit.*, p. 8.

57. In 2001—the first election in which the political influence of the movement came to wider attention—only 42 per cent of listeners voted for LPR. After Rydzyk's switching of horses, in 2005 PiS received 40 per cent, and in 2007, 62 per cent. However, in both 2001 and 2005 the majority of listeners voted for other parties, including the liberal enemy (8 per cent for UW in 2001; 16 per cent for PO in 2005), and in 2007 a full 20 per cent voted for PO (CBOS 2008, *op. cit.*, pp. 6–7). In the 2011 survey, 57 per cent of Radio Maryja listeners declared they had voted for Jarosław Kaczyński (compared with only 22 per cent of non-listeners), while 35 per cent declared they had voted for Bronisław Komorowski (compared with 70 per cent of non-listeners). After the 2011 parliamentary elections, 70 per cent of listeners declared that they had voted for PiS (compared with 20 per cent of non-listeners), while 14 per cent declared that they had voted for PO (compared with 46 per cent of non-listeners). (CBOS 2011, *op. cit.*, p. 9.)

58. *Ibid.*, p. 2.

59. Nicolet, Sarah, and Tresch, Anke, 'Changing Religiosity, Changing Politics? The Influence of "Belonging" and "Believing" on Political Attitudes in Switzerland', *Politics and Religion* 2(1) (2009), p. 81.

60. Gwiazda, Anna, 'Poland's Quasi-Institutionalized Party System: The Importance of Elites and Institutions', *Perspectives on European Politics and Society* 10(3) (2009), pp. 370–1.

61. Millard, Frances, 'Poland: Parties Without a Party System, 1991–2008', *Politics & Policy* 37(4) (2009), p. 795.

9. 'THE GOD OF HUNGARIANS': RELIGION AND RIGHT-WING POPULISM IN HUNGARY

1. See also Enyedi, Zsolt, 'Clerical and Religious Polarization in Hungary', in Broughton, David, and Ten Napel, Hans-Martin (eds), *Religion and Mass Electoral Behaviour*, London: Routledge 2000, pp. 157–76; Koesel, Karrie J., *Religion and Authoritarianism: Cooperation, Conflict, and the Consequences*, Cambridge: Cambridge University Press, 2014; Grzymala-Busse, Anna, *Nations under God: How Churches Use Moral Authority to Influence Policy*, Princeton: Princeton University Press, 2015.

2. See Chapter 5.

3. Lipset, Seymour M., and Rokkan, Stein (eds), *Party Systems and Voters' Alignments*, New York: The Free Press 1967.

4. Since the historic Hungarian Christian Democratic People's Party (KDNP—Kereszténydemokrata Néppárt) has practically became an inseparable part of Fidesz in the past decade, its ideology will not be discussed separately, but as part of Fidesz's public discourse on religion and religious values.

5. Bozóki, András (ed.), *The Roundtable Talks of 1989. The Genesis of Hungarian Democracy*, Budapest/New York: Central European University Press, 2002.

6. 'Two Decades after the Wall's Fall: End of Communism Cheered but Now with More Reservations'. *The Pew Global Attitudes Project*. Pew Research Center, 2 November 2009. (http://www.pewglobal.org/files/pdf/267.pdf)

7. *Ibid.*

8. Simon, Zoltán, 'Orbán Says He Seeks to End Liberal Democracy in Hungary', *Bloomberg*, 28 July 2014.

9. See also Bozóki, András, 'Occupy the State: The Orbán Regime in Hungary', *Debatte: Journal of Contemporary Central and Eastern Europe* 19(3) (2011), pp. 649–63; Korkut, Umut, 'A Conservative Putsch at EU's Periphery: Crisis of Democracy in Hungary', paper presented at the annual convention of Europeanists of the British Political Science Association, Gothenburg, 6 November 2014.

10. Kis, János, 'From the 1989 Constitution to the 2011 Fundamental Law', in Tóth, Gábor Attila (ed.), *Constitution for a Disunited Nation. On Hungary's 2011 Fundamental Law*, Budapest/New York: Central European University Press, 2012.

11. Chudziková, Alena, Kasprowicz, Dominika, and Vit, Michal, 'National Identities in Central-Eastern Europe', 2013, http://ceeidentity.eu/news/national-0.

12. Horthy, Miklós, governor of Hungary between 1919 and 1944, maintained a multi-party but authoritarian regime that was characterised by a 'Christian-nationalist' ideology. See Ungyáry, Krisztián, *A Horthy-rendszer mérlege* (An Evaluation of the Horthy Regime), Pécs/Budapest: Jelenkor-OSZK, 2012.

13. After the 2006 elections, both FKGP and MIÉP disappeared from the Hungarian political scene.

14. Oltay, Edith, *Fidesz and the Reinvention of the Hungarian Center-Right*, Budapest: Századvég, 2012.

15. Jobbik, 'Short Summary about Jobbik', 3 May 2010, http://jobbik.com/short_summary_about_jobbik, accessed 19 April 2016.

16. *Ibid.*

17. Jobbik ran together with MIÉP at the 2006 elections, but received less than 1 per cent of votes.

18. Jobbik, *op. cit.*

19. Jobbik, 'Manifesto of Jobbik', 24 October 2003, http://jobbik.com/manifesto_0.

20. *The Economist*, 'Right on Down: The Far Right in Eastern Europe', issue 8657, 14 November 2009.

21. See also Majtényi, László, and Szabó, Máté Dániel (eds.), *Az elveszett alkotmány*. (The Lost Constitution), Budapest: L'Harmattan/Eötvös Károly Intézet, 2011.

22. Fundamental Law of Hungary, 25 April 2011.

23. See also Bozóki, András, 'Broken Democracy, Predatory State, and Nationalist Populism' in Krasztev, Péter, and Van Til, Jon (eds), *The Hungarian Patient: Social Opposition to an Illiberal Democracy*, Budapest/New York: Central European University Press, 2015, pp. 3–36.

24. Orbán, Viktor, 'Minden magyar a turulba születik' (All Hungarians are born into the Turul bird), *Népszabadság*, 29 September 2012.

25. Orbán, Viktor, 'Magyarország keresztény lesz vagy nem lesz' (Hungary will be either a Christian country or will cease to exist), *Index.hu*, 18 May 2015, quoted by Balogh, Éva, 'Viktor Orbán and the Christian-National Idea', *Hungarianspectrum. org*, 22 September 2015.

26. For instance, Márton Gyöngyösi, the foreign affairs spokesman for Jobbik and its deputy leader in Parliament, criticised the pro-Israel position of the Hungarian government. He called on the government to 'tally-up' the number of influential Jews in Hungary, especially in Parliament and in the government. Jews, he said, represented 'a national security risk', which he linked to the conflict in the Middle East. Later he attempted to justify his comments on the party's website, explaining that Hungary's position in support of Israel was determined by the number of Jews in the country and that he was only targeting those with 'dual nationality'. See CEJI, 'Anti-Semitism in Hungary: Jobbik in Parliament', http://www.ceji.org/ anti-semitism-in-hungary-jobbik-in-parliament. According to the Medián Public Opinion Research Institute in March 2015, two-thirds of Jobbik voters are anti-Semites. Between 2009 and 2014 the percentage of those citizens who rejected Jews on emotional grounds grew from 10 per cent to 28 per cent. See www.origo. hu/itthon/20150331-a-fovarosban-nagyobb-merteku-az-antiszemitizmus-mint-videken.html, accessed 19 April 2016.

27. Pirro, Andrea L.P., *The Populist Radical Right in Central and Eastern Europe*, London: Routledge, 2015, pp. 67–86.

28. *Ibid.*, p. 71.

29. Thorpe, Nick, 'What happened when an anti-Semite found he was Jewish?' BBC. com News Magazine, 4 May 2015.

30. Vona, Gábor, 'Turanism instead of Euro-Atlantic Alliance', 23 January 2012, http://www.jobbik.com/jobbik_news/europe/3198.html.

31. Akcali, Emel, and Korkut, Umut, 'Geographical Metanarratives in East-Central Europe: Neo-Turanism in Hungary', Eurasian Geography and Economics 53(5) (2012), p. 600.

32. *Ibid.*

33. See also Cueva, Sarah A., 'Attack of the Radical Right: Incomplete Democratic Consolidation in Hungary and the Fidesz-Jobbik Convergence', manuscript, 2015; Dobszay, János, 'Egyet jobbra, kettőt jobbra' (One Step to the Right, Two Steps to the Right), *HVG*, 9 May 2015, pp. 6–9; Mudde, Cas, 'Is Hungary Run by the Radical Right?', *The Washington Post*, 10 August 2015.

34. Fidesz kept its two-thirds parliamentary majority at the 2014 general elections, labelled as free and unfair, but lost it in February 2015 as a result of a local by-election.

35. József Torgyán, an old-school populist politician, served as minister for agricul-

ture and the development of the countryside in the first Orbán cabinet between 1998 and 2001.

36. Bartlett, J., Birdwell, J., Krekó, P., Benfield, J., and Győri, G., *Populism in Europe: Hungary*. London: Demos Publishing, 2012, www.demos.co.uk/files/Demos_Hungary_Book_Web-1.pdf?1327923915, accessed 19 April 2016.

37. See Ungváry, Krisztián, A Horthy-rendszer mérlege (Evaluation of the Horthy regime), Budapest: Pécs—Budapest: Jelenkor & OSZK, 2012.

38. See Chapter 5.

39. Non-religious students can choose to study ethics instead.

40. 'The Constitutional Court in 2013 and the European Court of Human Rights in 2014 considered the deprivation of the status as a Church and recognition by Parliament as a rights violation, while the existence of two kinds of status for religious groups was considered discriminatory.' See Eötvös Károly Policy Institute, Hungarian Helsinki Committee, Hungarian Civil Liberties Union, Mérték Médiaelemző Műhely, 'Disrespect for European Values in Hungary 2010–2014. Rule of Law-Democracy-Pluralism-Fundamental Rights', Budapest, November 2014, http://helsinki.hu/en/disrespect-for-european-values-in-hungary-2010-2014, accessed 19 April 2016.

41. See also Novak, Benjamin, 'Lajos Simicska: "Orbán is a f*cker"', *The Budapest Beacon*, 6 February 2015.

42. Novak, Benjamin, 'Archbishop claims laws prevent Catholic Church from helping asylum seekers', *The Budapest Beacon*, 4 September 2015.

43. *Ibid*. As the Hungarian Helsinki Committee pointed out, state laws, in fact, did not preclude giving shelter to registered refugees and this did not constitute people trafficking.

44. Some smaller Christian Churches acted differently. The evangelical Faith Church in its media outlets conducted a strongly religion-based anti-immigration campaign. See Zolnay, János, 'A Hit Gyülekezetének Dzsihádja' (The Jihad of Faith Church), *Beszélő*, 19 October 2015. Other small Christian Churches helped the refugees.

45. Balogh, *op. cit.*

46. 'Prime Minister Viktor Orbán's Speech in the European Parliament', website of the Hungarian Government, http://www.kormany.hu/en/the-prime-minister/the-prime-minister-s-speeches/prime-minister-viktor-orban-s-speech-in-the-european-parliament, last accessed 20 May 2015.

47. The summer camp is located in Transylvania and it is an important event for Hungarian youth living in Romania.

48. Mudde, *op. cit.*

49. See also Mudde, Cas, 'The Hungarian PM made a "rivers of blood" speech ... and no one cares', *The Guardian*, 30 July 2015.

50. Boross, Péter, 'Americans Are Intellectually Unsuitable to Lead the World', *Budapest*

Sentinel, 20 August 2015. Boross wasted no time in mentioning the political role of Iran and Russia in this issue.

51. *Ibid.*

52. Some authors claim that the official idea of Christian nationalism, reminiscent of the interwar era, cannot simply be categorised as a part of non-ideological 'populism', but is increasingly close to a transmuted form of fascism and national socialism in Hungary. See also Ungváry, Rudolf, *A láthatatlan valóság: A fasisztoid mutáció a mai Magyarországon* (The Invisible Reality: Transmuted Fascism in Today's Hungary), Bratislava: Kalligram, 2013; Balogh, *op. cit.*

53. Krekó, Péter and Mayer, Gregor, 'Transforming Hungary—Together? An Analysis of the FIDESZ-JOBBIK Relationship', in Minkenberg, Michael (ed.), *Transforming the Transformation?: The East European Radical Right in the Political Process*, London: Routledge, 2015, pp. 183–205.

54. On Hungarian populism in more detail, see Enyedi, Zsolt, 'Plebeians, Citoyens and Aristocrats or Where Is the Bottom of the Bottom-up? The Case of Hungary', in Kriesi, Hanspeter, and Pappas, Takis (eds), *European Populism in the Shadow of the Great Recession*, Colchester: ECPR Press, 2015, pp. 242–57; Bozóki, András, 'The Illusion of Inclusion: Configurations of Populism in Hungary', in Kopecek, Michal, and Wcislik, Piotr (eds), *Thinking Through Transition: Liberal Democracy, Authoritarian Pasts, and Intellectual History in East Central Europe after 1989*, Budapest/New York: Central European University Press, 2015, pp. 275–311.

10. THE TEA PARTY AND RELIGION: BETWEEN RELIGIOUS AND HISTORICAL FUNDAMENTALISM

1. Abramowitz, Alan, 'Partisan Polarization and the Rise of the Tea Party Movement', paper presented at the 2011 American Political Science Association Conference.

2. The TP chose its name as a reference to the Boston Tea Party, a political revolt that took place in 1773 during which protesters destroyed supplies of tea in order to show their opposition to the taxation on tea imposed by the British Parliament.

3. The Moral Majority, a political organisation associated with the Christian right, was created in 1979 and played an influential role during the presidency of Ronald Reagan.

4. See Skocpol, Theda, and Williamson, Vanessa, *The Tea Party and the Remaking of American Conservatism*, New York: Oxford University Press, 2012.

5. For example, the Olin, Koch, and Scaife foundations. The John Olin Foundation, created in 1953 by John M. Olin, president of Olin Industries (manufacturing chemicals and munitions), supported conservative thinkers and activists through grants. The Charles Koch Foundation and the David Koch Charitable Foundation were founded by the two sons of Fred Koch, head of Koch Industries (involved in oil, gas and chemical industries). Through various grants, they support cultural, scientific and educational initiatives, informed by a libertarian worldview. The Scaife

Foundation belongs to the millionaire Richard Mellon Scaife (head of Mellon Industrial). It supports conservative think tanks such as the Heritage Foundation and the American Enterprise Institute.

6. Ron Paul was formerly a Republican representative for Texas in the House of Representatives. He was also the Libertarian Party candidate for the presidential elections in 1988, 2008 and 2012.

7. Kate Zernike shows that, even though the 'Santelli rant' has been viewed as the Tea Party's moment of creation, the first TP event actually took place three days earlier in Seattle, where Keli Carender, a twenty-nine-year-old woman of Mexican descent, organised a protest against Obama's stimulus plan. Santelli then 'gave the discontent a name and a bit of imagery'. See Zernike, Kate, *Boiling Mad: Inside Tea Party America*, New York: Time Books, 2010, p. 15.

8. Barone, Michael, 'The Transformative Power of Rick Santelli's Rant', http://www.creators.com/conservative/michael-barone/the-transformative-power-of-rick-santelli-s-rant.html, accessed 24 June 2014.

9. Burghart, Devin, and Zeskin, Leonhard, *Tea Party Nationalism: A Critical Examination of the Tea Party Movement and the Size, Scope, and Focus of Its National Factions*, Kansas City: Institute for Research and Education on Human Rights, 2010.

10. Tea Party Nation had 31,402 online members in August 2010, and differs from the Tea Party Express, which is not a membership organisation. Tea Party Patriots is the most 'grassroots' organisation, with about 2,200 local chapters, but has the smaller budget. FreedomWorks focuses mainly on its anti-tax agenda. By contrast, the 1776 Tea Party has close ties with the Minuteman project and the anti-immigrant movement. It describes itself as a 'Christian political organisation'.

11. Formisano, Ronald, *The Tea Party: A Brief History*, Baltimore: Johns Hopkins University Press, 2012; Carter, Jimmy, '1970s saw a Tea Party-like wave', *USA Today*, 29 September 2010.

12. Huret, Romain, 'Le mouvement Tea Party, une illusion', *Hérodote*, La Découverte, Paris, 2013/2, no. 149, pp. 105–14.

13. Kazin, Michael, *The Populist Persuasion: An American History*, New York: Cornell University Press, 1998.

14. Hofstadter, Richard, *The Paranoid Style in American Politics*, New York: Vintage, 1965.

15. The Pew Research Center for the People & the Press and the Pew Forum on Religion & Public Life, *The Tea Party and Religion*, 13 February 2011, http://www.pewforum.org/2011/02/23/tea-party-and-religion/, accessed 24 June 2014.

16. Montgomery, Peter, 'The Tea Party and the Religious Right Movements: Frenemies with Benefits', in Rosenthal, Lawrence, and Trost, Christine (eds), *Steep: The Precipitous Rise of the Tea Party*, Berkeley: University of California Press, 2012, pp. 242–75.

17. 'Pack's association with Robb's Klan in 1996 should not be read as an indication that the entire Tea Party movement is like the KKK. It does indicate, however, that a certain amount of overlap exists between the upfront racism of the Klan and the "we are not racists" denials of the Tea Parties.' Burghart, Devin, 'Karen Pack—Tea Party News and Analysis', Institute For Research and Education on Human Rights, http://www.irehr.org/news/latest-news/item/349-karen-pack, accessed 24 June 2014.

18. Pack, Karen, 'An Ardent Plea', *Tea Party 911*, http://www.teaparty911.com/articles/karen_pack_ardent_plea.htm, accessed 24 June 2014.

19. STAND, 'Mission', Staying True to America's National Destiny, http://www.standamerica.us/, accessed 1 July 2010.

20. See Wing, Nick, 'Sarah Palin: American Law Should Be "Based On The God Of The Bible And The Ten Commandments"', *Huffington Post*, http://www.huffingtonpost.com/2010/05/10/sarah-palin-american-law_n_569922.html, accessed 24 June 2014.

21. Gettys, Travis, 'Sarah Palin: "Angry atheists" are trying to "abort Christ from Christmas"', *TheRawStory*, http://www.rawstory.com/rs/2013/12/06/sarah-palin-angry-atheists-are-trying-to-abort-christ-from-christmas/, accessed 24 June 2014.

22. Bobic, Igor, 'Sarah Palin "Surprised" By Pope Francis' "Liberal" Sounding Statements', *Talking Points Memo*, www.talkingpointsmemo.com/livewire/sarah-palin-surprised-by-pope-francis-liberal-sounding-statements, accessed 24 June 2014.

23. Zaimov, Stoyan, 'Tea Party Advocate, Rush Limbaugh Criticize Pope Francis, Argue "Jesus Is a Capitalist"', *Christian Post*, http://www.christianpost.com/news/tea-party-advocate-rush-limbaugh-criticize-pope-francis-argue-jesus-is-a-capitalist-109958/, accessed 24 June 2014.

24. Ingersoll, Julie, 'Mobilizing Evangelicals: Christian Reconstructionism and the Roots of the Religious Right', in Brint, Steven, and Reith Schroedel, Jean, *Evangelicals and Democracy in America: Religion and Politics*, New York: Russell Sage Foundation, 2009, p. 180.

25. Worthen, Molly, 'The Chalcedon Problem: Rousas John Rushdoony and the Origins of Christian Reconstructionism', *Church History* 77(2), 2008.

26. Montgomery, Peter, 'Tea Party Senators Kick Off Ralph Reed's Faith & Freedom Conference', *Right Wing Watch*, http://www.rightwingwatch.org/content/tea-party-senators-kick-ralph-reed-s-faith-freedom-conference, accessed 24 June 2014.

27. Cited in http://www.religiondispatches.org/dispatches/sarahposner/3322/the_non-existent_tea_party_religious_right_god_gap/, accessed 24 June 2014.

28. In July 2010, Mark Williams and the Tea Party Express were expelled from the National Tea Party Federation in response to Williams' inflammatory comments about race, the NAACP and Barack Obama.

29. Williams, Mark, *Taking Back America One Tea Party at a Time*, MarkTalk.com, 2010, p. 80.

30. United States Department of Justice, *Report on the Tenth Anniversary of the Religious Land Use and Institutionalized Persons Act*, 22 September 2010; Ali, Wajahat *et al.*, *Fear, Inc.: The Roots of the Islamophobia Network in America*, Washington, DC: Muslim Public Affairs Council, 2011.

31. Nelson, Leah, 'Tea Party Patriots Wallow in Muslim-Bashing Gutter with Geller', Southern Poverty Law Center, http://www.splcenter.org/blog/2011/06/15/tea-party-patriots-wallow-in-muslim-bashing-gutter-with-geller/, accessed 24 June 2014.

32. *NewsCorpsWatch*, 'Memo to media: Pamela Geller does not belong on national television', *NewsCorpsWatch.org*, http://newscorpwatch.org/research/201007 140035, accessed 24 June 2014.

33. On this point, see Parker, Christopher S., and Barreto, Matt A., 'The Tea Party and Obamaphobia—Is the Hostility Real or Imagined?', in Parker, Christopher S., and Barreto, Matt A., *Change They Can't Believe In: The Tea Party and Reactionary Politics in America*, Princeton: Princeton University Press, 2013, pp. 190–217.

34. According to a Pew survey, 18 per cent of Americans thought that Obama was a Muslim in 2010. http://www.pewforum.org/2010/08/18/growing-number-of-americans-say-obama-is-a-muslim/, accessed 11 December 2015.

35. Zaitchik, Alexander, 'New Report Examines "Tea Party Nationalism", Charts Extremist Ties', Southern Poverty Law Center, http://www.splcenter.org/blog/2010/10/20/new-report-examines-tea-party-nationalism-charts-groups-history-and-extremist-ties-2/, accessed 24 June 2014.

36. The Muslim Brotherhood is a transnational religious organisation and social movement created in 1928 in Egypt by Hassan al-Banna, which has influenced many Islamist parties throughout the Arab world.

37. Volsky, Igor, 'Tea Party Congressman: Muslim Brotherhood Is Guiding Obama In Boston Bombings Investigation', *ThinkProgress.org*, http://thinkprogress.org/security/2013/04/27/1931051/tea-party-congressman-obama-bungled-investigation-of-boston-bombings-because-he-is-being-guided-by-muslim-brotherhood/, accessed 24 June 2014.

38. Volsky, Igor, 'Bachmann Stands By Widely Condemned Islamophobic Attack, Finds Ally In Glenn Beck', *ThinkProgress.org*, http://thinkprogress.org/security/2012/07/19/553361/bachmann-stands-by-widely-condemned-islamophobic-attack-finds-ally-in-glenn-beck/, accessed 24 June 2014.

39. Burghart, Devin, 'Tea Party Klansman Plotted to Kill Muslims with X-Ray Weapon', Institute for Research and Education on Human Rights, http://www.irehr.org/issue-areas/tea-party-nationalism/tea-party-news-and-analysis/item/499-tea-party-klansman-xray-plot, accessed 24 June 2014.

40. Morse, Samuel F.B., *Foreign Conspiracy against the Liberties of the United States*, 5th ed., New York: H.A. Chapin & Co., 1841.

41. Center for Security Policy, *Shariah: The Threat to America: An Exercise in Competitive Analysis—Report of Team B II*, Washington, DC: Center for Security Policy, 2010.

42. American Public Policy Alliance, 'American Laws for American Courts', http://publicpolicyalliance.org/legislation/american-laws-for-american-courts/, accessed 24 June 2014.

43. Brickman, Linda, 'Watching Sharia—NO to Sharia law!', Arizona Freedom Alliance, http://arizonafreedomalliance.ning.com/group/notosharialaw, accessed 24 June 2014.

44. Peck, Adam, 'Tea Party Senate Candidate Ted Cruz Jumps On The Sharia Conspiracy Bandwagon', *ThinkProgress.org*, http://thinkprogress.org/justice/2012/07/09/512075/cruz-sharia-problem/, accessed 24 June 2014.

45. Smietana, Bob, 'Tenn. bill criticized for targeting Muslims splits Tea Party', *USA Today*, http://usatoday30.usatoday.com/news/nation/2011–05–22-tennessee-bill-tea-party_n.htm, accessed 24 June 2014.

46. *Madville Times*, 'Keep Your Girls Away From Muslims, Says SD Legislator', http://madvilletimes.com/2011/02/keep-your-girls-away-from-muslims-says-sd-legislator/, accessed 24 June 2014.

47. Cockerham, Sean, 'Palmer lawmaker's bill aimed at Islamic law called divisive', *Anchorage Daily News*, http://www.adn.com/2011/03/30/1784015/bill-to-stop-sharia-law-called.html, accessed 24 June 2014.

48. Berg, Carl S., 'Muslim Tea Party Movement Challenges Islamophobia on Home Turf', *Illume*, http://www.illumemagazine.com/zine/articleDetail.php?Tea-Party-Gives-Rise-to-Surprising-American-Muslim-Movement-14153, accessed 24 June 2014.

49. Ben-Gedalyahu, Tzvi, 'Tea Party Preacher's "False Religion" Remark Upsets Jews', *The Jewish Press*, http://www.jewishpress.com/news/tea-party-preachers-false-religion-remark-upsets-jews/2013/10/23/, accessed 24 June 2014.

50. According to the Pew survey, 49 per cent of Jews say they disagree with the Tea Party movement, and only 15 per cent agree with it. http://www.pewforum.org/2011/02/23/tea-party-and-religion/, accessed 11 December 2015.

51. Krieger, Hilary Leila, '"Tea Party's Christian ties will alienate Jewish voters"', *The Jerusalem Post*, http://www.jpost.com/International/Tea-Partys-Christian-ties-will-alienate-Jewish-voters, accessed 24 June 2014.

52. As required by the Patient Protection and Affordable Care Act, signed into law by President Obama in 2010, employers have to cover their employees' expenses for some contraceptives. In 2012, this mandate triggered a heated controversy due to the protest of some religious organisations (notably the US Conference of Catholic Bishops) who argued that this mandate was contrary to the principle of religious liberty.

53. Ford, Kristin, 'Ohio Catholic Leaders to Speaker Boehner: Listen to Catholic

Church, not Tea Party', *FaithinPublicLife.org*, http://www.faithinpubliclife.org/newsroom/press/ohio_catholic_leaders_to_speak/, accessed 24 June 2014.

54. Smith, Jan, 'US Catholic Bishops Vs. Tea Party', Rainbow Sash Movement, http://rainbowsashmovement.wordpress.com/2011/07/30/us-catholic-bishops-vs-tea-party/, accessed 24 June 2014.

55. Lepore, Jill, *The Whites of their Eyes: The Tea Party's Revolution and the Battle over American History*, Princeton: Princeton University Press, 2010, p. 16.

56. Skousen, W. Cleon, *The Five Thousand Year Leap*, National Center for Constitutional Studies, 1981.

57. Vanel, Chrystal, *Des mormonismes: une étude historique et sociologique d'une fissiparité religieuse américaine (1805–2013)*, doctoral thesis under the direction of Jean-Paul Willaime, Ecole Pratique des Hautes Etudes, Paris, 2013, pp. 488–95.

58. New York, Simon & Schuster, 2015.

59. Bail, Christopher A., *Terrified: How Anti-Muslim Fringe Organizations Became Mainstream*, Princeton: Princeton University Press, 2015.

60. Spellberg, Denise A., 'Ben Carson Would Fail U.S. History', http://time.com/4042435/ben-carson-would-fail-u-s-history/, accessed 30 November 2015.

61. Henderson, Nia-Malika, 'After Call to Ban Muslims, is the GOP Ready to Unite against Trump?', 8 December 2015, http://edition.cnn.com/2015/12/08/politics/donald-trump-muslim-republicans-2016/, accessed 11 December 2015.

62. Sobieraj, Sarah, and Berry, Jeffrey M., 'From Incivility to Outrage: Political Discourse in Blogs, Talk Radio, and Cable News', *Political Communication* 28(1) (2011), p. 20.

63. Norman, Jim, 'In U.S., Support for Tea Party Drops to New Low', http://www.gallup.com/poll/186338/support-tea-party-drops-new-low.aspx?g_source=Politics&g_medium=newsfeed&g_campaign=tiles, accessed 30 November 2015.

11. 'WE ARE ALSO THE (CHOSEN) PEOPLE, YOU ARE NOT': THE CASE OF SHAS' POPULISM

1. Wiles, Peter, 'A Syndrome not a Doctrine: Some Elementary Theses on Populism', in Ionescu, Ghita, and Gellner, Ernest, *Populism: Its Meaning and National Characteristics*, London: Macmillan, 1969.

2. Tessler, Ricky, *In the Name of God: Shas and the Religious Revolution*, Jerusalem: Keter (Hebrew), 2003.

3. Tessler, *op. cit.*

4. www.shas.org.il, accessed 11 December 2015.

5. Yadgar, Yaacov, 'Shas as a Struggle to Create a New Field: A Bourdieuan Perspective of an Israeli Phenomenon', *Sociology of Religion* 64(2) (2003), p. 242.

6. Peled, Yoav, 'Towards a Redefinition of Jewish Nationalism in Israel: The Enigma of Shas', *Ethnic and Racial Studies* 21(4) (1998), pp. 703–27; Shalev, Michael, and Levy, Gal, 'Winners and Losers in 2003 Elections: Ideology, Social Structure and

Political Change', in Arian, Asher, and Shamir, Michal, *Elections in Israel 2003*, Jerusalem: IDI (Hebrew), 2005.

7. http://www.shas.org.il/Web/He/About/AboutUs/Default.aspx, accessed 11 December 2015.

8. *Ibid.*

9. *Ibid.*

10. http://www.shas.org.il/Web/He/About/ChairmanMessage/Default.aspx, accessed 11 December 2015.

11. Laclau, Ernesto, *The Populist Reason*, New York: Verso, 2005.

12. Kamil, Omar, 'The Synagogue as Civil Society, or How Can We Understand the Shas Party', *Mediterranean Quarterly* 12(3) (2001), p. 136.

13. Benizri, Shlomo, http://www.shas.org.il/Web/He/Party/Vaknin/Default.aspx (Hebrew), accessed 11 December 2015.

14. Benizri, *op. cit.*

15. Yadgar, *op. cit.*, p. 81.

16. *Ibid.*

17. Yishai, Eli, http://www.nrg.co.il/online/1/ART1/801/558.html, accessed 4 May 2014.

18. See, for example, http://www.mako.co.il/news-military/politics-q1_2015/Article-b640a73be2dfa41004.htm, accessed 30 April 2015.

19. Mudde, Cas, *Populist Radical Right Parties in Europe*, Cambridge: Cambridge University Press, 2007, p. 19.

20. Yadgar, *op. cit.*

21. Tessler, *op. cit.*; Yadgar, *op. cit.*

22. www.shas.org.il/party/ammsalem/Default, accessed 11 December 2015.

23. Yishai, Eli, http://israblog.nana10.co.il/blogread.asp?blog=613076, 2009, accessed 17 November 2012.

24. Quoted in Tessler, *op. cit.*, p. 78.

25. Yadgar, *op. cit.*

26. Caplan, Kimi, 'Mizrahi Ultra-orthodoxy and Popular Religion', in Ravitzky, Aviezer (ed.), *Shas: Cultural and Ideological Perspectives*, Tel Aviv: Am Oved (Hebrew), 2006, p. 456.

27. Kopelowitz claims that 'the "softer" effect of the assertion of rabbinical authority on Shas' politics is [due to] the more lenient tendency of the Sephardic rabbinical tradition. [...] The Sephardic style of legal interpretation tends to stress the fact that controversial public issues do not have a single authoritative solution.' Kopelowitz, Ezra, 'Religious Politics and Israel's Ethnic Democracy', *Israel Studies* 6(3) (2001), pp. 166–90.

28. Tessler, *op. cit.*, p. 99.

29. On the eve of the 2015 elections, Yishai left Shas and ran as the leader of a new party initially called 'Together, the People With Us'.

30. Kalim, *op. cit.*, p. 137.

31. Quoted in Feldman, Anat, 'The Emergence of Shas: Aims and Means', in Ravitzky, Aviezer (ed.), *Shas: Cultural and Ideological Perspectives*, Tel Aviv: Am Oved (Hebrew), 2006, p. 412.

32. Feldman, *op. cit.*, p. 423.

33. *Ibid.*

34. http://www.shas.org.il/Web/He/About/History/Default.aspx, accessed 4 May 2014.

35. Zohar, Zion, 'Oriental Jewry Confronts Modernity: The Case of Rabbi Ovadiah Yosef', *Modern Judaism* 24(2) (2004), pp. 120–49.

36. Tessler, *op. cit.*

37. Caplan, *op. cit.*

38. Peled, *op. cit.*

39. Quoted in Cohen, Asher, 'Shas and the Religious-Secular Cleavage', in Peled, Yoav (ed.), *Shas: The Challenge of Israelness*, Tel Aviv: Yediot Aharonot (Hebrew), 2000, p. 96.

40. Ben Hayiim, Avishai, 'Interview with Aryeh Deri', *Ynet*, www.ynet.co.il/articles/0,7340,L-2099674,00.html (Hebrew), 2002, accessed 13 September 2013.

41. *Ibid.*

42. Bilsky, Leora, 'Political Indictment and Collective Memory', in Peled, Yoav (ed.), *op. cit.*, p. 307.

43. *Ibid.*, p. 468.

44. http://www.shas.org.il/Web/He/About/Platform/Default.aspx, accessed 11 December 2015.

45. *Ibid.*

46. *Ibid.*

47. *Ibid.*

48. Quoted in Baum, Roni, and Tepe, Sultan, 'Shas, a Likkud with Kippa? A Comparative Study on Transformation Processes in Political Parties', in Aryan, Asher, and Shamir, Michal (eds), *Elections in Israel 2006*, Jerusalem: IDI (Hebrew), 2008, p. 103.

49. Quoted in Baum and Tepe, *op. cit.*, p. 103.

50. Horodniceanu, Maya, 'Shas presents: we do not care for the middle classes but for the 2000000 "unseen" people', *Haaretz*, 18 January 2015.

51. Chetrit, Sami, 'Catch 17: Between Ultra-orthodox and "Orientals"', in Peled, Yoav (ed.), *Shas: the Challenge of Israelness*, Tel Aviv: Yediot Aharonot (Hebrew), 2001.

52. Chetrit, *op. cit.*.

53. Kalim, *op. cit.*; Tessler, *op. cit.*

54. While conversion is possible in principle, ultra-orthodox Jews discourage it.

55. Leon, Nissim, 'Ethno-religious Nationalism and Theo-ethnocratic Politics in Israel', *Studies in Ethnicity and Nationalism* 14(1) (2014), pp. 20–35.

56. Shafir, Moshe, quoted in *Sudanese Shas Journal*, 2012, http://www.plitim. co.il/2427.html, last accessed 30 November 2015.

57. http://www.moit.gov.il/NR/exeres/B0B48981–357D-446F-AFAC-91A358E93C87.htm, accessed 14 September 2013.

58. Yishai, Eli, http://www.nrg.co.il/online/1/ART1/031/048.html?hp=1&cat=478, 2006, accessed 13 May 2014.

59. http://www.shas.org.il/Web/He/About/Platform/Default.aspx, accessed 11 December 2015.

60. Yishai, Eli, http://www.ynet.co.il/articles/0,7340,L-4288197,00.html, 2012, accessed 13 May 2014.

61. Yishai, Eli, 'Infiltrators will Return, Every Last One', *Mako*, http://www.mako. co.il/news-military/politics/Article-74bb292eddc1431017.htm, accessed 13 September 2013.

62. Leon, *op. cit.*

63. Quoted in Reiner, Joshua, 'Likud Beiteinu—the Party of Russians and White', *Walla! News*, http://news.walla.co.il/elections/?w=/2780/2601061 accessed 13 September 2013.

64. This clip is still available at http://www.shas.org.il/Web/He/About/Platform/ Default.aspx, accessed 11 December 2015.

65. Leon, *op. cit.*

66. Quoted from Novick, Akiva, 'Deri's Shas Party Conference', *Ynet*, http://www. ynet.co.il/articles/0,7340,L-4301965,00.html (Hebrew), 2012, last accessed 13 September 2013. This approach was reflected in the results of the 2013 elections. Shas was the non-Arab party which obtained the most votes among Israeli Arabs. Shas' success was especially significant among the Bedouins in southern Israel. One of the local family leaders, Suliman Tarabin, explained support for Shas as resulting from the fact that 'they are the only party that supports the lower classes. [...] Only Shas took care of the Bedouins, they are religious, they are credible and they care for the weak.' Yagna, Yanir, 'When the Bedouin Vote, They Often Vote Shas', *Haaretz*, 27 January 2013, http://www.haaretz.com/news/ israeli-elections-2013/when-the-bedouin-vote-they-often-vote-shas.pre-mium-1.496401, accessed 13 September 2013.

67. Kopelowitz, *op. cit.*, p. 175.

68. Tepe, Sultan, 'Moderation of Religious Parties: Electoral Constraints, Ideological Commitments, and the Democratic Capacities of Religious Parties in Israel and Turkey', *Political Research Quarterly* 65(3) (2012), pp. 467–85.

69. *Ibid.*; Kopelowitz, *op. cit.*

12. BEYOND POPULISM: THE CONSERVATIVE RIGHT, THE COURTS, THE CHURCHES AND THE CONCEPT OF A CHRISTIAN EUROPE

1. See Chapter 2.

2. Administrative Court, Stuttgart (Verwaltungsgericht Stuttgart, 2000), relating to the judgment of 24 March 2000.

3. For an in-depth discussion of the Ludin case, see http://www.nylslawreview.com/wordpress/wp-ontent/uploads/2013/11/51–3.Fogel_.pdf, accessed 11 December 2015.

4. See Chapter 4.

5. Roy, Olivier, *Holy Ignorance*, London: Hurst, 2010.

6. This question in the original French was: *France, fille aînée de l'Eglise, es-tu fidèle aux promesses de ton baptême?*

7. *Le Figaro Magazine*, 13 August 2004. He added in this interview: 'Christian faith has something to say for the common morale and for the constitution of society. Faith is not just a private and subjective issue. It is a great spiritual power that should touch and illuminate public life.'

8. 'L'Europa ha sviluppato una cultura che, in un modo sconosciuto prima d'ora all'umanità, esclude Dio dalla coscienza pubblica', http://chiesa.espresso.repubblica.it/articolo/27262, accessed 11 December 2015.

9. *Die Presse*, 'Kardinal Schönborn liest Strache die Leviten', *Die Presse*, 21 May 2009.

10. Le Monde, http://abonnes.lemonde.fr/politique/article/2013/04/20/pour-les-sondeurs-l-opinion-demeure-majoritairement-favorable-au-mariage-gay_3163404_823448.html, accessed 11 December 2015.

11. *La Repubblica*, 'La Padania attacca Tettamanzi "Ma è un vescovo o un imam?"', 6 December 2009.

12. Although it is not usually made explicit, Evangelical Protestant Church leaders also promote a view of their religion's superiority over both Judaism and Catholicism.

13. http://www.religionnews.com/2014/06/16/meet-evangelical-catholics-remaking-gop/, accessed 11 December 2015.

14. Of course, although right-wing populists are the most vocal promoters of this idea, they are not the only ones to endorse it—a number of mainstream centre-right and conservative parties have also done so.

15. Arrêt no. 612, 'Baby-Loup', Cour de Cassation, 25 June 2014. In his interview in *Le Devoir* (Montreal) on 4 December 2013, the rabbi said, *Nous, Juifs, ne trouvons pas d'inconvénient à dire à nos enfants d'ôter la kippa en entrant à l'école* (We Jews don't have a problem with telling our children to take off the kippa before going into school).

16. In fact, new priests are coming from Africa in increasing numbers to staff the deserted parishes of old Europe.

17. http://www.slate.fr/story/30535/evangeliques-fer-de-lance-du-protestantisme-en-france, accessed 11 December 2015.

18. http://www.rue89strasbourg.com/index.php/2012/04/03/politique/pour-les-protestants-dalsace-ce-sera-a-droite-toute/, accessed 11 December 2015.

BIBLIOGRAPHY

Aarts, Kees, and Thomassen, Jacques, 'Dutch Voters and the Changing Party Space 1989–2006', *Acta Politica* 43(2–3) (2008), pp. 203–34.

Abramowitz, Alan, *Partisan Polarization and the Rise of the Tea Party Movement*, paper presented at APSA, 2011.

Adamson, Fiona, Triadfilos, Triadafilopoulos, and Zolberg, Aristide, 'The Limits of the Liberal State: Migration, Identity and Belonging in Europe', *Journal of Ethnic and Migration Studies* 37(6) (2011), pp. 843–59.

Akcali, Emel, and Korkut, Umut, 'Geographical Metanarratives in East-Central Europe: Neo-Turanism in Hungary', *Eurasian Geography and Economics* 53(5) (2012), pp. 596–614.

Akkerman, Tjitske, 'Anti-immigration parties and the defence of liberal values: The exceptional case of the List Pim Fortuyn', *Journal of Political Ideologies* 10(3) (2005), pp. 337–54.

Albertazzi, Daniele, and McDonnell, Duncan, 'The Lega Nord in the second Berlusconi government: In a league of its own', *West European Politics* 28(5) (2005), pp. 952–72.

———, *Twenty-First Century Populism. The Spectre of Western European Democracy*, Basingstoke: Palgrave Macmillan, 2008.

———, 'Introduction: The Sceptre and the Spectre', in Albertazzi, D., and McDonnell, D. (eds), *Twenty-First Century Populism: The Spectre of Western European Democracy*, Basingstoke: Palgrave Macmillan, 2008, pp. 4–5.

———, 'The Lega Nord back in government', *West European Politics* 33(6) (2010), pp. 1318–40.

———, *Populists in Power*, London: Routledge, 2015.

Alduy, Cécile, and Wahnich, Stéphane, *Marine Le Pen prise aux mots, décryptage du nouveau discours frontiste?*, Paris: Le Seuil, 2015.

Ali, Wajahat *et al.*, *Fear, Inc.: The Roots of the Islamophobia Network in America*, Washington DC: Muslim Public Affairs Council, 2011.

Altermatt, Urs, 'Die Christlichdemokratische Volkspartei der Schweiz. 1945–1999', in Veen, Hans-Joachim (ed.), *Christlich-demokratische und konservative Parteien in Westeuropa*, Munich: Schöningh, 2000, pp. 37–118.

American Public Policy Alliance, *American Laws for American Courts*, http://publicpolicyalliance.org/legislation/american-laws-for-american-courts/, accessed 24 June 2014.

Amselle, Jean-Loup, *Les nouveaux rouges-bruns. Le racisme qui vient*, Paris: Editions Lignes, 2014.

Andeweg, Rudy B., and Irwin, Galen A., *Governance and Politics of the Netherlands*, 3rd ed., Basingstoke: Palgrave Macmillan, 2009.

Bail, Christopher A., *Terrified: How Anti-Muslim Fringe Organizations Became Mainstream*, Princeton: Princeton University Press, 2015.

Bale, Tim, van Kessel, Stijn, and Taggart, Paul, 'Thrown Around with Abandon? Popular Understandings of Populism as Conveyed by the Print Media: A UK Case Study', *Acta Politica* 46(2) (2011), pp. 111–31.

Balogh, Éva S., 'Viktor Orbán and the "Christian-National" Idea', 22 September 2015, http://www.hungarianspectrum.org/2015/09/22/viktor-orban-and-the-christian-national-idea/, accessed 7 December 2015.

Barone, Michael, 'The Transformative Power of Rick Santelli's Rant', http://www.creators.com/conservative/michael-barone/the-transformative-power-of-rick-santellis-rant.html, accessed 24 June 2014.

Bartlett, Jamie, Birdwell, Jonathan, Krekó, Péter, Benfield, Jack, and Győri, Gabor, *Populism in Europe: Hungary*, London: Demos, 2012.

Bauman, Zygmunt, *Community. Seeking Safety in an Insecure World*, Cambridge: Polity Press, 2001.

Baumann, Martin and Stolz, Jörg, 'Vielfalt der Religionen. Risiken und Chancen des Zusammenlebens', in Baumann, Martin, and Stolz, Jörg (eds), *Eine Schweiz—viele Religionen. Risiken und Chancen des Zusammenlebens*, Bielefeld: Transcript Verlag, 2007, pp. 344–78.

Baum, Roni, and Tepe, Sultan, 'Shas, a Likkud with Kippa? A Comparative Study on Transformation Processes in Political Parties', in Aryan, Asher, and Shamir, Michal (eds), *Elections in Israel 2006*, Jerusalem: IDI (Hebrew), 2008.

BBC News, 'Racist voters "spitting at God"', 28 May 2004, http://news.bbc.co.uk/1/hi/england/west_midlands/3756201.stm, accessed 10 December 2015.

———, 'BNP rejects church boycott call', 24 May 2009, http://news.bbc.co.uk/1/hi/uk_politics/8066000.stm, accessed 13 September 2013.

———, 'David Cameron says the UK is a Christian country', 16 December 2011, http://www.bbc.co.uk/news/uk-politics-16224394, accessed 10 December 2015.

———, 'Stand up for our Christianity, David Cameron tells UK', 16 April 2014, http://www.bbc.co.uk/news/uk-politics-27053112, accessed 10 December 2015.

Behloul, Samuel-Martin, 'Discours Total! Le débat sur l'Islam en Suisse et le positionnement de l'Islam comme religion publique', in Schneuwly Purdie, Mallory, Gianni, Matteo, and Magali, Jenny (eds), *Musulmans d'aujourd'hui. Identités plurielles en Suisse*, Geneva: Labor et Fides, 2009, pp. 53–72.

———, 'Religion und Religionzugehörigkeit im Spannungfeld von normativer Exklusion und Zivilgesellschaftlichem Bekenntnis. Islam und Muslime als öffentliches Thema in der Schweiz', in Allenbach, Birgit, and Sökefeld, Martin (eds), *Muslime in der Schweiz*, Zurich: Seismo, 2010, pp. 43–65.

Ben Hayiim, Ayishai, 'Interview with Aryeh Deri', *Ynet*, 2002, www.ynet.co.il/articles/0,7340,L-2099674,00.html, accessed 13 September 2013.

Ben-Gedalyahu, Tzvi, 'Tea Party Preacher's "False Religion" Remark Upsets Jews', *The Jewish Press*, 23 October 2013, http://www.jewishpress.com/news/tea-party-preachers-false-religion-remark-upsets-jews/2013/10/23/, accessed 24 June 2014.

Benoist, Alain de, 'Gramsci et la conquête du pouvoir culturel', *Le Figaro Magazine*, 11/12 March 1978.

———, Interview in *Terre et Peuple*, September 2001.

Ben-Porat, Guy, *Between State and Synagogue: The Secularization of Contemporary Israel*, Cambridge: Cambridge University Press, 2013.

Berg, Carl S., 'Muslim Tea Party Movement Challenges Islamophobia on Home Turf', *Illume*, 10 May 2013, http://www.illumemagazine.com/zine/articleDetail.php?Tea-Party-Gives-Rise-to-Surprising-American-Muslim-Movement-14153, accessed 24 June 2014.

Berger, Peter L. (ed.), *The Desecularization of the World: Resurgent Religion and World Politics*, Michigan: Eerdmans, 1999.

Berizzi, Paolo, 'La Lega assapora la rivincita e prepara la crociata in Padania', *La Repubblica*, 4 March 2006.

Berliner Tagesspiegel, 'Interview mit Jörg Haider', 11 June 2000.

Betz, Hans-Georg, and Johnson, Carol, 'Against the current—stemming the tide: the nostalgic ideology of the contemporary radical populist right', *Journal of Political Ideologies* 9(3) (2004), pp. 311–27.

Betz, Hans-Georg, and Meret, Susi, 'Revisiting Lepanto: the political mobilization against Islam in contemporary Western Europe', *Patterns of Prejudice* 43(3–4) (2009), pp. 313–34.

Biffi, Giacomo, *La città di San Petronio nel terzo millennio*, pastoral letter, 12 September 2000, http://www.toscanaoggi.it/Documenti/Altri-episcopati/Card.-Biffi-La-citta-di-San-Petronio-nel-terzo-millennio-12-09–2000, accessed 10 December 2015.

Bilsky, Leora, 'Political Indictment and Collective Memory', in Peled, Yoav (ed.), *Shas: The Challenge of Israelness*, Tel Aviv: Yediot Aharonot (Hebrew), 2000.

Bingham, John, 'Britain's Christians are being vilified, warns Lord Carey', *The Daily Telegraph*, 13 April 2012, http://www.telegraph.co.uk/news/religion/9203953/Britains-Christians-are-being-vilified-warns-Lord-Carey.html, accessed 13 September 2013.

Biorcio, Roberto, *La Padania promessa: La storia, le idee e la logica d'azione della Lega Nord*, Milan: il Saggiatore, 1997.

British National Party, *Rebuilding British democracy: British National Party general election 2005 manifesto*, Welshpool: British National Party, 2005.

———, *Democracy, freedom, culture and identity: British National Party general elections manifesto 2010*, Welshpool: British National Party, 2010.

———, *Putting local people first: Local election manifesto 2011*, Turriff: British National Party, 2011.

Bobic, Igor, 'Sarah Palin "Surprised" By Pope Francis' "Liberal" Sounding Statements', *Talking Points Memo*, 12 November 2013, http://www.talkingpointsmemo.com/livewire/sarah-palin-surprised-by-pope-francis-liberal-sounding-statements, accessed 24 June 2014.

Bonney, Norman, 'Established Religion, Parliamentary Devolution and New State Religion in the UK', *Parliamentary Affairs* 66(2) (2013), pp. 425–42.

Boross, Péter, 'Americans Are Intellectually Unsuitable to Lead the World', *Budapest Sentinel*, 20 August 2015.

Bouchacourt, Christian, 'Une nouvelle ère?', *TradiNews*, 29 April 2013, http://tradinews.blogspot.fr/2013/04/abbe-christian-bouchacourt-fsspx-une.html?utm_source=feedburner&utm_medium=feed&utm_campaign=Feed:+Tradinews+(TradiNews), accessed 10 December 2015.

Bozóki, András (ed.), *The Roundtable Talks of 1989: The Genesis of Hungarian Democracy*, Budapest/New York: Central European University Press, 2002.

———, 'Occupy the State: The Orbán Regime in Hungary', *Debatte: Journal of Contemporary Central and Eastern Europe* 19(3) (2011), pp. 649–63.

———, 'Broken Democracy, Predatory State, and Nationalist Populism' in Krasztev, Péter, and Van Til, Jon (eds), *The Hungarian Patient: Social Opposition to an Illiberal Democracy*, Budapest/New York: Central European University Press, 2015, pp. 3–36.

———, 'The Illusion of Inclusion: Configurations of Populism in Hungary' in Kopecek, Michal, and Wcislik, Piotr (eds), *Thinking Through Transition: Liberal Democracy, Authoritarian Pasts, and Intellectual History in East Central Europe after 1989*, Budapest/New York: Central European University Press, 2015, pp. 275–311.

Brickman, Linda, 'Watching Sharia—NO to Sharia law!', Arizona Freedom Alliance, http://arizonafreedomalliance.ning.com/group/notosharialaw, accessed 24 June 2014.

Brown, Jonathan, 'Far-right activists hand out Bibles outside mosques in Bradford', *The Independent*, 12 May 2014, http://www.independent.co.uk/news/uk/home-news/farright-activists-hand-out-bibles-outside-mosques-in-bradford-9352271.html, accessed 22 May 2014.

Bruce, Steve, *Politics and Religion in the United Kingdom*, London: Routledge, 2012.

Brückmüller, Ernst, 'Die Entwicklung des Österreichbewusstseins', in Kriechbaumer, Robert (ed.), *Österreichische Nationalgeschichte nach 1945. Die Spiegel der Erinnerung: Die Sicht von innen*, vol. 1, Wien/Köln/Weimar: Böhlau, 1998, pp. 369–96.

Burchianti, Flora, and Itcaina, Xabier, 'Between Hospitality and Competition. The Catholic Church and Immigration in Spain', in Haynes, Jeffrey and Hennig, Anja (eds), *Religious Actors in the Public Sphere-Means, Objectives, and Effects*, London/New York: Routledge, 2011, pp. 57–76.

Burdziej, Stanisław, 'Radio Maryja a społeczeństwo obywatelskie', *Znak*, issue 640, 2008, pp. 17–28.

Burghart, Devin, 'Karen Pack—Tea Party News and Analysis', Institute For Research and Education on Human Rights, 2010, http://www.irehr.org/news/latest-news/item/349-karen-pack, accessed 24 June 2014.

———, 'Tea Party Klansman Plotted to Kill Muslims with X-Ray Weapon', Institute For Research and Education on Human Rights, 2013, http://www.irehr.org/issue-areas/tea-party-nationalism/tea-party-news-and-analysis/item/499-tea-party-klansman-xray-plot, accessed 24 June 2014.

——— and Zeskin, Leonard, *Tea Party Nationalism: A Critical Examination of the Tea Party Movement and the Size, Scope, and Focus of Its National Factions*, Kansas City: Institute for Research and Education on Human Rights, 2010.

Burgos, Elie, Mazzoleni, Oscar, and Rayner, Hervé, *La Formule Magique: conflits et consensus partisans dans l'élection du Conseil Fédéral*, Lausanne: Presses Polytechniques et Universitaires Romandes, 2011.

Butt, Riazat, 'Church of England votes to ban BNP clergy', *The Guardian*, 10 February 2009, http://www.guardian.co.uk/politics/2009/feb/10/general-synod-bnp-vote, accessed 13 September 2013.

Campiche, Roland J., *Les deux visages de la religion. Fascination et désenchantement*, Geneva: Labor et Fides, 2004.

Canovan, Margaret, *Populism*, New York: Harcourt Brace Jovanovich, 1981.

Caplan, Kimi, 'Mizrahi Ultra-orthodoxy and Popular Religion', in Aviezer, Ravitzky (ed.), *Shas: Cultural and Ideological Perspectives*, Tel Aviv: Am Oved (Hebrew), 2006.

Carter, Jimmy, '1970s saw a Tea Party-like wave', *USA Today*, 29 September 2010.

Cavalera, Fabio, 'Bossi: questo Papa fa politica per Roma', *Corriere della Sera*, 17 August 1997.

CBOS, *Religijność Polaków Na Przełomie Wieków*, Warsaw: Centrum Badania Opinii Społecznej, 2001.

———, *Słuchacze Radia Maryja*, Warsaw: Centrum Badania Opinii Społecznej, 2008.

———, *Wiara i Religijność Polaków Dwadzieścia Lat Po Rozpoczęciu Przemian Ustrojowych*, Warsaw: Centrum Badania Opinii Społecznej, 2009.

———, *Dwadzieścia Lat Radia Maryja*, Warsaw: Centrum Badania Opinii Społecznej, 2011.

BIBLIOGRAPHY

Center for Security Policy, *Shariah: The Threat to America: An Exercise In Competitive Analysis—Report of Team B II*, Washington, DC: Center for Security Policy, 2010.

Cesari, Jocelyne, 'Islam, Secularism and Multiculturalism After 9/11: A Transatlantic Comparison', in Cesari, Jocelyne, and McLoughlin, Séan (eds), *European Muslims and the Secular State*, Aldershot: Ashgate, 2005, pp. 39–54.

CFP, *Christlich Freiheitliche Plattform für ein freies Europe souveräner Völker, Über uns*, 2012, http://www.cfp.co.at/index.php/ueber-uns, accessed 8 October 2012.

Chetrit, Sami, 'Catch 17: Between Ultra-orthodox and "Orientals"', in Peled, Yoav (ed.), *Shas: the Challenge of Israelness*, Tel Aviv: Yediot Aharonot (Hebrew), 2001.

Christmann, Anna, Danaci, Deniz, and Krömler, Oliver, 'Ein Sonderfall? Das Stimmverhalten bei der Minarettverbots-Initiative im Vergleich zu andern Abstimmungen und Sachfragen', in Vatter, Adrian (ed.), *Vom Schächt- zum Minarettverbot. Religiöse Minderheiten in der direkten Demokratie*, Zurich: NZZ, 2011, pp. 171–90.

Chudziková, Alena, Kasprowicz, Dominika, and Vit, Michal, 'National Identities in Central-Eastern Europe', *CEE Identity*, 2013, http://ceeidentity.eu/news/national-0, accessed 8 December 2015.

CIDI, *Mythe ontzenuwd: Joden stemmen amper PVV*, http://www.cidi.nl/Nieuwsberichten-in-2010/-Mythe-ontzenuwd-Joden-stemmen-amper-PVV.html, accessed 25 October 2012.

Clavien, Gaëtan, 'Médias et discours islamophobe: au croisement du dicible et du recevable', in Schneuwly Purdie, Mallory, Gianni, Matteo, and Magali, Jenny (eds), *Musulmans d'aujourd'hui. Identités plurielles en Suisse*, Geneva: Labor et Fides, 2009, pp. 95–109.

Cockerham, Sean, 'Palmer lawmaker's bill aimed at Islamic law called divisive', *Anchorage Daily News*, 30 March 2011, http://www.adn.com/2011/03/30/1784015/bill-to-stop-sharia-law-called.html, accessed 24 June 2014.

Cohen, Stuart A., 'Shas and the Religious-Secular Cleavage', in Peled, Yoav (ed.), *Shas: The Challenge of Israelness*, Tel Aviv: Yediot Aharonot (Hebrew), 2000.

Copsey, Nigel, *Contemporary British Fascism: The British National Party and the Quest for Legitimacy*, Basingstoke: Palgrave Macmillan, 2004.

———, 'Changing Course or Changing Clothes? Reflections on the Ideological Evolution of the British National Party 1999–2006', *Patterns of Prejudice* 41(1) (2007), pp. 61–82.

———, 'Sustaining a mortal blow? The British National Party and the 2010 general and local elections', *Patterns of Prejudice* 46(1) (2012), pp. 16–39.

Cueva, Sarah A., *Attack of the Radical Right: Incomplete Democratic Consolidation in Hungary and the FIDESZ—Jobbik Convergence*, New York: Columbia University Press (Unpublished manuscript), 2015.

Czapiński, Janusz, 'Stosunek Do Przemian Systemowych i Ocena Ich Wpływu Na Życie Badanych', in Czapiński, Janusz, and Panek, Tomasz (eds), *Diagnoza*

Społeczna 2005: Warunki i jakość życia Polaków, Warsaw: Wyższa Szkoła Finansów i Zarządzania w Warszawie, 2006, pp. 182–89.

Dazzi, Zita, 'La Lega Nord attacca Tettamanzi', *La Repubblica*, 5 September 2010.

—— and Monestiroli, T., 'La Padania attacca Tettamanzi', *La Repubblica*, 7 December 2009.

Della Frattina, Giannino, 'Ma c'è chi approfitta di Francesco per le proprie squallide battaglie', *Il Giornale*, 8 July 2013.

Der Standard, 'FPÖ auf antiklerikalen Kurs. "Ehre, Freiheit, Vaterland statt Armut, Keuschheit, Gehorsam"', 8 August 1997.

Destro, Adriana, 'A New Era and New Themes in Italian Politics: The Case of Padania', *Journal of Modern Italian Studies*, 2(3) (1997), pp. 358–77.

Diamanti, Ilvo, 'Lega Nord: un Partito per le Periferie', in Ginsborg, Paul (ed.), *Stato dell'Italia*, Milan: il Saggiatore, 1994.

Die Presse, 'Kardinal Schönborn liest Strache die Leviten', 21 May 2009.

——, 'Österreich nimmt 1000 weitere syrische Flüchtlinge auf. FPÖ-Generalsekretär Harald Vilimsky fordert, dass verfolgte Christen bevorzugt werden', 20 April 2014.

Dmowski, Roman, *Kościół, Naród i Państwo*, Wrocław: Wydawnictwo NORTOM, 2000.

Dobszay, János, 'Egyet jobbra, kettőt jobbra' (One Step to the Right, two Steps to the Right), *HVG*, 9 May 2015, pp. 6–9.

Dolezal, Martin, Helbling, Marc, and Hutter, Swen, 'Debating Islam in Austria, Germany and Switzerland: Ethnic Citizenship, Church-State Relations and Right-Wing Populism', *West European Politics* 33(2) (2010), pp. 171–90.

EJC Team, *Anti-Semitism in Hungary: Jobbik in Parliament*, CEJI, 2012, http://www.ceji.org/anti-semitism-in-hungary-jobbik-in-parliament, accessed 8 December 2015.

Ekklesia, 'BNP hits back against churches', 2004, http://www.ekklesia.co.uk/content/news_syndication/article_040428bnpchc.shtml, accessed 13 September 2013.

El Tayeb, Fatima, *European Others. Queering Ethnicity in Postnational Europe*, Minnesota: Minnesota University Press, 2011.

Enyedi, Zsolt, 'Clerical and Religious Polarization in Hungary', in Broughton, David, and Ten Napel, Hans-Martin (eds), *Religion and Mass Electoral Behaviour*, London: Routledge, 2000, pp. 157–76.

——, 'Plebeians, Citoyens and Aristocrats or Where is the Bottom of Bottom-up? The Case of Hungary', in Kriesi, Hanspeter, and Pappas, Takis (eds), *European Populism in the Shadow of the Great Recession*, Colchester: ECPR Press, 2015, pp. 242–57.

Eötvös Károly Policy Institute, Hungarian Helsinki Committee, Hungarian Civil Liberties Union, Mérték Médiaelemző Műhely, *Disrespect for European Values in Hungary 2010–2014. Rule of Law—Democracy—Pluralism—Fundamental Rights*,

Budapest, November 2014, http://helsinki.hu/en/disrespect-for-european-values-in-hungary-2010–2014, accessed 10 December 2015.

Federation of Swiss Protestant Churches, *Background paper on Switzerland's vote on Minarets*, Bern, 2010.

Feldman, Anat, 'The Emergence of Shas: Aims and Means', in Ravitzky, Aviezer (ed.), *Shas: Cultural and Ideological Perspectives*, Tel Aviv: Am Oved (Hebrew), 2006.

Field, Clive D., 'Islamophobia in Contemporary Britain: The Evidence of the Opinion Polls, 1988–2006', *Islam and Christian-Muslim Relations* 18(4) (2007), pp. 447–77.

Ford, Kristin, 'Ohio Catholic Leaders to Speaker Boehner: Listen to Catholic Church, not Tea Party', *FaithinPublicLife.org*, http://www.faithinpubliclife.org/newsroom/press/ohio_catholic_leaders_to_speak/, accessed 24 June 2014.

Ford, Robert, and Cutts, David, 'Strategic Eurosceptics and Polite Xenophobes: Support for the UK Independence Party (UKIP) in the 2009 European Parliament Elections', *European Journal of Political Research* 51(2) (2012), pp. 204–34.

———— and Goodwin, Matthew J., *Revolt on the Right: Explaining Support for the Radical Right in Britain*, London: Routledge, 2014.

Formisano, Ronald P., *The Tea Party. A Brief History*, Baltimore: Johns Hopkins University Press, 2012.

Fortuyn, Pim, *De Puinhopen van acht jaar paars. Een genadeloze analyse van de collectieve sector en aanbevelingen voor een krachtig herstelprogramma*, Uithoorn-Rotterdam: Karakter Uitgevers-Speakers Academy, 2002.

Fourquet, Jerôme, 'Présidentielle 2012: l'analyse du vote catholique par l'Ifop', *Famille Chrétienne*, 23 April 2012, http://www.libertepolitique.com/Actualite/Decryptage/Presidentielle-2012-l-analyse-du-vote-catholique-par-l-Ifop, accessed 10 December 2015.

FPÖ, *Das Parteiprogramm der Freiheitlichen Partei Österreichs*, 23 April 2005 (1997 programme with changes), http://www.fpoe-bildungsinstitut.at/documents/10180/20998/Parteiprogramm+der+FP%C3%96%201997+mit+den+2005+beschlossenen+%C3%84nderungen.pdf/abf304e8–3871–4dfc-80d3–6ee60259bf93, accessed 10 December 2015.

————, *Wir und der Islam. Freiheitliche Positionen zur Religionsfreiheit, zur islamischen Welt und zur Problematik des Zuwanderungs-Islam in Europa*, Vienna, 22 January 2008, https://rfjfreistadt.files.wordpress.com/2009/02/wir_und_der_islam_-_freiheitliche_positionen1.pdf, accessed 10 December 2015.

————, *SOS-Abendland: "Sind entsetzt über Werteverfall in der Europäischen Union"*, 4 November 2009, www.fpoe.at, accessed 2 July 2013.

————, *Parteiprogramm der Freiheitlichen Partei Österreichs*, 18 June 2011, https://www.fpoe.at/fileadmin/user_upload/www.fpoe.at/dokumente/2015/2011_graz_parteiprogramm_web.pdf, accessed 10 December 2015.

————, *Handbuch freiheitlicher Politik*, Vienna, 2013, https://www.fpoe.at/fileadmin/user_upload/www.fpoe.at/dokumente/2015/Handbuch_freiheitlicher_Politik_WEB.pdf, accessed 10 December 2015.

Friesl, Christian, Polak, Regina, and Harmachers-Zuba, Ursula, *Die Österreicherinnen. Wertewandel 1990–2008*, Vienna: Czernin Verlag, 2009.

Frischenschlager, Friedhelm, 'Das Verhältnis der FPÖ zu den Kirchen', in *Österreichisches Jahrbuch für Politik 1983*, Vienna: ÖVP Bildungsakademie, 1984.

Frölich-Steffen, Susanne, 'Die Identitätspolitik der FPÖ: Vom Deutschnationalismus zum Österreich-Patriotismus', *Österreichische Zeitschrift für Politikwissenschaft* 33(3) (2004), pp. 281–95.

Gazeta.pl, 'Co Powiedział O. Rydzyk?—Zapis Nagrań', 9 July 2007, http://wiadomosci.gazeta.pl/kraj/1,34308,4300292.html, accessed 1 December 2012.

———, 'Kaczyński: Ich Zwycięstwo Będzie Nowym 13 Grudnia 1981 Roku', 22 September 2007, http://wiadomosci.gazeta.pl/wiadomosci/1,114873,4511730.html, accessed 1 December 2012.

———, '"Ustawa o in vitro to zwycięstwo wolności", "prezydent po stronie ludzi". A prawica dalej swoje: "Komorowski za cywilizacją śmierci"', 22 July 2015, http://wyborcza.pl/1,75478,18403640,komentarze-po-podpisaniu-ustawy-o-in-vitro-prezydent-wybral.html, accessed 9 August 2015.

Gettys, Travis, 'Sarah Palin: "Angry atheists" are trying to "abort Christ from Christmas"', *TheRawStory*, http://www.rawstory.com/rs/2013/12/06/sarah-palin-angry-atheists-are-trying-to-abort-christ-from-christmas/, accessed 24 June 2014.

Giannatasio, Maurizio, 'Bossi: abbiamo chiuso la moschea di Milano', *Corriere della Sera*, 5 July 2008.

Gianni, Matteo, *Vie musulmane en Suisse. Profils identitaires, demandes et perceptions des musulmans en Suisse. Rapport réalisé par le Groupe de Recherche sur l'Islam en Suisse*, Bern: Commission Fédérale pour les Questions de Migration, 2010.

Giertych, Roman, 'List Romana Giertycha Do Przełożonego Ojca Rydzyka', *Gazeta. pl*, http://wyborcza.pl/1,75478,13186919,List_Romana_Giertycha_do_przelozonego_ojca_Rydzyka.html, accessed 10 September 2013.

Gillissen, Daniël, and Houtman, Wim, 'PVV-aanhang in kerken blijft beperkt', *Nederlands Dagblad*, 25 February 2010, http://www.nd.nl/artikelen/2010/februari/25/-christen-kan-geen-wilders-stemmen-, accessed 22 October 2012.

Gingrich, Andre, 'A man for all seasons. An anthropological perspective on public representatives and cultural politics of the Austrian Freedom Party', in Wodak, Ruth, and Pelinka, Anton (eds), *The Haider Phenomenon in Austria*, New Brunswick/London: Transaction Publishers, 2002, pp. 67–94.

Goodwin, Matthew J., *New British Fascism: Rise of the British National Party*, London: Routledge, 2011.

Gowin, Jarosław, *Kościół Po Komunizmie*, Kraków: Wydawnictwo Znak, 1995.

———, 'Gowin w Radiu Kraków o imigrantach: Przyjmijmy chrześcijan, ale nie muzułmanów. "Wystarczą setki tysięcy niezasymilowanych, żeby roznosić zarazę terroryzmu"', *wPolityce.pl*, 2015, http://wpolityce.pl/polityka/259191-gowin-w-radiu-krakow-o-imigrantach-przyjmijmy-chrzescijan-ale-nie-muzulmanow-wystarcza-setki-tysiecy-niezasymilowanych-zeby-roznosic-zaraze-terroryzmu, accessed 10 August 2015.

Grabowska, Mirosława, *Podział Postkomunistyczny: Społeczne Podstawy Polityki w Polsce Po 1989 Roku*, Warsaw: Scholar, 2004.

Grochal, Renata, 'Ciemnogród w polskiej polityce trzyma się mocno', *wyborcza.pl*, 14 July 2015, http://wyborcza.pl/politykaekstra/1,147093,18359428,ciemnog rod-w-polskiej-polityce-trzyma-sie-mocno.html, accessed 9 August 2015.

Groll, Verena, 'Die Wahrnehmung von Migration und WählerInnen mit Migrationshintergrund durch die österreichischen Parteien', Master's thesis, University of Vienna, 2010.

Grzymala-Busse, Anna, *Nations under God: How Churches Use Moral Authority to Influence Policy*, Princeton: Princeton University Press, 2015.

Guolo, Renzo, *Chi impugna la croce? Lega e Chiesa*, Rome: Laterza, 2012 (Kindle edition).

Gwiazda, Anna, 'Poland's Quasi-Institutionalized Party System: The Importance of Elites and Institutions', *Perspectives on European Politics and Society* 10(3) (2009), pp. 350–76.

Hadj-Abdou, Leila, Rosenberger, Sieglinde, Saharso, Sawitri, and Siim, Birte, 'The Limits of Populism. Accommodative Headscarf Policies in Austria, Denmark, and the Netherlands', in Rosenberger, Sieglinde, and Sauer, Birgit (eds), *Politics, Religion and Gender. Framing and Regulating the Veil*, Oxford: Routledge, 2012, pp. 132–49.

Haider, Jörg, '*Österreich-Erklärung zur Nationalratswahl 1994*', FPÖ, Vienna, 1994.

———, 'Grundsätzliches zum Verhältnis FPÖ und katholische Kirche', in Wilhelm, Michael, and Wuthe, Paul (eds), *Parteien und Katholische Kirche im Gespräch*, Graz/Vienna: Verlag Zeitpunkt, 1999, pp. 33–41.

Hajdukiewicz, Lech, 'Uwarunkowania Demograficzno-społeczne Rozwoju Polski', in Jacyna-Onyszkiewicz, Zbigniew (ed.), *Ku odnowie Polski*, Warsaw: Liga Polskich Rodzin, 2005, pp. 11–36.

Hakkenes, Emiel, 'De tweede christelijke partij van Nederland', *Trouw*, 26 November 2009, http://www.trouw.nl/tr/nl/4324/Nieuws/article/detail/1179389/2009/11/26/De-tweede-christelijke-partij-van-Nederland.dhtml, accessed 25 October 2012.

Hasan, Mehdi, 'The Great UKIP Racism Debate—Debunking the Six Main Myths', *The Huffington Post*, http://www.huffingtonpost.co.uk/mehdi-hasan/ukip-racism-myths_b_5271986.html?utm_hp_ref=uk, accessed 22 May 2014.

Heinisch, Reinhard, *Populism, Proporz, Pariah: Austria Turns Right: Austrian Political Change, its Causes and Repercussions*, New York: Nova Science, 2002.

Helms, Ludger, 'Right-wing Populist Parties in Austria and Switzerland: A

Comparative Analysis of Electoral Support and Conditions of Success', *West European Politics* 20(2) (1997), pp. 37–52.

Henderson, Nia-Malika, 'After Call to Ban Muslims, is the GOP Ready to Unite against Trump?', 8 December 2015, http://edition.cnn.com/2015/12/08/politics/donald-trump-muslim-republicans-2016/, accessed 11 December 2015.

Hill, Mark, 'Religious Symbolism and Conscientious Objection in the Workplace: An Evaluation of Strasbourg's Judgment in Eweida and others v United Kingdom', *Ecclesiastical Law Journal* 15(2) (2013), pp. 191–203.

Hödl, Klaus, 'Islamophobia in Austria: The Recent Emergence of Anti-Muslim Sentiments in the Country', *Journal of Muslim Minority Affairs* 30(4) (2010), pp. 443–56.

Hofstadter, Richard, *The Paranoid Style in American Politics*, New York: Vintage, 1965.

Hołub, Jacek, 'Radio Maryja Mobilizuje: "Bojówki Lewicowe Chcą Zabrać Krzyż"', *Gazeta Wyborcza*, http://wyborcza.pl/Polityka/1,103835,8231658,Radio_Maryja_mobilizuje___Bojowki_lewicowe_chca_zabrac.html, accessed 13 February 2012.

Horodniceanu, Maya, 'Shas presents: we do not care for the middle classes but for the 2000000 "unseen" people', *Haaretz*, 18 January 2015.

Huntington, Samuel P., *The Clash of Civilizations and the Remaking of World Order*, New York: Simon and Schuster, 1996.

Huret, Romain, 'Le mouvement Tea Party, une illusion', *Hérodote*, La Découverte, Paris, 2013/2, no. 149, pp. 105–14.

IFOP, 'Les Français et les manifestations sur le mariage et l'adoption pour les couples de même sexe après le vote de la loi', FD/EP N° 111316, May 2013.

Ignazi, Piero, *Extreme Right Parties in Western Europe*, Oxford: Oxford University Press, 2006.

IKON, *Plaisier: denkbeelden Wilders onverenigbaar met kerk*, http://www.kerknieuws.nl/nieuws.asp?oId=12863, accessed 11 October 2012.

———, *Raad van Kerken: 'Fitna is eenzijdig en provocerend'*, http://www.kerknieuws.nl/nieuws.asp?oId=12815, accessed 11 October 2012.

Il Fatto Quotidiano, 'Migranti, Papa: "Perdono per chi chiude porte". Salvini: "Non abbiamo bisogno"', http://www.ilfattoquotidiano.it/2015/06/17/migranti-il-papa-perdono-per-chiude-le-porte-salvini-non-abbiamo-bisogno/1787505/, accessed 10 December 2015.

Imhof, Kurt, and Ettinger, Patrik, 'Religionen in der Medienvermittelten Öffentlichkeit der Schweiz', in Baumann, Martin, and Stolz, Jörg (eds), *Eine Schweiz—viele Religionen. Risiken und Chancen des Zusammenleben*, Bielefeld: Transcript Verlag, 2007, pp. 284–300.

Immerzeel, Tim, Jaspers, Eva, and Lubbers, Marcel, 'Religion as Catalyst or Restraint of Radical Right Voting?', *West European Politics* 36(5) (2013), pp. 946–68.

Ingersoll, Julie, 'Mobilizing Evangelicals: Christian Reconstructionism and the Roots of the Religious Right', in Brint, Steven, and Reith Schroedel, Jean (eds), *Evangelicals and Democracy in America: Religion and Politics*, New York: Russell Sage Foundation, 2009.

Instytut Statystyki Kosciola Katolickiego, *Dominicantes 1992–2010—Wykresy*, http://www.iskk.pl/kosciolnaswiecie/75-dominicantes.html, accessed 11 December 2012.

Janicki, Mariusz and Władyka, Wiesław, *Cień Wielkiego Brata: Ideologia i Praktyka IV RP*, Warszawa: POLITYKA Spółdzielnia Pracy, 2007.

Jędrzejczak, Aleksandra, 'Młodzież Wszech Stanowisk', *Przekrój*, 26, 2006.

Jobbik, *Manifesto of Jobbik*, 24 October 2003, http://jobbik.com/manifesto_0, accessed 10 December 2015.

———, *Short Summary about Jobbik*, 3 May 2010, http://jobbik.com/short_summary_about_jobbik, accessed 10 December 2012.

Jong, Ron de, van der Kolk, Henk, and Voerman, Gerrit, *Verkiezingen op de kaart, 1848–2010. Tweede Kamerverkiezingen vanuit geografisch perspectief*, Utrecht: Matrijs, 2011.

Kamil, Omar, 'The Synagogue as Civil Society, or How Can We Understand the Shas Party', *Mediterranean Quarterly*, 12(3) (2001), pp. 128–43.

Karnowski, Michał, and Zaremba, Piotr, *O Dwóch Takich... Alfabet Braci Kaczyńskich*, Kraków: Wydawnictwo M, 2006.

Kazin, Michael, *The Populist Persuasion: An American History*, New York: Cornell University Press, 1998.

Keman, Hans and Pennings, Paul, 'Oude en nieuwe conflictdimensies in de Nederlandse politiek na 1989: een vergelijkende analyse', in Andeweg, Rudy B., and Thomassen, Jacques (eds), *Democratie Doorgelicht, het functioneren van de Nederlandse democratie*, Leiden: Leiden University Press, 2011, pp. 247–66.

Kis, János, 'From the 1989 Constitution to the 2011 Fundamental Law', in Tóth, Gábor Attila (ed.), *Constitution for a Disunited Nation. On Hungary's 2011 Fundamental Law*, Budapest/New York: CEU Press, 2012.

Klei, Ewout, and Lemm, Jeffrey, 'Een nieuwe Messias? Christenen en het fenomeen Geert Wilders', *Liberaal Reveil*, http://vriendklei.blogspot.de/2010/12/een-nieuwe-messias-christenen-en-het.html, accessed 10 December 2015.

Kleine Zeitung, 'Ökumenischer Rat der Kirchen kritisiert FPÖ', 5 May 2009.

Kobach, Kris W., *The Referendum: Direct Democracy in Switzerland*, Aldershot: Dartmouth Publishing, 1993.

Koesel, Karrie J., *Religion and Authoritarianism: Cooperation, Conflict, and the Consequences*, Cambridge: Cambridge University Press, 2014.

Kopelowitz, Ezra, 'Religious Politics and Israel's Ethnic Democracy', *Israel Studies* 6(3) (2001), pp. 166–90.

Korkut, Umut, 'A Conservative Putsch at EU's Periphery: Crisis of Democracy in Hungary', paper presented at the annual convention of Europeanists of the British Political Science Association, Gothenburg, 6 November 2014.

Krekó, Péter, and Mayer, Gregor, 'Transforming Hungary—Together? An Analysis of the Fidesz-Jobbik Relationship', in Minkenberg, Michael (ed.), *Transforming the Transformation? The East European Radical Right in the Political Process*, London: Routledge, 2015, pp. 183–205.

Krieger, Hilary Leila, 'Tea Party's Christian ties will alienate Jewish voters', *The Jerusalem Post*, http://www.jpost.com/International/Tea-Partys-Christian-ties-will-alienate-Jewish-voters, accessed 24 June 2014.

Krzemiński, Ireneusz, 'Radio Maryja i Jego Przekaz. Analiza Treści Wybranych Audycji "Rozmowy Niedokończone" z Sierpnia 2007 Roku', in *Czego nas uczy Radio Maryja?*, Warsaw: Wydawnictwo Akademickie i Profesjonalne, 2009.

Kucharczak, Przemysław, and Stopka, Artur, 'Na Pewno Jestem Patriotą', interview with Lech Kaczyński, *Gość Niedzielny*, 40, 2005.

Le Pen, Marine, Interview with *La Vie*, 16 June 2011, http://www.lavie.fr/hebdo/2011/3433/marine-le-pen-les-cures-devraient-rester-dans-leur-sacristie-15–06–2011–17717_231.php, accessed 10 December 2015.

———, Speech for the 600th anniversary of Joan of Arc's birthday, 6 January 2012, http://www.frontnational.com/2012/01/discours-de-jean-marie-le-pen-lors-de-la-celebration-du-600eme-anniversaire-de-la-naissance-de-jeanne-darc/, accessed 10 December 2015.

———, Interview at the French broadcast station RTL, 4 April 2014, http://tempsreel.nouvelobs.com/video/20140404.OBS2693/marine-le-pen-ne-veut-plus-de-menus-sans-porc-dans-les-cantines.html, accessed 10 December 2015.

La Repubblica, 'Bossi promette alla Lega "Trionferemo Alle Elezioni"', 9 December 1989.

———, 'Vignette, 11 morti durante la protesta davanti al consolato italiano di Bengasi', 17 February 2006.

———, 'La Lega va all' attacco Non c'è un Islam moderato', 6 March 2006.

———, 'La Padania attacca Tettamanzi "Ma è un vescovo o un imam?"', 6 December 2009.

———, 'Le polemiche sui campi rom, Salvini rivela: "Facebook mi ha sospeso per la parola zingari"', 9 April 2015, http://milano.repubblica.it/cronaca/2015/04/09/news/milano_salvini_dopo_le_polemiche_sui_campi_rom_ho_usato_la_parola_zingari_facebook_mi_ha_sospeso_-111501066/, accessed 10 December 2015.

———, 'Galantino (Cei): "Contro i migranti piazzisti da 4 soldi". Salvini: "Chi difende invasione o non capisce o ci guadagna"', 10 August 2015, http://www.repubblica.it/vaticano/2015/08/10/news/immigrati_galantino_cei_contro_loro_piazzisti_da_4_soldi_-120738402/?ref=search, accessed 10 December 2015.

Laclau, Ernesto, *The Populist Reason*, New York: Verso, 2005.

Lange, Sarah L. de, and Art, David, 'Fortuyn versus Wilders: An Agency-Based Approach to Radical Right Party Building', *West European Politics* 34(6) (2011), pp. 1229–49.

Lange, Sarah L. de, and Rooduijn, Matthijs, 'Een populistische Zeitgeist in Nederland? Een inhoudsanalyse van de verkiezingsprogramma's van populistische en gevestigde politieke partijen', in Andeweg, Rudy B., and Thomassen, Jacques (eds), *Democratie Doorgelicht, het functioneren van de Nederlandse democratie*, Leiden: Leiden University Press, 2011, pp. 319–34.

Lega Nord, *La Costituzione europea e le radici cristiane*, 2003.

———, *Proposte e Obiettivi*, 2009.

———, *Scuola Quadri Politica*, 2012.

Lentin, Alana, and Titley, Gavan, *The Crises of Multiculturalism: Racism in a Neoliberal Age*, London: Zed Books, 2011.

Lepore, Jill, *The Whites of their Eyes: The Tea Party's Revolution and the Battle over American History*, New Jersey: Princeton University Press, 2010.

L'Express, 'Avec l'invitation de Marion Maréchal-Le Pen, l'évêque du Var brise un tabou', 27 August 2015.

Liga Polskich Rodzin, 'Skrót Programu Gospodarczego', in Słodkowska, Inka, and Dolbakowska, Magdalena (eds), *Wybory 2005: Partie i ich programy*, Warszawa, 2006.

Lijphart, Arend, *The Politics of Accommodation: Pluralism and Democracy in the Netherlands*, 2nd ed., Berkeley: University of California Press, 1975.

Lijst Pim Fortuyn, 'Lijst Pim Fortuyn. Zakelijk met een hart', in *Documentatiecentrum Nederlandse politieke partijen*, http://dnpp.eldoc.ub.rug.nl/FILES/root/programmas/vp-per-partij/lpf/lpf02.pdf, accessed 19 July 2011.

Lipset, Seymour M., and Rokkan, Stein (eds), *Party Systems and Voters' Alignments*, New York: The Free Press, 1967.

Lucardie, Paul, 'Prophets, Purifiers and Prolocutors: Towards a Theory on the Emergence of New Parties', *Party Politics* 6(2) (2000), pp. 175–85.

———, 'The Netherlands: Populism versus Pillarization', in Albertazzi, Daniele, and McDonnell, Duncan (eds), *Twenty-First Century Populism. The Spectre of Western European Democracy*, London: Palgrave Macmillan, 2008, pp. 151–65.

——— and Voerman, G., *Populisten in de Polder*, Amsterdam: Boom, 2012.

Luther, Kurt Richard, 'Die Freiheitliche Partei Österreichs (FPÖ) und das Bündnis Zukunft Österreichs (BZÖ)', in Dachs, Herbert, Gottweis, Herbert, Lauber, Volkmar, and Müller, Wolfgang C. (eds), *Politik in Österreich. Das Handbuch*, Vienna: Manz, 2006, pp. 364–88.

——— 'The Revival of the Radical Right. The Austrian Parliamentary Election of 2008', Working Paper 29, Keele European Parties Research Unit, 2008.

Lynch, Philip, Whitaker, Richard, and Loomes, Gemma, 'The UK Independence Party: Understanding a Niche Party's Strategy, Candidates and Supporters', *Parliamentary Affairs* 65(4) (2012), pp. 733–57.

Madville Times, 'Keep Your Girls Away From Muslims, Says SD Legislator', http://madvilletimes.com/2011/02/keep-your-girls-away-from-muslims-says-sd-legislator/, accessed 24 June 2014.

Majtényi, László, and Szabó, Máté Dániel (eds), *Az elveszett alkotmány* (The Lost Constitution), Budapest: L'Harmattan/Eötvös Károly Intézet, 2011.

Mammone, Andrea, and Peace, Timothy, 'Cross-national Ideology in Local Elections: The Case of Azione Sociale and the British National Party', in Mammone, Andrea *et al.* (eds), *Mapping the Extreme Right in Contemporary Europe: From Local to Transnational*, London: Routledge, 2012.

Mamoń, Marek, 'Tu Jest Polska Kaczyńskiego', *Gazeta Wyborcza*, 2007.

March, Luke, *Radical Left Parties in Europe*, London: Routledge, 2011.

Mason, Rowena, 'Ukip MEP says British Muslims should sign charter rejecting violence', *The Guardian*, 4 February 2014, http://www.theguardian.com/politics/2014/feb/04/ukip-mep-gerard-batten-muslims-sign-charter-rejecting-violence, accessed 22 May 2014.

———, 'Ukip urged to cut ties with Christian group over gay "depravity" comments', *The Guardian*, 3 February 2015, http://www.theguardian.com/politics/2015/feb/03/christian-soldiers-ukip-gay-depravity, accessed 5 March 2015.

——— 'Nigel Farage: UK mosques have been infiltrated by hate preachers', *The Guardian*, 26 February 2015, http://www.theguardian.com/politics/2015/feb/26/nigel-farage-uk-mosques-have-been-infiltrated-by-hate-preachers, accessed 5 March 2015.

Massetti, Emanuele, 'Mainstream Parties and the Politics of Immigration in Italy: A Structural Advantage for the Right or a Missed Opportunity for the Left?', *Acta Politica* 50(4) (2015), pp. 486–505.

Mazzoleni, Oscar, *Nationalisme et populisme en Suisse. La radicalisation de la 'nouvelle' UDC*, Lausanne: Presses Polytechniques et Universitaires Romandes, 2008.

———, 'Between Centralisation and Nationalisation: The Case of the Swiss People's Party', in Pallaver, Günther, and Wagemann, Claudius (eds), *Challenges for Alpine Parties. Strategies of Political Parties for Identity and Territory in the Alpine Regions*, Innsbruck/Vienna/Bozen: Studien Verlag, 2012, pp. 17–33.

———, 'Between Opposition and Government. The Swiss People's Party', in Grabow, Karsten, and Hartleb, Florian (eds), *Exposing the Demagogues. Right-wing and National Populists in Europe*, Brussels: CES-KAS, 2013, pp. 237–60.

——— and Skenderovic, Damir, 'The rise and impact of the Swiss People's Party: Challenging the rules of governance in Switzerland', in Delwit, Pascal, and Poirier, Philippe (eds), *Droites nouvelles et pouvoir en Europe/The New Right-wing Parties and Power in Europe*, Brussels: Editions de l'Université de Bruxelles, 2007, pp. 85–115.

McDonald, Henry, 'BNP seeks anti-abortion Catholic votes', *The Observer*, 4 March 2007, http://www.guardian.co.uk/uk/2007/mar/04/thefarright.otherparties, accessed 13 September 2013.

McDonnell, Duncan, 'A Weekend in Padania: Regionalist Populism and the Lega Nord', *Politics* 26(2) (2006), pp. 126–32.

——, 'Abbott, Rudd and de Blasio: Many Things, But Not Populists', *The Conversation*, 19 September 2013, https://theconversation.com/abbott-rudd-and-de-blasio-many-things-but-not-populists-18390, accessed 25 August 2014.

Medián, 'A Jobbik szavazóinak kétharmada antiszemitának mondható' (Two-thirds of Jobbik voters can be considered as anti-Semitic), *Origo.hu*, 31 March 2015, http://www.origo.hu/itthon/20150331-a-fovarosban-nagyobb-merteku-az-antiszemitizmus-mint-videken.html, accessed 10 December 2015.

Meijer, David, *FPÖ und Christentum. Zwischen Gegnerschaft und Vereinnahmung*, Master's thesis, University of Vienna, 2012.

Millard, Frances, 'Poland's Politics and the Travails of Transition After 2001: The 2005 Elections', *Europe-Asia Studies* 58(7) (2006), pp. 1007–31.

——, 'Poland: Parties Without a Party System, 1991–2008', *Politics & Policy* 37(4) (2009), pp. 781–98.

Montgomery, Peter, 'The Tea Party and the Religious Right Movements: Frenemies with Benefits', in Rosenthal, Lawrence, and Trost, Christine (eds), *Steep: The Precipitous Rise of the Tea Party*, Berkeley: University of California Press, 2012, pp. 242–75.

——, 'Tea Party Senators Kick Off Ralph Reed's Faith & Freedom Conference', *Right Wing Watch*, 13 June 2013, http://www.rightwingwatch.org/content/tea-party-senators-kick-ralph-reed-s-faith-freedom-conference, accessed 24 June 2014.

Morrow, Duncan, 'Jörg Haider and the New FPÖ: Beyond the Democratic Pale?', in Hainsworth, Paul (ed.), *The Politics of the Extreme Right: From the Margins to the Mainstream*, London: Pinter, 2000, pp. 33–63.

Morse, Samuel F.B., *Foreign Conspiracy against the Liberties of the United States*, 5th ed., New York: H.A. Chapin & Co., 1841.

Mourão Permoser, Julia, *Between Privatization and Politicization: Assessing the 'Return of Religion' in the Attitudes of Austrian MEPs*, workshop report, 'Religion at the European Parliament' research project, unpublished, 2013, www.releur.eu/index.html, accessed 1 November 2013.

Movsesian, Mark L., *Defining Religion in American Law: Psychic Sophie and the Rise of the Nones*, EUI working paper, RSCAS 2014/19, Robert Schuman Centre for Advanced Studies, RELIGIOWEST.

Mudde, Cas, 'The Populist Zeitgeist', *Government and Opposition* 39(4) (2004), pp. 542–63.

——, *Populist Radical Right Parties in Europe*, Cambridge: Cambridge University Press, 2007.

——, 'The Hungarian PM made a "rivers of blood" speech ... and no one cares', *The Guardian*, 30 July 2015.

——, 'Is Hungary Run by the Radical Right?', *Washington Post*, 10 August 2015.

—— and Kaltwasser, Cristóbal, 'Populism', in Freeden, Michael, and Stears, Marc (eds), *The Oxford Handbook of Political Ideologies*, Oxford: Oxford University Press, 2013.

Müller, Felix, and Tanner, Matthias, 'Muslime, Minarette und die Minarett-Initiative in der Schweiz: Grundlagen', in Tanner, Matthias *et al.* (eds), *Streit um das Minarett. Zusammenleben in der religiös pluralistischen Gesellschaft*, Zurich: Theologischer Verlag, 2009, pp. 21–44.

Neiyyar, Dil, 'UKIP holds meetings to win over British Asians', BBC News, 21 September 2013, http://www.bbc.co.uk/news/uk-politics-24175687, accessed 22 May 2014.

Nelson, Leah, 'Tea Party Patriots Wallow in Muslim-Bashing Gutter with Geller', Southern Poverty Law Center, http://www.splcenter.org/blog/2011/06/15/tea-party-patriots-wallow-in-muslim-bashing-gutter-with-geller/, accessed 24 June 2014.

News.at, 'Nach Strache-Sager zur Fristenlösung: Heftige Kritik der ÖVP, der SPÖ & den Grünen', 13 January 2006, www.news.at, accessed 12 July 2013.

NewsCorpsWatch.org, 'Memo to media: Pamela Geller does not belong on national television', http://newscorpwatch.org/research/201007140035, accessed 24 June 2014.

Nicolet, Sarah, and Tresch, Anke, 'Changing Religiosity, Changing Politics? The Influence of "Belonging" and "Believing" on Political Attitudes in Switzerland', *Politics and Religion* 2(1) (2009), pp. 76–99.

Niggli, Peter, and Frischknecht, Jürg, *Rechte Seilschaften. Wie die 'unheimlichen Patrioten' den Zusammenbruch des Kommunismus meisterten*, Zurich: Woz im Rotpunktverlag, 1998.

Nijakowski, Lech, *Polska Polityki Pamięci: Esej Socjologiczny*, Warsaw: Wydawnictwo Akademickie i Profesjonalne, 2008.

Nissim, Leon, 'Ethno-religious Nationalism and Theo-ethnocratic Politics in Israel', *Studies in Ethnicity and Nationalism* 14(1) (2014), pp. 20–35.

Norman, Jim, 'In U.S., Support for Tea Party Drops to New Low', *Gallup*, 26 October 2015, http://www.gallup.com/poll/186338/support-tea-party-drops-new-low.aspx?g_source=Politics&g_medium=newsfeed&g_campaign=tiles, accessed 10 December 2015.

NOS, 'Wilders: aanpak islam prioriteit 2013', http://nos.nl/artikel/455673-wilders-aanpak-islam-prioriteit-2013.html, accessed 09 March 2012.

Novak, Benjamin, 'Lajos Simicska: "Orbán is a f*cker"', *The Budapest Beacon*, 6 February 2015.

———, 'Archbishop claims laws prevent Catholic Church from helping asylum seekers', *The Budapest Beacon*, 4 September 2015.

Novick, Akiva, 'Deri's Shas Party Conference', *Ynet*, 2012, http://www.ynet.co.il/articles/0,7340,L-4301965,00.html, accessed 13 September 2013.

Oltay, Edith, *Fidesz and the Reinvention of the Hungarian Center Right*, Budapest: Századvég, 2012.

Orbán, Viktor, 'Minden magyar a Turulba születik' (All Hungarians are born into the Turul bird), *Népszabadság*, 29 September 2012.

———, 'Magyarország keresztény lesz vagy nem lesz' (Hungary will be either a Christian country or it will cease to exist), *Index.hu*, 18 May 2015, http://index.hu/belfold/2015/05/18/orban_magyarorszag_kereszteny_lesz_vagy_nem_lesz/, accessed 10 December 2015.

———, Speech in the European Parliament, 19 May 2015, http://www.kormany.hu/en/the-prime-minister/the-prime-minister-s-speeches/prime-minister-viktor-orban-s-speech-in-the-european-parliament, accessed 20 May 2015.

ORF, 'Deutlicher Rückgang: 58.603 Kirchenaustritte 2011', http://religionv1.orf.at/projekt03/news/1201/ne120110_statistik_fr.htm, accessed 9 October 2012.

———, 'Asyl: Strache attackiert Schönborn', 17 January 2013, http://wien.orf.at, accessed 15 July 2013.

———, 'Kirchliche Kritik an FPÖ-Wahlplakaten', 12 August 2013, http://religion.orf.at/stories/2597798/, accessed 22 April 2014.

Österreichische Bundesregierung, 'Verantwortung für Österreich—im Herzen Europas', Government Declaration, 3 February 2000,

OTS0051, 'FP-Sichrovsky: Religionsfreiheit muß in Österreich garantiert werden', 11 October 2001.

OTS0079, 'HC Strache: Terror-Camps—Grenzkontrollen zum Schutz vor IS dringlicher denn je', 22 July 2015.

OTS0128, 'FPÖ: Strache und Wilders warnen vor Islamisierung Europas', 27 March 2015.

OTS0361, 'Strache: Gegenschlag gegen Kirche', 19 May 2009.

Ozzano, Luca, and Giorgi, Alberta, 'The Debate on the Crucifix in Public Spaces in Twenty-First Century Italy', *Mediterranean Politics* 18(2) (2013), pp. 259–75.

Pace, Enzo, 'La questione nazionale fra Lega e Chiesa cattolica', *Il Mulino*, no. 5, September–October 1997, pp. 857–64.

Pack, Karen, 'An Ardent Plea', *Tea Party 911*, http://www.teaparty911.com/articles/karen_pack_ardent_plea.htm, accessed 24 June 2014.

Panizza, Francesco, 'Introduction: Populism and the Mirror of Democracy', in Panizza, Francesco (ed.), *Populism and the Mirror of Democracy*, London: Verso, 2005.

Pankowski, Rafal, *The Populist Radical Right in Poland: The Patriots*, Oxford: Routledge, 2011.

Paradowska, Janina, 'Tercet Egzotyczny', *Polityka* 19 (2006), p. 2553.

Parker, Christopher S., and Barreto, Matt A., 'The Tea Party and Obamaphobia—Is the Hostility Real or Imagined?', in Parker, Christopher S., and Barreto, Matt A., *Change They Can't Believe In: The Tea Party and Reactionary Politics in America*, Princeton: Princeton University Press, 2013, pp. 190–217.

Parool, 'Wilders wil dat kerken kiezen tegen de Islam', http://www.parool.nl/parool/nl/224/BINNENLAND/article/detail/285523/2010/03/23/Wilders-wil-dat-kerken-kiezen-tegen-de-Islam.dhtml, accessed 22 October 2012.

Peace, Timothy, 'Muslims and Electoral Politics in Britain: The Case of Respect', in Nielsen, J. (ed.), *Muslims and Political Participation in Europe*, Edinburgh: Edinburgh University Press, 2013, pp. 426–54.

Peck, Adam, 'Tea Party Senate Candidate Ted Cruz Jumps On The Sharia Conspiracy Bandwagon', *ThinkProgress.org*, http://thinkprogress.org/justice/2012/07/09/512075/cruz-sharia-problem/, accessed 24 June 2014.

Peled, Yoav, 'Towards a Redefinition of Jewish Nationalism in Israel: The Enigma of Shas', *Ethnic and Racial Studies* 21(4) (1998), pp. 703–27.

Pelinka, Anton, 'Die FPÖ in der vergleichenden Parteienforschung. Zur typologischen Einordnung der Freiheitlichen Partei Österreichs', *Österreichische Zeitschrift für Politikwissenschaft* 31(3) (2002), pp. 281–90.

Perchinig, Bernhard, 'Ein langsamer Weg nach Europa. Österreichische (Arbeits)migrations- und Integrationspolitik seit 1945', in Leibnitz Institut für Sozialwissenschaften/Bundesamt für Migration und Flüchtlinge (ed.), *Sozialwissenschaftlicher Fachinformationsdienst (SoFid) 2010/1, Migration und ethnische Minderheiten*, Mannheim: GESIS, 2010, pp. 11–32.

Pew Research Center, 'Two Decades after the Wall's Fall: End of Communism Cheered but Now with More Reservations', *The Pew Global Attitudes Project*, 2 November 2009, http://www.pewglobal.org/files/pdf/267.pdf, accessed 10 December 2015.

Pew Research Center for the People & the Press and Pew Forum on Religion & Public Life, *The Tea Party and Religion*, 13 February 2011, http://www.pewforum.org/2011/02/23/tea-party-and-religion/, accessed 24 June 2014.

Pidd, Helen, 'George Galloway hails "Bradford spring" as Labour licks its wounds', *The Guardian*, 30 March 2012, http://www.guardian.co.uk/politics/2012/mar/30/george-galloway-bradford-spring-labour, accessed 10 December 2015.

Pirro, Andrea L., *The Populist Radical Right in Central and Eastern Europe*, London: Routledge, 2015.

Plasser, Fritz, and Ulram, Peter A., 'Electoral Change in Austria', in Plasser, Fritz, and Ulram, Peter A. (eds), *The Changing Austrian Voter*, New Brunswick: Transaction Publishers, 2008, pp. 54–78.

Polak, Bogusław, 'W Sprawie Wychowania Patriotycznego Młodych Polaków i Wyzwań Dla Historyków. Kilka Uwag i Propozycji', in Jacyna-Onyszkiewicz, Zbigniew (ed.), *Ku odnowie Polski*, Warsaw: Liga Polskich Rodzin, 2005, pp. 171–85.

Polak, Regina, and Schachinger, Christoph, 'Stabil in Veränderung: Konfessionsnahe Religiosität in Europa', in Polak, Regina (ed.), *Zukunft. Werte. Europa: Die Europäische Wertestudie 1990–2010: Österreich im Vergleich*, Böhlau, 2011, pp. 191–222.

Poorthuis, Frank, and Wansink, Hans, 'Pim Fortuyn op herhaling: "De islam is een achterlijke cultuur"', *Volkskrant*, http://www.volkskrant.nl/vk/nl/2824/Politiek/

article/detail/611698/2002/02/09/De-islam-is-een-achterlijke-cultuur.dhtml, accessed 25 October 2012.

Potz, Richard, 'State and Church in Austria', in Robbers, Gerhard (ed.), *State and Church in the European Union*, Baden-Baden: Nomos, 2005, pp. 391–418.

Prawo i Sprawiedliwość, *Polska Katolicka w Chrześćijańskiej Europie*, Warsaw: Komitet Wyborczy Prawo i Sprawiedliwość, 2005.

———, Samoobrona Rzeczypospolitej Polskiej, and Narodowe Koło Parlamentarne, *Koalicyjna Deklaracja Programowa "Solidarne Państwo" z 27 Kwietnia 2006 R., Załącznik Nr.1, Cele i Zadania Rządu Koalicyjnego w Latach 2006–2009*, 2006, http://www.pis.org.pl/download.php?g=mmedia&f=zalacznik_nr_1.pdf, accessed 13 September 2013.

Partij voor de Vrijheid, *Verkiezingspamflet*, Partij voor de Vrijheid parliamentary election manifesto, 2006.

———, *Partij voor de Vrijheid: De agenda van hoop en optimisme. Een tijd om te kiezen*, Partij voor de Vrijheid parliamentary election manifesto, 2010.

———, *Hún Brussel, óns Nederland*, Partij voor de Vrijheid parliamentary election manifesto, 2012.

Radiomaryja.pl, 'O. Rydzyk o PiS-ie i Szambie', 8 March 2007, transcript of broadcast by Radio Maryja, http://www.radiomaryja.pl.eu.org/nagrania/20070308-rydzyk/20070308-rydzyk.html, accessed 4 April 2013.

Ramet, Sabrina, 'The Catholic Church in Post-Communist Poland: Polarization, Privatization, and Decline in Influence', in Ramet, Sabrina (ed.), *Religion and Politics in Post-Socialist Central and Southeastern Europe. Challenges since 1989*, Basingstoke: Palgrave Macmillan, 2014.

Reiner, Joshua, 'Likud Beiteinu—the Party of Russians and White', *Walla! News*, http://news.walla.co.il/elections/?w=/2780/2601061, accessed 13 September 2013.

RKK, 'Bisschop vraagt Wilders om fatsoen', http://www.rkk.nl/actualiteit/2008/detail_objectID666796_FJaar2008.html, accessed 11 October 2012.

———, 'Brabantse priesters steunen Wilders', http://www.rkk.nl/actualiteit/2008/detail_objectID668982_FJaar2008.html, accessed 11 October 2012.

———, 'Rabbijn Soetendorp: kerken moeten zich mengen in Wilders-debat', http://www.rkk.nl/actualiteit/2008/detail_objectID663067_FJaar2008.html, accessed 13 October 2012.

Rosaspina, Elisabetta, 'Un rito celtico per le prime nozze padane', *Corriere della Sera*, 21 September 1998.

Rosenberger, Sieglinde, and Hadj-Abdou, Leila, 'Islam at Issue. Anti-Islamic Mobilization of the Extreme-Right in Austria', in Mammone, Andrea, Godin, Emmanuel, and Jenkins, Brian (eds), *Varieties of Right-wing Extremism in Europe*, New York: Routledge, 2012, pp. 149–63.

Roy, Olivier, *La Sainte ignorance. Le temps de la religion sans culture*, Paris: Le Seuil, 2008.

———, *Holy Ignorance*, London: Hurst, 2010.

———, 'The Closing of the right's mind', *New York Times*, 4 June 2014.

Ryba, Mieczysław, 'O Przełom Cywilizacyjny w Europie i w Polsce', in Jacyna-Onyszkiewicz, Zbigniew (ed.), *Ku odnowie Polski*, Warsaw: Liga Polskich Rodzin, 2005, pp. 77–96.

Saint-Blancat, Chantal, and Schmidt di Friedberg, Ottavia, 'Why are Mosques a Problem? Local Politics and Fear of Islam in Northern Italy', *Journal of Ethnic and Migration Studies* 31(6) (2005), pp. 1083–1104.

Sanders, Charles, 'Joodse sponsors woest op Wilders', *Telegraaf*, http://www.telegraaf.nl/binnenland/verkiezingen2012/12796867/__Sponsors_woest_op_Wilders__.html, accessed 25 October 2012.

Scharsach, Hans-Henning, *Strache. Im braunen Sumpf*, Vienna: Kremayr & Scheriau, 2012.

Schweizerische Volkspartei, *SVP—The Party for Switzerland. Party Programme 2011–2015*, http://www.svp.ch/display.cfm/id/101395, accessed 13 September 2013.

———, *SVP—The Party for Switzerland. Party Programme 2015–2019*, Bern, 2015.

Schwengler, Bernard, *Le vote Front National: L'Alsace: un cas particulier? Sociologie d'un vote complexe*, Strasbourg: Éditions Oberlin, 2003.

Segal, Jérôme, and Mansfield, Ian, 'Contention and Discontent Surrounding Religion in Noughties' Austria', *Austrian Studies* 19 (2011), pp. 52–67.

Sejm Rzeczypospolitej Polskiej, *Sprawozdanie Stenograficzne z Posiedzeń Sejmu RP II Kadencji*, 1997, http://orka2.sejm.gov.pl/Debata2.nsf, accessed 3 August 2012.

———, *Sprawozdanie Stenograficzne z Posiedzeń Sejmu RP V Kadencji*, 2007, http://orka2.sejm.gov.pl/Debata5.nsf, accessed 4 January 2012.

Shafir, Moshe, quoted in *Sudanese Shas Journal*, 2012, http://www.plitim.co.il/2427.html, accessed 13 September 2013.

Shalev, Michael and Levy, Gal, 'Winners and Losers in 2003 Elections: Ideology, Social Structure and Political Change', in Aryan, Asher, and Shamir, Michal (eds), *Elections in Israel 2003*, Jerusalem: IDI (Hebrew), 2005.

Simon, Zoltán, 'Orbán Says He Seeks to End Liberal Democracy in Hungary' *Bloomberg*, 28 July 2014, http://www.bloomberg.com/news/articles/2014-07-28/orban-says-he-seeks-to-end-liberal-democracy-in-hungary, accessed 10 December 2015.

Skenderovic, Damir, 'Campagnes et agenda politiques. La transformation de l'Union démocratique du centre', in Mazzoleni, O., and Rayner, H. (eds), *Les partis politiques en Suisse. Traditions et renouvellements*, Paris: Michel Houdiard Editeur, 2009, pp. 378–409.

Skocpol, Theda, and Williamson, Vanessa, *The Tea Party and the Remaking of American Conservatism*, New York: Oxford University Press, 2012.

Skousen, Cleon, *The Five Thousand Year Leap*, National Center for Constitutional Studies, 1981.

Smietana, Bob, 'Tenn. bill criticized for targeting Muslims splits Tea Party', *USA Today*, 22 May 2011, http://usatoday30.usatoday.com/news/nation/2011–05–22-tennessee-bill-tea-party_n.htm, accessed 24 June 2014.

Smith, Jan, 'US Catholic Bishops Vs. Tea Party', *Rainbow sash movement*, 30 July 2011, http://rainbowsashmovement.wordpress.com/2011/07/30/us-catholic-bishops-vs-tea-party/, accessed 24 June 2014.

Sobieraj, Sarah, and Berry, Jeffrey M., 'From Incivility to Outrage: Political Discourse in Blogs, Talk Radio, and Cable News', *Political Communication* 28(1) (2011), p. 20.

Sonntagszeitung, 'Maurer und Spuhler gegen Minarett-Verbot. Warnung vor Boykotten', 25 October 2009.

Spektorowski, Alberto, 'Ethnoregionalism: The Intellectual New Right and the Lega Nord', *The Global Review of Ethnopolitics* 2(3) (2003), pp. 55–70.

Spellberg, Denise A., 'Ben Carson Would Fail U.S. History', *Time*, 21 September 2015, http://time.com/4042435/ben-carson-would-fail-u-s-history/, accessed 10 December 2015.

STAND, 'Mission', *Staying True to America's National Destiny*, http://www.standamerica.us/, accessed 1 July 2010.

Stanley, Ben, 'The Thin Ideology of Populism', *Journal of Political Ideologies* 13(1) (2008), pp. 95–110.

Stavrakakis, Yannis, 'Antinomies of Formalism: Laclau's Theory of Populism and the Lessons from Religious Populism in Greece', *Journal of Political Ideologies* 9(3) (2004), pp. 253–67.

Sun News Network, 'Geert Wilders on the Islamic terror attacks on Charlie Hebdo cartoonists', Interview with Geert Wilders, 8 February 2015, https://www.youtube.com/watch?v=vzDCeWNObBo, accessed 25 May 2015.

Swiss Bishops' Conference, *L'initiative contre la construction de minarets*, 9 September 2009, press release, http://www.eveques.ch, accessed 27 October 2012.

Swiss Federation of Jewish Communities, *Pas de loi d'exception. Non à l'interdiction des minarets*, press release, 28 October 2009.

Szczerbiak, Aleks, '"Social Poland" Defeats "Liberal Poland"? The September–October 2005 Polish Parliamentary and Presidential Elections', *Journal of Communist Studies and Transition Politics* 23(2) (2007), pp. 203–32.

Taggart, Paul, *Populism*, Buckingham/Philadelphia: Open University Press, 2000.

Tambini, Damian, *Nationalism in Italian Politics: The Stories of the Northern League, 1980–2000*, London: Routledge, 2001.

Tarchi, Marco, *L'italia populista: Dal qualunquismo ai girotondi*, Bologna: il Mulino, 2003.

Taylor, Matthew, 'BNP seeks to bury antisemitism and gain Jewish votes in Islamophobic campaign', *The Guardian*, 10 April 2008, http://www.guardian.co.uk/politics/2008/apr/10/thefarright.race, accessed 13 September 2013.

Tepe, Sultan, 'Moderation of Religious Parties: Electoral Constraints, Ideological Commitments, and the Democratic Capacities of Religious Parties in Israel and Turkey', *Political Research Quarterly* 65(3) (2012), pp. 467–85.

Terpstra, Doekle, '"Nee" tegen kwade boodschap Wilders', *Trouw*, 30 November 2007, http://www.trouw.nl/tr/nl/4324/Nieuws/article/detail/1369213/2007/11/30/rsquo-Nee-rsquo-tegen-kwade-boodschap-Wilders-opinie.dhtml, accessed 9 March 2013.

Tessler, Riki, *In the Name of God: Shas and the Religious Revolution*, Jerusalem: Keter (Hebrew), 2003.

TgCom, 'Salvini shock: "Milioni di musulmani pronti a sgozzare in nome dell'Islam"', 10 January 2015, http://www.tgcom24.mediaset.it/mondo/speciale-attacco-charlie-hebdo/salvini-shock-milioni-di-musulmani-pronti-a-sgozzare-in-nome-dell-islam-_2088784–201502a.shtml, accessed 11 December 2015.

The Economist, 'Right on Down: The Far Right in Eastern Europe', 12 November 2009.

The Huffington Post UK, 'Heino Vockrodt Is Yet Another Ukip Candidate In Outrageous Anti-Muslim Rant', 15 May 2014, http://www.huffingtonpost.co.uk/2014/05/15/heino-vockrodt-ukip-musli_n_5329311.html, accessed 22 May 2014

Thorpe, Nick, 'What happened when an anti-Semite found he was Jewish?', BBC.com News Magazine, 4 May 2015.

Trouw, 'Bisschop De Korte: Wilders drijft mensen uiteen', http://www.trouw.nl/tr/nl/5009/Archief/archief/article/detail/3278827/2012/06/29/Bisschop-De-Korte-Wilders-drijft-mensen-uiteen.dhtml, accessed 22 October 2012.

UK Independence Party, *Party Election Broadcast: Common Sense on Immigration*, 23 April 2013, http://www.youtube.com/watch?v=Zt9uDZF24x8, accessed 11 September 2013.

——, *UKIP Manifesto April 2010: Empowering the People*, Newton Abbot: UK Independence Party, 2010.

Ungváry, Krisztián, *A Horthy-rendszer mérlege* (Evaluation of the Horthy regime), Budapest: Pécs—Budapest: Jelenkor & OSZK, 2012.

Ungváry, Rudolf, *A láthatatlan valóság: A fasisztoid mutáció a mai Magyarországon* (The invisible reality: Transmuted fascism in today's Hungary), Bratislava: Kalligram, 2013.

United States Department of Justice, *Report on the Tenth Anniversary of the Religious Land Use and Institutionalized Persons Act*, 22 September 2010.

van de Griend, Robert, 'Wilders' diepe denker uit België', *Vrij Nederland*, http://www.vn.nl/Archief/Politiek/Artikel-Politiek/Wilders-diepe-denker-uit-Belgie.htm, accessed 6 March 2013.

van der Brug, Wouter, Hobolt, Sara, and Vreese, Claes de, 'Religion and Party Choice in Europe', *West European Politics* 32(6) (2009), pp. 1266–83.

van der Kolk, Henk, Aarts, Kees, Rosema, Martin, and Brinkman, Martha, *Dutch Parliamentary Election Study 2010*, The Hague: CBS/SKON, 2012.

van der Kolk, Henk, Tillie, Jean N., van Erkel, Peter, van der Velden, Mariken, and Damstra, Alyt, *Dutch Parliamentary Election Study 2012*, The Hague: DANS, 2013.

van der Meer, Tom, Lubbe, Rozemarijn, van Elsas, Erika, Elff, Martin, and van der Brug, Wouter, 'Bounded volatility in the Dutch electoral battlefield: A panel study on the structure of changing vote intentions in the Netherlands during 2006–2010', *Acta Politica* 47(4) (2012), pp. 333–55.

van Holsteyn, Joop, and Irwin, Galen A., 'Never a Dull Moment: Pim Fortuyn and the Dutch Parliamentary Election of 2002', *West European Politics* 26(2) (2003), pp. 41–66.

van Kersbergen, Kees and Krouwel, André, 'A double-edged sword! The Dutch centre-right and the "foreigners issue"', *Journal of European Public Policy* 15(3) (2008), p. 398.

van Kessel, Stijn, *The Dutch General Election of June 2010*, European Parties Elections and Referendums Network, Election Briefing Paper no. 54, 2010.

——— and Hollander, Saskia, *Europe and the Dutch Parliamentary Election, September 2012*, European Parties Elections and Referendums Network, Election Briefing Paper, no. 71, 2012.

Vanel, Chrystal, *Des mormonismes: une étude historique et sociologique d'une fissiparité religieuse américaine (1805–2013)*, doctoral thesis under the direction of Jean-Paul Willaime, Ecole Pratique des Hautes Etudes, Paris, 2013.

Vecchi, Gian G., 'Fisichella: l' intervento dei vescovi era necessario', *Corriere della Sera*, 30 March 2010.

Volsky, Igor, 'Bachmann Stands By Widely Condemned Islamophobic Attack, Finds Ally In Glenn Beck', *ThinkProgress.org*, 19 July 2012, http://thinkprogress.org/security/2012/07/19/553361/bachmann-stands-by-widely-condemned-islamophobic-attack-finds-ally-in-glenn-beck/, accessed 24 June 2014.

———, 'Tea Party Congressman: Muslim Brotherhood Is Guiding Obama In Boston Bombings Investigation', *ThinkProgress.org*, 27 April 2014, http://thinkprogress.org/security/2013/04/27/1931051/tea-party-congressman-obama-bungled-investigation-of-boston-bombings-because-he-is-being-guided-by-muslim-brotherhood/, accessed 24 June 2014.

Vona, Gábor, *Turanism Instead of Euro-Atlantic Alliance*, 23 January 2012, http://www.jobbik.com/jobbik_news/europe/3198.html, accessed 10 December 2015.

Vossen, Koen, 'Populism in the Netherlands after Fortuyn: Rita Verdonk and Geert Wilders Compared', *Perspectives on European Politics and Society* 11(1) (2010), pp. 22–38.

———, 'Classifying Wilders: The Ideological Development of Geert Wilders and His Party for Freedom', *Politics* 31(3) (2011), pp. 179–89.

Vuijst, Freke, 'Op zoek naar dollars', *Vrij Nederland*, 13 June 2009, http://www.vn.nl/

Meer-dossiers/Wilders-en-de-PVV/Artikel-Wilders/Op-zoek-naar-dollars.htm, accessed 9 March 2013.

Waber, Christian, 'Facts', *Schweizer Nachrichten*, 20, 2007, p. 26.

Wainwright, Martin, 'Sheffield UKIP candidate sacked over Breivik comments', *The Guardian*, 2 May 2012, http://www.guardian.co.uk/uk/the-northerner/2012/may/02/ukip-steve-moxon-whistleblower-home-office-beverley-hughes, accessed 13 September 2013.

Wälti, Carole, 'Minaret vote was a "lesson in civic spirit"', Swissinfo.ch, 16 December 2009, accessed 29 November 2012.

Weiss, Gilbert, 'A.E.I.O.U.—Austria Europe Imago, Onus, Unio?', in Malmborg, Mikael af, and Strath, Bo (eds), *Meanings of Europe*, Oxford: Berg, 2000, pp. 263–84.

Weseman, Pauline, 'Muskens: "Wilders misbruikt angstgevoelens in crisistijd"', *Nieuwwij*, 01 May 2009, http://www.nieuwwij.nl/index.php?pageID=13&messageID=2187, accessed 11 October 2012.

Wever, Robin de, 'Wilders' joodse, christelijke en anti-islamitische geldschieters', *Trouw*, 3 July 2012, http://www.trouw.nl/tr/nl/5091/Religie/article/detail/3281078/2012/07/03/Wilders-joodse-christelijke-en-anti-islamitische-geldschieters.dhtml, accessed 22 October 2012.

———, 'Een kerkdienst tegen Wilders? Zo moet je het niet zien', *Trouw*, 21 March 2014, http://www.trouw.nl/tr/nl/5091/Religie/article/detail/3620085/2014/03/21/Een-kerkdienst-tegen-Wilders-Zo-moet-je-het-niet-zien.dhtml, accessed 27 May 2015.

Wilders, Geert, *Groep Wilders. Onafhankelijkheidsverklaring*, party document, Groep Wilders, The Hague, 2005.

———, 'Inbreng Geert Wilders bij terreurdebat', *PVV*, 11 February 2015, http://www.pvv.nl/index.php/36-fj-related/geert-wilders/8168-inbreng-geert-wilders-bij-debat-over-inzet-en-capaciteit-in-de-veiligheidsketen.html, accessed 25 May 2015.

———, 'Speech Geert Wilders for US Congressmen, Washington DC, Conservative Opportunity Society', *PVV*, 29 April 2015, http://www.pvv.nl/index.php/36-fj-related/geert-wilders/8324-speech-geert-wilders-for-us-congressmen-washington-dc-conservative-opportunity-society-29-april-2015.html, accessed 25 May 2015.

Wiles, Peter, 'A Syndrome not a Doctrine: Some Elementary Theses on Populism', in Ionescu, Ghita, and Gellner, Ernest (eds), *Populism: its Meaning and National Characteristics*, London: Macmillan, 1969.

Williams, Mark, *Taking Back America One Tea Party at a Time*, Online: MarkTalk.com, 2010.

Windisch, Uli, *Suisse-immigrés. Quarante ans de débats 1960–2001*, Lausanne/Paris: L'Age d'Homme, 2002.

Wing, Nick, 'Sarah Palin: American Law Should Be "Based On The God Of The Bible And The Ten Commandments"', *The Huffington Post*, 10 May 2015, http://www.

huffingtonpost.com/2010/05/10/sarah-palin-american-law_n_569922.html, accessed 24 June 2014.

Wiśniewska, Katarzyna, 'Lech Kaczyński Wysłał Proboszczom List', *Gazeta Wyborcza*, 2005.

Wodak, Ruth and Köhler, Katharina, 'Wer oder was ist "fremd"? Diskurshistorische Analyse fremdenfeindlicher Rhetorik in Österreich', *SWS-Rundschau* 50(1) (2010), pp. 33–55.

Wojtas, Kinga, 'Poland', in Havlík, Vlastimil (ed.), *Populist Political Parties in East-Central Europe*, Brno: MUNI Press, 2012.

Wood, Chris, and Finlay, William M. L., 'British National Party Representations of Muslims in the Month after the London Bombings: Homogeneity, Threat, and the Conspiracy Tradition', *British Journal of Social Psychology* 47(4) (2008), pp. 707–26.

Woodbridge, Steven, 'Christian Credentials? The Role of Religion in British National Party Ideology', *Journal for the Study of Radicalism* 4(1) (2010), pp. 25–54.

Worthen, Molly, 'The Chalcedon Problem: Rousas John Rushdoony and the Origins of Christian Reconstructionism', *Church History* 77(2) (2008).

Wroński, Paweł, 'Dmowskiego Do Ligi Bym Nie Przyjął', interview with Roman Giertych, *Gazeta.pl*, http://serwisy.gazeta.pl/wyborcza/1,68586,3484547.html, accessed 12 September 2013.

Yadgar, Yaacov, 'Shas as a Struggle to Create a New Field: A Bourdieuan Perspective of an Israeli Phenomenon', *Sociology of Religion* 64(2) (2003), pp. 223–46.

Yagna, Yanir, 'When the Bedouin Vote, They Often Vote Shas', *Haaretz*, 27 January 2013, http://www.haaretz.com/news/israeli-elections-2013/when-the-bedouin-vote-they-often-vote-shas.premium-1.496401, accessed 13 September 2013.

Yishai, Eli, 'Infiltrators will Return, Every Last One', *Mako*, http://www.mako.co.il/news-military/politics/Article-74bb292eddc1431017.htm, accessed 13 September 2013.

Zaimov, Stoyan, 'Tea Party Advocate, Rush Limbaugh Criticize Pope Francis, Argue "Jesus Is a Capitalist"', *Christian Post*, http://www.christianpost.com/news/tea-party-advocate-rush-limbaugh-criticize-pope-francis-argue-jesus-is-a-capitalist-109958/, accessed 24 June 2014.

Zaitchik, Alexander, 'New Report Examines "Tea Party Nationalism", Charts Extremist Ties', Southern Poverty Law Center, 20 October 2010, http://www.splcenter.org/blog/2010/10/20/new-report-examines-tea-party-nationalism-charts-groups-history-and-extremist-ties-2/, accessed 24 June 2014.

Zając, Marek, 'Między Zdradą Judasza i Drzemką w Ogrójcu', *Tygodnik Powszechny*, 4, 2005.

Załuska, Wojciech, 'Dlaczego Jarosław Kaczyński Zaprzyjaźnił Się z Ojcem Rydzykiem?', *Gazeta Wyborcza*, 2005.

Zernike, Kate, *Boiling Mad: Inside Tea Party America*, New York: Time Books, 2010.

Zohar, Zion, 'Oriental Jewry Confronts Modernity: The Case of Rabbi Ovadiah Yosef', *Modern Judaism* 24(2) (2004), pp. 120–49.

Zolnay, János, *A Hit Gyülekezetének Dzsihádja* (The Jihad of Faith Church), *Beszélő*, 19 October 2015.

Zubrzycki, Genevieve, *The Crosses of Auschwitz: Nationalism and Religion in Post-Communist Poland*, new ed., Chicago: University of Chicago Press, 2006.

Zulehner, Paul, 'Über die religiöse Verbuntung Österreichs', *Die Presse*, 3 June 2011.

Zúquete, José Pedro, 'The European Extreme-Right and Islam: New Directions?', *Journal of Political Ideologies* 13(3) (2008), pp. 321–44.

Zuser, Peter, *Die Konstruktion der Ausländerfrage in Österreich. Eine Analyse des öffentlichen Diskurses 1990*, Working Papers no. 35, Institute for Advanced Studies, Vienna, 1996.

INDEX